W9-BVH-814

THE JEWISH COMMUNITY IN AMERICA

Library of Jewish Studies

THE JEWISH COMMUNITY IN AMERICA

Edited, with introductions and notes, by

MARSHALL SKLARE

BEHRMAN HOUSE, INC. | PUBLISHERS | NEW YORK

ACKNOWLEDGMENTS

The author and publisher thank the following for permission to reprint:

The American Jewish Committee for selections from Lucy S. Dawidowicz and Leon J. Goldstein, *Politics in a Pluralist Democracy;* Charles S. Liebman, "Orthodoxy in American Jewish Life"; and selections from Seymour Martin Lipset, ed., *Group Life in America—A Task Force Report.* Copyright © 1963, 1965, 1972 by the American Jewish Committee.

Basic Books, Inc., and the American Jewish Committee for Daniel J. Elazar, "Decision-Making in the American Jewish Community"; selections from Benjamin B. Ringer, *The Edge of Friendliness;* and selections from Marshall Sklare and Joseph Greenblum, *Jewish Identity on the Suburban Frontier.* Copyright © 1973, 1967 by the American Jewish Committee.

Combined Jewish Philanthropies of Greater Boston for selections from Morris Axelrod, Floyd J. Fowler, and Arnold Gurin, *A Community Survey for Long Range Planning.* Copyright © 1967 by the Combined Jewish Philanthropies of Greater Boston.

The Jewish Journal of Sociology for Nathan Glazer, "The New Left and the Jews." Copyright © 1969 by the World Jewish Congress.

The Macmillan Company for Herbert J. Gans, "The Origin and Growth of a Jewish Community in the Suburbs: A Study of the Jews of Park Forest." Copyright ©1958 by the Free Press.

Schocken Books, Inc., for selections from Marshall Sklare, *Conservative Judaism: An American Religious Movement.* Copyright ©1955, 1972 by Marshall Sklare.

Teachers College Press for selections from Lloyd P. Gartner, ed., *Jewish Education in the United States: A Documentary History.* Copyright © 1969 by Teachers College, Columbia University.

The Theodor Herzl Foundation and *Midstream* for Walter I. Ackerman, "The Present Moment in Jewish Education." Copyright © 1972 by the Theodor Herzl Foundation.

The Union of American Hebrew Congregations for selections from Leonard J. Fein, Robert Chin, Jack Dauber, Bernard Reisman, and Herzl Spiro, *Reform is a Verb: Notes on Reform and Reforming Jews.* Copyright © 1972 by the Union of American Hebrew Congregations.

Library of Congress Cataloging in Publication Data

Sklare, Marshall, date. comp.
The Jewish community in America.

(Library of Jewish studies)
Bioliography: p.
1. Jews in the United States—Political and social conditions—Addresses, essays, lectures. 2. Jews in the United States—Politics and government. 3. Judaism—United States. 4. Jews in the United States—Education. I. Title.
E184.J5S5478 301.45'19'24073 74-8678
ISBN 0-87441-204-8

Published by Behrman House, Inc., 1261 Broadway, New York, N.Y. 10001
Manufactured in the United States of America

CONTENTS

PREFACE

ALL OF THE aspects of Jewish communal life treated in this book—the informal community, the formal community, religious movements in the American Jewish community, Jewish education, and the interaction of the Jewish community (or, more properly, of the Jewish sub-community) with the general society—derive their significance from the unique historical destiny of American Jewry. The momentous historical developments and challenges of the recent past constitute the backdrop against which the selections following should be read. In the Introduction, I have tried to sketch the contours of these developments and place them in perspective.

American Jewry can profitably be studied from the vantage point of the behavior, attitude, and sociological character of the individual American Jew. This vantage point is employed in the companion volume to this one, *The Jew in American Society*. But communal behavior is as significant as individual behavior, and perhaps to no group in American Society does this general rule apply with greater force than to the Jews, whose communal structure and range of activity are both complex and various. The fact, in addition, that American Jewry as a whole has fallen heir to unique responsibilities has made a volume focusing on the development and structure of the community seem all the more desirable.

Not all of the authors represented in this volume see the historical destiny of the American Jewish community from my own particular stance. So much the better; diversity in interpretation can be an aid rather than an impediment to learning. I have been concerned with selecting authors who have a serious concern with understanding the functioning of the Jewish community in American society whether or not they share my own proclivities. And I have sought also to enlist those scholars who base themselves on sociological or historical data. Speculation and conjecture have their place, but if they are unsupported by data they can confuse more than they clarify, and in so doing retard understanding of American Jewish life.

I am fortunate that my wife Rose is not only an inspiration to my work but as an experienced editor she has cheerfully assisted me with my own manuscripts after a long day spent with the manuscripts of others. I rely heavily on her expert eye for makeup and design and for aid in the numerous details that go into the making of a book.

As with *The Jew in American Society,* it is my pleasant duty to acknowledge the help of Neal Kozodoy, editor of the Library of Jewish studies; Joshua Rothenberg and Daniel Lourie of the Goldfarb Library of Brandeis University, and Nathan Kaganoff and his staff at the Library of the American Jewish Historical Society; Arden J. Geldman, my research assistant; Doris Lelchook; and Mrs. Gerry Gould of the Behrman House staff.

I am deeply grateful to the authors and publishers who have permitted their works to be utilized in this volume. I am also grateful to the National Endowment for the Humanities for a senior fellowship which allowed me the opportunity to review the scholarly literature on Jewish communal structure. The assistance of the Lucius N. Littauer Foundation and the interest of Harry Starr, its president, are also gratefully acknowledged.

Marshall Sklare
Waltham, Massachusetts

INTRODUCTION

IT IS FAIR to say that the dominant tone in the writing of concerned Jews about the American Jewish community is one of criticism. Jewish organizations, year after year, raise large sums of money to assist the settlement of Jews in Israel and their integration into Israeli society, yet many feel that the response of the American Jewish community to Israeli needs is inadequate. Similarly, American Jewish organizations have in a variety of ways brought pressure to bear on the Soviet Union, both to alleviate the condition of Jews in that country and particularly to win for them the right of emigration; yet here too many concerned Jews feel that not enough has been done. And if the organized response to the overseas concerns of American Jewry has been called inadequate, the response of the community to its domestic concerns has drawn forth a veritable symphony of criticism.

A major motif in this criticism is the lagging development of Jewish education. Critics emphasize that despite the fact that Jewish education requires extensive communal support, the financial burden of educating the Jewish young continues to fall mainly upon the individual parent. Furthermore, despite the stress placed by Jewish tradition on Jewish education as a life-long concern, only the smallest efforts, it is charged, have been made in the area of adult Jewish education.

The condition of the Jewish poor and the safety of Jews living in older urban neighborhoods are additional subjects of criticism. Some say that the Jewish communal agencies are tied to their middle- and upper-class constituencies and as a consequence have lost touch with the public which was once the special focus of their concern. The agencies have also been accused of blindly pursuing left-liberal policies even when the consequences of such policies may be seen to run counter to Jewish interests; from the viewpoint of the critics, Jewish communal agencies are inadequate defenders of Jewish interests and are in danger of losing their creditability.

Even the American synagogue has its detractors. There are those who feel that the American synagogue looks inward rather than outward—that each congregation selfishly concerns itself with the needs of its own particular constituency and is unresponsive to the totality of Jewish needs—be they local, national, or international. Others object that the American synagogue does not even serve its own constituency adequately—it does not contribute significantly to the congregants' spiritual development or enhance their pride in being Jewish. American synagogues in this view are cold and distant institutions, and it is thus understandable why so few are actively committed to them.

But if critics abound within the Jewish community, their view of things is not that of most outside observers. More often than not, such observers are amazed at the amount of money raised in Jewish drives. They are highly impressed with the intricate network of social services which the Jewish community has developed. They point out that synagogues have suffered fewer defections than have the churches. And far from thinking Jewish organizations ineffectual, they see them as possessing great thrust and vitality, as worthy models of emulation for other minority groups as well as for the American community at large.

This discrepancy in perception reflects the difference between an outsider's and an insider's view of the same phenomenon. The outsider measures achievement by a yardstick based on his experiences with his own group and a casual acquaintanceship with the Jewish group. The insider, on the other hand, measures achievement by a yardstick based on an intimate understanding of the needs and situation of his own group. In the present instance, as we shall see, the insider's yardstick may well be the more accurate instrument.

Unique and unforeseen responsibilities have been thrust upon the present-day American Jewish community. In the eighteenth century it seemed that America would be only one among a number of different countries to receive an influx of population from the Jewish heartland of Central and Eastern Europe, but by the first half of the nineteenth century it became clear that the United States was fated to become a central area of Jewish concentration. The tidal wave of immigrants from Eastern Europe at the turn of this century had a profound effect both on American society and on the worldwide shape of the Jewish people.

It is true that some Jews did not consider emigration from Central and Eastern Europe; they had faith in the eventual improvement of the Jewish situation there. But a strong current of opinion held that leaving Europe was the better part of wisdom, if not of necessity. Where to go? Palestine, late in the nineteenth century, was proposed by some, but these were a minority. For most Jews of Central Europe (and eventually for those of Eastern Europe as well), the slogan was "On to America." This phrase served as the title of an article published in 1848 by Leopold Kompert, a prominent Jewish writer from Bohemia. Kompert expressed the belief that whatever beneficial changes the revolutions of his time might bring to the general populace, the Jewish condition would not be substantially improved. Rather, revolution would give rise to counter-revolution and reaction, and any freedom the Jews won would be short-lived. He wrote:

> No relief has been brought to us. The sun of liberty is up for the Fatherland; but for us it is a blood-red Northern Light. The larks of deliverance warble in the free air; but for us it is like the screaming of mews during a storm. Because servile hordes and sordid-minded people have not understood and do not understand the spirit of liberty, we have to suffer. . . . There is no other desire among us than to get away from this "freedom." Our goal must, therefore, be emigration, the founding of a new fatherland, the immediate achievement of freedom. . . . Let us go to America![1]

Kompert not only believed that America was indispensable to the Jews but he also held that the Jews would be indispensable to

[1]See Mark Wischnitzer, *To Dwell in Safety: The Story of Jewish Migration Since 1800* (Philadelphia: Jewish Publication Society of America, 1948), pp. 18-19.

America: "The Jews possess the qualities and virtues so indispensable for reconstruction in [America]: foresight, sobriety, economy, discipline, and loyalty."[2]

Despite the effort of Zionist groups to encourage emigration to Palestine, "to build and to be rebuilt there," the Jews of Eastern Europe followed those of Central Europe in their attraction to America. After the Russian pogroms in the spring of 1881, Simon Dubnow—later to become the leading historian of East European Jewry and an advocate of Diaspora nationalism—came to the conclusion that the United States was the only feasible land for mass Jewish migration. Dubnow believed that America was destined to be ". . . the new fatherland of the Russian and German Jews who form two-thirds of European Jewry."[3]

Kompert and Dubnow were borne out in their preferences by the migrants themselves. By the last quarter of the nineteenth century the steady stream of Jews to America had enlarged into a flood; America was more attractive than all other countries to which Jews were then migrating: Australia, Canada, South Africa, and the nations of Central and South America. And even at that time, although more so later, some of those who went to other countries did so not because they preferred them but because they could not get admitted to the United States. A variety of beliefs fed the Jewish attraction to the United States: America was seen as a country of freedom, of great economic opportunity, of unlimited frontiers, and perhaps above all as a place where Jews would be able to reconstruct their lives in security and dignity.

Immigration to the United States reached such proportions at the turn of the century that it alarmed some of the leaders of the American Jewish community. As they saw it, if immigration were not controlled, America's capacity to absorb Jews would be exceeded and grave repercussions would follow. Both newcomers and those already settled would be in jeopardy, and even the physical security of the community might be undermined. The private debates of the time about the desirability of continued Jewish immigration, and the confidential exchanges between officials of American Jewish organizations and their counterparts in Europe—on the need to channel migrants to other countries—do

[2] *Ibid.*, p. 19.

[3] *Ibid.*, p. 52.

not make pleasant reading today. Still, whatever its fears about the effect of additional Jewish immigration to the United States, the leadership of American Jewry did refuse to support restrictive immigration laws; in fact, it worked to defeat the passage of such legislation. Thus, in 1891, when Congress passed a bill providing for the rejection of immigrants who were paupers or in danger of becoming public charges, four leading Jewish organizations submitted a joint memorandum of protest, rejecting the allegation that Jewish immigrants had become public charges and protesting the denial of refuge to those in need of a haven:

> To deny them [i.e. the refugees] a resting-place on God's footstool because [they are] temporarily devoid of material wealth, would be an endorsement of cruelty and an encouragement to its continuance. It is apposite to mention that about ten years since, in consequence of the cruel edicts recently being again carried out, a very large number of Russian Jews sought this land of liberty as a haven of rest. They have been assimilated in the mass of the citizenry, and, so far as can be ascertained, not a single one has become a public burden.[4]

Even more restrictive legislation was passed by Congress in 1921 and 1924. This legislation distributed admission according to the percentage of the American population coming from specific foreign countries. The impact of the 1924 law was especially drastic, for quotas were determined on the basis of the census of 1890. The law drastically limited immigration from countries with large Jewish populations like Poland, Russia, and Rumania. Yet despite such hindrances the future of America as a Jewish community had already been determined: the Jews of the United States were fated to become the largest Jewish community in the world—in fact, the largest single community in the millennial history of the Jewish people.

In 1973 the *American Jewish Year Book* estimated the Jewish population of the United States at 6,115,000. World Jewish population was estimated at 14,370,000.[5] No single country approached the United States in the size of its Jewish population. Even Israel, with a Jewish population of 2,723,000, had less than half the number of Jews in the United States.

[4] *Ibid.*, p. 77.

[5] *American Jewish Year Book* 1973, Vol. 74, pp. 307, 523.

The dominance of the American Jewish community means that its survival has become crucial to the future of the Jewish people. Indeed, it is hard to imagine Jewish existence in the Diaspora without a viable and vital American Jewish community. But the importance of the American Jewish community is related not only to its size but to the awesome circumstances of recent Jewish history.

Some 6,000,000 Jews were put to death in the Nazi Holocaust during World War II. In recent years, in the United States and elsewhere, Jews have begun to grapple with the manifold implications of this catastrophe. However, even before it was possible to discuss the Holocaust on the conscious level, one of its implications came to be understood implicitly: in the late 1940's American Jewish leaders began to stress the responsibility of American Jewry for Jewish survival. The Holocaust had thrust the leadership of Diaspora Jewry upon the Jewish community of the United States. For some the new role represented as much a burden as an opportunity. But even those not especially eager to grasp the responsibility were at least dimly aware that they had become trustees of the Jewish people and would play a major role in determining its future.

The responsibilities of American Jewry came to be greatly magnified by another development. The Jewish community of the Soviet Union—at 2,648,000, the third largest in the world—has for the past half-century been prevented from playing its proper role in Jewish affairs. Though the suppression of Jewishness in the Soviet Union has at some periods been more brutal than at others since the Communist revolution, the most that could be expected of Soviet Jewry is that it would somehow preserve the will to remain Jewish, and manage somehow to pass on a feeling for Jewishness to the younger generation. In any case the predicament of Soviet Jewry has greatly heightened the responsibilities of Jews living in the United States—a nation where there was never a barrier to the free expression of Jewish identification and where there has always existed every possibility of passing on the Jewish heritage to the next generation.

Before 1947 the responsibilities which had been thrust upon American Jewry by the Holocaust and by the predicament of Soviet Jewry could have been displaced upon the Jews of Palestine, and after 1948 they could have been set upon the doorstep of the new State of Israel. To some extent this in fact occurred, particularly inasmuch as the Jewish leaders of Palestine, and later of Israel, saw their community as central to world Jewry, and went to great lengths to save Jewish lives during World War II and to encourage the settlement of Jews in the land. Despite the fact that in the 1930's the United States did receive an influx of Jews fleeing Nazi persecution, later augmented by survivors of the Holocaust, the main focus of immigration from the European continent during the most recent past has been Palestine-Israel. The same holds true for Jews leaving the Arab countries of North Africa or the Middle East, and the process is being repeated in the latest migration of Jews from the Soviet Union: so far, migration is predominantly to Israel rather than to the United States or to other Diaspora communities.

The facts of Jewish migration patterns during recent decades, together with the establishment of Israel as a sovereign Jewish state, should have served to diminish the leadership role that had come to the American Jewish community on account of the Holocaust and the restrictive policy of the Soviet Union toward its Jewish citizens. That diminishment was in fact ardently desired by Zionist leadership and later by officials of the State of Israel, who saw themselves as preeminently responsible for the destiny of world Jewry. While some Jewish leaders in the United States contested these claims, others were not altogether unwilling to relinquish the heavy burdens they had fallen heir to.

Resignation or relinquishment was easier said than done, however, for Israel's ambitions in this regard have yet to be fulfilled. Israel has been able to assist world Jewry in new and manifold ways, by providing a haven free from immigration restrictions, supplying teachers of the Hebrew language as well as religious specialists, and in general improving the self-esteem of Diaspora Jews. But Israel has also been a beleaguered state for over a quarter-century now, and this condition has militated against its capacity to become the sole center of Jewish life, just as it has greatly retarded the relinquishment by American Jewry of its own particular leadership role. Zionist ideology held that the establishment of a Jewish state would spell the end of Jewish dependency and Jewish vulnerability, but in the case of Israel this hoped-for self-sufficiency has not come to pass. Israel has been forced to look to world Jewry for both financial assistance and political support, and for all practical purposes this has meant an unwanted reliance upon American Jewry.

The overwhelming need constantly to defend the very existence of the State has made Israel dependent on Gentile as well as on Jewish support. Its viability has rested at least as much upon the will of the great powers as upon its own resources and resolve. And of the great powers only the United States has shown itself to be a long-time and reliable friend. This dependence on American political and military support has served to magnify further the leadership role of the American Jewish community, whose steadfast endorsement of an activist American policy in the Middle East has been a significant factor in the continued pursuit of that policy. The role which has been thrust upon the American Jewish community, then, is not only a result of its great numbers, of the awful consequences of the Holocaust, and of the tragic situation of Soviet Jewry. American Jewry's role has also been vastly enlarged by the circumstances under which the State of Israel has been forced to exist.

The combination of all of these historical developments and forces means that while the optimism of outsiders about the state of the Jewish community is understandable, it is the insiders whose assessment has been in accord with Jewish needs. The constant dunning of the Jewish community, the restless urging that it do more and more, is not simply the voice of a few malcontents. This criticism is sensitive to the changing tides of history; it reflects an awareness, however unarticulated, of the awesome responsibilities which have befallen American Jewry, and as often as not, it is directed at encouraging actions which will help to assure the survival of Jewish life.

THE INFORMAL COMMUNITY

THE ORIGIN OF A JEWISH COMMUNITY IN THE SUBURBS

by HERBERT J. GANS

INTRODUCTION

PARK FOREST, ILLINOIS—one of the largest of the post-World-War II housing developments—happens to be located within easy commuting distance of the University of Chicago and as a result has been intensively investigated by social scientists. Herbert J. Gans, a leading urbanologist, was a graduate student at the university when Park Forest was founded and he took on the task of studying Jewish life in the new community.

Since the outward direction of Chicago Jewry was almost entirely to the northern and northwest suburbs, for a time it seemed unlikely that there would be anything worth studying in Park Forest. However, despite its location southwest of the city, Park Forest did succeed in attracting some Jewish families for several possible reasons: Park Forest was itself developed by Jews who were widely known in the Jewish community, it offered housing at a time of critical shortage, its private dwellings and apartments cost less than comparable housing in suburbs which were attracting large numbers of Jews, and for some breadwinners transportation from Park Forest to their jobs was more convenient than from the northern suburbs.

The Jews who were attracted to Park Forest tended to be

somewhat marginal to the Jewish community.* Their marginality was compounded by the fact that there was no preexistent Jewish community—or for that matter, any real community at all—in Park Forest to which they might attach themselves. Thus in theory, and perhaps in reality as well, the Jews who settled in Park Forest had the option of integrating themselves into the life of the newly forming general community and, if not themselves assimilating, at least encouraging their children to do so. The other available option was to pursue group survival by seeking to establish a Jewish community in the inhospitable territory of the southwestern suburbs.

The predominant response was to pursue the goal of group survival, and a Jewish community soon came to be established in Park Forest. While some Jews did very little to advance the cause, the activists were sufficiently numerous and influential to achieve their goal. (In any case there was no organized group dedicated to preventing the emergence of a Jewish community; given the pluralism and permissiveness of American social structure, it would have been difficult to organize one.) To be sure, the kind of community which emerged in Park Forest was far from traditional—it accorded instead with the patterns of Jewish culture and identity practiced by members of the community themselves. No mikvah was built in Park Forest, and indeed the early pioneers of the community were in no hurry even to establish a synagogue, the one institution which symbolized Jewish affirmation in so many other suburban communities. But despite the indifference to a mikvah and the hesitancy to form a synagogue, very soon after the first Jewish residents arrived it was clear that the question of whether there was to be a Jewish community had been resolved in the affirmative.

What did the Jewish pioneers of Park Forest establish? Gans discovered that the community consisted of two layers—what he calls the informal community and the formal community. The formal community was established second—indeed it was made possible by the existence of an informal community and was erected on its foundation. At the outset the formal community was rudimentary in structure and consisted of little more than a single

*It is quite possible that one of Park Forest's attractions was that it would not become a Skokie—a northwestern suburb of Chicago which was transformed in a relatively few years from an all-Gentile community to a thickly populated Jewish area.

organization for men and another organization for women. (When Gans returned to Park Forest in the mid-1950's he found the formal community to be much more elaborate; for example, it had come to include a synagogue much like those in other communities settled by highly acculturated Jews after World War II.)

That the organized Jewish community in general might rest on the base of an informal community had escaped most observers, who as a rule saw a community well after its establishment and whose attention was drawn to the formal structure: the synagogues, the offices of Jewish organizations, the Jewish community centers, the hospitals. Since the clique structure which undergirded the formal community (and which itself was undergirded by a Jewish kinship network) was invisible, the eye naturally focused on the formal aspects of the community. Gans, however, had the good fortune to witness the Park Forest Jewish community at its birth and being an unusually gifted field observer he not only detected the significance of the informal community but came to understand how its existence led to the establishment of a formal community.

Gans distinguishes four stages in the organization of the informal community: contact, recognition, acquaintance, and friendship. Since movement from stage to stage was exceedingly rapid in Park Forest we must draw the conclusion that ethnic identity has salience even for marginally situated Jews. The cycle from contact to friendship is particularly impressive if we remember that the Jews of Park Forest were not only a minuscule group but were scattered throughout the sprawling development—in the early days of Park Forest there was no one area with a concentration of Jewish population. In addition, whether because they were detached from Jewish tradition or because they were unwilling to distinguish themselves publicly from their neighbors, the Jews of Park Forest did not "advertise" their Jewishness: Gans does not mention a single instance of a mezuzah being fastened to a door frame. Nevertheless the initial 150 Jewish families (out of a total of 1,800 families then in Park Forest) speedily discovered each other; the devices they used are delineated by Gans with particular clarity. The process, which began with contact, culminated in the formation of an informal Jewish community—cliques that were all or predominantly Jewish in composition.

As Gans points out, even individuals who maintained the irrelevancy of the Jewish-Gentile distinction in choosing their friends came to belong to predominantly Jewish cliques. The *informal Jewish community thus consisted of Jews who varied in the level and type of their Jewish identity. Although in the earliest days of Park Forest these differences were not reflected in the formal community, as that community became more elaborate they did come to take on public significance.*

M. S.

. . . PARK FOREST, ILLINOIS, the scene of the study described here, is not an ordinary suburb but rather a partially planned garden city.[1] Located thirty miles south of Chicago's Loop, it was envisioned both as a dormitory for Chicago white-collar workers (which it is), and a partially self-sufficient community with its own industries (which it still hopes to be). The plan called for 3,000 rental garden apartments, for 4,500 single-family homes available for sale, as well as for shopping centers, schools, churches, playgrounds, and other community facilities.[2] The conversion of

[1]The garden-city movement—founded by Ebenezer Howard in England at the turn of the century—advocated the building of small communities with their own industries, to combine what were considered to be the social and psychological advantages of small-town living with the requirements of an urban economy (see Howard's book, *Garden Cities of Tomorrow*, [London: 1902]). Leaders of this movement were instrumental in the construction of two garden cities in England. They have influenced, either directly or indirectly, the new towns built near London after World War II, the U.S. government's greenbelt towns built during the 1930's, and private developments such as Radburn (New Jersey), Park Forest, the Levittowns, and several industry-built communities. Some of these are analyzed in Clarence Stein, *Towards New Towns for America* (Chicago: 1951).

[2]The plans for Park Forest (which were revised during construction) are described in "American Community Builders," *The Architectural Forum*, August 1948, pp. 70–74, and by H. Henderson and S. Shaw, "City to Order," *Collier's*, 14 February 1948. Many other articles on the community have appeared in various architectural journals and general magazines since that time. The best report on life in Park Forest is an insightful journalistic-sociological study by William H. Whyte, Jr., "The Transients," *Fortune*, May-August 1953. See also, Herbert J. Gans, "Planning and Political Participation," *Journal of the American Institute of Planners*, Winter 1953, pp. 1–9, and "Political Participation and Apathy," unpublished M.A. thesis, Division of the Social Sciences, University of Chicago, June 1950.

For studies of English communities similar to Park Forest, see Ruth Durant, *Watling* (London: 1939); Harold Orlans, *Utopia Limited* (New Haven: 1953), and Leo Kuper *et. al., Living in Towns* (London: 1953). For studies of American communities, see Robert K. Merton, "Social Psychology of Housing," in Wayne Dennis (ed.), *Current Trends in Social Psychology* (Pittsburgh: 1948), pp. 163–217, and his forthcoming *Patterns of Social Life: Explorations in the Sociology and Social Psychology of Housing*, with P. S. West, and M. Jahoda; William Form, "Status Stratification in Low and Middle Income Housing Areas," in "Social Policy and Social Research in Housing," *Journal of Social Issues*, Issues 1 and 2, 1951, pp. 109–131, and "Status Stratification in a Planned Community," *American Sociological Review*, October 1945, pp. 605–613. Two as yet unpublished studies of the Levittowns are Marie Jahoda *et. al., Community Influences on Psychological Health* (tentative title), and John Liell, *"Levittown: A Study in Community Development and Planning,"* Ph.D. dissertation, Department of Sociology, Yale University, 1952.

the golf course and farmland which were to be the site of the new town began in 1947, and the first tenants moved in on August 30, 1948. By April 1949, the community had been incorporated as a village.

Like other postwar suburbs, Park Forest first attracted the people most sorely pressed for shelter—young couples with one or two children of preschool age.[3] In 1949, the median age of the men was thirty-two, of the women somewhat less; anyone over forty was generally considered old. Many of the men were beginning their careers, and most of them were in professional, sales, or administrative and other business fields. . . . It seemed probable that the village was attracting the socially and geographically more mobile members of the generation of returning veterans.

In November 1949, when the interviewing for this study was completed, about 1,800 families were living in the village. About 25 percent of them were Catholic. The Jewish community then numbered just under 150 families. Of these, about twenty (fifteen of them mixed marriages) rejected all relationships with the formal Jewish community.[4] Another thirty families had not been in Park Forest long enough to have made contact with the established Jewish community. We interviewed a sample which consisted of forty-four of the remaining group of 100 families.[5] This sample was subdivided into families of people who had been *active* in the formation of Jewish organizations or were now in leadership positions, and those *inactive*, whether or not they were members of organizations.[6] Within the total sample, the median age of heads of

[3]This description of the residents of Park Forest is based on participant observation as well as some fifty interviews with residents chosen at random (though not from a statistically designed random sample), for a study of political participation.

[4]The total number of known "mixed marriages" was estimated at twenty-four, or 17 percent of the Jewish population. Despite the efficiency of the community grapevine, this estimate is probably conservative. Of the twenty-four couples, about a third participated in the Jewish community.

[5]This group of one hundred also included twenty who said they were not interested in the Jewish community. However, they had Jewish friends and were at least part of the communication network of the Jewish group.

The data presented here are based on about six months of observation in the village, including attendance at many meetings, on conversations with Jewish residents, and on full interviews with one person in each of forty-four Jewish families and partial ones with ten more. . . .

[6]The sample on which the data presented in this section is based was stratified between a group of leaders and actives selected from all factions of the community for the analysis of community processes, and a group of residents most of whom were

households was thirty-five, and of their wives, thirty. Some 43 percent of the families had one or more school-age children, while 57 percent had only younger children or were still childless. Although there were no age differences between the actives and the inactives, the former had a slightly higher proportion of older children. . . .

About 90 percent of the men in the sample had some college training. Some 57 percent had graduated from college, and 32 percent held graduate or professional degrees. . . . Some 36 percent of the sample were professionals. A total of 48 percent were in business and industry, though only 14 percent were owners.

Eighty-eight percent of the adults in the sample were native-born. Most of the parents of this group were foreign-born. Overwhelmingly, the families came from Eastern Europe. All but a few of our interviewees were brought up in large cities (60 percent of them in Chicago); they came primarily from working-class or lower-middle-class areas of second settlement. While Park Foresters are mainly "second generation," they are the children of later immigrants or of immigrants who themselves came to America as children, and must be distinguished from second-generation descendants of Jews in the first waves of Eastern European immigration (before 1900) whose own children (third generation) are already adolescents or young adults. . . .[7]

In summary, the Jewish sample can be described as a group of young, highly educated, second-generation Jews of Eastern European parentage, most of whom have already achieved—or are likely to achieve—upper-middle-class income status, given con-

known not to be leaders, chosen at random from the mailing list. In the original sample, actives were overrepresented; but with a knowledge of the proportion of actives and inactives in the total community (based on the judgments of a number of informants), this sample was brought closer to representativeness, *post facto*, by the random elimination of some interviews with actives.

[7]The generational analysis using formal genealogical categories is complicated by the fact that Jewish immigration from Eastern Europe lasted over two generations. Furthermore, the immigrants were themselves of two generations, being either children or adults. Also, since Eastern European Jewry was then already acculturating in the wake of urban-industrial change and Western cultural influences, immigrants may have been of two or more *cultural generations* (i.e., "generations" defined in terms of deviation from the traditional culture). Consequently, an analytically meaningful concept of generation would have to include several factors, and a generational description of a second generation Jew would not be complete without an analysis of his parents' age at arrival and their cultural orientation at the time of his upbringing. Such an analysis of the Park Forest material remains to be done.

tinued prosperity. The active members of the community rate somewhat higher on socio-economic characteristics than do the inactives.

Turning to the problem of cultural distinctiveness, it is apparent that many of the Jewish residents could not easily be distinguished from other Park Foresters. Although many of them could be said to "look Jewish," they wore the same fashions, ate the same dishes (except on special occasions), and participated with other Park Foresters in the ubiquitous American class- and leisure-culture of the "young moderns." They observed few of the old cultural and religious traditions. The village's isolation from synagogues and kosher butcher shops discouraged observant Jews from becoming tenants, and brought problems to those who did.

Not only did Park Forest Jews live like other Park Foresters; they lived *with* them. Whereas most American cities have neighborhoods which are predominantly Jewish (if not always in numbers, at least in atmosphere and institutions), such was not the case with Park Forest. The Jewish families were scattered at random, and only rarely were two Jewish families to be found in adjacent houses. The tenants, Jewish and non-Jewish, lived in so-called "courts"—*cul-de-sac* parking bays encircled by twenty to forty two-story garden apartments, built together in rows of five to seven, and renting in 1949 for $75–$100 per month.[8]

The occupants of the courts described themselves as living in a goldfish bowl in which privacy was at a minimum. Depending on the makeup of the group, this court life ranged from that of "one big happy family" to a tense collection of unwilling neighbors, although with the passing of time people learned how to find privacy in a high-density world of picture windows. For many of the non-Jewish Park Foresters, the court was almost an independent social unit in which they found most, if not all, their friends, and from which they ventured only rarely, at least during the first year or two.[9]

[8]Some of the Jewish families showed a decided preference for end-units, which were slightly more expensive. The extent to which this choice was due to desire for isolation rather than the need for an extra bedroom for older children or the ability to pay higher rents, was not studied. The homeowners who came later live on a more traditional but curved street plan. For a highly generalized description of the court life see William H. Whyte, Jr., "How the New Suburbia Socializes," *Fortune,* August 1953, pp. 120–122, 186–190. For a rigorous study of certain limited aspects of the social life of a housing project, see Leon Festinger, Stanley Schachter, and Kurt Back, *Social Pressures in Informal Groups* (New York: 1950).

[9]A systematic stratification analysis would probably show that those with upper-middle-class aspirations tended to find friends outside the court; this in part also explains the behavior of the Jewish residents.

The Formation of the Jewish Community

The Jews who came to Park Forest were impelled by the same need for housing, and a desire for a suburban environment in which to raise their children, as were their neighbors.[10] (Some of them also came to learn how to live in the suburbs before buying a house.) Soon after they arrived, they aligned themselves into a number of cliques. In a remarkably short period these formed an interrelated network by which news, gossip, and rumor could be communicated. Out of this informal community there developed a formal community of voluntary associations and religious organizations.

A. *Evolution of the Informal Community.* The developmental processes of this informal community can be described in four stages: *contact, recognition, acquaintance,* and *friendship.*

Contact is the opportunity for face-to-face meeting. In order for interaction to develop beyond this point, there had to be the mutual recognition of each other's Jewishness and status position. *As an ethnic group, the Jews form a cohesive ingroup and tend to behave differently toward a member of the ingroup than toward a non-Jew, in many cases reserving the intimacy of friendship for the former.* Thus, before two persons can act in terms of the more personal ingroup norm, they must have a sign that identifies them to each other as fellow ingroup members. Without this recognition there can be no progress toward the formation of acquaintance and the regular interaction of an intimate nature (i.e., the exchange of personal facts, attitudes, and feelings which we call friendship).

Due to the fact that most of the officers of American Community Builders, Inc. (A.C.B.), the corporation that built Park Forest, are Jewish, and the further fact that several have long been active in Jewish affairs, a Jewish community in Park Forest was

[10]No one has ever studied why one community or subdivision gains Jewish residents while another area is avoided. Dr. Julian L. Greifer reported that in the Philadelphia area:

> Some of the new private housing developments have become almost exclusively populated by Jews, as friend followed friend, and relative moved near relative. . . . I know of several pioneering Jewish families that settled in new suburban communities but after a few years moved back, at great personal loss, to localities more heavily populated by Jews. Apparently the failure of additional Jewish families to settle in the new communities isolated the pioneers from Jewish contacts and communal institutions.

"Relationships in a Large City," *Jewish Social Studies,* July 1955, pp. 269–270. One factor in this decision is probably the ethnic identity of the developer. If he is Jewish he is likely to advertise in Anglo-Jewish papers, as well as invite friends to move into his project.

almost predestined.[11] Before the opening of the development, its officers had invited several friends to move out, and these were among the first tenants.

For those not personally known to the officers, the recognition process began in each court, as families stood beside their moving van and eyed the strangers who were to be their neighbors. Recognition was initiated even before contact was made, for with the first glance, Jewish people were attempting to figure out whether one or another person could be Jewish. This hypothesizing sometimes went on for days; or, if there was relative certainty, and one person was aggressive enough, it lasted a matter of minutes. Mrs. H. described it thusly:

> Mrs. F. came over and talked to me while we were outside with the moving van. It was not a question of religion, but of recognition, I knew she was Jewish by her name, and she looked Jewish, I don't know if the thing was ever discussed, I don't know if she knew I was Jewish that first day.

Mrs. F. said of that meeting:

> I didn't know Mrs. H. was Jewish, I kind of thought as much, by her looks.

In this case there were two signs of recognition, the Jewish "look" and a Jewish "name." Frequently people used a customary request for each other's names to test hypotheses of recognition based on the Jewish "look."

Anthropologists are agreed that there is no Jewish race. Nevertheless, many people, and especially Jews, tend to identify Mediterranean and Armenoid facial features as Jewish. This, plus the fact that certain names are almost monopolized by Jews, has created a stereotypical recognition formula which is realistic enough to be correct more often than it is not. This formula was used in a large number of cases for determining who were the other Jews in the court; its role in the formation of the Jewish community cannot be underestimated.

The look and the name were sometimes reinforced by what might be described as Jewish mannerisms, that is, a set of gestures or verbal expressions that are—again stereotypically—ascribed to Jews:

[11]In 1953 the president of A.C.B. became the international president of B'nai B'rith.

It was obvious he was Jewish, by name and appearance. I thought he was from New York, by his speech and action. I've run into a lot of Brooklyn people and can tell them apart. Then I went into his house, and saw the candlesticks.

As the above respondent indicated, there were other signs of recognition, for some people displayed Jewish ritual objects which quickly resolved all doubts.

Sometimes, however, people turned to systematic techniques of exploration. For example, initial conversations were skillfully directed toward attempts to discover the other's religion, or to offer clues as to one's own. When that failed, or seemed imprudent, the conversation turned to food habits:

. . . we have a taste for Jewish food . . . we told them what kind of food it was we liked: cornbeef, lox [smoked salmon]. . . .

The day I moved in I advertised that I was Jewish by asking for Jewish women who kept kosher. . . .

Sometimes there were no symbols or formulas which could be applied, and people found out by accident:

My next door neighbors, they didn't look Jewish, nothing Jewish about them, but then I asked before Passover if they wanted to try some macaroons, and we found out.

I knew them as neighbors, knew them for a month, then the name was given me on a mailing list. I was amazed, I didn't know they were Jewish.

The recognition process was somewhat facilitated by the presence of a minister who conducted a religious survey soon after each court was occupied, and informed curious Jews who the other Jews in the court were. In addition, there were a number of Jewish men who made a point of getting to know the entire Jewish community, and thus they were able to introduce individuals to each other.[12]

There was no automatic progression from recognition to *acquaintance* without a desire for further association. In many

[12]In most cases, however, the recognition as well as many other parts of the community formation process were handled by the women, for they were in the community all day long while the men commuted to Chicago. This sexual division of the social labors held also in the non-Jewish community.

cases, however, this desire for association with Jews was implied if not expressed already at the recognition stage, by the aggressiveness of one person or the other in creating conditions that allowed recognition when the Jewish-look-or-name formula alone was not conclusive.

Mutual recognition was followed by further exploration of each other's ethnic characteristics and affiliations. Neighbors asked each other where they were from, where they lived last, whom they knew there, what congregation or groups they belonged to, and later turned to discussing their attitudes toward Jewish traditions and observances. The question, "Did you know the So-and-So's in ———?" was perhaps most important. People who had mutual friends, or even mutual acquaintances in previous places of residence, very quickly passed to the acquaintance and friendship stages, thus accelerating the rate of community formation.

The abundance of these prior contacts is a function of the fact that the world of the middle-class Jew is comparatively small. Even in the larger cities, there are only a limited number of Jewish organizations, temples, and neighborhoods. Furthermore, Jewish families are still extensive, and maintain communication contacts even when kinship solidarity is much reduced. Consequently, people who are socially active tend to meet, or at least know about, a considerable proportion of their community's Jewish group. Many Park Forest Jews thus encountered neighbors with whom they could initiate relationships on the basis of some previous bond, even if it was nothing more than an introduction at some social function. In a new community of strangers, these prior contacts were invested with a greater significance than they would have elsewhere, and the relationships which grew from them achieved regularity and stability rather quickly. They became the foundations for the informal community, which was then completed by the slower development of social relationships among total strangers. The exchange of names also provided an opportunity for the parties involved to measure each other's social status and interests by those of the mutual acquaintance.

While it is difficult to determine at what point an acquaintance relationship became one of *friendship,* the overall timetable of the process of informal community development was fairly uniform. Usually ten days to two weeks passed before any but the exceptionally gregarious and mobile people made any serious attempts at getting out of the house to make contacts. However, after this moving-in period, contact, recognition, and acquaintance relationships developed quickly. In general it was a matter of only four to eight weeks before people said they had friends whom they saw regularly. Some residents suggested that regularity did not yet mean intimacy: "We see the So-and-So's regularly but you really can't call them friends, we haven't been here that long." Nor was it certain that these relationships would persist. Nevertheless, in November of 1949 almost all of the families who were living in the village by July of that year had established some regular and stable sociability relationships with their fellow Jews.[13]

B. Development of Formal Organizations. The development of the formal community began with the organization of a B'nai B'rith lodge and a chapter of the National Council of Jewish Women.

Among the first arrivals in Park Forest were a handful of "Jewish professionals," men who work for American-Jewish agencies. They were interested in setting up Jewish organizations, and while their activity was voluntary, like that of any other resident, their interest was still more than purely social or civic. In March of 1949, when fifty Jewish families were living in the village, one of these professionals (employed as an organizer in Chicago) considered the time to be ripe and invited a small group of men to discuss the formation of a lodge. Several of the men had met each other previously in the course of a local political campaign. Many of those present at the meeting, although vaguely in favor of a group, were not interested in any specific organization. One of them said:

> We were contemplating some kind of a social club, recreational, then we hit on . . . B'nai B'rith. The fact is that we were influenced, I guess, by fellows who are with B'nai B'rith.

Consequently, the group decided to form a lodge. Some thirty-five men were invited to the next meeting. There the lodge was organized, with the professionals and a handful of other actives taking over the decision-making positions.

[13]The kind of friendship relationship discussed here is not the intimate lifetime friendship as it is classically defined, but rather a companionship in transitory surroundings (like a college dormitory or army camp) which is intimate while the surroundings are shared but may end when they are not. On the other hand, it may lead to permanent relationships, especially if the parties involved are traveling toward the same social goals. It would be interesting to discover whether contemporary social trends encourage such companionship rather than the permanent type of friendship.

The organization of the women's group took place about a month later. It was initiated by two women who had just entered the village. While they knew the Jewish residents of their court, they wanted to make contact with others. Through a mailing list already compiled by the men's group,[14] the women were contacted and invited to an organizational meeting. At this gathering the process which took place at the men's meeting was repeated. Most of those present expressed the desire and need for a women's group. The initiators proposed affiliation with Council. Their choice was approved, and they were named to leadership positions.

Attendance and active participation in the Council of Jewish Women was immediately greater than in B'nai B'rith, reflecting the women's greater desire for Jewish companionships. Furthermore, the Council meetings provided an efficient and easily available method for newcomers to make contacts with the older settlers. It facilitated the recognition process, and initially this was perhaps the group's major—though latent—function.

The early leadership structure of both groups in its relationships with the informal community was quite similar. The top leaders in both organizations were "lone wolves"—they belonged to no set clique in the village. The rest of the officers in both groups were drawn largely from a clique of the older, well-to-do people who had been active in formal organizational life elsewhere. This clique had become fairly well stabilized by the time the two formal groups were organized; consequently clique members worked actively together in the structuring of the formal community.

After the organizational period, both groups evolved in the direction of their urban counterparts. Thus B'nai B'rith had speakers, played poker, and offered refreshments; the Council ran a number of study groups, heard other speakers, conducted charity programs, and gave the Jewish women of the community a chance to dress up and meet. In November 1949, each had enrolled about fifty members. . . .

[14]Some comment should be made about the cohesive and social pressure functions of the mailing list. This list was carefully compiled soon after the formation of the lodge, and kept up to date so as to include everyone known or suspected to be Jewish. The existence of the community was stressed by frequent mailings which went even to people who rejected all contact with the Jewish group. Later, Sunday school announcements were sent to everyone, as its caretaker reported:

> Just to show people what was being done in the Jewish community and to keep their interest up. No names should be taken off the list just because people hadn't shown interest.

The Informal Community— The Ethnic Cohesion of Sociability

While [some] Jewish Park Foresters . . . avoided involvement with adult Jewish activities, they were nevertheless willing and desirous of associating with other Jews. Groups were formed consisting usually of another couple or a clique[15] of couples. Together they composed the informal Jewish community.

A. *Sociability Patterns.* On the whole, the informal community existed only at night. In the daytime, Park Forest was inhabited by housewives and the ever present children, and the Jewish women participated in the social life of the courts in which they lived. They interrupted their household duties to chat and "visit with" a neighbor over a morning cup of coffee, or while watching the children in the afternoon. They also belonged to the bridge and sewing clubs that were established in many courts. In these nonintimate, quasi-occupational relationships, which in many ways resembled their husbands' relationships at the office, ethnic distinctions were minimized.[16]

In the evening and weekend social relationships of couples, however, the Jewish husband and wife turned primarily to other Jews. One housewife summarized matters as follows:

> My real close friends are Jewish, my after-dark friends in general are Jewish, but my daytime friends are Gentile.

Table 1 shows the sociability choices of thirty respondents who volunteered the names of their friends living in the village.

Although the figures are small, it is apparent that the actives chose their friends among other Jews to a greater extent than the inactives. *However, about half the people who named both Jews and non-Jews pointed out that their best friends were Jewish,* and

[15]For a useful definition of clique, see W. Lloyd Warner and Paul Lunt, *The Social Life of a Modern Community* (New Haven: 1941), pp. 110–111.

[16]Ethnic distinctions were almost nonexistent in the all-male activities. Bowling teams, baseball leagues, and poker clubs were organized on a court basis. In this connection one of the women observed:

> The boys are real friendly, I imagine they don't think about it [ethnic distinctions] but the women have different feelings. Women have little to do; they talk about it in the afternoons.

The extent to which class factors rather than ethnic factors determined participation in these activities was not studied.

two of the inactives who "saw" mainly non-Jews explained that they were merely visiting with nearby neighbors and implied that the search for friends had not yet begun in earnest. Two of the respondents who named only non-Jews were attempting to avoid all relationships with Jews. Thus, for the purpose of "friendship" as distinguished from "neighboring," and especially for close relationships, the Jewish residents seemed to prefer other Jews. The informal Jewish community existed primarily for this function.

The cliques into which this community was subdivided varied in size from two to six couples. Sociometric factors as well as living-room size set this as an upper limit. A superficial sociometric analysis indicated that these cliques were connected into a network (which existed primarily for communication) by people who belonged to more than one clique, and by a few others who maintained loose memberships with a large number. These latter people, who made few close friends, chose to get to know as many people as possible and derived pride and satisfaction from the acquisition of such relationships. During the time of the study, the informal community came together only once. This was at a village dance. As both Jews and non-Jews later reported, the Jews at this affair congregated in one section of the hall.

The formation of cliques was accelerated by the people with previous acquaintances. However, loose as these contacts may have

TABLE 1
Sociability choices by activity status

"See regularly socially"	*Actives*		*Inactives*		*All*	
	No.	*%*	*No.*	*%*	*No.*	*%*
Jews only	4	57	6	26	10	33
Mainly Jews, some non-Jews	1	14	9	39	10	33
Mainly non-Jews, some Jews	1	14	5	22	6	20
Non-Jews only	1	14	3	13	4	14
TOTAL	7	99	23	100	30	100

been (a fleeting introduction at a meeting or party sufficed), such people established friendship relationships much more quickly than strangers who had first to explore each others' social attributes and interests. They generally became "charter members" of a clique which then attracted strangers into its circle. Of the approximately twenty-five cliques and combinations isolated in the sample, twenty had been formed, at least in part, on the basis of previous or mutual acquaintance. In this respect, the Jews differed sharply from other Park Foresters, most of whom knew no one when they arrived in the village.

Cliques were formed primarily on the basis of class, status, age, and ethnic background criteria. One of the largest and most powerful of the cliques was made up predominantly of relatively older, higher-income Park Foresters, many of them previously active in big-city Jewish congregations and groups. Most of the men held supervisory positions in business or industry, or were in the nonacademic professions. A second clique consisted largely of academicians, researchers, scientists, writers, and their wives (many of whom were active on the community newspaper). A third was made up of families who had come to Park Forest from areas of second and third settlement. They were torn between their lower-middle-class and still partially tradition-oriented ways of life, and the upper-middle-class ways of the first clique.

Despite the class-status homogeneity of the cliques, members often harbored the most diverse attitudes toward Jewishness. Respondents reported frequent clique discussions on Jewish topics, and commented:

> I don't start these discussions; it's a beautiful subject to steer away from; there are more fights about religion than anything else.
>
> There's a couple with whom we're very friendly; we like each other very much. They don't believe the way we do, and if we discuss it, it would just lead to arguments.

Whereas most non-Jewish Park Foresters chose their friends from within their courts, Jews tended to wander outside the court for their social relationships. Sometimes this was due to the absence of other Jews, but when this was not the case, clique membership and associated status- and age-criteria were more important than locational ones. One respondent described her relationship with the other Jewish women in the court:

> We've never spent an evening together. Mrs. F. and I are good friends, we walk together, but she is a bit older. . . . She travels in a different circle of people . . . with an older, more settled crowd, better off; if they have children, they're beyond the preschool age. . . .

B. Friendship and Ingroup Behavior. Many factors must be considered in the explanation of this intraethnic friendship pattern. A fundamental one is the age-old segregation between Jew and non-Jew in Western society. Despite political emancipation, this segregation has been maintained by cultural differences. While many of these differences are being eliminated by acculturation, not enough time has elapsed for this change to affect adult social, and especially peer-group, relationships. As a consequence, current Jewish–non-Jewish relationships are still based largely on the historic segregation. Most Jews seem to assume its continued existence. Also, some feel they would be rejected in non-Jewish society, while others are not much interested in primary relationships with non-Jews.[17]

Perhaps most often, the long segregation has made association solely with other Jews almost habitual. The interview material indicated that most Park Forest Jews grew up in urban Jewish neighborhoods. Their parental circle, and their own childhood, adolescent, and adult peer groups, were predominantly Jewish. In the absence of any strong incentives or socio-economic and ideological pressures for greater social intimacy with non-Jews, these patterns of association were rarely questioned.

An important functional basis for the choice of Jewish friends was contained in the attitude shared by many Park Forest Jews that "it's easier being with Jews." *Since sociability is primarily a leisure activity, and in a suburban community one of the major forms of relaxation and self-expression, the belief that there is likely to be less tension in social relationships with other Jews becomes all-important.* A respondent who had both Jewish and non-Jewish friends pointed out:

> You can give vent to your feelings. If you talk to a Christian and say you don't believe in this, you are doing it as a Jew; with Jewish friends you can tell 'em point blank what you feel.

[17]For a discussion of Jewish–non-Jewish relationships, and of anti-Semitism in Park Forest, see the writer's "Park Forest: Birth of a Jewish Community," *Commentary*, April 1951, pp. 337–338.

However ambivalent their feelings toward Judaism, in a group of friends the Jews form a strong ingroup, with well-verbalized attitudes toward the non-Jewish outgroup.[18]

The group cohesion, the ingroup attitude, and the anti-outgroup feeling that often accompanies it, are expressed frequently at the informal parties and gatherings where the friendly atmosphere and the absence of non-Jews creates a suitable environment. These feelings are verbalized through the Jewish joke, which expresses aspects of the Jew's attitude toward himself as well as toward the outgroup, or through direct remarks about the outgroup. At parties which are predominantly Jewish, it is necessary to find out if everyone is Jewish before such attitudes can be expressed overtly. When someone in the gathering who is assumed to be Jewish turns out to be otherwise, the atmosphere becomes very tense and the non-Jewish person may be avoided thereafter.

The manifestation of this ingroup attitude was described by one respondent who was converted to Judaism in his twenties. He told of becoming disturbed over a discussion at an informal party, the subject being how to inculcate Judaism into the children "and keep them away from the *goyim* (non-Jews)." This resident was very active in the Jewish community and feared the consequences of revealing his origin. Nevertheless, he felt the time had come to announce that he had been born and raised a Christian. The declaration broke up the party, and shocked many people. He said afterward:

> From now on, they'll be on their guard with me in their presence. They've lost their liberty of expression, they don't express themselves without restriction now. At a party if anybody says something, everybody looks to see if I've been offended and people are taken into a corner and explained about me.

Despite the fact that this person had adopted the Jewish religion, was raising his children as Jews, and was active in Jewish life, he was no longer a member of the ingroup although he remained a member both of the community and of his clique.

[18]Some of the respondents had rejected Judaism as a culture and religion, had not joined any of the formal organizations of the Park Forest Jewish community, but yet remained in the informal community. However, since the cliques were not formed on ideological bases, those alienated from Jewishness and from participation in the formal community were not excluded.

In summary, ingroup feelings provided a solid base of emotional security for group members of the type which they felt they could not receive from strictly organizational and religious activities. It gave a cohesive function to the informal community.

C. Ethnic Cohesion Through Intellectual Positions and Leisure-Time Preferences. Some of the more highly educated members of the community rejected these ingroup feelings as "chauvinistic"; they pointedly responded that they did not distinguish between Jews and non-Jews in choosing friends. Nevertheless, they remained in the ingroup.[19] They made statements like the following:

> The funny thing is, most of our friends are Jewish even though we say we don't care.

Or they said, on a note of guilt:

> I think we should try to have friends that aren't Jewish. I don't like the fact that all my friends are Jewish.

Such Jews sensed that their failure to associate with non-Jews was not due to ethnic differences, but rather to their own special orientation toward American society and middle-class culture. Several reported such differences with honest misgivings and alarm:

> I think most Jews feel they are a little better than others . . . they won't admit it, they think they're smarter than the rest. I almost guess Jews live by brain more than anyone else.
>
> We're smarter, that's a prejudice . . . we have better intuition, but I know it's not true.
>
> The Jews are more conscientious, they get more involved as in the League of Women Voters. . . .

These feelings were summarized in extreme form by one respondent:

> I have a friend who is not Jewish who told me how fortunate I was in being born Jewish. Otherwise I might be one of the sixteen to eighteen

[19]Compare the letter, "Jews and the Community," by Deborah Dorfman, *Commentary,* January 1955, p. 85.

> out of twenty Gentiles without a social conscience and liberal tendencies. . . . Being Jewish, most of the Jews, nine out of ten, are sympathetic with other problems; they sympathize, have more culture and a better education; strictly from the social and cultural standpoint a man is lucky to be born a Jew.

These attitudes had some basis in reality, for there seemed to be proportionately more Jews than non-Jews in Park Forest who expressed strong feelings of social consciousness, a personal concern in the political, social, and economic problems of the larger society, some interest in intellectual questions, and a tendency toward humanistic agnosticism.[20] Similarly, more Jews seemed to be interested in serious music and the fine arts, or at least the "highbrow" or "upper-middle brow" mass media fare,[21] in the so-called "higher quality" magazines, in the reading of books, and in membership in a Park Forest Cinema Club which showed foreign and art films.[22]

As a result, Jews who sought people sharing this subculture of intellectual interests and leisure preference tended to find them more easily among other Jews. In part this was due to the greater accessibility of other Jews. However, this was not a sufficient factor. Jews came together not only because they were Jews but because they shared the subculture, though it was actually devoid of Jewish

[20]No systematic comparative study was made of this phenomenon; the generalization is based on participant observation of Jewish and non-Jewish leisure activities of various "brow" levels, and the examination of close to 200 living-room bookshelves in the community. Note also the comments by Nathan Glazer, "Social Characteristics of American Jews 1654–1954," in the *American Jewish Year Book* Vol. 56 (New York: 1955), p. 33.

[21]See Russell Lynes' classic essay, "Highbrow, Middlebrow, Lowbrow," in *The Tastemakers* (New York: 1954), Ch. 13.

[22]Compare this with Berelson's description of the typical library user:

> From related investigations, the most probable interpretation of the differences in interest and activity involves a general characteristic which might be called cultural alertness. Studies . . . have repeatedly identified a certain group of people who engage in all sorts of cultural activities, in the broad sense, more than does the rest of the community. They read more, and listen more and talk more; they have opinions and feel more strongly about them, they join more organizations and are more active in them, and they know more about what is going on and . . . they are generally more sensitive and responsive to the culture in which they live.

"The Public Library, Book Reading and Political Behavior," *Library Quarterly*, October 1945, pp. 297–298, quoted in his *The Library's Public* (New York: 1949), p. 49.

themes. Furthermore, when Jewish problems were discussed by this group (and they *were* discussed), these were seen from a generalized world view rather than from the ingroup perspectives described above.[23] Since the reasons for associating with other Jews were not primarily ethnic, ethnic distinctions were not made.[24] The Jewish scientists and academicians in the village formed a number of cliques organized on the basis of this shared culture. Membership, though predominantly Jewish, included non-Jews as well.[25]

The explanation for the fact that Jews seem to be more predominant in this culture than non-Jews is a complex one which can only be suggested here. In part, it stems from the fact that the second generation Jew is frequently a marginal person whose upbringing makes him sensitive to the world around him.[26] Furthermore, this culture is associated with upper- and upper-mid-

[23]These Jews shared many of the characteristics which Robert K. Merton has attributed to the cosmopolitan influentials. While Merton made no distinctions between Jews and non-Jews, the Jew's historic role on the fringe of the social structure has perhaps directed him into cosmopolitan (if not influential) roles. Some of the conflicts within the Park Forest Jewish community (and also in Park Forest generally) can be understood in terms of conflicts between locals and cosmopolitans. Park Forest differed from the community studied by Merton in that a large number of cosmopolitans who were among the first arrivals in Park Forest saw the then unformed community as a place in which they might attempt to implement some of their cosmopolitan ideals. They thus took on many of the characteristics of "locals." In time, these cosmopolitans relinquished their positions to more genuine locals, for their utopian aspirations were rejected by the more conservative residents. See Robert K. Merton, "Patterns of Influence, A Study of Interpersonal Influence and of Communication Behavior in a Local Community," in *Communications Research 1948–1949*, ed. by Paul F. Lazarsfeld and Frank N. Stanton (New York: 1949), pp. 180–219.

[24]Milton Gordon has described these as "passive ethnic intellectuals." See his "Social Class and American Intellectuals," *Bulletin of the American Association of University Professors*, Winter 1954–1955, p. 527.

[25]The role of the non-Jewish intellectual in the Jewish group is discussed in Chandler Brossard's "Plaint of a Gentile Intellectual," *Commentary*, August 1950, pp. 154–156.

[26]Robert Park originally applied the concept to the Jews in his essay "Human Migration and the Marginal Man," *American Journal of Sociology*, May 1928, pp. 881–893. This is reprinted in his *Race and Culture* (Glencoe: 1950), pp. 345–356. See also Everett Hughes, "Social Change and Status Protest; An Essay on the Marginal Man," *Phylon*, First Quarter 1949, pp. 58–65; Everett Stonequist, "The Marginal Character of the Jews," in Isaque Graeber and Steuart H. Britt, *Jews in a Gentile World* (New York: 1942), pp. 296–310; and Thorstein Veblen's perceptive essay, "The Intellectual Pre-Eminence of Jews in Modern Europe," in *Political Science Quarterly*, March 1919, pp. 33–42. David Riesman has elaborated on the theme in "Some Observations Concerning Marginality," reprinted in his *Individualism Reconsidered* (Glencoe: 1954), pp. 153–165.

dle class circles,[27] and in Park Forest was shared by Jews who were either already upper-middle class, or moving in that direction. However, people did not choose this culture for its status implications, for they did not choose it consciously. Rather, they were drawn to it as much by their marginality as their mobility. . . .

[27]See, for example, the analysis of reading and class in the Yankee City class structure in Warner and Lunt, op. cit., Ch. 19, and similar analyses in *Middletown, Middletown in Transition, Elmtown's Youth,* and other community studies.

THE FRIENDSHIP PATTERN OF THE LAKEVILLE JEW

by MARSHALL SKLARE and JOSEPH GREENBLUM

INTRODUCTION

If THE INFORMAL COMMUNITY is fundamental to group cohesion and survival we need to know why it is that most Jews make friends with other Jews rather than with Gentiles, at which point in the life-cycle such friendships emerge, which segment of the Jewish group is most likely to form such friendships, and what the prognosis is for the maintenance of the present pattern of clique interaction.

These questions are analyzed by Marshall Sklare and Joseph Greenblum in their study of the Jews of Lakeville, The Lakeville study focused on many aspects of Jewish identity but what Sklare and Greenblum call the phenomenon of "associational Jewishness" (the same phenomenon which Gans labels the "informal community") turned out to be a central feature of their analysis. Sklare and Greenblum found that while many aspects of Jewishness had declined, and that while Jews were reshaping their style of life and in the process were increasingly coming to resemble non-Jews, associational Jewishness continued to maintain itself.

One of the central shifts in Jewish life has been the sharp decline in kinship interaction: Lakeville Jews are not involved with extended kin with anything like the frequency and intensity of their parents. Lakeville Jews are considerably less observant of religious*

*To be sure Lakeville Jews are still highly involved if judged by the prevailing standards among their counterparts in the Gentile community.

ritual than were their parents, and the culture patterns they follow are much less Jewish than those of their parents. Furthermore, even if the area in which they happen to live has as high a proportion of Jews as was true of the neighborhoods in which they were reared in Lake City or in some other metropolis, Lakeville has no "Jewish" neighborhoods—that is, Jews have not affected a fundamental change in Lakeville's Gentile ambience.

All of these changes make the level of associational Jewishness crucial to the continuance of group cohesion. Sklare and Greenblum find that despite a weakening of kinship interaction, a decline in Jewish observance, and a sharp rise in the level of acculturation to Gentile norms and styles, Lakeville Jews maintain a strong pattern of associational Jewishness. Despite the fact that Lakeville Jews have Gentile acquaintances, on the whole they make their close friendships among Jews. Furthermore, Lakeville Jews do so with virtually the same frequency as was true of their parents. As Lakeville Jews move away from the pattern in which they were reared—that of intense involvement with kin—they appear to substitute in its place an intense involvement with Jewish friends. The pattern is all the more remarkable given the fact that in adolescence a significant percentage of Lakeville Jews had close friends who were Gentile. Furthermore, subsequent to their high-school days Lakeville Jews lived in environments such as college dormitories or Army barracks where Gentiles predominated. In sum, given the erosion of many significant aspects of Jewish identity among Lakeville Jews in comparison with their parents, it seems evident that a high level of associational Jewishness has been crucial for the development of a formal Jewish community in Lakeville and for its continued maintenance.

In a sense the high level of associational Jewishness prevailing in Lakeville is of greater significance than the same pattern in Park Forest. While Park Forest is a minor center of Jewish life whose residents could assimilate without vitally affecting the future of Jews in the metropolitan region, Lakeville is quite another matter. Located in the mainstream of Jewish suburbia, Lakeville is one of several communities on the Heights—a chain of elite suburbs located outside of Lake City, a large Midwestern metropolis. The price of its homes as well as the educational and professional status of its residents make Lakeville beyond the reach of the mass of middle-class Jews of Lake City, but it is also the object of their envy and aspiration.

Lakeville, unlike Park Forest, was a town long before it became a suburb. In the last quarter of the nineteenth century it began to lose its industrial and commercial importance but its favorable location and its combination of beaches and wooded hills ensured its future as an elite summer colony, and later, with the development of rail commuter service and the improvement of cars and roads, a year-round place of residence for upper- and upper-middle-class businessmen of Protestant extraction. Since Lakeville had once been a town, certain sections of the community were still inhabited by working-class people, whose numbers now increased as Lakeville came to function as a service center both for its own prosperous residents and for similarly-situated families in other Heights communities.

It was Lakeville's mixed character that made it the most hospitable of all the Heights communities to the settlement of Jews. Unlike neighboring suburbs which barred Jewish residents, Lakeville was comparatively open, and Lake City's German-Jewish elite proceeded to build or buy large summer homes and small estates in the community. In conformity with the pattern of the time they were excluded from country clubs and other facilities patronized by the Gentile elite, but they soon established a golf club of their own—the Wildacres Country Club—which became the first Jewish institution in the area.

In the course of time Jewish summer residents also became year-round commuters. After World War I the Jewish elite was joined by other prosperous Jewish families and a Reform synagogue—the Isaac Mayer Wise Temple—was established on the Heights. However, German-Jewish dominance could not long endure. While East European Jews were excluded from Wildacres and were given a lukewarm reception at the Wise Temple, in the 1940's East Europeans began to move out to Lakeville in significant numbers. Lakeville soon became a mixed Jewish community, with upper-class German and East European Jews, an upper-middle-class of both German and East European extraction, and a continual inflow of young families who were prosperous but not yet wealthy. These families were attracted by the community's physical surroundings as well as by the excellent reputation of its school system.

While Lakeville continued to be dominated numerically by Protestants the influx of Jews had the effect of making it unattractive to young Gentile upper-class couples who had been raised in Lakeville or in other suburbs on the Heights. Gentiles who did settle in Lakeville tended to be new to the Lake City area and to be less prosperous than many of Lakeville's Jewish residents. In contrast to the Jews some of the Gentile residents were organization men—they worked for giant corporations and in the normal course of events would be transferred to another community.

Despite its loss of social éclat Lakeville has retained its elite reputation among Jews. The blighting of several important Jewish residential districts in Lake City has meant a steady influx of upper- as well as of middle-class Jews. Some of the wealthiest Jews of the Lake City metropolitan area reside in Lakeville, together with a heavy representation of upper-middle-class Jews. There is even a section of Lakeville which—Jewishly speaking—is on the wrong side of the tracks although it also includes some Jews of considerable wealth and/or high education—individuals who consider themselves superior to the "strivers" who live in the more prestigious areas of Lakeville. Most Jewish oldtimers have remained in the area, although a small number of great wealth and high acculturation have left. There has also been something of an exodus of elderly Jews who find it burdensome to maintain an elaborate home; some have bought cooperative apartments in the most exclusive area of Lake City (luxury high-rise apartment buildings have also been put up on the Heights).

Lakeville is a community of well-educated Jews. As many as 34 percent of the men have attended graduate school—they are lawyers, judges, internists, surgeons, psychiatrists, and dentists. And even the 11 percent who have gone no further than high school are almost without exception members of the upper-class—German Jews who inherited considerable wealth but lacked the taste for higher education, or self-made East European millionaires whose families could barely manage to help them through high school. Lakeville Jews tend to be much more diverse in their Jewish identity than Park Forest Jews. Some are religiously observant (at least by Park Forest standards), while others are indifferent, if not hostile. Most of the leaders of Lake City's philanthropic, educational, and pro-Israel organizations who reside in the suburbs live in Lakeville. On the other hand there is also a definable group in Lakeville with no connection to the formal Jewish community. The twin facts of wide diversity in Jewish identity and elite status among Lake City Jews make the study of the friendship patterns of Lakeville residents of considerable significance in gaining an understanding of the foundations of communal sentiment among American Jewry as a whole.

M. S.

LIKE ANY SIMILAR collectivity, the specifically Jewish friendship group exists for the satisfaction of personal needs and interests, rather than for advancing any special group purpose. Nevertheless, the Jewish friendship group may constitute an important influence in developing and solidifying in-group sentiment: by providing a mode of Jewish association in a predominantly non-Jewish society, it is capable of confirming Jewish identity and consequently contributing to Jewish survival. The fact that the friendship group lacks many of the characteristics of an organization—a set time for meetings, an annual election of officers, a machinery which both advances the cause espoused by the agency and assures its perpetuation—is one of its greatest strengths; it can confirm and strengthen Jewish identity in a much more personal manner than an organization. Indeed, the overriding personalism of the friendship group is one of the most significant elements in its attractiveness. Thus the Jewish friendship group can work indirectly but nevertheless effectively to preserve group identity. It may constitute as great an influence, or an even greater influence, on the preservation of that identity than instrumentalities whose manifest purpose is the advancement of group survival.

The Character of Friendship Ties

. . . when our respondents were growing up, 42 percent of their parents spent more time socializing with friends than they did with relatives. On the other hand, as many as 88 percent of our respondents spend more time socializing with friends than with relatives. A shift of this magnitude occurring within the space of a single generation carries with it the potentiality of fragmenting patterns of in-group interaction, for a high level of interaction with a family group minimizes the possibility of meaningful involvement with members of the out-group. The shift to a group which is self-selected rather than inherited may portend the end of in-group solidarity.

This potentiality is particularly high given the fact that Jews constitute a rather small segment of the population in the Lake City area. Even if adjustments are made for factors which strongly delimit the choice of friends—race, class, educational level, and the like—Gentiles still outnumber Jews by a substantial ratio. Furthermore, most of our respondents have spent extended periods of time—particularly during the period of their late adolescence and early adulthood—detached from traditional familial and neighborhood relationships. Frequently, Jews constituted a minority in such settings. New patterns of shared experiences in such settings may give rise to cross-ethnic friendships that might endure long after these experiences have passed.

One example of such a setting is the Armed Forces, in which many of our male respondents have served. A better example—because it encompasses a more like-minded population and also includes the great majority of our female respondents—is the college or university.[1] While the schools which our respondents attended had a much higher proportion of Jews than was true for the Armed Forces, in most cases they were in a decided minority on their particular campus. The state universities which our respondents attended drew on the varied segments of the population of the area in which they were situated; the private institutions of higher learning generally chose their students on a variety of criteria which operated to select a so-called "balanced" student body. Furthermore, many respondents who attended colleges distant from their homes were almost completely dependent on the social life that they found in such campus situations. Taking into account, then, the shift from family to friends, as well as the exposure to environments where people of diverse backgrounds associate, what is the character of the friendship ties of the Lakeville Jew?

We find that such ties are predominantly—almost overwhelmingly—with other Jews. Some 42 percent of our respondents report that their circle of close friends[2] is composed exclusively of Jews.

[1]More than eight out of ten women and almost nine out of ten men had at least some college education.

[2]While such terms as "friendship circle," "friendship group," or "clique" generally refer to a distinguishable set of persons who are bound together by friendship ties, our data refer only to the aggregate of persons considered as "close friends" by the respondent. These data do not tell us, of course, the extent to which such friendship choices are reciprocated or whether the respondent's collection of close friends constitutes a functioning group.

We employed the following item for the purpose of distinguishing between close friends and others: "When you think of all the persons you are friendly with at this moment, about how many of them are people you consider really close friends?" Respondents were then probed as to the religious identity of their close friends. They

Another 49 percent say that their circle is composed of a majority of Jews. Only 7 percent report that Gentiles constitute a majority in their circle of close friends or that their circle is equally divided between Jews and Gentiles.[3] The Jewish character of the friendship circle of the Lakeville resident is clearly revealed when we look more closely at the 49 percent who say that their circle includes a minority of one or more Gentiles. We discover that approximately one-half of these respondents report that all or most of their Gentile friends are married to Jews.[4]

Perhaps the most remarkable aspect of this pattern of pervasive Jewish friendship ties is that in spite of being more acculturated than their parents and moving in a more mixed environment, our respondents make their close friendships with Jews virtually as often as did their parents. Thus, while 87 percent of the parents had most or all of their close friendships with Jews, the same holds true for 89 percent of our respondents (Table 1).[5] To realize the significance of this overlap between the generations, it is only necessary to recall the amount of disjunction in the area of religious behavior. And the continuity in friendship patterns between the generations is all the more remarkable, given such strong differences in the level of involvement with the family group.

Since friendship ties with Gentiles who are married to Jews are frequent enough to be of significance and will presumably bulk even larger in the future, a detailed analysis of them is required. The phenomenon suggests that a certain proportion of intermarried couples have found a place inside the Jewish group—that they have not assimilated into the non-Jewish world in a meaningful sense.

were also asked a series of questions regarding the type of relationship they had with the person whom they considered their closest Jewish friend as well as with the person whom they considered their closest Gentile friend.

[3]Some 2 percent did not know the religious identity of their close friends or did not report any close friends.

[4]Four in ten of these respondents say that all such Gentile friends are married to Jews. Another one in ten say that *most* such Gentile friends are married to Jews. If these cases, which constitute about one-fourth of all respondents, are added to those whose friendship circle is exclusively Jewish, we find that as many as two-thirds of Lakeville Jews make all their close friendships either with Jews or with Gentiles who are all or mostly married to Jews.

[5]The comparison with parents required that "most" friendships be defined as over 60 percent, rather than over 50 percent, and that "about half" be defined as 41 to 60 percent (Table 1). Therefore, the 89 percent figure is slightly less than the comparable total of the relevant percentages in the previous paragraph.

TABLE 1
Proportion of close friends Jewish among respondents and among their parents

Percent with following proportion of Jews among their close friends[b]	*Parents*[a]		*Respondents*	
All (100%)	30	87	42	89
Almost all (91-99%)	31		10	
Most (61-90%)	26		37	
About half (41-60%)	5		6	
Some (1-40%)	2		—	
None (0%)	2		—	
N.A., no close friend	1		2	

[a]During the period when respondent was growing up.
[b]The proportions stated in percentages apply to respondents. These have been calculated from data supplied by respondents in answer to separate questions on the total number of their close friends and the total number of their close Gentile friends. These percentages are grouped in intervals which most approximate the descriptive categories used in the question applicable to the parents.

Furthermore, we discover the startling fact that some of the spouses identified by our respondents as Gentile have actually been converted to Judaism. Of course, their categorization as Gentile indicates incomplete assimilation, this time into the Jewish group. Such categorization is also an aspect of the remarkable influence of ethnicity on our respondents—an influence which persists in spite of the prevalence of an extremely high level of acculturation.

While our respondents may not categorize all converts as Jewish, there is no question that they feel that such individuals, as well as non-Jews married to Jews, are quite different from the average Gentile. The distinction mentioned most frequently is that these intermarried Gentiles have adopted a Jewish identity and a Jewish way of life. In some instances, the attitudes and behavior of Gentile friends who are married to Jews are felt to be so typically Jewish that respondents are prompted to remark—as does a pharmacist's wife who is active in ORT—that their Gentile friend is "more Jewish than anyone else is." And according to a prosperous salesman whose only ethnic affiliation is with a local Jewish country club,

> This Gentile woman considers herself a Jew. We will kid her that: "We know you're not a Jew, so you don't have to bother acting like one." Yet in fact she does act like a Jew as much as the rest of us do.

A young and highly observant insurance broker, a member of the Schechter Synagogue who is quite active in B'nai B'rith, says of still another Gentile woman, "She has a warmth and attachment to things Jewish and follows its customs." And a lawyer's wife who is active only in non-sectarian groups and does not follow Jewish rituals in her own home details some of these customs and "things Jewish": "After her marriage this Italian girl started keeping a kosher house. She encourages her husband to go to temple and sends her kids to Jewish Sunday School."

Our respondents also emphasize that not only have such Gentiles become acculturated to Jewish ways, but they have become detached from Gentile clique groups. The insurance broker quoted above says of the Gentile woman whom he includes in his circle of close friends, "She primarily associates with Jews, and most of her friends are Jewish." An affluent salesman who does not feel entirely comfortable in the company of Gentiles nevertheless experiences no anxiety with his two close Gentile friends who are married to Jews: "[It is because] they move in a Jewish circle and are outside the pale of circle of their own kind." A further indication of the movement of such Gentile friends into Jewish clique relationships is the fact that when the most intimate of such friends is entertained, in seven out of ten cases most or all of the other persons present are Jewish.[6]

With respect to those whose friendship circle is predominantly Jewish but whose Gentile friend is not married to a fellow Jew, several types of relationships with such Gentiles are possible. For example, such a friend could be a detached Gentile who feels alienated from his peers and who as a consequence is willing, even eager, to join a Jewish clique group. Or the friend could be a Gentile

[6]When the most intimate Gentile friend who is not married to a Jew is entertained, in only a third of the cases are most or all of the other persons likely to be Jewish. Such information was gathered only in respect to the most intimate Gentile friend, the person who is referred to in the relevant questionnaire item as "the one with whom you are most friendly."

who is well integrated with his traditional group and as a consequence may be eager to have the Jewish friend join *his* Gentile clique group. In the first instance, the character of the Jew's friendship ties would not be shifted, while in the second instance they could be strongly affected. There is also a third possibility, however: that the Gentile to whom the Jew is close is neither well attached to nor strongly alienated from his traditional group and that in any case this aspect is not a significant element in the relationship. Rather, for both Jew and Gentile their friendship is a very special relationship—a relationship which does not disturb their respective friendship ties. Tending to see each other alone, neither Jew nor Gentile becomes incorporated in the other's homogeneous friendship group.

While further analysis is needed to discover the character and dynamics of such relationships, what is presently apparent is that most Lakeville Jews who have Gentile friends who are not married to Jews do not seem to be in the process of shifting their friendship circle. Instead of utilizing their contacts in the Gentile world to build a new pattern of friendship ties, they appear to pursue their interfaith relationship apart from their Jewish network. In summary, there tends to be no disruption of the predominantly Jewish friendship circle, even among those who have a Gentile friend who is not married to a Jew. . . .

The Shift to a Homogeneous Friendship Circle

While the pattern of friendship ties of our respondents is so strongly Jewish as to duplicate the one prevalent in the parental generation, it was not always so. During adolescence, our respondents had many more Gentile friends than they do today. To be sure, in the majority of cases teenage friendship ties were predominantly with Jews. However, almost four in ten of our respondents report that in adolescence only half, or less than half, of their circle of close friends consisted of Jews (Table 2). In actuality, the increased homogeneity of friendship ties is greater than these figures indicate, for, as we have noted, some of the present Gentile friends of our respondents have ties to Jewish life through marriage to a Jew.

While close friendships with Gentiles are much more exceptional today than they were in the past, adolescent patterns still retain their influence. Thus the greater the proportion of Jewish friends in adolescence, the greater the proportion today (Table 3). However, the trend is toward a homogeneously Jewish pattern for

TABLE 2

Proportion of close friends Jewish during adolescence and today

*Percent with following proportion of Jews among their close friends**	*Adolescence*		*Today*	
All (100%)	14		42	
Almost all (91-99%)	20	63	10	89
Most (61-90%)	29		37	
About half (41-60%)	18		6	
Some (1-40%)	15		3	
None (0%)	4		–	
N.A., no close friend	–		2	

*The proportions stated in percentages apply to respondents as adults and were calculated and grouped as described in Table 1. The matched descriptive categories were used in the question referring to their teen-age period.

all, even for those who had only some or no Jewish friends in adolescence, with those who had more Jewish friends to begin with having the highest proportion of all-Jewish friendships.

It appears that our respondents acquired and stabilized a relatively homogeneous pattern of close Jewish friendships while emerging from adolescence to adulthood, or at least before achieving parenthood. We find that throughout the parental phase of the life cycle, their sociability pattern remains stable: there is little difference between our younger and older respondents with respect to the ethnic composition of their friendship circles. Thus the friendship pattern acquired in the earliest phase of the parental life cycle remains constant through the mature years.

The trend to homogeneity in friendship behavior is comparable in some aspects to that which obtains in respect to religious behavior. Religious behavior is also at minimal levels during the adolescent and early adulthood years—transitional phases of the life cycle when the individual is in the process of loosening his bonds to

TABLE 3

Proportion of close friends Jewish today by proportion of close friends Jewish during adolescence

	Proportion of close teen-age freinds Jewish			
Percent with following proportion of Jews among their close friends	*All or almost all*	*Most*	*About half*	*Some or none*
All	55	47	31	27
Most: Gentiles married to Jews	23	29	24	20
Most: Gentiles not married to Jews	21	23	37	31
Half or less	1	1	8	22
Number	(149)	(123)	(78)	(81)

his parental home, but has yet to establish his own household. Nevertheless, the trend to homogeneity of association occurs earlier than the maximization of the religious aspect of Jewishness. Thus the intensification of Jewish association may constitute a kind of preview of the reintegration of the young Jew into a variety of other aspects of his Jewish identity.

What accounts for the increase in homogeneous friendship ties before the onset of parenthood as well as for their maintenance through the ensuing years? This question is deserving of extended research; we are only able to supply preliminary answers along one or two of many relevant dimensions.

If we focus on those whose present circle is composed exclusively of Jews, we find that in many cases they once had Gentile friends. These Gentile friendships were often formed in a mixed setting into which they had been thrust for a relatively limited period. When the situation terminated, their relationships with Gentiles ended. We cannot be certain why these friendships never deepened; all that we can say is that the relationship was not firm enough to withstand separation. A young woman who is very active in non-sectarian organizations recalls that when she attended a small women's college in the East, she had friends who were "Christians and Negroes. I went to their parties . . . and I also dated Gentile boys." While she describes her college chums as "old friends" and retains membership in her alumnae association, she has not seen her college friends in some years; she considers none of them to be her close friends today. A professional man recalls the peculiar quality of the relationships with his Gentile friends in the Army and later in dental school. In each instance, the friendships were terminated after his connection with the respective institution came to an end: "At the time, it's like being on a desert island. . . . But when it's over, you just break up." A young matron who had a mixed group of close friends as a teenager reports that she also had mostly Gentile friends when she accompanied her husband during his military service. She sums up the situational nature of these relationships: "Of course, we broke up as we went from post to post. In making friends, I guess you take the path of least resistance, and these people were there."

Another relevant factor is that relationships with Gentiles did not receive the institutional, communal, or familial reinforcement that occurred with respect to relationships with Jews. Such reinforcement was apparently a factor which helped such relationships to endure long after the situation in which they developed had passed. Jewish friendships that have persisted since childhood and adolescence are especially instructive in this connection. We find cases where respondents trace their present homogeneous Jewish associations to the Jewish neighborhood of their childhood or even to their parents. For example, an executive in the entertainment industry who is somewhat active in Wise Temple soon lost contact with the close Gentile friends he made in adolescence. However, with respect to the Jewish friends he made during the same period, with some of whom he currently associates, he recalls, "Most of us came out of the same neighborhood; our communities were Jewish, and our families were heavily Jewish and traditional." Although as a teenager she had some Gentile boyfriends, a young fourth-generation wife of a buyer—a woman who is active only in non-sectarian groups—says much the same thing about her Jewish circle: "Most of us grew up together. Our parents knew each other, and we are all Jewish." A sales executive who also has little attachment to Jewish religious or organizational life points out how his Jewish friendships were formed in the close world of the neighborhood in which he was raised in Lake City:

> Most of this circle [of friends] is an old-time relationship dating back to public school and Hebrew school where our activities kept us close together. Why should we bring newcomers into the group? One of the important things about it is that it's such an old group.

The tendency to homogeneity becomes particularly discernible in late adolescence. Some of the all-Jewish cliques formed during this period have no institutional connections, while others have as their locus formal organizations such as high-school or college fraternities and sororities. The wife of a prosperous salesman, who is equally active in Jewish and non-sectarian groups, traces her Jewish friendship circle to her sociability pattern as a teenager: "It all goes back to the local high-school sorority that was all Jewish." A minimally observant woman with a similar pattern of organizational involvement had many close Gentile friends as a teenager, including those of the opposite sex, but she lost these contacts after joining a Jewish sorority in college. She says of her Jewish clique, "We are a closed group from college. Most of us are sorority sisters or fraternity brothers. We've been together for years." The young owner of an automobile parts business, a minimally observant second-generation man who is not affiliated with any Jewish organization, relates how his clique group became increasingly Jewish as he grew from adolescence to adulthood:

> I was active in a high-school fraternity—all Jewish. Until high school, I had more non-Jewish friends than Jewish ones. Though I held on to the non-Jewish friends, they decreased in proportion; we weren't in the same fraternity and we did little or no double dating. . . . This pattern increased as I got older, dated, and got married.

. . . while some of our respondents account for their homogeneous friendship pattern by highlighting factors that operated at an earlier period of their life, in the majority of cases it appears that present ties were formed during adulthood. Queried as to how they developed an all-Jewish circle, about half of our respondents feel that it results from the fact that Jews are more available and accessible to them. "There's more opportunity to make friends with Jews. We're with them a thousand times more: the Jews are around," explains a publisher who is somewhat active in Wise Temple and in a Jewish community-relations group. As a teenager, most of his close associations were with Gentiles, including a serious relationship with a Gentile girl. Such ties were dissolved, however, when he joined a Jewish fraternity at college. Another man who gives much the same type of response is a minimally observant advertising agency executive whose Jewish organizational affiliations are limited to a Jewish city club and to the Einhorn Temple. He grew up in a prestigious suburb on the Heights among predominantly Gentile friends, but he joined a Jewish fraternity at college. Today his close friends are all Jewish. He says, "I'm thrown into contact with [Jews] in many places and in many ways. It's easier. I don't feel the need to cultivate people. Proximity is the thing."

While many respondents allude to these Jewish associational opportunities in a general way, some specify the settings in which they occur: chiefly the neighborhood in which they live, the Jewish organization with which they are affiliated, and the synagogue in which they are active. "We all came into the neighborhood at around the same time about five years ago and have known each other as long," remarks a young second-generation mother of two children, who was reared in a small town on the West Coast where her close friendships were mainly with Gentiles. She has few ties to Jewish religious and organizational life. A physician's wife, a relative newcomer to the community, states that she "became friendly [with an all-Jewish friendship group] through organizations." She is a member of several Jewish women's groups, including the Sisterhood of Wise Temple. And a highly observant middle-aged owner of a men's clothing business states that he developed his friendships as a result of his activity in a Conservative synagogue in Lake City:

> I haven't had the occasion to mix with any [Gentiles] socially. I've never been in mixed community affairs. I developed a social life through the [X] Synagogue—the one place where I had causes plus friends and social activities.

While it is true that such associational opportunities are part of the situation in which individual Jews find themselves, in another fundamental sense they can be the outcome of individual preferences—the result of an attraction to fellow Jews and a desire for personal contact with them. It is apparent that because of this attraction many of our respondents place themselves in situations where it is Jews, rather than Gentiles, who are more available and accessible to them.

Jewish accessibility could, of course, be the result of nothing more than Gentile inaccessibility. This is not the picture which our respondents present, however. While one in ten of those who have a homogeneous Jewish friendship circle accounts for the pattern on the basis of exclusion by Gentiles, some four in ten say that it is a result of a preference for Jews. Some of these respondents consider such a preference to be self-evident, as does a moderately observant accountant who had some close Gentile friends as a teenager, but feels that "it's normal that Jewish people befriend other Jewish people." A college-educated and religiously unobservant wife of an executive in the construction industry, who also associated with Gentiles in adolescence, presents a more thoughtful formulation: "Today . . . Jews and Gentiles have much in common. But somehow a social barrier exists. Jews don't go seeking people different from themselves."

Other respondents emphasize that Jews are predisposed to social contact and intimate association with other Jews because of a common religio-ethnic heritage and a pervasive group identity. "It's because Jews go with Jews and Gentiles go with Gentiles. My background is so Jewish and my life is so Jewish that I'm happier surrounded by Jews," explains a young salesman's wife who is now active in Lilienthal Temple, although as an adolescent she had some close friends who were Gentile. "It's the identity, the background, the religion. It would be hard for a Gentile to be comfortable without these common bonds," elaborates an affluent lawyer and business executive who came to the United States from Russia when he was a youngster and is quite active in a variety of Jewish organizations. "There's a common notion of 'fate,' so we don't seek out non-Jews," is the concise reason given by a mother of three school-age children, who finds time for activity in several Jewish welfare groups despite her intense involvement in her local PTA group.

Some account for their preferences for Jewish social contacts by emphasizing life styles and manners which they believe are more commonly encountered among Jews. "There are cultural differences; we have common backgrounds, interests, and standards as Jews," is the general and somewhat cautious comment made by an affluent businessman, a member of Einhorn Temple, who did not receive a Jewish upbringing by his parents and claims to be entirely uninterested in religious matters. He considers none of the many Gentiles with whom he mixes socially to be a close friend. A more specific explanation is offered by a prosperous accountant highly active in a Jewish youth welfare group: "It's just our way of life—our parental background, our closer family and home ties, and our social tastes." He is no longer friendly with the Gentiles whom he met in college and in the Navy. And a young businessman who observes almost none of the traditional religious practices to which he was exposed in childhood mentions similar reasons to account for the fact that he lost contact with the non-Jewish friends he had before marriage:

> They went different paths because of differences in economics, education, and a different mode of living. The others bought homes earlier, but homeowning is only a recent thing for Jews.

Seeking out other Jews with whom one shares common attitudes and a way of life results in the strengthening of feelings of ethnic solidarity. Such solidarity, in turn, contributes to the formation of homogeneously Jewish cliques. "Jews seem to stick together. There's more security that way. It makes for a feeling of belonging," notes the wife of a prosperous businessman, whose intimate friends since childhood have been Jewish and is quite active in the PTA of the Wise Temple. A young salesman with a business degree who had some Gentile friends at college refers to "that family feeling" among Jews; his religious observance is minimal, but he is about to join the Schechter Synagogue. A fairly observant housewife who was close with several Gentile girls with whom she worked before marriage and is now active in the PTA and the Scouts summarizes the emotional basis of in-group solidarity in the following terms:

> My association with non-Jews has been good. But there's a warmth amongst Jews that couldn't be in a Gentile. A Gentile can't be as warm; he would have a different philosophy.

While this respondent and many others whose close friends are all Jewish account for their pattern by stressing the "positive" fact of attraction to Jews rather than such "negative" reasons as alienation, suspicion, or uncomfortableness with Gentiles, the possibility exists that their explanations contain an element of rationalization. In response to a direct query, we find that less than one in ten of those who have homogeneous Jewish friendship ties reports that either he or his friends would have an unfavorable reaction if a Gentile were to join the circle. On the other hand, we find respondents who, in trying to account for the fact that all their close friends are Jewish, are frank to admit that the presence of a Gentile would create strain. Thus a middle-aged housewife affiliated with a variety of Jewish groups, who recalls that half of her close friends during adolescence were Gentile, states:

> We have Gentile friends, but we'd never think of mixing them. It wouldn't work. We're very small drinkers. We like to have a nice dinner and play cards. We'd feel self-conscious, especially if they'd lose.

The presence of Gentiles would mean that conversation would have to be guarded. A woman who is highly active in the Schechter Synagogue as well as in ORT and is married to an attorney says of her Jewish clique, "They wouldn't be able to speak as freely about politics and religion if non-Jews were present." She is familiar with the ways of both groups, for as an adolescent she had close friends among Gentiles, and she still has Gentile acquaintances. . . .

We see, then, that the Lakeville Jew who has an all-Jewish circle explains his pattern of friendship ties in a variety of ways. What seems to charaterize these respondents, and others as well, is that they feel more comfortable with Jews than with Gentiles—a feeling which they experience in spite of their high level of acculturation and their affirmation of the value of Jewish-Gentile integration. The sense of feeling comfortable with another person is, of course, a precondition for intimacy; it is difficult to establish a close and abiding relationship without such rapport.[7]

The varied responses of these Lakeville Jews who have homogeneous Jewish friendship ties not only are characterized by

[7]See Vol. II of the Lakeville Studies for a discussion of the relationship between comfortableness, social anxiety, and integration-mindedness (Benjamin B. Ringer, *The Edge of Friendliness* [New York: Basic Books, 1967], pp. 138–154). It should be remembered that this material refers to any social contact with Gentiles, rather than to close friendships.

feelings of being at ease with Jews but also appear to involve a deep sense of kinship with other Jews. The composition of clique groups aside, if we take our respondents as a whole and compare their most friendly Gentile relationship with their most intimate Jewish one, we find that 76 percent say that they are closer to their best Jewish friend and only 9 percent say they are closer to their best Gentile friend. Some 14 percent claim that they are as close to their best Gentile friend as they are to their best Jewish friend. Indeed, while our respondents generally refer to their best Gentile friend as a "friend," they frequently speak of their best Jewish friend as being like a "sister" or "brother." An active alumna of a leading Eastern women's college, who is also involved in several Jewish and non-sectarian groups, characterizes her relationship with her most intimate Gentile friend as "friendly" and finds the Gentile friend as stimulating as her closest Jewish friend: "They're both intellectually stimulating. Both are very good for my ego; I feel like a whole person when I'm with them." But she states that she has a "deeper relationship" with the Jewish friend. Her insightful characterization of the relationship with the Jewish friend is as follows: "It's like being [in] a family without the tension."

The Alienated Jew and the Homogeneous Friendship Circle

It is clear from the personal information which has been supplied about the respondents whom we have been quoting that some are apathetic to traditional Jewish concerns and affirmations. Since they are nevertheless involved in homogeneous friendship groups, it is apparent that the kind of group solidarity demonstrated by their "associational Jewishness" is not necessarily related to what may be described as more "positive" expressions of Jewish identity. Such solidarity can and does exist apart from any commitment to Jewish religious or organizational life and even apart from any affirmation of the concept of Jewish peoplehood as manifested in pro-Israel sentiment. While "associational Jewishness" may go hand in hand with strong Jewish attachments . . . associationalism is highly prevalent even among alienated Jews.

Thus we find that those who are uninvolved in religion and synagogue life have almost as Jewish a friendship circle as those who possess religious commitments. As many as six in ten of the unobservant, compared with about seven in ten of the most observant, claim that all their close friends are Jewish or are

Gentiles married to Jews.[8] Barely more than one in ten of the unobservant claim that their circle of close friends is either ethnically balanced or predominantly Gentile. Furthermore, almost six in ten of those who lack an affiliation with a synagogue, although they have already reached that stage in the life cycle where the great majority join, report a homogeneously Jewish friendship circle.[9] This is not much different from the seven in ten among active synagogue members who have such a circle. Furthermore, only one in eight of the unaffiliated claim that Gentiles constitute half or more of their circle of close friends. . . .

It is only in respect to involvement in Jewish organizations that the situation is different. While 73 percent of those who are active in such organizations, whether they be less or more active, have homogeneous ties, only 56 percent of the unaffiliated possess such friendship ties.[10] Furthermore, a larger percentage of the unaffiliated—although no more than 14 percent—in contrast to the actives have a circle of close friends which is not predominantly Jewish or all-Jewish.[11] These findings highlight the function of the Jewish organization as a framework for social relationships; they suggest that the organization reinforces the tendency toward homogeneous friendship ties.

This pattern is accentuated among women. . . . Among men, there is only a slight difference between the unaffiliated and the actives with respect to homogeneous friendship ties: while the unaffiliated less often report exclusively Jewish friends, more often they have a minority of Gentile friends who are married to Jews. Among women, however, homogeneous Jewish cliques are found among as many as 75 percent of the actives, but only among 45

[8]The "most observant" group here are those who observe five or more home rituals. The finding remains the same even if we compare the unobservant with those who observe seven or more rituals. A strikingly similar finding emerges when those who never attend synagogue services are compared with those who attend quite regularly.

[9]In this section, a homogeneously Jewish circle of friends refers to a collection of close friends which is either all Jewish or includes a minority of Gentiles who are all or mostly married to Jews.

[10]The "unaffiliated" are persons who do not hold membership in either a general Jewish organization or a synagogue-related organization. Some, however, may belong to a synagogue.

[11]Only among a small segment who are consistently alienated from Jewish organizations is there a sizable proportion who participate in ethnically balanced or mostly Gentile cliques. Among those who are not affiliated with a Jewish organization or with a synagogue (despite the fact that their children have reached or passed the peak age for religious education), as many as 31 percent claim such friendship circles, while only 54 percent are part of homogeneously Jewish cliques.

percent of the unaffiliated. It should be noted that the divergence between the sexes occurs chiefly among the unaffiliated; men and women who are active or nominal members resemble each other fairly closely with respect to their pattern of friendship ties. Thus while most unaffiliated men retain a homogeneously Jewish circle of friends, most unaffiliated women have one or more Gentile intimates who are married to Gentiles. It should be remembered, however, that an overwhelming majority of those of both sexes who are alienated from Jewish organizational life have their friendship ties primarily or exclusively with their fellow Jews.

One of the remarkable aspects of the friendship pattern of the Lakeville Jew is that it remains so Jewish despite the pervasiveness of integrationist sentiment. Almost without exception, Lakeville Jews tend in the direction of integration, but an all-Jewish or predominantly Jewish friendship circle is even characteristic of more than nine in ten of those who score extremely high on our measure of integration-mindedness (Table 4).[12] Such respondents do differ from others, however, in respect to the ties which their minority of close Gentile friends have with Jewish life: as many as half of the integrationists, in contrast to only two or three in ten among others, have Gentile friends who are not married to Jews.

Why does the Jew who is highly alienated or strongly integrationist-minded tend to make so many of his close friendships within the Jewish group? Some would answer this question in a suprasocial framework, viewing associational Jewishness as a kind of Jewish affirmation and stressing that it is characteristic of the "wondering Jew." According to this perspective, associational Jewishness expresses a desire to preserve a link with Jewish tradition with its basis in inspiration in God; the individual hesitates to sever his one remaining link with the group lest he foreclose all possibility of encounter with God.

The conventional sociological approach shies away from such a perspective. Instead, it highlights the function which Jewish

[12]The measure of "integration-mindedness" is a composite index summarizing several dimensions of Jewish attitudes and behavior vis-à-vis the Gentile community. The index has five component items: 1) attitudes with respect to whether it is essential for a Jew to promote civic improvement in the community and to gain the respect of Christian neighbors; 2) feelings and behavior with respect to having a Christmas tree in one's home; 3) the ratio of Gentiles to Jews desired in the neighborhood; 4) involvement in non-sectarian organizations; and 5) participation in leisure-time activities that are characteristic of non-Jews in Lakeville.

TABLE 4
Proportion of close friends Jewish by level of integration-mindedness

Percent with following proportion of Jews among their close friends	*Integration-mindedness score*						
	High 8–9	*7*	*6*	*5*	*4*	*3*	*Low 1–2*
All	33	44	33	46	44	50	50
Most: Gentiles married to Jews	10	25	22	26	31	21	25
Most: Gentiles not married to Jews	50	23	33	23	21	24	20
Half or less	7	8	12	5	4	5	5
Number	(30)	(52)	(80)	(86)	(77)	(60)	(40)

friendship ties serve for the alienated. Accordingly, such ties may be seen as a buttress compensating for weak attachment to Jewish life. Thus the Jewish friendship circle might be viewed in the framework of the contribution it makes to Jewish survival.

The function of such ties aside, we are still left with the problem of explaining the persistence of a relatively homogeneous friendship pattern among strongly alienated and highly integrationist-minded Jews. Thoroughgoing research on this type of individual is necessary if we are to arrive at a definitive explanation for his puzzling behavior. However, our knowledge of the psychological orientation of the Lakeville Jew vis-à-vis the Gentile places us in a position to suggest an approach to such an explanation.

Earlier . . . we described one aspect of the orientation of those whose friendship circle is composed entirely of Jews: their feeling of greater comfort with Jews than with Gentiles. Comfortableness may arise from a variety of sources. One is the belief that the style of life and values of the Jewish group are closer to one's own. Another is the fear that Gentiles hold negative attitudes about Jews. However, almost half of our respondents—among them many alienated and highly integrationist-minded individuals—claim that they are as comfortable with Gentiles as with Jews. But while they are sufficiently comfortable in more casual social contacts with members of the out-group to maintain a relationship, we suggest that their level of comfort drops sharply in more intimate social relationships. Thus we reason that their lack of ease in truly intimate relationships with Gentiles explains their peculiar pattern. While we have no direct evidence to support this conclusion, the indirect evidence is strong indeed. We find that the majority of Lakeville Jews see themselves as ambassadors to the Gentile world.[13] We also find that our alienated and integration-minded respondents are even somewhat more committed to this role than other Jews.

To specify this idea further, if the Lakeville ambassador performs his duties well, his lot, and that of his children as well as of Jews generally, will improve. If not, the relationship between the Jewish "world" and the Gentile "world" will deteriorate. It is apparent that the assumption of an ambassadorial role places a strain on the individual, for in his contacts with Gentiles he must constantly manipulate himself so that he may succeed in manipulating them. Such manipulative conduct is acceptable in a variety of secondary relationships, but inappropriate in the context of intimacy. Even strongly alienated and highly integrationist-minded respondents, then, find it difficult to establish and maintain the type of close contact with Gentiles which their ideological proclivities suggest. Like all people, they are most at ease in a psychological climate characterized by candor and trust, and it is precisely such a climate which favors the growth of intimate association. Thus, given their orientation to intergroup relations, they find it easier to develop such a climate with fellow Jews than with Gentiles.

Because the Lakeville Jew sees himself as a representative of the Jewish group, he feels that he shares responsibility for its public image. As a consequence, he tends to become extremely self-conscious in the presence of Gentiles, which is another way of saying that he becomes highly aware of being Jewish. Such a fixed attitude of group consciousness and responsibility encompasses the range of manners by which the Lakeville Jew attempts to alter and

[13]Note, for example, our respondents' image of the "good Jew," particularly their feeling about gaining the respect of Christian neighbors (see Chapter 10).

redeem the Gentile stereotype. "I have to be careful with my manners, my dress, my expressions," says a middle-aged lawyer. He is active only in non-sectarian organizations, but he claims no close Gentile friends. "I'm always on my guard as to whether I laugh too loud or my voice is too shrill," says a minimally observant woman whose close friends are all Jewish. "I feel that I have to count my words," says a chemist's wife who observes hardly any religious practices, but has a predominantly Jewish friendship circle.

One aspect of inhibition and self-consciousness is the fear of the Jew that in the encounter with the Gentile he may be regarded stereotypically and not appreciated as an individual; in the eyes of the Gentile, he will be a Jew first and an individual a poor second. Thus an unobservant businessman who believes it "fitting and proper" to have a Christmas tree each year, but confines his organizational life to a Jewish city and country club and his clique participation to Jewish friends, observes about Gentiles, "You have to be on guard and careful about subjects you discuss. I don't have the freedom of personality I have with Jews." This crucial aspect of psychological climate is described even more insightfully by a thoughtful young housewife who is a newcomer to Lakeville. A college graduate and the wife of a prosperous businessman, she is completely alienated from Jewish organizational and religious life and highly integration-minded. One of those respondents constituting the 7 percent who do not have a predominantly or all-Jewish friendship circle, she has such a tenuous in-group connection that even the Jewish friend to whom she feels closest is intermarried. But with all that, this woman confesses, "I'm less comfortable with non-Jews because you feel that they think of you as a Jew. Jews don't really think of you as a Jew."

While the persistence of Jewish friendship ties among the alienated may contribute to Jewish survival, the pattern may not continue indefinitely. The ambassadorial function and the self-consciousness of the Jew in intergroup relationships is, among other things, related to the prevalence of prejudice and discrimination in the immediate past. Thus the involvement of the alienated in a Jewish clique structure not only grows out of the psychological situation which we have delineated but is also related to the fact that such cliques were reinforced by anti-Jewish sentiment and behavior on the campus, in public life, in business and professional affairs, and in club life.

Some of this prejudice and discrimination was experienced personally, more was experienced through significant others, and even more was experienced vicariously through exposure to various channels of communication.

Since it is an unresolved question whether the old pattern of prejudice and discrimination will occur in the future (it has already declined sharply), the Jewish clique may represent a residual form of Jewishness, a "holding operation" preliminary to the assimilation of the individual—or of his offspring—into the majority community.[14] It may be assumed that even with the trend to a more open society, those who are less integration-minded—and who are closely attached to religion, the synagogue, Israel, and the network of Jewish organizations—will retain friendship ties with their Jewish peers. But at the very minimum, the trend to openness suggests that the remarkable discrepancy between the real and the ideal betrayed by the alienated will become ever more apparent. Those who are most firmly committed to the ideal of a mixed society and whose ties to Jewish life are extremely attenuated will be confronted more directly with the choice of transforming their associational life in accordance with their value system or of continuing to journey along the Jewish "Indian path" which they presently tread.

Even if they demur to affect any substantial change in clique behavior, it is questionable whether their offspring will tolerate—or find it necessary to abide—the same disparity between the real and the ideal. Presumably, the children of most alienated Jews will be no more firmly involved in traditional aspects of Jewishness, and it may also be assumed that they will be at least as integrationist-minded as their parents. The open society having been achieved, members of the younger generation may feel free to shed the ambassadorial role and with it their Jewish self-consciousness. At that juncture, close friendships with Gentiles might burgeon, many more Jews finding it psychologically possible to take their place as members of otherwise all-Gentile or predominantly Gentile cliques. Significant numbers might enter such cliques as the spouses of Gentiles, thus reversing the situation of the present Lakeville Jew whose friendship circle, as we have noticed, sometimes includes the Gentile spouse of a Jew.

[14]Regarding the relevance of religious and ethnic identity in assimilating successful members of minority groups to elite social life, see E. Digby Baltzell, *The Protestant Establishment* (New York: Random House, 1964). See also Richard L. Rubenstein, "The Protestant Establishment and the Jews," *Judaism*, XIV (Spring 1965), 131–145.

THE FORMAL COMMUNITY

DECISION-MAKING IN THE AMERICAN JEWISH COMMUNITY

by DANIEL J. ELAZAR

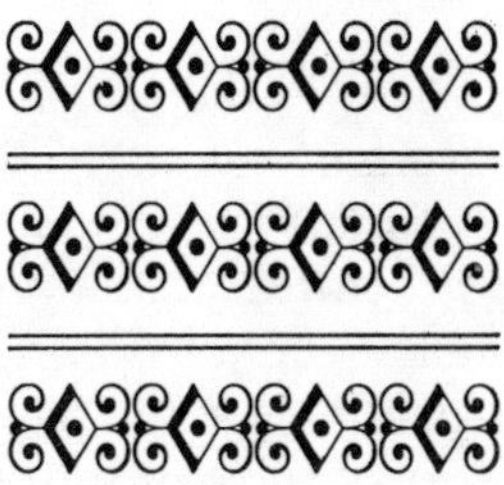

INTRODUCTION

EUROPEAN OBSERVERS of the American scene have long commented upon the unique role of the voluntary association in American society—how citizens join together for the most diverse purposes, and how they seek to meet needs which in other societies are considered to be the responsibility of official bodies. Although it has not received similar attention, a related development of equal significance is the existence of "sub-communities" based on common descent and on feelings of a common religious, ethnic, or racial identity. While the legal system of the nation takes note of the existence of sub-communities it does not grant them a corporate status. Thus it comes about that the sub-community has no coercive powers. Nevertheless, despite its unofficial character and status, the sub-community has proved to be an enduring phenomenon in American society.

The sub-community—especially its communal structure—has not been the object of concentrated scholarly attention, perhaps because of the pervasiveness of the melting-pot ideology. For many decades it was assumed that the sub-communities were either European holdovers or defensive structures erected as a response to prejudice and discrimination. In either case it was thought that the sub-community would wither away with the passing of the immigrant generation and as barriers to fuller participation in American life were removed. As we know from the present concern with pluralism, these assumptions were grounded more in wishful thinking than in social reality.

Among American sub-communal structures the Jewish one is extremely elaborate, composed of a network of voluntary associations appealing to diverse constituencies. Part of the reason for the high development of Jewish communal structure is that it predates the American experience, though to be sure the Jewish organizations of the present are not duplicates of those of the past. The elaboration of a specifically Jewish network of social institutions is characteristic in Jewish history not only when Jews were excluded from the majority institutions but when they regarded such institutions as unacceptable on religious or cultural grounds. The fact that historically Jews had developed an institutional network of their own undoubtedly prepared them for the American experience of voluntarism and pluralism. Thus in addition to the factors of prejudice and discrimination, historical experience—and the feelings of Jews about their group identity—were elements which helped in the creation of an elaborate sub-communal structure in the United States.

The structure of the American Jewish sub-community is not a single entity; rather, it is a network of organizations. One becomes part of the formal community by affiliation with an organization—by joining a synagogue, contributing to a Jewish philanthropy, or participating in a Jewish voluntary association. However, those who do not participate in the formal community—or do so irregularly—are not outside of the community in the usual sense. Since the community rests on the kinship principle that Jews are Jews by virtue of birth and common descent, those who fail to participate in the formal community are not outcasts but rather "inactives" who can assume their place in the formal community at any time, at their own desire. Participation in the informal community is crucial, for it can easily be transformed into affiliation with the formal community.

Histories of local Jewish communities often include considerable detail about their voluntary associations, but there has been a dearth of knowledge concerning the basic structural features of the American Jewish community. Daniel Elazar, a political scientist interested in Jewish communal structure both in the United States and abroad, has analyzed the associations which make up the

Jewish community on the local and national levels. He has clarified the objectives of such associations, the roles played by various types of people, and the trends responsible for shifts in the status and direction of given voluntary associations.

It should be pointed out that while scholarly literature is sparse there has been considerable writing about the Jewish community by those active in it, as well as by those who would like to assume leadership. Much of this writing is critical in tone—for decades Jewish periodicals have published articles decrying the state of Jewish communal life and suggesting plans for its improvement. One chronic complaint centers on what is assumed to be the uncoordinated nature of Jewish communal structure, its tendency toward duplication. Another is that the Jewish community is undemocratic, that it is controlled by plutocrats who are said to rule by virtue of their fiscal potency.

Elazar's approach is different. He sees two large factors which have determined the shape of the community. The first is the growth of the federations, which he regards as a healthy development, accurately expressing the will, not of plutocrats, but of American Jewry as a whole. Federation leadership is made up, in his view, by a "trusteeship of doers" intensely committed to Jewishness. On the other hand, Elazar sees the main structural weakness of the Jewish community in the growth and development of the second large factor, the American synagogue. In his view the synagogue is localistic—it looks inward to its own constituency rather than outward toward the larger Jewish world. In an age of large and strong congregations, such localism becomes a significant factor in preventing the American Jewish community from effectively discharging the responsibilities thrust upon it by virtue of its numbers, wealth, and talent. Elazar's central proposals for the reform of American Jewish community structure center on the demand that congregational leaders come to consider their institutions as public rather than private institutions, and that the two key structures of the American Jewish community—the federations and the synagogues—be brought together in closer articulation.

M. S.

ENVIRONMENTAL AND CULTURAL FACTORS

The Character of American Jewry

AMERICAN JEWRY forms the largest Jewish community in Jewish history and, indeed, is the largest aggregation of Jews ever located under a single government, with the possible exception of Czarist Russia on the eve of the mass migration. Its major local communities are larger than all but a handful of countrywide communities in the past.

The spread of Jews from East Coast to West and from far North to Deep South, despite the unevenness of the distribution, has given the Jewish community major concentrations of population at the farthest reaches of the country. Moreover, the density of Jewish population in the Northeast has been declining, at least since the end of World War II. California now has more Jews than any country in the world other than the United States itself, the Soviet Union, and Israel. Los Angeles, the second largest local Jewish community in the world, has as many Jews as all of France, which is ranked as the country with the fourth largest Jewish population. Simple geography serves to reinforce all other tendencies to disperse decision-making in the American Jewish community as in American society as a whole. It has proved difficult for any "central office" to control countrywide operations in the United States regardless of who or what is involved.

The five largest Jewish communities[1] in the United States contain close to 60 percent of the total Jewish population and the top sixteen communities[2] (all those containing 50,000 Jews or more) contain over 75 percent of the total. At the same time Jews are

[1]New York City, Los Angeles, Nassau County (N.Y.), Philadelphia, and Chicago.

[2]The aforementioned communities, plus Boston, Miami, Bergen County (N.J.), Essex County (N.J.), Westchester County (N.Y.), Baltimore, Washington, Cleveland, Detroit, San Francisco, and St. Louis.

distributed in over 800 communities ranging in size from just under two million in New York City down to a handful of families in the more remote towns and cities. Those 800 are organized into 225 local federations or their equivalent, of which only 27 have more than 20,000 Jews and only ten over 100,000. (Greater New York City, while really a region rather than a local community, is organized under a single limited-purpose federation, which includes the five boroughs plus Nassau, Suffolk, and Westchester counties.)

Local community size contributes directly to the organization of decision-making on the American Jewish scene. New York is not only in a size-class by itself but maintains its own—highly fragmented—organizational patterns while holding itself substantially aloof from all other communities. The federation system, which has become the norm throughout the rest of the country, is limited in New York City. There the major Jewish institutions and organizations, beginning with the United Jewish Appeal, conduct their own fund-raising campaigns and operate their own local programs outside of any overall planning or coordinating framework, often from their own national offices.

The major Jewish communities outside of New York are all structured so that the federations play a major, if not dominant, role in communal fund-raising and decision-making. All the significant ones among them are members of the Large City Budgeting Conference (LCBC) of the Council of Jewish Federations and Welfare Funds. While the LCBC itself is essentially an information-gathering body, its members together represent the single most powerful influence on communal fund-raising on the American Jewish scene and the leaders of its constituent federations are the major source of American Jewry's leadership across the spectrum of functional spheres. The communications network that is generated out of the interaction of those communal leaders may well be the heart of the countrywide Jewish communal decision-making system. Significantly, New York is not a member of the LCBC.

Communities too small or too weak to be members of the LCBC stand on the peripheries of the countrywide decision-making processes, no matter how well-organized and active they may be locally. Occasionally notable individuals from such communities do attain national prominence, but that is rare. Only in the last few years have the stronger of these communities begun to devise ways to enhance their national visibility in the manner of the LCBC.

Local decision-making has not been systematically studied in more than a handful of these organized communities. What we do know, however, is that there are variations among cities simply as a result of the differences in scale that change the magnitude of the communications problems. The ways in which patterns of communication are organized vary in communities of different sizes, not to speak of other cultural, historical, social, and economic factors. Size, for example, does much to determine who knows whom and how comprehensive or exclusive are friendship and acquaintanceship nets. These, in turn, determine who speaks to whom on communal matters.

There is also considerable evidence that the percentage of those affiliated with and active in communal life stands in inverse ratio to community size. Since there is always a certain minimum of positions to be filled, regardless of community size, smaller communities will, *ipso facto,* involve a greater proportion of their population than larger ones, not to speak of the greater social pressures for participation often manifested in smaller communities where people know who is and who is not participating.

The size factor works in other ways as well. To some extent, the number and spread of Jewish institutions is dependent upon the size of the community. A community of 10,000 Jews is not likely to have the range of institutions of a community of 100,000. Consequently it will not have the complexity and diversity of decision-making centers or channels nor the problems of separated leadership that are likely to prevail in a very large community where people can be decision-makers in major arenas without knowing or working with their counterparts in others.

The impact of size of place also has a dynamic quality. From the early eighteenth century, when Jews first arrived in the American colonies, until the mid-nineteenth century, Jews lived in a number of small communities of approximately the same size, none of which were able to support more than the most rudimentary congregational institutions. All this changed with the subsequent mass immigration of Jews from Eastern Europe, who settled overwhelmingly in the major urban centers. At the same time, the Jews in the hinterland communities continued to migrate to the metropolises because that is where the opportunities lay.

Since the end of World War II there has been another shift in the scale of Jewish settlement that is only now beginning to be fully reflected in the structure of local decision-making. Increasingly, Jews have been moving out of the big cities into suburbs which, while nominally parts of the same metropolitan area, in fact have fully separate governmental structures and substantially distinctive socio-economic characteristics, both of which they guard jealously. This migration is leading the Jews back once again to small communities where, unless they are involved with a great metropolitan federation, they are able to maintain only the minimum in the way of local Jewish institutions. Scattered widely among many small towns, they are tied together at most by a common fund-raising system for overseas needs. From the available data it would seem that 60 percent of American Jews today live in separate suburban communities or in metropolitan communities of less than 20,000 Jews.

New York, with its 31 percent of the total American Jewish population, is the *de facto* capital of the American Jewish community. Moreover, because New York is really a region rather than a single community, and is additionally surrounded by perhaps another 15 percent of American Jewry living within the orbit of Manhattan, the Jews of New York tend to believe that all Jewish life in the United States is concentrated in their city and environs. At the same time, what would be considered very large Jewish communities in their own right are well-nigh buried within the metropolitan area and maintain only those institutions that meet local needs.

The other very large Jewish communities are regional centers of Jewish life as well as major communities in their own right. Los Angeles is clearly the center of Jewish life west of the Rocky Mountains and the second city of American Jewry institutionally as well as in numbers, with branches of all the countrywide Jewish organizations and institutions located within its limits. Because of its distance from the East Coast it has a greater degree of independence from "New York" than any other regional center in the United States. Chicago is the capital of the Jewries of mid-America in much the same way, although in its case relative proximity to New York has prevented it from developing the same range of national institutions or local autonomy as Los Angeles. Once the great western anchor of American Jewish life, its overall position has been lost to Los Angeles along with so much of its Jewish population.

Philadelphia and Boston, although now almost within commuting distance of New York, remain equally important secondary national centers for American Jewry because of historical circumstance. Philadelphia's old, established Jewish community has long played a national role that at one time even rivaled that of the Empire City. It continues to maintain some institutions of national significance. Perhaps more important, as the first major Jewish community outside of the New York metropolitan area, its leaders have easy access to the national offices of Jewish organizations where they frequently represent the point of view of the rest of American Jewry (insofar as there is any common one) vis-à-vis that of "New York."

Boston Jewry, though a far younger Jewish community, has capitalized on its city's position as the Athens of America to create major Jewish academic institutions of national scope and to become the home of whatever Jewish academic brain trust exists in the United States.

Only in the South is the largest city not the regional center. Greater Miami, still a very new community, the product of the post-World War II migration southward and heavily weighted with retirees, has had no significant national impact as a community (as distinct from a location for the conduct of the winter business of American Jewry as a whole). The capital of Jewish life in the South is Atlanta, the region's general capital. Despite its small Jewish population of 16,500, it possesses the panoply of regional offices associated with much larger Jewish communities in other parts of the country. The pattern of Jewish activity in Atlanta is markedly different from that of any of the other regional centers because of the intimacy and proximity within which the regional offices and local institutions must live.

Jewish communities of medium size (here defined as 20,000 to 100,000 population) all play tertiary roles (as communities) in the hierarchy of American Jewish communities. They are generally able to provide the full range of local institutions and organizations found in any American community, although often in rudimentary form, but serve no particular national functions except as a result of historical accident. Among them, national importance is determined by factors other than size. The subsidiary regional centers, all located between the Mississippi and the Pacific, represent nodes of Jewish population. These centers serve wide areas, sparsely settled by Jews, and thus occupy a more important role in the overall scheme than either their size or, in most cases, the quality of Jewish life within them would otherwise warrant. . . .

Associational Framework

Still another environmental factor that is vital in shaping decision-making in the American Jewish community is the extraordinary variety of forms of Jewish association possible. Any organized interconnections within the maze of institutions and organizations of American Jewry have had to be forged in the face of many obstacles, including the lack of any inherent legitimacy attaching to any coordinating institutions, the penchant for individualism inherent in the American Jewish community derived from both American and Jewish sources, and the difficulties of enforcing any kind of coordinating effort within the context of American society which treats all Jewish activities as private, voluntary ones.

Thus the pattern of relationships within the matrix of American Jewish life must be a dynamic one. There is rarely a fixed division of authority and influence within American Jewry but, rather, one that varies from time to time and usually from issue to issue with different elements of the matrix taking on different "loads" at different times and in relation to different issues. Moreover, since the community is a voluntary one, persuasion rather than compulsion, influence rather than power, are the tools available for making decisions and implementing policies. All this works to strengthen the character of the community as a communications network since the character, quality, and relevance of what is communicated and the way in which it is communicated frequently determine the extent of the authority and influence of the parties to the communication.

The World Jewish Environment

Decision-making in the American Jewish community is further shaped by the impact of the world Jewish environment. This is most immediately evident in the role which Israel plays in American Jewish life. Israel has become the major unifying symbol in the community, in effect replacing traditional religious values as the binding ties linking Jews of varying persuasions and interests. Fund-raising for Israel has not only come to dominate all communal activity, but has been the stimulus for the general increase in funds raised for across-the-board Jewish purposes in the United States since the end of World War II. . . .

Indeed, Israel has become, *de facto,* the authority-giving element in Jewish life today in the way that the Torah was in the pre-modern world. The ascendancy of Israel appears to have ended a period of well over a century in which there was no clear-cut source of authority in Jewish life at all. The fact that Israel has become the new source of authority is not without problems of its own, but nevertheless this new situation provides a means for uniting a people with very diverse beliefs.

The authoritative role of Israel functions in two ways. First, Israel is itself authoritative. Those who wish to dissent from any particular Israeli policy or demand must be very circumspect when they do so. Those Jews who reject Israel's claims upon them are more or less written off by the Jewish community. They are certainly excluded from any significant decision-making role in the community. Second, leaders who can claim to speak in the name of Israel or on behalf of Israel gain a degree of authority that places them in very advantageous positions when it comes to other areas of communal decision-making. Even the synagogues, which are expected to be bastions of support for the Torah as the primary source of authority in the community, have come increasingly to rely upon Israel and Israel-centered activities to legitimize their own positions.

INSTITUTIONS AND ORGANIZATIONS

Institutional Roles

The organizations and institutions within which the decisions of the American Jewish community are made group themselves into four categories based on the kinds of roles they play within the community as a whole. They are: *1) government-like institutions; 2) localistic institutions and organizations; 3) general-purpose, mass-based organizations;* and *4) special-interest institutions and organizations.*

Government-like institutions are those that play roles and provide services on a countrywide, local, or (where they exist) regional basis which, under other conditions, would be played, provided, or controlled, predominantly or exclusively, by governmental authorities. The Jewish federations and their constituent agencies are the most clear-cut examples of government-like institutions in the American Jewish community. Locally, the federations themselves have become something like roof organizations. They are constantly expanding their role in community planning, coordination, and financing. While they are not always comprehensive in the sense of embracing all organizations in the community directly, in most cases, they do maintain some formal connections with all significant ones performing government-like services which are either their constituent agencies, beneficiaries, or affiliates. Thus the bureaus of Jewish education, the Jewish community centers, Jewish community-relations councils, the community-wide welfare institutions, and the like, all of which perform functions which would otherwise be performed by government, are generally linked to the federation.

On the countrywide plane the analogous organizations are not as easily identifiable. The Council of Jewish Federations and Welfare Funds, the Synagogue Council of America, the National Jewish Welfare Board, the National Community Relations Advisory Council, and the American Association for Jewish Education at least make claims in that direction. In fact, however, the Jewish communities of the United States are no more than leagued together; they are not really federated on a countrywide basis in a sufficiently comprehensive manner to have generated comprehensive institutions that are comparable to those on the local scene.

Localistic institutions and organizations, primarily synagogues now that the *landsmanshaften* have virtually disappeared, are those whose first and foremost task is to meet the primary personal and interpersonal needs of individual Jews and Jewish families. By their very nature, synagogues are geared to be relatively intimate associations of compatible people. While the growth of the large American synagogue has led to a confusion of functions (which has contributed to the present difficulties of the synagogue as an institution), it still retains primary responsibility for meeting those needs.

General-purpose, mass-based organizations are those that function to a) articulate community values, attitudes and policies;

b) provide the energy and motive force for crystallizing the communal censensus that grows out of those values, attitudes, and policies; and c) maintain institutionalized channels of communication between the community leaders and "actives" ("cosmopolitans") and the broad base of the affiliated Jewish population ("locals") to deal with the problems and tasks facing the community in light of the consensus. These mass-based organizations provide the political structural parallel to the government-like ("cosmopolitan") and localistic institutions, bridging the gaps between them, providing a motivating force to keep them running, and also functioning to determine their respective roles in the community as a whole. In a sense these organizations function as the equivalent of political parties in a full-fledged political system (in some Jewish communities in other countries they are indeed political parties) to aggregate and mobilize interests in the community.

In the American Jewish community, these organizations are to be found in three varieties. First, there are the quasi-elite organizations which have begun to reach out to develop a larger membership base but in such a way that only people with special interests or backgrounds are likely to find their place within them. The American Jewish Committee is perhaps the best example of such an organization and in many respects is the most important of these organizations. Beginning as a small select group, the Committee has developed a larger membership base as it has become more democratized, but its base still includes a relatively select group of people (even if they are more self-selected than they used to be). At the same time, it is a very powerful group since its major principle of inclusion seems to be influential or potentially influential leaders. It, more than any other organization, has a membership strategically placed in the ranks of the leadership of the government-like institutions and the major synagogues.

The American Jewish Congress is another organization of this type. Its history has followed exactly the reverse pattern of that of the Committee. It was founded with the intention of becoming a mass-based organization but has instead become the preserve of a self-selected group interested in a particular kind of civil-libertarian approach to Jewish communal affairs.

The second variety consists of mass-based organizations that remain widely open to all types of Jews but have not been able to develop the mass base they desire. The Zionist organizations in the United States (with the exception of Hadassah) are the principal examples of this group. They have not only fallen short of their basic aim but have also failed to develop an elite cadre that would place them in the first group.

Finally, there are the truly mass-based organizations of which two stand out: B'nai B'rith and Hadassah. These organizations, whose members number in the hundreds of thousands each, reach out to the lowest common denominator in the American Jewish community on one hand, while at the same time speaking for the most sophisticated and complex communal needs.

Special-interest institutions and organizations are what their name indicates. They reflect the multitude of special interests in the community, either by maintaining programs of their own or functioning to mobilize concern and support for the various programs conducted by the government-like institutions in the community by exerting pressure for their expansion, modification, or improvement. The number of special-interest organizations is well-nigh myriad and they cover the gamut of interests which any Jewish community could possibly possess. They perform the important functions of concentrating on specific issues and trying to raise those issues before the larger Jewish public on the one hand, and before the leaders and decision-makers of the Jewish community on the other. No one of these special-interest groups is likely to have a great deal of influence in the community as a whole, though some will be of decisive importance in those specific areas of interest in which they are involved. A whole host can wield some influence on communal decision-making, depending on the character of the interest they represent, the degree of sympathy it invokes as an interest among the decision-makers in the community, and the caliber of leadership attached to the special-interest group.

It should be noted that the description presented here is idealized to the extent that particular organizations and institutions have functions that overlap the categories. For historical reasons that relate to the evolution of the American Jewish community from discrete institutions, functions were assumed in unsystematic ways. Thus B'nai B'rith is responsible for welfare institutions and the Hillel Foundations because, at the time they were founded, no more appropriate organization was available to initiate, finance, or operate them. Today they are slowly being transferred to more appropriate communal bodies.

The patterns of decision-making in the American Jewish community must be traced in light of the foregoing four-fold division which contributes so much to the shaping of the community's structural matrix. However it does not do so alone but only in combination with the territorial and non-territorial patterns of organization that inform the community.

Territorial and Non-Territorial Organization

The American Jewish community, like every Jewish community before it, is organized on a mixture of territorial and non-territorial bases. The territorial organizations are invariably the most comprehensive ones, charged with providing overall direction for the community as a whole or some otherwise fragmented segment of it, while the ideological, functional, and interest organizations generally touch the more personal aspects of Jewish life. One consequence of this has been that Jewish reformers in the United States seeking to improve the organization of the American Jewish community have constantly emphasized the need to strengthen territorial organization as against other kinds, while partisans of particular interests in the Jewish community have emphasized non-territorial forms of organization as the most appropriate forms in a voluntary community.

At the same time, because of the nature of the Jewish community, the territorial organizations rarely have fixed boundaries except by convention. Furthermore because ideological commitment in American Jewish life tends to be very weak, the ideological groupings have little internal strength of their own except insofar as they serve the interests of their members by taking on specific functional roles.

Ideologically based organizations have had more success on a countrywide basis where the absence of comprehensive territorial institutions has been marked until recently. Such countrywide organizations as developed prior to the 1930's became committed to specific ideological trends whether they were founded that way or not. However the impact of American life constantly serves to emphasize the territorial over the non-territorial elements wherever given half a chance and to reduce ideologically based organizations to functional specialists responsible for specific tasks. A major result of this has been to limit the powers of the countrywide organizations and to make the primary locus of decision-making for the American Jewish community local.

With the exception of a few institutions of higher education (and, once upon a time, a few specialized hospitals which are now non-sectarian), all Jewish religious, social, welfare, and educational institutions are local both in name and in fact. Some are casually confederated on a supra-local basis but most are not, and those claiming national status with no local base soon find themselves without a constituency. Indeed, the major institutions of the American Jewish community—the federations and the synagogues—developed their countrywide bodies after their local institutions had become well-established. Among the organizations which have been built out of a national headquarters, the only ones that have succeeded are those which have been able to develop meaningful local operations under local leadership.

The three great synagogue movements which are conventionally viewed as the primary custodians of Jewish affiliation in the United States since the end of World War II are excellent cases in point. All are essentially confederations of highly independent local congregations linked by relatively vague persuasional ties and a need for certain technical services such as professional placement, the organization of intercongregational youth programs, and the development of educational material. The confederations function to provide the requisite emotional reinforcement of those ties and the desired services for their member units. They have almost no direct influence on crucial congregational policies and behavior except insofar as the congregations themselves choose to look to them as guides. Short of expulsion from the movement, they have no devices which they can use to exercise any authority they might claim even in those cases where the congregation was originally established by the parent movement (which is not the usual pattern but does occur). Once a congregation is established it becomes as independent as all the rest.

The other great countrywide institutions of American Jewry are similarly organized. The Council of Jewish Federations and Welfare Funds is an equally loose confederation of hundreds of local Jewish federations which have emerged in the past four decades as the most powerful institutional forces in Jewish life. The role of the CJFWF is definitely tributary to that of its constituents who do not hesitate to give it direction. As in the case of the synagogue movements, the power of the national organization flows from its ability to provide services to the local affiliates, generate ideas for them, and manage the flow of professionals.

So, too, the National Jewish Welfare Board is the countrywide service agency of the clearly autonomous local community centers, the American Association for Jewish Education is the service agency of the local bureaus of Jewish education plus the countrywide organizations that claim to have a major interest in Jewish education, and the National Jewish Community Relations Advisory Council is the service agency of the local Jewish community-relations councils and the umbrella agency for the countrywide community-relations agencies and organizations. Exercise of these service functions brings with it a certain power which the professionals who staff the national agencies have developed in various ways, but it is a limited power, usually more visible at conferences than in the daily affairs of the local bodies. In recent years, the countrywide federations have been supplemented by even more loosely knit confederations of national bodies such as the Synagogue Council of America, a confederation of the major synagogue movements and, most recently, the Presidents' Conference, a loose league of the presidents of major Jewish organizations organized for "foreign-relations" purposes.

Whether the federative arrangements involved are of near-universal scope and have broad-based, multipurpose goals or are limited to single functions with rarely more than consultative or accreditation power, it is the consistent use of such arrangements that enables American Jewry to achieve any kind of structured communal unity at all. What emerges is not a single pyramidal structure, nor even one in which the "bottom" rules the "top" as in the case of Jewish communities with representative boards in other parts of the world. There is no "bottom" and no "top" except on a functional basis for specific purposes (if then). Thus it is the absence of hierarchy which is the first element to recognize in examining the decision-making process.

The Role of Functional Groupings

The institutions of the American Jewish community can properly be grouped into five spheres based primarily on function: 1) religious-congregational; 2) educational-cultural; 3) community relations; 4) communal-welfare; and 5) Israel–overseas. Decision-making in the community is organized accordingly.

Religious-Congregational Sphere: Even the synagogues can be seen as a functional grouping since American Jews' ideological commitment to a particular synagogue movement is very weak except at the extremes of Orthodoxy and Reform. In essence, they provide the immediately personal and interpersonal ritual- *cum*-social functions demanded by the community and do so primarily through individual congregations. They have an essential monopoly on those functions locally while the synagogue confederations, rabbinical associations, seminaries, and *yeshivot* maintain a parallel monopoly over the community's theological and ritual concerns countrywide.

Nationally, the three great synagogue confederations dominate the religious-congregational sphere. Over the years, each has expanded its scope and intensified its efforts on the American Jewish scene. In their common quest for an expanded role in American Jewish life, they leagued themselves into the Synagogue Council of America which, for a few years during the height of the "religious revival" of the 1950's, tried to capture the leading role as spokesman for American Jewry and which remains the Jewish religious counterpart to the national church bodies.

Each of the synagogue confederations has a seminary of its own which, because of its academic character, projects itself on the American Jewish scene in a quasi-independent way. Even with the growth of Judaic studies programs in academic institutions, these seminaries remain the backbone of organized Jewish scholarship in the United States. Their alumni lead the congregations of American Jewry and, through their rabbinical associations, link seminaries and the confederations. In addition, there are a growing number of yeshivot in New York and many of the other major Jewish communities that reflect the great growth and proliferation of the new ultra-Orthodox elements in the community. They preserve and extend traditional Jewish scholarship on a scale never before experienced in American Jewish history.

Since World War II, there has been an increasing involvement of power centers outside of the United States in the religious-congregational spheres. The Israeli rabbinate is a growing force on the American scene by virtue of its role in deciding the personal status of individual Jews. In an age of jet travel between Israel and the Diaspora, such decisions have ramifications which reverberate throughout the Jewish world. In this connection, the Knesset is also acquiring influence in the religious-congregational sphere and, indeed, is the first "secular" body anywhere to do so, simply because of its central role in defining the question of "Who is a Jew"? in a setting where separation of "church" and state does not prevail.

The controlling power of the synagogue in the religious-congregational sphere means that a very large share of Jewish activity—involving perhaps half of the total revenue and expenditure of American Jewry—is managed outside of any communal decision-making system. American synagogues have traditionally considered themselves (and have been considered) to be private institutions, like clubs or fraternal lodges, accountable to no one but their own members for the decisions they make. This reflects their status in American law and has simply been carried over unquestioningly into Jewish communal affairs.

Educational-Cultural Sphere: The synagogues also play a major role in educational matters, having acquired that role after a contest of some forty years' duration during which the non-synagogue schools were defeated in the struggle over who was to assume responsibility for elementary and secondary Jewish education. Today the great majority of Jewish Sunday and afternoon schools at the elementary level and a large number of those at the secondary level are housed in and controlled by synagogues. Synagogue control is so complete where it exists that we do not even have decent estimates of how much is spent on Jewish education since they do not make their budgets public.

Management of elementary and secondary Jewish education carried on outside of the synagogues is vested in three categories of institutions. There are a few surviving "secular" schools, usually Yiddishist in orientation, managed by what are secularistic equivalents of congregations, that is to say, groups of families that carry out the same functions together that conventional congregations do, eliminating their overtly "religious" character. There are also some remnants of older non-congregational school systems, generally confined to serving the older neighborhoods. Finally, there are a handful of communal school systems, the largest of which are in Detroit, Minneapolis, and St. Paul, that function as the comprehensive educational arms of the Jewish community and dominate Jewish educational activity locally.

Aside from the latter, the only movement in Jewish elementary and secondary education outside of the synagogue that is growing is the day-school movement. Day schools, whether formally attached to some national "ideology" or not, tend to develop with communal support by default, though, because few communities have any well-defined way to deal with them, they are rarely tied to the central institutions of communal governance but remain nominally "private" schools that receive subsidization to some degree.

Central agencies of Jewish education in the larger Jewish communities do have some formal responsibility for developing curricula, setting professional standards and the like for the synagogue schools, and in some cases have acquired responsibility for directly managing secondary afternoon schools and colleges of Jewish studies. Occasionally, they even maintain "experimental schools" which usually provide such intensive supplementary Jewish education as exists in a given community. While their operational role is limited, they usually represent the only links between the synagogue educational programs and the central institutions of the local Jewish community.

Higher Jewish education is also divided into three segments, the colleges of Jewish studies, the seminaries and yeshivot, and the emerging Jewish-studies programs in general colleges and universities. The latter, whatever their name and format, are beginning to acquire a certain amount of importance within the overall scheme of Jewish education locally and are even beginning to affect the character and content of the traditional institutions of Jewish education. It would be wrong, however, to overestimate the importance of such programs—as against the seminaries and yeshivot—as sources of Jewish scholars or to view the colleges of Jewish studies as influences on local communal life.

If anything, Jewish educational activities are even more localized than the religious-congregational activities. The American Associaton for Jewish Education, the umbrella body for the central agencies and itself a confederation of local and national groups, is limited in the technical services it renders to studies of local needs and problems. The Orthodox day schools are somewhat more clearly linked to their countrywide bodies, particularly in the case of the *Torah Umesorah* schools. The Conservative day schools are linked formally to umbrella bodies which exist in name only and many such schools have no extra-community ties at all. The most important ties linking any Jewish schools are the professional associations linking Jewish educators. Increasingly, the Council of Jewish Federations and Welfare Funds is becoming involved in the educational and cultural sphere in an attempt to develop some countrywide input, but its role must still be considered peripheral at this point.

Worldwide bodies involved in the educational-cultural arena

include the Jewish Agency, which represents the Zionist point of view and Israel's interests and which works most extensively in the realm of adult education and in linking Jewish students with Israel. The Memorial Foundation for Jewish Culture, an international body with headquarters in New York, has become the most potent source of support for Jewish scholarly and cultural activities since its resources exceed those of any other institution on the scene.

Among the scholarly associations and research institutes, the YIVO Institute for Jewish Research and the American Jewish Historical Society are probably the most potent independent bodies actually engaged in projects and their activities are distinctly limited, if only because of monetary limitations. In general, these bodies are small, independent, and outside the mainstream of American Jewish life.

Except for the Jewish Publication Society and the small seminary and movement publication programs, publication is a private enterprise in American Jewish life. The JPS is the most significant publishing force on the American Jewish scene and the only one seriously linked with other institutions in the Jewish community. Only recently has the publication of Jewish books for profit expanded much beyond the textbook business.

What is important about the cultural activities of American Jewry is how peripheral they and those engaged in them are in the context of American Jewish public affairs. Since the cultural institutions do not even have the advantage of feeling needed by the decision-makers, as is true of Jewish education, and rarely have the prestige of Jewish academics in general universities, they are at a great disadvantage in a community that is not much oriented to scholarly or cultural concerns.

Community-Relations Sphere: Most major Jewish communities have a Jewish Community Relations Council which considers itself the central agency for handling community-relations problems. In addition, communities often have local offices or chapters of the American Jewish Committee, the Anti-Defamation League of B'nai B'rith, the American Jewish Congress, the Jewish War Veterans, and the Jewish Labor Committee that also engage in community-relations work, whether in cooperation with the Jewish Community Relations Council or independently. Indeed, the classic pictures of fragmentation in American Jewish life are usually drawn in regard to the community-relations field, and it was in that field that the most publicized countrywide efforts have been made to bring order out of chaos, beginning with the development of the National Community Relations Advisory Council in the 1940's. The latter is a confederation of independent agencies combining both local agencies and countrywide bodies in one common league. Of course it is limited in its role precisely because it is a confederation of what are powerful and independent bodies, each in its own right.

In the educational-cultural and religious-congregational spheres the situation is so structured that the many separate organizations engage in relatively little direct competition. In the community-relations sphere, on the other hand, the smaller number of separate organizations overlap one another because they deal with the same problem—often the same explicit issues. The effects of that competition are potentially great because they are directed toward "foreign affairs" matters, that is to say, matters that reach outside of the Jewish community and directly affect its relations with the larger world. Consequently, a considerable amount of self-policing and specialization has developed within the sphere in the past two decades.

The American Jewish Committee, the Anti-Defamation League, and the American Jewish Congress, conventionally recognized as the "big three" in community-relations work, are the most centralized of all countrywide Jewish organizations. Their role in American Jewish life was once enhanced by their centralized structures at a time when the local Jewish communities were barely organized and the individual institutions within them were far too parochial to reach out to the general community. Today, their situation is reversed. Only those that have managed to decentralize are thriving. The American Jewish Congress, perhaps the most centralized among them, has not properly taken root on the local plane and as a result is suffering tremendously as a countrywide organization. The Anti-Defamation League and the American Jewish Committee began earlier to achieve substantial decentralization with greater success, though in both cases the national office still plays a very great role even in local activities.

More recently, the synagogue movements have attempted to enter the community-relations field as part of their drive toward dominance in American Jewish life. Bodies such as the Synagogue Council, the Commission on Social Action of Reform Judaism, and the National Commission on Law and Public Affairs of the Orthodox movement reflect this. However, they still play a relatively limited role on the overall scene.

Increased American Jewish involvement in the concerns of the

Jewish people as a whole has sharpened the need for a communal voice that speaks as one, at least in the foreign-relations field. This, in turn, has led to the establishment of the Presidents' Conference, consisting of presidents of the major countrywide Jewish organizations who meet together to make policy decisions that the more institutionalized consultative bodies cannot. Since the Presidents' Conference must make all decisions unanimously, it is limited in the degree in which it can play an active role in its prescribed area, but it has brought some order at least in matters strictly pertaining to foreign relations.

Since support and assistance for Israel have become key items on the community-relations agenda, the Israel government has become a prime mover in this sphere. Despite occasional protests to the contrary, official American Jewish action on behalf of Israel in the public-relations field is conducted in close consultation with and in response to the initiatives of the Israel authorities. In certain respects, Israel's role in the community-relations sphere may well be greater than its role in any other sphere of decision-making in the American Jewish community.

Communal-Welfare Sphere: The communal-welfare sphere has undergone the greatest change in the past generation. As late as the 1950's it was simply another functional grouping among several, considerably better organized internally; the various Jewish social service and welfare agencies plus the Jewish community centers had federated with one another a generation or more earlier. While the local federations had already expanded to include fund-raising for overseas needs, their pretensions to centrality in the community were limited by the fact, that on the domestic scene, they remained primarily concerned with the traditional social service functions.

By the end of the 1950's, the federations had been transformed into the major fund-raising bodies in the community and stood on the threshold of a whole new world of responsibilities. The latter transformation came as federations realized that proper execution of their role as allocating agencies necessitated greater involvement in community planning of a scope that at least touched all the activities defined as being communitywide in character in any given locality. At the same time, the old "German" leadership in the communal-welfare field was being broadened to include "Eastern European" elements as well, selected from the same income, occupational, and observance levels.

The decade of the 1960's saw the federations undertake

community planning on a large scale, beyond that required for the simple allocation of funds. They also acquired greater responsibility for and interest in Jewish education as well as continuing and even deepening their relationships with their constituent social-service and welfare agencies. In the process, most made strong efforts to broaden their leadership base to include new segments of the community.

All this has served to enhance the central role of the federations locally and to give them the best—if not the unrivaled—claim to being the umbrella organizations. There is no question that the key to the growth of the power of the local federations is that they have become the major fund-raising bodies on the American scene. Even though money and influence are not necessarily correlated on a one-to-one basis, there is unquestionably a relationship between the two. Locally, as agencies become more dependent upon the federation for funds, they are more likely to be included in the ambit of federation planning and policy-making.

The same pattern has repeated itself on the countrywide plane though in a less clear-cut way. The difference is that the Council of Jewish Federations and Welfare Funds does not have the fund-raising power which the local federations have and consequently has no such monetary power to exercise over the parallel national associations. The Jewish Welfare Board, for example, is funded the way the CJFWF is—by grants from its local constituents and the local federations directly, thus limiting the possibilities of CJFWF influence on indirect grants. The national community-relations and religious organizations are even more independent.

A new addition to the communal-welfare scene is the Israeli element, the result of the large role played by the federations in raising funds for Israel's needs. The government of Israel has its special concerns in American Jewish life which it pursues in many ways, but is finding it increasingly advantageous to pursue within the context of the communal-welfare sphere. The Jewish Agency, particularly since its recent reconstitution, has virtually coopted the federation leadership as its "non-Zionist" representatives, creating an even tighter bond between the institutionalized representatives of the World Zionist movement and the American Jewish community than ever before. In both cases, the institutionalization of relationships is still in its incipient stages.

Israel-Overseas Sphere: This area is both the best organized and the best integrated of all the spheres. Integration here dates back to

World War I and the founding of the American Jewish Joint Distribution Committee (JDC). In general, the sphere has two interlocking wings, one concerned with fund-raising and the other with political-*cum*-educational activity. Responsibilities for fund-raising are divided between the federations which handle the United Jewish Appeal (UJA) the Israel Bonds Organization, the Jewish National Fund, and the various "friends" of Israeli or overseas institutions. Political-*cum*-educational activities are conducted primarily through the Zionist organizations that are now at least nominally united (except for the Zionist Organization of America [ZOA]) into an American Zionist Federation, locally and country-wide.

Since the potentiality for competition among these organizations is great and the need to cooperate for the common good of Israel felt universally among them, a system of negotiated sharing has been developed through a network of agreements dividing the funds and/or the campaign arenas. The basic agreements are those reached nationally between the representatives of the federations working through the CJFWF and the UJA on an annual basis, dividing the funds raised in the local campaigns. A second agreement, between the UJA, the Israel Bond Organization, and the various "friends" groups more or less spells out their respective jurisdictions and claims to various methods of fund-raising. Thus Israel Bonds has a right to make synagogue appeals, while direct solicitation is a province of the UJA through the federations. The problem of cooperation among the Zionist organizations has consistently been more difficult. Since, with the exception of Hadassah and the ZOA, they are tied to the great "national" (read "worldwide" Jewish) Zionist parties that participate in the political life of Israel, they have been less than willing to cooperate on the local scene until very recently.

Naturally, the Israel-overseas sphere is substantially influenced by sources outside of the United States. The Israel government and the Jewish Agency take a very active role in the fund-raising process. Similarly, the Jewish National Fund and the *Keren Hayesod* become active participants both through the Jewish Agency and to some extent directly on the American scene as well. Aside from these Israel-based bodies, the JDC, the Organization for Rehabilitation and Training (ORT), and the Claims Conference are also involved in the worldwide activities of the Jewish people, both as beneficiaries and constituents of the American Jewish bodies functioning in the field. Their role has been of great significance in the postwar period. The JDC in particular has become the bearer of American Jewish "know-how" as well as money wherever there are Jewish communities in need of redevelopment.

BASIC DIVISIONS IN THE DECISION-MAKING ARENAS

Religious and Secular

The division between the "religious" and the "secular" developed out of the American milieu and was enhanced in the early days of the twentieth century by the relatively sharp division between those Jews who concerned themselves with their *shuls* and those who, while members of synagogues and temples, were really far more interested in welfare and community-relations activities which they saw as divorced from "religion" *per se.* This led to the rise of two separate groups of decision-makers. By their very nature, synagogues were localistic institutions, while the secular services became the province of the cosmopolitans.

Despite all the forces making for separation, the division could not and did not remain a hard and fast one. Indeed, it has been breaking down since the end of World War II. In the first place, there was the great expansion of those educational and cultural functions which could not be neatly divided between the two. Moreover, as the synagogues grew in power in the 1950's and began to see themselves as the true custodians of American Jewish life, they began to claim authoritative roles in areas previously reserved to the "secular" side. Finally, the whole thrust of Jewish tradition militated against such a separation as artificially enforced. As those concerned with the "secular" side became more involved in Jewish life and began to see their services as functions that had a specifically Jewish content, they began to think of them as no less religious in the traditional Jewish sense than the functions of the synagogues. Nevertheless, while ideologically and functionally the lines between the two are weakening, structurally the separation between "religious" and "secular" institutions remains as strong as ever.

Public and Private

While there is little conscious perception of the distinction between "public" and "private" (partly because there is some notion that vis-à-vis governmental activities all Jewish communal activities are private), nevertheless the activities sponsored or funded by the federations and their constituent agencies are implicitly understood to be the public activities of the American Jewish community. The argument for "communal responsibility" essentially has been an argument designed to define them in that manner.

Synagogues, on the other hand, have continued to be regarded as "private." Only in the last few years has the notion of the synagogues as private enterprises been questioned within Jewish communal circles, and then only privately, in a belated recognition of the fact that a congregation of 1,000–2,000 families, providing a range of services far beyond simple maintenance of the weekly and yearly prayer schedule, is not the same as a collection of twenty or forty men gathered together primarily for a *minyan*. In part, this recognition is a response to the synagogues' encroachment upon the traditionally communal sector. In part, it is also a reflection of the suburbanization of American Jewry whereby synagogues have become major centers of community activities in their respective suburbs—if not the *only* centers—and where movement of a major synagogue from one neighborhood to another affects the whole course of Jewish life within a particular locale.

"Cosmopolitans" and "Locals"

The "public-private" distinction as it is implicitly recognized in Jewish life today follows very much along the lines of the dichotomy between "cosmopolitans" and "locals" described by social scientists. Briefly, cosmopolitans are those who see the whole community as a single entity and maintain connections and involvements across all of it. While their cosmopolitanism is first defined in relation to a particular local community, once they develop a cosmopolitan outlook toward the local community, they almost invariably take a cosmopolitan view of the larger world of which that community is a part, as well. Locals, on the other hand, are those whose involvement and connections are confined to a small segment of the total community—a neighborhood, a particular social group or, in Jewish life, a particular synagogue, organization, or club. Their involvement rests overwhelmingly on their commitment to that point of attachment and does not extend to the community as a whole except indirectly. Moreover, their perceptions of the larger world are also quite limited, based as they are on their localistic involvements.

To a very real extent, this is a natural division in society. At the same time, all cosmopolitans have clearly localistic needs—to be tied to something more intimate than the community in the abstract, or even to a set of institutions which must inevitably be depersonalized to some degree. Similarly, locals can be mobilized for essentially cosmopolitan purposes when those purposes are made to strike home at the source of their involvement. Thus every community needs institutions devoted to serving both cosmopolitan and local needs as well as the local needs of cosmopolitans and the cosmopolitan needs of locals.

In the Jewish community, the organizations and agencies that fall within the federation family generally represent the cosmopolitan interest and consequently attract cosmopolitans to leadership positions within them. The synagogues, on the other hand, represent localistic needs and interests first and foremost. Indeed, that is their primary role (if one that is often neglected in the large contemporary American congregation). Consequently, the leadership they attract consists of a very high percentage of locals.

Professionals and Volunteers

The other major division among decision-makers in the American Jewish community is that between professional and voluntary leaders, with the professionals further subdivided into those whose training is obtained through religious institutions and those whose training is through secular ones. The American Jewish community has the most professionalized leadership of any in the world, probably the most of any in Jewish history. The roots of this undoubtedly lie in the commitment to professionalization which envelops the larger American society.

Today, the day-to-day business of the Jewish community is almost exclusively in the hands of professionals or, at the very least, people who are paid for their services even if they do not meet professional standards or consider themselves as forever committed to Jewish careers. Because these professionals are involved on a daily basis with the problems of the community, they exercise great influence in the decision-making of the community. On the other hand, there has been no diminution in the number of voluntary leaders. Parallel roles for professionals and volunteers have developed in virtually every Jewish organization and institution, allowing for extensive participation by both. What is not fixed is the way in which they relate to each other.

In some cases, the relationship between professionals and volunteers is resolved by separation of functions and in some by a mixing of functions. As a general rule, wherever the requirements of the profession are most exclusive and demanding, and the need for professional expertise established, separation of functions tends to be the norm. Wherever the line between professional competence and volunteer talent is least distinct, sharing tends to be the norm. Thus, in the rabbinate, Jewish education, and certain of the Jewish social services, not only operations, but many policy-making powers are placed in the hands of professionals who are viewed as specially trained experts, bringing to their tasks an expertise that endows them with a special role. In such cases, the voluntary leadership often confines itself to endorsing or ratifying policies suggested by professionals, developing and approving very general organizational goals and principles, and finding the necessary monetary and community support for their enterprise, only intervening more actively when the professionals fail to provide the requisite leadership.

On the other hand, in community relations and fund-raising, the lines that divide professionals and volunteers tend to be relatively weak. Professionals are often treated as if they cannot claim very much in the way of special expertise (other than the expertise of experience) for handling what are essentially political tasks. In fact, they gain their substantial influence because they, too, are specially trained and, most important, spend all of their working time at what they do, enabling them to know the situation better than the voluntary leadership. Like all professionals, their special power is based on the extent to which they control (willy-nilly, deliberately, or for traditional reasons) the amount and kind of information that reaches their volunteer counterparts. In addition, their control of in-house planning, their ability to strongly influence the appointment of voluntary leaders to particular committees, and the fact that they provide continuity in the life of the organization adds to their power. At the same time, some of the volunteers may indeed have special talents, capabilities, or positions, particularly political ones, which place them in very strategic positions within the organizations and give them major roles in the decision-making process hardly different from those of the professionals in those arenas where their talents, capabilities, or positions are useful. In fact, the process usually finds volunteers and professionals working in tandem on common problems with minimum conflict.

The sources of professional and volunteer leadership in the community themselves help to mark the division. By and large, the volunteers are recruited from among the wealthier elements associated with any particular function or institution. This is partly because the hierarchy of influence among the voluntary leadership is often set in terms of the size of their contributions and partly because the costs of playing a leadership role are such that only the well-to-do can afford the time and the money to do so. Aside from successful businessmen and professionals and perhaps young lawyers associated with law firms where there is a tradition of participation in Jewish communal life, the only people who can contribute the requisite time are academicians and they are limited by their inability to spend the money required to maintain an active role. Thus, willy-nilly, wealth becomes an important factor in determining the voluntary leadership.

This situation is not quite as stark as it seems. Obviously it is far less true in the case of small synagogues and clubs (the most localistic institutions of all) and most true in the case of the UJA. Even where wealth is of great importance, it does not function as the only measure of leadership. The wealthiest men are not necessarily the most important leaders. There is apparently some threshold of prosperity past which most men are relatively equal in the pursuit of leadership roles. A man of still modest means from the perspective of the very wealthy may choose to allocate a high proportion of his resources to the Jewish community and get recognized accordingly, while a man of very great means may not be willing to make such a major allocation and remains unrecognized accordingly. Moreover, beyond the willingness to give there must be a willingness to serve.

THE DECISION-MAKERS: THEIR ROLES AND FUNCTIONS

There are at least five categories of decision-makers functioning in the Jewish community today. Three of these are dominated by professionals: rabbis, communal workers, and Jewish educators. Two are dominated by lay personnel: congregational boards and volunteers. These categories, in turn, fall into two divisions: congregational decision-makers (rabbis, congregational boards) and communal decision-makers (communal workers, volunteers). (The educators, as we shall see, form a kind of class of their own.)

Congregational Decision-Makers

Rabbis: At the very least, rabbis function as decision-makers within their congregations, while the more talented, important, well-known or cosmopolitan among them are able to build upon their rabbinical roles to become decision-makers in the larger Jewish communal life as well. In general, rabbis tend to be restricted to their congregations or to their synagogue movements by the secular sector and by their own reluctance to venture outside of the arena in which their authority is rarely questioned.

It is very difficult for rabbis to shift roles when they leave the congregational setting, as they would have to do if they were to participate, say, in communal-welfare activities. There they would have to participate as if among equals, but with neither the special competence of professionals in the particular field nor with any claim to special recognition by virtue of their rabbinical positions. A relationship of equality in such a situation is uncomfortable for both sides, since neither knows how properly to respond to the other. Thus it is more convenient for a rabbi simply not to participate.

The field of education and culture however, is one area in which rabbis can participate fully. At the same time, rabbis are not especially eager to become professional leaders in this area for at least two reasons. First, Jewish education tends to enjoy a relatively low status in the eyes of the voluntary leaders who control their destinies as rabbis; second, American rabbis rarely have the training or the time to develop excellence in Jewish scholarship to a degree that would give them the kind of status they demand—and get—in the pulpit.

When the Jewish community was smaller, its leadership concentrated in fewer hands, and its functions (and finances) more limited, a few dynamic rabbis could rise to positions of communal eminence by dint of their virtuosity. None of those conditions prevails today and the virtuoso rabbi has gone the way of his secular counterpart. Another reason why rabbis are not found in the forefront of American Jewish leadership is that synagogues are essentially localistic institutions and rabbis, no matter how cosmopolitan in outlook, in order properly to maintain their congregational bases must adapt themselves to localistic needs and interests.

Congregational Boards: Since synagogues account for so much of Jewish activity in the United States today, the men and (in some instances) women who comprise the congregational boards of trustees must be considered important decision-makers, though they are rarely recognized as such. The lack of recognition stems from the fact that there are so many congregations in the United States, each a little empire in itself, controlling its own budget, hiring its own personnel, establishing its own program, and building its own facilities with barely any reference to any outside body.

The congregations spend no less than $100 million a year and perhaps as much as $500 million. Nobody knows the exact figure, or even knows how to make a proper estimate. This is an amount of money equal to that contributed to the federations and the UJA in the very best years of their drives.

There are over 4,500 Jewish congregations in the United States according to the fragmentary figures available. Should the average size of the congregational board be ten members (probably an underestimate), this would mean that there are at least 45,000 congregational board members. In fact, the number is probably larger than that. When we add to the congregational boards the number of men who serve on congregational committees, the number of potential decision-makers increases even further and our knowledge of what they do and how they do it diminishes even more.

Every form of decision-making is to be found in the government of Jewish congregations in America, ranging from the most autocratic, where one man decides all congregational policy, holds the rabbi in the palm of his hand, so to speak, hires, fires, and decides as he pleases on all issues, to situations where the most open forms of town-meeting democracy prevail and the congregation governs itself without the mediation of any board.

In the larger congregations, with boards of thirty or more, actual policy-making may be confined to an even smaller group. Assume that decision-making is shared among five people in each congregation—again, probably an underestimate. That means that there are still 20,000 significant decision-makers governing the synagogues of the United States, all of whom function within their respective congregations with minimal, if any, ties among congregations.

At this stage of our knowledge, it would be difficult to describe the "typical" congregational board member or even the typical congregational board. What unites them all is their essentially localistic commitment to the primary needs of their own particular congregations. It is rare to find a congregational board that, in its official capacity, will concern itself with the needs of the larger community, even when its members may, in other capacities, be the major communal leaders.

This fragmentation of outlook has great consequences for the community as a whole, particularly in the case of the largest congregations, those with membership of a thousand families or more. The consequences are obviously far less important in connection with congregations of fifty families. What is most important is that even congregations of medium size, whose actions are not likely to jolt the Jewish community as a whole in the manner of the largest ones, have a tremendous impact on the character of the community by virtue of their control over the education of their children.

Relations between rabbis and congregational boards obviously stand at the heart of the congregational decision-making process. While, again, the variety is great, three general models can be found. On one hand, the congregational board, or the dominant authority figure in the congregation, may simply dominate the rabbi, confining him to a role that involves conducting services and carrying out similar ritual chores. In some cases, rabbis are not even allowed to attend congregational board meetings. In other situations, the diametrically opposite condition prevails: the rabbi is so strong that he dominates the congregational board, which exists primarily to mediate between him and the congregation as a whole or to carry out his wishes in areas where he does not want to be directly or extensively involved. Finally, there is the situation which prevails more normally, where some kind of division of functions is worked out between the congregational leadership and the rabbi, with decision-making shared in certain relatively clear-cut areas.

Communal Decision-Makers

Communal Workers: Communal workers gain their power on the basis of either expertise or their day-to-day involvement with the problems of the community. Their technical knowledge and perennial availability give them important decision-making roles unless they are directly challenged by the voluntary leadership. This rarely happens because, in most cases, the voluntary leadership does not feel interested or competent enough to challenge them.

At the present time it is likely that the majority of Jewish communal workers are drawn from the social-work professions and have been trained as social workers, with legal training in second place. In relatively few cases were the senior civil servants of the Jewish community trained specifically for Jewish positions. In most cases they simply fell into such positions as a result of happenstance or circumstance. This is less true among the younger members where Jewish agencies, in an effort to overcome the personnel problem, have made some effort to recruit people and provide them with the resources needed to attend secular schools to get social-work training on condition that they then serve the agencies for a specified period of time.

For the most part, the communal workers are not well-grounded in traditional Jewish learning or even in rudimentary knowledge of Jewish history, law, society, or customs. Consequently, their deficiencies are most glaring when it comes to making decisions involving the Jewishness of their programs. Since their expertise in other respects tends to be among the very best available in the country, the contrast is rendered even sharper than it might otherwise be. This is not to say that many—or most—of them have not become seriously and sincerely interested in fostering the Jewish aspects of their work, but they are in a difficult position when it comes to translating attitudes into concrete programs.

Volunteers: We have almost no data on the voluntary leaders of the American Jewish community, but one thing that does mark them is their relative wealth, although this is not the only criterion. They are very heavily confined to community-relations, communal-welfare, and Israel-overseas activity. Volunteers are a group for whom Jewish activity is a means of expressing Jewishness, no more and no less than synagogue worship or observance of Jewish tradition is for others. In effect, their activity becomes their religion, and their observance is conditioned by the demands of communal life. Some of them are involved in communal leadership primarily for the honor, but many others work as persistently as their professional counterparts for little recognition. Moreover, they expend large sums of money for the pleasure of participating.

Money and energy are thus key sources of such influence over decision-making as the volunteers have, although neither replaces talent when it comes to the actual decision-making process itself. Money may buy a man the presidency of an organization or agency. Energy may put a man in a leadership position, but some kind of talent is necessary if a person is actually to have a share in making decisions. This is true if only because of the role of the professionals in screening the advancement of the voluntary leadership.

In at least one area—that of fund-raising—volunteers are the dominant decision-makers. No matter how much professional help is provided, it is only the voluntary leadership—the men who give the money themselves—who are able to influence others to give money. Moreover, with respect to fund-raising they usually feel that they have as much expertise as any one else and therefore are less likely to defer to the ideas or demands of the professionals.

By and large, the volunteers are probably representative of the more Jewishly committed elements in the mainstream of the American Jewish community, this despite the fact that they are rarely elected to the offices they occupy in any meaningful sense of the term. (The elections, though not always formalities, are usually simply means of formally ratifying the choices of nominating committees and, even when contested, are rarely contested by candidates representing seriously different characteristics or points of view.) They are representatives because there is a certain sameness in American Jewry; their desires, tastes, attitudes, interests, and educational backgrounds probably depart very little from the norm among the majority of American Jews.

Jewish Educators: Jewish educators are here considered apart from rabbis and communal workers because they generally pass through different forms of training and pursue different career lines. While some men trained as rabbis become Jewish educators, most of the educators are men who had decided upon Jewish education as a career before entering rabbinical school. It can fairly be said that the educators' decision-making role is confined to the sphere of Jewish education, that is to say, to schools or camps where they exercise authority as professionals. However, their authority is limited by various external factors. Chief among these are the problems inherent in Jewish education in the United States—namely, the ambivalence of parents regarding the amount of Jewish education they wish their children to acquire, the problems of obtaining qualified teachers and adequate financial support, and the fact that education is lodged in the synagogue whose leadership has other priorities.

Still, within this framework there is usually little interest in what the Jewish educators teach except on the part of the rabbi who may intervene to assure that "loyalty to the institution" is given the first priority. Beyond that, even the rabbis tend to pay little attention to the day-to-day operations of "their" schools. A Jewish educator who wishes may do more or less what he pleases in his school with little outside interference, provided he does not do anything that violates the Jewish communal consensus.

DECISION-MAKING TASKS AND MODES

The tasks to which the various categories of decision-makers address themselves are all ultimately geared to the question of Jewish survival. Given this overriding interest, the Jewish community's two most important concerns are defense and education.

Defense: The major defense concerns have changed radically within recent years. From the 1870's through the 1930's domestic anti-Semitism was the dominant defense concern of the community. Beginning with the 1930's, however, this was gradually replaced by efforts to defend Jews in other parts of the world. However, after 1948, Israel became the major focus of Jewish attention; and since 1967 particularly, insuring the survival of Israel has become the heart of the defense function of the American Jewish community.

Even the community-relations agencies are now spending a high proportion of their time and resources trying to increase support for Israel in the United States. As a result, the most important decision-makers in the community are those who are related to the defense of Israel, namely the federation and UJA leadership, voluntary and professional.

Education: Education is now being recognized as an equally essential concern. Meeting Jewish educational needs is a somewhat problematic matter for the community since it exposes all the ambivalences of contemporary Jewish life, creating a clash between the desire for survival as a people with the desire for full integration into the general society. Jewish education therefore requires a great measure of commitment to the notion that Jews are different and must educate their children to be different. All agree that Jewish education is important, but the character of the commitment is something else again. American Jewish education reflects all the ambiguities, and that is one reason why major decision-makers rarely play any real role in the educational field and why those who are professionally involved in Jewish education are not major decision-makers in the community.

Since these ambivalences are not easily overcome there is not likely to be any dramatic change in the foreseeable future although there has been a consistent and gradual increase in support for Jewish schools over the last twenty years. It is now clear that the major decision-makers are willing to provide some kind of "minimum base" support for Jewish education locally through the federations and their appropriate constituent agencies. This minimum base is progressively being defined upward but it remains a base line, not an aggressively advancing one. Moreover, the federations are discouraged from moving beyond the minimum by the unresolved division over control of Jewish education between the community as a whole and the individual synagogue.

Social Services and Welfare: The decision-makers who are most involved in this area have been losing importance on the communal scene. This is partly because the social services themselves have become progressively less Jewish in appearance, if not in fact, and partly because the rise of the welfare state has reduced their significance in American Jewish life. Jewish hospitals, for example, are now simply institutions sponsored by the Jewish community as one of its contributions to the welfare of American society as a whole. The Jewish community maintains its stake in such institutions partly because it is a customary way of making a contribution to the life of the general community, partly because it provides a bridge to other minority groups with whom the Jewish community wants to maintain good relations, and partly because there is some strong, if unspoken, sentiment in the Jewish community that it is well for Jews to have such institutions under their supervision "just in case."

Pressures are also mounting for the social welfare agencies to give representation on their governing bodies to their non-Jewish clients. While most Jewish communities have resisted those pressures, the fact that the institutions are supported only partially from Jewish funds and heavily by United Fund and government contributions or grants makes it more difficult to hold the line.

Certain of the institutions which are presently considered to be within the social-service sphere are now seeking to broaden their interests, usually by moving into the area of education and culture as well. This is particularly true of the Jewish community centers whose social-service functions have been reduced as their educational and cultural functions have increased. Today some Jewish community centers often appear to be secular rivals of the synagogues.

Finance: Community finance is obviously a central task of the American Jewish community and the raising of money is a continuing and unrelenting activity. Indeed, such is its importance in determining the organization of Jewish communal life that from a strictly organizational point of view it may be considered the most important task of all.

Two major struggles have developed and have been essentially resolved in the area of fund-raising, both of which have had significant consequences for the organizational structure and the patterns of decision-making in the community. The first was the struggle within each locality as to whether or not to centralize the raising of funds for Jewish communal purposes. By and large, the decision has been to centralize fund-raising for all purposes other than those that fall within the religious-congregational sphere. This struggle led to the creation of the Jewish federations which by standing astride of general fund-raising have acquired the central decision-making role in the community.

The second struggle that took place was between local and

national organizations over who should be responsible for the raising of funds. The local organizations won the lion's share of the victory, gaining control over fund-raising for even the most national and international purposes. This victory has substantially strengthened the power of the local communities in the overall framework of American Jewish life.

Decision-Making Modes

In the final analysis, what can we say about the decision-making modes of the American Jewish community? A number of modes may be identified. We will consider six of these: 1) the penchant for government by committee; 2) the urge to avoid conflict; 3) the legitimacy of tension between the "national office" and the "local affiliates"; 4) the patterns of "duplication" and inter-organizational competition; 5) the sources of innovation and the initiation of programs; and 6) the role of personalities in the decision-making process.

Government by Committee: The immediate organizational tool of decision-making in the American Jewish community is the committee. Committees—in all shapes, sizes, and forms—carry out all the variegated business of the community. The multiplicity of committees within organizations and institutions provides for a certain degree of diffusion of power among many decision-makers and something akin to an intra-institutional "checks and balances" system.

Power and influence accrue to those who can control the committees and their work. Personality conflicts may well be focused more sharply in committees but, then, the business of the community is conducted through committees, from the smallest synagogue to the President's Conference (itself simply a high-level committee). Consequently, the dynamics of committee behavior are at least a partial factor in any decision taken by the leadership of the American Jewish community.

Conflict Avoidance: Despite the existence of conflict as part of life's reality, conflict avoidance is a major principle in American Jewish decision-making. By and large, especially where voluntary leaders are involved, every effort is made to avoid open conflict. Where issues are such that they are likely to provoke conflict there is every tendency to avoid raising them in the first place. Where an issue is likely to provoke conflict and must be raised, every effort is made to develop a decision in such a way that there is no chance for the conflict to be expressed.

In part, this avoidance of conflict reflects the traditional desire of a minority to avoid risking any weakening of the ties that bind its members together. But, in part, it also reflects the fact that the voluntary leaders in the American Jewish community are overwhelmingly recruited from the world of business and commerce where open conflict is considered "bad form" and decisions are reached in such a way as to minimize the appearance of conflict if not its reality.

The desire to avoid open conflict clearly rules out some issues from consideration no matter how important they might be. It also enhances the role of the professional leadership since it enables them to administer the community rather than requiring the voluntary leaders to *govern* it. In such situations, the tendency is to rely upon the men trusted with the administration to make what still are, in the end, political decisions. Thus the professionals continue to gain power simply because they can organize decision-making in such a way as to minimize the emergence of conflict, thereby earning the appreciation of the voluntary leadership.

Local Affiliates vs. the "National Office": One perennial conflict which is considered legitimate, provided that it is not allowed to spread beyond limited tactical skirmishes, is the tension between the "national office" and the local "affiliates". In part, it reflects the simple difference in constituency and interest of the national office and the local affiliates or branches. In part, it reflects a difference in the situation between Jews in the New York metropolitan area with its particular set of problems and Jews in other smaller communities which have a different scale of operations.

This tension is a perennial one which, by its very nature, can never finally be resolved. But shifts do take place in the structure of the tension, and these bring about immediate changes in the community's decision-making patterns. What can be said about the present situation, in general terms, is that those organizations which have traditionally been New York-centered are losing power in the community as a whole, while those whose locus of power is in the localities are gaining.

"Duplication" and Inter-Organizational Competition: Inter-organizational competition within the same sphere (duplication) is

another perennial feature of the American Jewish scene, stemming from the voluntary and associational character of the community. The attack on duplication is part of the standard rhetoric of American Jewish community life. At the same time, competition itself is not always a negative phenomenon. Moreover, on the local plane, organizations functioning within the same sphere often develop patterns of sharing that effectively divide tasks so as to minimize overlapping. Duplication is not likely to disappear on the American Jewish scene nor even to be substantially reduced in the ways in which reformers usually suggest because there is no realistic way to curb the proliferation of organizations. When organizational consolidation does take place, it usually reflects a tightening of the organizational belt to cope with decline, a retreat rather than a step forward, such as in the case of the recent formation of the American Zionist Federation.

This is not to say that all efforts to control duplication reflect weakness. Within the sphere of community relations, for example, coordination came about at a time when the individual organizations were all fluorishing. Furthermore, even though some of the same organizations are now doing poorly, they are not interested in consolidation. Rather they are redoubling their efforts to survive.

Recognition of the realities of interorganizational competition is not the same as condoning the semi-anarchy which prevails in some sectors of American Jewish life and which is justified in the name of a specious "pluralism" that is no more than a reflection of organizational self-interest. What is needed are better means of enhancing coordination and limiting harmful duplication in ways that are consonant with the American situation.

Innovation and Program Initiation: While decision-making in connection with established programs is more or less shared by the professional and voluntary leadership, innovation and program initiation are more often than not dominated by the professionals, if only because they are involved in organizational and institutional affairs on a day-to-day basis and are recognized as the custodians of programmatic expertise. Their positions, then, make them the initiators of a very high proportion of new activities and programs and the prime generators of new ideas. This is not to say that they are the only innovators and initiators; but there is no question that they bear a disproportionate share of the responsibility in these areas.

Personalities: The role of personalities in decision-making is not to be underestimated even though there have been substantial changes in this regard in recent years. Ironically, personality conflicts are particularly significant at the highest levels in the national organizations. Perhaps because they are so detached from operational responsibilities, the top leaders can indulge in the luxury of personality conflicts. In the local communities, operational necessities lead to greater efforts to control such conflicts.

Problems and Prospects

Despite the limitations of the data, it is not unfair to conclude that the American Jewish community is governed by what may be termed a "trusteeship of doers" in which decision-makers who are generally self-selected on the basis of their willingness to participate hold the reins of communal life in all of its facets. They perceive of their function as managing the community's affairs in trust for its members, the Jewish people as a whole, just as earlier generations of leaders saw themselves as managing the community's affairs as trustees of God. It is this sense of trusteeship which keeps the communal leadership from being an oligarchy, or a small body that manages the community for its own profit. Every significant Jewish interest has the right to claim a place in the trusteeship of doers and is accorded that place once it brings its claim to the attention of the appropriate leadership by "doing."

Although it is not elected in any systemically competitive manner, the trusteeship is representative of American Jewry in that it reflects the attitudes, values, and interests of the community—except perhaps in one respect: the leaders are probably more positively Jewish then the community's rank and file.

A trusteeship of doers seems to be the system that is fated for American Jewry and probably for any Jewish community living in a voluntaristic environment like the United States. Those modern Jewish communities which have experimented with communal elections have not found them any better a solution to the problem of representation, because the turnout in these elections tends to be extremely low. Moreover, a voting procedure does not guarantee the election of statesmen to communal leadership either. Elections do have one important consequence, however. They raise to the inner circles of leadership men whose qualifications are not simply financial. In most cases these are men who have gained leadership of some important organizational bloc within the community which is able to turn out its members to vote. As such they are more likely to be attuned to straightforward political considerations than big donors who do not have to conciliate constituencies in any way. . . .

The fact that elections are not likely to accomplish the purposes for which they are instituted does not mean that ways cannot be developed better to involve a wider segment of the American Jewish community in its crucial decision-making bodies. In any case, efforts in that direction must be founded on the recognition that oligarchy is likely to be the persistent form in American Jewish life. What is called for, then, is an attempt to make the oligarchies properly representative.

This might involve the encouragement of a whole host of tendencies already present on the American scene and the addition of others. The strengthening of the federation movement, for example, might offer the best opportunity for creating a systematic decision-making structure on the American Jewish scene. In this connection, it is absolutely vital that the synagogues cease to be considered the private property of their members and be recognized for what they are—public institutions bearing significant communal responsibilities. This is not an argument against congregationalism; indeed, there is every reason to want to foster true congregational spirit in synagogues of proper scale, provided that it is not a euphemism for communal anarchy.

If this could be accomplished, it might then be possible to devise ways in which elections conducted through the congregations would form a major part of the basis of representation in the federations, so that the leadership recruitment process would reach down into every segment of the community. Under such circumstances federations would become more completely and thoroughly communal agencies. Moreover, under such circumstances it will be possible to make better determinations as to who should conduct and finance the different activities of the Jewish community. The advances suggested here should be made on a proper federal basis . . . not through a centralization of power either locally or nationally, as is often suggested. . . .

THE JEWISH COMMUNITY OF BOSTON/ MEMBERSHIP IN SYNAGOGUES AND JEWISH ORGANIZATIONS

by MORRIS AXELROD, FLOYD J. FOWLER, and ARNOLD GURIN

INTRODUCTION

COMMUNAL SURVEYS sponsored by federations constitute an excellent source of data on American Jewry. However, the utility of the surveys is limited by the fact that so few have been done in the larger communities and of those, some have sampling problems which result in underrepresenting important segments of the community. Such surveys may also exhibit a rate of response below acceptable standards.

The sampling design of the survey of Boston, which is utilized here, was carefully conceived and executed. Boston is one of the nation's major Jewish communities—the survey, done in 1965, estimates the size of the Jewish population of the Greater Boston area as 208,000. Boston's Jewish community resembles that of most other large cities, for it includes first- and second-generation Americans as well as those in the third or later generations. While there are pockets of Jewish concentration in Boston, the area has the same characteristic as other large communities: there are several centers of Jewish population located at some distance from each other.

The occupational structure of Boston Jewry includes the usual preponderance of managers, proprietors, and clerical and sales personnel. However, Boston also has an unusually high number of professional Jews, a significant percentage of whom are not self-employed. They work for nonprofit institutions or for large corporations where their peers are predominantly Gentile. In addition to its large student population, Boston also attracts many recent graduates of colleges and graduate schools, and it has an intellectual community which in theory could provide alienated Jews with an alternative to the Jewish community. Thus, Boston has some of the features of the large Jewish community while at the same time it previews some of the features of the changing occupational and educational distribution of American Jewry. Boston is of unusual interest not only because it is large but also because it has features which make for communal alienation and disintegration.

The excerpt which follows from the Boston survey does not give a full picture of the communal participation of Boston Jewry. For example, it does not include material on funds contributed to Jewish philanthropies; such contributions constitute an important aspect of Jewish communal membership and participation. Furthermore, data on the use of Jewish communal facilities like community centers, hospitals, old-age homes, or family agencies are not included. Our excerpt concerns two significant aspects of communal participation: affiliation with synagogues and membership in Jewish organizations.

The picture which emerges is of a community in which the synagogue has assumed a leading role. Not only do half of the respondents claim to be members of synagogues but brotherhoods and sisterhoods attached to synagogues attract more members than any single non-synagogal organization. As we shall see in the section of this volume devoted to religious movements, the synagogues are not without problems of their own. But the Boston statistics make clear why Daniel Elazar and others are so concerned with the issues of congregational independence, localism, and privatization.

The Boston study presents figures on membership in ten Jewish organizations exclusive of synagogue sisterhoods and brotherhoods. All ten of these organizations are national agencies having Boston chapters. In addition, many other national agencies sponsor Boston chapters or seek to attract members in Boston. There are also numerous Jewish organizations in Boston which are strictly confined to the local scene. As is apparent from the data, no single membership organization dominates the community. Even the synagogues, theoretically capable of such domination, are independent agencies loosely federated into Orthodox, Conservative, and Reform coordinating bodies (in addition to bodies which aspire to coordinate all three groups). Hadassah too has not succeeded in enlisting a majority of the women of the area.

In theory the lack of a single dominating body might be compensated for by the diversity afforded by the wide spectrum of organizations offering affiliation to individuals of various ideological commitments or "background" differences such as brow-level, income, occupation, and generation. The organizations undoubtedly do provide alternatives for a differentiated population. However, despite this variety fully half of the Jewish population of Boston does not belong to any Jewish organization. Furthermore, membership in a Jewish organization is not an alternative to synagogue membership, for congregational and organizational memberships tend to overlap. Most individuals who do not join a congregation also fail to affiliate with an organization.

If communal affiliation in Boston is to continue at its present level, members of the more advanced generations—third or later—must come to assume the pattern of the first and second generations. Also, at a later point in their lives younger individuals must reach the level of affiliation of their older contemporaries. Furthermore, the less prosperous (many of whom are young and have yet to reach their peak income) must achieve the level of affiliation of their more prosperous peers. As modest as they are, these targets constitute ambitious goals—at the moment the young, the members of the third or a later generation, and the less prosperous lag in Jewish communal affiliation and involvement.

It could of course be claimed that the weaknesses in affiliation and involvement with the formal community evident in the Boston data are of limited significance—that the informal community is the crucial one, that kinship relationships are more significant than institutional ties, and that the culture of the Jewish neighborhood is more important in identity formation and maintenance than are congregational or organizational ties. There is validity in this line of reasoning, but the strength of the formal community is crucial from two perspectives. First, certain functions—such as the furtherance of Jewish interests in the sphere of public affairs or the raising of funds for Jewish causes—cannot be exercised (except on an

MEMBERSHIP IN SYNAGOGUES

THE SYNAGOGUE clearly is central to Judaism for a large portion of the Jewish population. More Jews are affiliated with synagogues than any other form of Jewish organizational life. . . . One-third of the Jewish households in the Boston Area report contributing $200 or more to a synagogue during 1965 (Table 1). . . .

Table 2 shows the distribution of synagogue membership among adult Jews in Greater Boston. Fifty-three percent report presently belonging to a synagogue, and an additional 26 percent report previously belonging to a synagogue. Thus, only a fifth of the Jewish community has never belonged to a synagogue.

Table 3 shows the relationship between present synagogue membership and age. This shows that those under 30 years old are unlikely to belong to a synagogue at present. This includes, of course, those who are recently out of school, those who are

TABLE 1

Amount of synagogue contributions among Greater Boston Jews

Amount	*Percent*
Nothing	34
$5–$49	14
$50–$99	8
$100–$199	7
$200–$499	23
$500 or more	7
Not ascertained	7
TOTAL	100

TABLE 2

Synagogue membership of Jewish population in Greater Boston

Synagogue membership	*Percent*
Presently belongs	53
Belonged in past, but not presently	26
Never belonged	20
Not ascertained	1
TOTAL	100

TABLE 3

Present synagogue membership of Greater Boston Jews by age

	Age				
Membership	*21–29*	*30–39*	*40–49*	*50–64*	*65 & over*
Belongs	24%	55%	65%	59%	57%
Does not belong	76	45	35	41	42
Not ascertained	*	*	*	*	1
TOTAL	100%	100%	100%	100%	100%

*Less than 0.5 percent

beginning their careers, and those who are not fully settled in a community. For those who are over 30, there is little difference between age groups in the rate of membership.

There is a rather marked relationship between the generation of the respondent and synagogue membership (Table 4). Immigrants, in addition to being more Orthodox and more observant of tradition, are also more likely than others to belong to a synagogue. . . .

What other characteristics are related to whether or not a person belongs to a synagogue? Table 5 shows that one of the important factors is the family income. For all generations, except immigrants, the likelihood of having a synagogue membership is markedly increased as income increases. . . . The relatively high cost of some synagogue memberships may be a barrier for those who are financially less well off. This is particularly evident among those of the third generation and later. Only a quarter of this group with incomes under $10,000 per year presently belong to a synagogue.

Overall, the rate of synagogue membership is about the same for Conservative and Orthodox Jews. Reform Jews are somewhat less likely to have a synagogue membership; and less than one-fifth of those who have no preference among the denominations held a synagogue membership (Table 5A).

TABLE 4

Present synagogue membership of Greater Boston Jews by generation

	Generation		
Membership	*Immigrant (First)*	*Second*	*Third or later*
Belongs	62%	53%	45%
Does not belong	38	47	55
TOTAL	100%	100%	100%

TABLE 5

Present synagogue membership of Greater Boston Jews by family income within generation

Present synagogue membership	*Family income*				
	Under $6,000	*$6,000-9,999*	*$10,000-14,999*	*$15,000-19,999*	*$20,000 or over*
Immigrant (First)					
Belongs	65%	54%	54%	*	67%
Does not belong	35	46	46	*	33
TOTAL	100%	100%	100%	*	100%
Second generation					
Belongs	37%	45%	53%	67%	78%
Does not belong	63	55	47	33	22
TOTAL	100%	100%	100%	100%	100%
Third generation or later					
Belongs	28%	24%	54%	55%	87%
Does not belong	72	76	46	45	13
TOTAL	100%	100%	100%	100%	100%

*Too few cases to be meaningful

TABLE 5A
Present synagogue membership of Greater Boston Jews by preference for branch of Judaism

	Preference for branch of Judaism			
Present synagogue membership	*Orthodox*	*Conservative*	*Reform*	*Other*
Belongs	62%	61%	52%	19%
Does not belong	38	39	48	81
TOTAL	100%	100%	100%	100%

MEMBERSHIP IN JEWISH ORGANIZATIONS

The basic facts about participation will be considered with a view to answering three questions:

1) What is the extent of membership in the various prominent Jewish organizations?
2) What are the characteristics of those who are most active in the formal Jewish community?
3) What are the characteristics of those who are relatively more active in specifically Jewish than in non-Jewish or general organizations?

Specific Memberships

Table 6 presents the percentage of adults in the Greater Boston Area Jewish community who report belonging to selected Jewish organizations. In looking at the figures in Table 6, at least four qualifications should be brought to mind before generalizing to the total membership of a particular organization. First, some organizations have dues as a requirement for membership. A person who supports such an organization may pay the dues and,

TABLE 6
Rate of membership among adult Greater Boston Jews in selected Jewish organizations

Organization	*Percent*
American Jewish Committee	*
American Jewish Congress	1
Arbeiter Ring (Workman's Circle)	*
B'nai B'rith	9
Brandeis Women	5
Council of Jewish Women	1
Hadassah	15
Jewish War Veterans	3
Labor Zionists	*
ORT	3
ZOA	*
Synagogue Sisterhood or Brotherhood	24

*Less than 0.5 percent

therefore, be a member, but never attend meetings or do anything active. When asked about memberships, this person looks upon his "membership" as a contribution rather than a membership and, consequently, may not report it. For example, the American Jewish Congress and American Jewish Committee may be organizations which a person might support financially without considering himself a member.

Second, some organizations have "family memberships," whereby they count all family members or all adults in a family as members; yet in some cases, it may be only one adult who actually considers himself to be a member. Thus, again, membership rolls of any given organization may reflect a larger number of people than report being members.

Third, some of these organizations are restricted to one sex. The figures in Table 6, however, reflect the percentage of all adults in the Boston Area who report membership. Thus, while five percent of the Boston adult population reports belonging to Brandeis Women, a more meaningful figure might be that 10 percent of the women in the area belong to Brandeis Women.

Fourth, like all figures in this report, the figures in Table 6 . . . could vary by chance by one or two percent. Such variation would have considerable effect when the rate of membership is less than five percent.

With these considerations in mind, the data are clear, nonetheless, that four organizations stand out as being the main channels of participation in the Jewish community. The largest single type of membership is the synagogue sisterhoods and brotherhoods. . . . Hadassah, despite the fact that it is restricted to women, has the next largest membership and is the largest single organization in the area, as reported by respondents. Over one-fourth of the women in the Boston area report belonging to Hadassah. B'nai B'rith and Brandeis Women follow, in that order, as being the next largest Jewish organizations by reported membership.

Characteristics of Members

The number of Jewish organizations to which Boston Jews belong is presented in Table 7. It can be seen that 50 percent, however, do not report belonging to any Jewish organizations. . . .

TABLE 7

Number of memberships in Jewish organizations of Greater Boston Jews

Memberships	*Percent*
None	50
One	22
Two	13
Three or more	14
Not ascertained	1
TOTAL	100

TABLE 8

Number of memberships in Jewish organizations of Greater Boston Jews by age

Number of memberships	*Age* 21–29	30–39	40–49	50–64	65–69	70 or over
None	71%	54%	42%	45%	33%	43%
One	21	22	23	18	18	29
Two	6	15	17	15	13	8
Three or more	2	9	18	22	35	17
Not ascertained	*	*	*	*	1	3
TOTAL	100%	100%	100%	100%	100%	100%

*Less than 0.5 percent

Table 8 shows that those under 30 years of age are decidedly less likely to belong to any Jewish organizations, and those between 30 and 40 years old show a lower rate of participation in the formal Jewish community than persons who are older. In Table 9, it can be seen that memberships are highest among immigrants, lowest among those of the third and fourth generations. . . .

The data in Tables 9A and 10 are also relevant to understanding the relationship of age and generation to Jewish memberships. In Table 9A, it can be seen that those with annual incomes over $20,000 belong to markedly more Jewish organizations than those with lower incomes. Interestingly, other differences in income do not seem to affect the rate of membership. The next table (Table 10) shows that synagogue membership is strongly related to membership in other Jewish organizations. Only one out of three adult Jews who are not synagogue members belong to any Jewish organization. Two out of three synagogue members, however, belong to at least one other Jewish organization.

TABLE 9

Number of memberships in Jewish organizations of Greater Boston Jews by generation

Number of memberships	*Generation* *Immigrant (First)*	*Second*	*Third or later*
None	41%	49%	60%
One	27	20	23
Two	13	15	10
Three or more	19	16	7
TOTAL	100%	100%	100%

TABLE 9A

Number of memberships in Jewish organizations of Greater Boston Jews by family income

Number of memberships	*Family income* *Under $6,000*	*$6,000-9,999*	*$10,000-14,999*	*$15,000-19,999*	*$20,000 and over*
None	53%	60%	45%	50%	31%
One	25	18	24	27	17
Two	10	10	18	13	18
Three or more	12	12	13	9	34
Not ascertained	*	*	*	1	*
TOTAL	100%	100%	100%	100%	100%

*Less than 0.5 percent

TABLE 10

Number of memberships in Jewish organizations of Greater Boston Jews by present synagogue membership

Number of memberships	*Present synagogue membership* Belongs	*Does not belong*
None	32%	70%
One	25	18
Two	19	7
Three or more	23	5
Not ascertained	1	*
TOTAL	100%	100%

*Less than 0.5 percent

These tables, together with other data in the report, provide the basis for some tentative conclusions. There are two distinctive characteristics of those who do not participate in the formal Jewish community: they do not have a preference for a particular branch of Judaism (Orthodox, Conservative, or Reform) and they do not belong to a synagogue. Both of these characteristics are markedly more prevalent among those under 40 and those of the third and fourth generations. Both no doubt reflect on the degree of commitment to being Jewish and integration into the Jewish community. It is virtually tautological to say that those who are more committed participate more. It may not have been predicted, however, that the synagogue is an important indicator of other forms of formal participation, as the data suggest.

Income is not as strongly related to participation as one might have predicted. Considering the marked relationship between income and synagogue membership, a strong relationship between income and memberships in Jewish organizations was expected. Yet only those in the highest income category stand out as more active in the Jewish community.

Table 10A shows that women report notably more member-

TABLE 10A

Number of memberships in Jewish organizations of Greater Boston Jews by sex

Number of memberships	*Sex*	
	Male	*Female*
None	60%	42%
One	25	20
Two	8	17
Three or more	7	20
Not ascertained	*	1
TOTAL	100%	100%

*Less than 0.5 percent

ships in Jewish organizations than do men. None of the preceding tables accounts for this tendency. The fact that Hadassah and Brandeis Women are two of the largest Jewish organizations in the area is consistent. The data on identification do not lead one to conclude that women are more committed than men. It may be that women have more time for community activities, however.

Relative Participation in Jewish and General Organizations

Extent of participation in Jewish organizations is of interest by itself, but the relative number of Jewish vis-à-vis general organizations to which a person belongs may be a better cue to the degree to which he is oriented toward the Jewish community. Some people belong to a number of organizations of all kinds, while others belong to a few organizations, Jewish or non-Jewish.

Overall, it is found that Jews belong to Jewish and non-Jewish organizations in about the same numbers; but this is not true for all segments of the population.

In Tables 11, 12, and 13, the Index of Jewish Participation is

TABLE 11

Index of relative participation in Jewish and non-Jewish organizations of Greater Boston Jews by sex

Sex	*Index of participation**
Male	–20
Female	40

*Percent belonging to at least one Jewish organization minus percent belonging to at least one non-Jewish organization. An index score of "O" means equal participation in Jewish and non-Jewish organizations. Positive index score indicates more participation in Jewish organizations.

TABLE 12

Index of relative participation in Jewish and non-Jewish organizations of Greater Boston Jews by age

Age	*Index of participation*
Under 40	–14
40–64	1
65 or over	21

presented by sex, age and generation. It can be seen that women participate much more in the Jewish community than in the non-Jewish community; whereas men are likely to have more memberships in general organizations than in Jewish ones.

Those who are youngest are more likely to belong to general than Jewish organizations. This is true for all those under 50. Over 50, however, people are more likely to belong to Jewish than general organizations—a tendency which increases in degree with age.

TABLE 13

Index of relative participation in Jewish and non-Jewish organizations of Greater Boston Jews by generation

Generation	*Index of participation*
Immigrant (First)	22
Second	–4
Third or later	–14

By generation, it can be seen in Table 13 that only the immigrant generation is more likely to belong to Jewish than non-Jewish organizations. Subsequent generations belong to more general organizations than Jewish.

Summary

The following points are the highlights of the data we have presented:

1) Two main factors affect the probability of belonging to a synagogue: generation and income. More recent immigrants and those who have higher incomes are more likely to belong to a synagogue. In addition, those under 30 years of age are less likely than others to presently belong to a synagogue.

2) The main reason for the decrease in synagogue membership by generation appears to be the increased numbers of Jews with no denominational preference.

3) Hadassah, B'nai B'rith, and Brandeis Women are the three organizations to which more than five percent of the adult Boston Jewish population report belonging.

4) Whether or not a person belongs to a synagogue is a major sign of whether or not he will belong to any other Jewish organization.

5) Women are more likely to be active in formal Jewish organizations than men.

RELIGIOUS MOVEMENTS

ORTHODOXY IN AMERICAN JEWISH LIFE
by CHARLES S. LIEBMAN

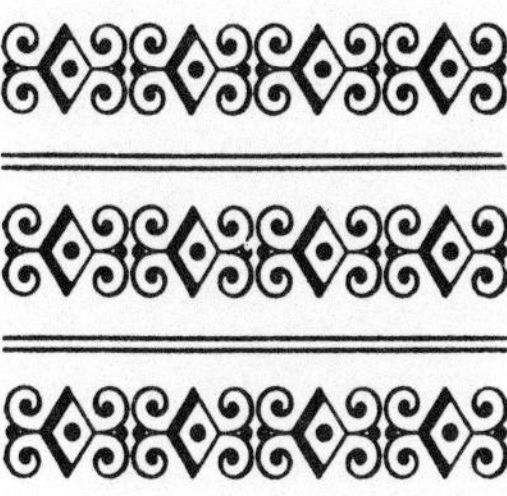

INTRODUCTION

ONE OF THE MOST *surprising trends in American Jewish life has been the emergence of Orthodoxy as a "third force" competing with Reform and Conservative Judaism. In less than three decades Orthodoxy has transformed its image from that of a dying movement to one whose strength and opinions must be reckoned with in any realistic appraisal of the Jewish community.*

Behind this shift in image lies a sociological reality. Earlier American Orthodoxy was pervaded with elements of folk religion and was dominated by what Charles Liebman has called the "uncommitted Orthodox" and the "residual Orthodox"; in recent decades this has given way to a new Orthodoxy dominated by what Liebman calls the "committed Orthodox." The material which follows is selected from Liebman's larger analysis of Orthodoxy and centers on the committed group. As Liebman demonstrates, committed Orthodoxy comprises an intricate network of organizations and institutions. Such institutions not only compete with each other but also relate themselves to the Jewish community as a whole and to the larger non-Jewish society.*

*See Charles S. Liebman, "The Religion of American Jews," in Marshall Sklare, ed., *The Jew in American Society* (New York: Behrman House, Inc., 1974), pp. 223–252.

Understanding the Orthodox world is no simple task. A separate monograph would be required to comprehend just the Orthodox synagogue, although Liebman says enough about the institution to convey its infinite variety. But he focuses his analysis on the significant non-synagogal organizations and institutions in American Orthodoxy: the yeshivot, the rabbinical associations, the synagogal unions, the hasidic groups. Liebman also helps us understand the intricate leadership structure of American Orthodoxy.

The structure of Orthodoxy differs quite sharply from that of the Reform and Conservative movements. Instead of a comparatively well-integrated and coordinated structure, Orthodoxy's is highly proliferated and weakly coordinated. Part of the reason for this lies in the continuity Orthodoxy maintains with the European past (and in the case of some Sephardic Jews, with the Near-Eastern past). Furthermore, Orthodoxy's structure is not based exclusively on traditions and models generated on American soil. For example, instead of the Reform and Conservative model of a single institution serving as rabbinical school and source of Jewish learning, Orthodoxy preserves the European model of multiple yeshivot, each founded by an outstanding leader, independent of others, and free to emphasize a particular approach to Talmudic learning.

The study of Orthodox organizations and institutions presents formidable difficulties. As Liebman emphasizes, Orthodoxy has a strong sectarian element which is suspicious of outsiders. Even the "modern Orthodox," as Liebman designates them, are not particularly anxious to be studied by the social scientist. The world of modern Orthodoxy necessarily represents a delicate balance between the imperatives of Jewish tradition and the demands of the larger Jewish and Gentile worlds. Such a fine balance is not only inherently unstable but is especially vulnerable to attack by sectarians. Thus the modern Orthodox group fears that however fair-minded the social scientist may be, his findings may be used by sectarians for their own partisan purposes. The modern Orthodox group is in the difficult position of approving of research in principle but fearing that, in practice, research may work to its detriment.

The Orthodox sectarian can overcome his suspicion of the outsider by realizing that whether or not the outsider penetrates what he, the sectarian, feels is the essence of his religious perspective, publicity may be a positive good—it may serve the purpose of magnifying the importance of his sectarian group. The modern Orthodox group, having better access to the media of communication, looks for publicity on its own terms. It is dubious of the value of exposing differences in the Orthodox camp. Unlike the sectarians the modern Orthodox are concerned with building unity, and as they see it, the building of unity can only be harmed by public discussion.

In his analysis of the institutions and organizations of the committed Orthodox group Liebman, who is himself a committed Orthodox Jew, discusses both those who are close to him and those located at a greater remove. He relies on diverse concepts and different kinds of data, both in the general field of the sociology of religion and in the special area of the study of Jewish society. Convinced of the correctness of the Orthodox position and believing that it constitutes the only hope of American Jewry, Liebman succeeds in preventing his value judgments from working to the detriment of his analysis, as he critically evaluates each Orthodox institution, highlighting both its weaknesses as well as its strengths.

M. S.

. . . ORTHODOXY perceives itself as the only legitimate bearer of the Jewish tradition; to Orthodoxy this tradition is expressed almost exclusively in religious form (which is not to say that all elements of the tradition are necessarily religious in their essence). While Conservative and Reform see themselves as legitimate heirs to the Jewish tradition, neither claims to be its exclusive bearer. This distinction between Orthodoxy and the other denominations has analytically separable consequences which only seem to operate at cross-purposes. Since neither the Reform nor the Conservative lays claim to exclusive doctrinal "truth," they are free to cooperate with one another, with Orthodoxy, and even with secular Jewish groups; they risk only institutional losses. The doctrines of Orthodoxy, on the other hand, are more precise and are by definition beyond compromise or even the appearance of compromise. Hence Orthodoxy must be constantly on guard against appearing to surrender or water down its doctrine.

But there is a second consequence that flows from Orthodoxy's exclusive claim to the truth and its major tenet that it is the obligation of every Jew to observe the *mitzvot* (religious commandments). While Conservatives and Reformists are under no obligation to do anything about the matter, the Orthodox are doctrinally obligated to encourage the observance of Jewish law here and now. In addition, the doctrine of *ahavat Yisrael* (love of Israel), particularly as elaborated by the late Rabbi Abraham Isaac Kook, chief rabbi of Palestine until his death in 1935, impels Orthodoxy to extend itself to the non-Orthodox. If non-Orthodox Jews were unorganized, the consequences of Orthodoxy's doctrinal position would not be contradictory. It could simply undertake missions to the non-Orthodox. But when, in fact, about half of the non-Orthodox are organized in the Conservative and Reform movements, and the remainder are almost beyond reach of any religious group in Jewish life, then Orthodoxy is confronted with two mutually exclusive mandates—to promote faith and observance among non-Orthodox Jews, while giving no recognition and comfort to the only existing institutions which can reach those Jews.

In practice, different groups within Orthodoxy have emphasized one mandate or the other, and most of the divisions within Orthodoxy, in practice, reflect this division. But the point to be stressed is that, with the possible exception of the Satmar *hasidim*, all Orthodox groups consider both mandates as binding. (The Satmar probably do, too, but feel that the obligation to promote observance is simply impractical in this day among all but a handful of Jews and that their own piety is not so secure as to justify undertaking "missions" to other Jews.) Hence, no matter how zealous the right wing may be in its stress on religious continuity, maximal observance, and condemnation of the non-Orthodox, it hesitates to characterize the non-Orthodox as beyond hope of redemption. And no matter how outgoing and conciliatory the left wing may be toward the nonobservant and the institutions of the non-Orthodox, it is always restrained by its acceptance of the basic doctrinal principles as being beyond compromise.

Orthodoxy and the Demands of Society

The differences within Orthodoxy are best understood in the broad framework of the sociology of religion. While the concepts here developed are not directly applicable to Judaism, they are suggestive of differences among Jewish groups and serve heuristic purposes.

Students of religion, drawing their data primarily from the development of Christianity, have developed a typology of religions based on distinctions between church and sect. Following Yinger's refinement of Troeltsch,[1] church and sect are defined as ideal types, that is, end points on a continuum along which religious groups can be placed and compared with one another as they approach one end or the other.

The central problems to which the church-sect dichotomy is addressed are how a religious body confronts the secular world and how it provides a religious response to the personal needs of its adherents. The *church* "recognizes the strength of the secular world and rather than either deserting the attempt to influence it or losing its position by contradicting the secular powers directly, accepts the main elements in the social structure as proximate goods." The major function of the church is its effort to insure social cohesion and order and to do so it must extend its ministry to

[1]John Milton Yinger, *Religion, Society and the Individual* (New York: 1957).

everyone. As a result it must be willing to "compromise with the wide ranges of behavior that may be found in a society."[2]

The *sect* is a smaller group, arising from the inability of the church to meet some members' needs by virtue of its very flexibility and adaptability. The sect "repudiates the compromises of the church, preferring isolation to compromise."[3] Hence, unlike the church, it is hostile or indifferent to the secular order. It seeks primarily to satisfy individual religious needs rather than societal ones.

It is apparent that the church-sect dichotomy is not applicable in this form to Judaism today. The typology assumes a closed society in which the religious order is confronted only by the secular order and the individual needs of its members. When Judaism represented a basically closed society, before Emancipation, the dichotomy appears to have been more applicable. Where the definition of church or sect says "society," we can read "Judaism" or "Jews." Thus, the early development of hasidism appears to fit the definition of sectarian growth and development.

But religious groups within Judaism today are confronted with problems of the larger Jewish society—what we may call the secular (or non-religious) institutionalized Jewish order—as well as the non-Jewish society, and the problems of the religious denomination are not only to adapt to Jewish society and insure social cohesion and order within Judaism, but also to adapt to general society and insure cohesion and order within it. Furthermore, Judaism must meet not only the individual needs of members as they arise by virtue of Jewishness, but also those that arise by virtue of membership in the general society. An effort to solve one kind of problem frequently exacerbates another. To sum up—the Christian denomination plays a double role: vis-à-vis the social order or general society, and vis-à-vis the individual needs of its membership. To the extent that the Christian denomination stresses the solution to one order of problems it raises questions for the other. Judaism faces not two but four problems. It must meet the needs or demands of the broader society and of the narrower, Jewish society. It must meet the needs that arise from an individual's problems in the general society and those that arise from his problems in the Jewish society.

[2] *Ibid.*, p. 144.

[3] *Ibid.*, p. 146.

Let us be specific about the nature of these problems as they have emerged in the United States:

1) To meet the needs of the general society, it is necessary to affirm the democratic political structure and to develop a symbolism (transcendental or not) for its transmission; to affirm the unity of all Americans and the primacy of American national interests and needs.

2) To meet the needs of the Jewish society, it is necessary to achieve unity among Jews and to maintain Jewish identification in a permissive gentile society; to maintain defenses against prejudice and discrimination.

3) To meet the individual's needs in the general society, it is necessary to confront the problems of good and evil, of reward and punishment, and of alienation and anomie in an urban, heterogeneous society.

4) To meet the individual's needs in Jewish society, it is necessary to interpret traditional Jewish beliefs and practices in the light of the individual's present needs and problems.

Bearing in mind these four types of demands or needs, we can classify all Jewish organizations by the problem or combination of problems to which they have addressed themselves. Each of these classifications can, in turn, be refined according to the *manner* in which the problem is approached. Within any given organization there is bound to be some conflict or tension over which problem should assume priority. A general theory of Jewish organizational life would have to take account of the manner in which social status, education, accommodation to the American milieu, and other such factors cut across the leadership and constituent groups of each organization, determining the perspective in which problems are viewed and solutions chosen.

Our concern here is with Orthodoxy, but first we must look briefly into the Conservative and Reform groups, which today come closer than Orthodoxy to assuming the characteristics of church rather than sect. By and large, Conservatism and Reform address themselves to problems arising from societal demands. The application is made at an individual level and to individual problems, but the context out of which the problem emerges is generally societal—social cohesion and moral order—rather than individual. Until recently, Reform was more oriented toward general societal problems and Conservatism toward those of Jewish society. This is changing somewhat as Conservatism becomes more self-conscious about its role as a church and Reform, with a longer church experience, becomes more aware of the limitations of a church in reaching its membership directly. . . .

In contrast to Conservative and Reform Judaism, much of Orthodoxy's energy has been addressed to finding solutions within a halakhic framework for individual problems arising in contemporary life. Orthodoxy has been the least churchlike of all Jewish religious groups. In part this stems from the absence (until recently) of any self-consciousness. Only recently has Orthodoxy begun to define itself as a particular movement in the United States and been brought into contact with the broader society by the accelerated acculturation of its adherents and its own institutional growth. This new confrontation has raised problems that formerly did not exist for Orthodoxy or were overlooked. Thus, Orthodox leaders have been much slower than other Jewish leaders to define their attitude toward problems of civil rights or labor.

Since 1960 much of this has changed. In 1964, speaking to a Young Israel meeting in New York, Rabbi Aaron Soloveitchik, one of the leading Talmudic authorities in Jewish life, delivered a major address on civil rights from a halakhic perspective. In that same year a joint conference of the Industrial Union Department, AFL-CIO, and the Social Action Committee of the Rabbinical Council of America (RCA) heard a series of papers by young Orthodox rabbis on religion and labor. Such developments were a portent of serious stirrings within Orthodoxy. . . .

. . . some of the divisions within [Orthodoxy's] camp are best understood by analyzing the different positions of Orthodox leaders and institutions as they approach the church or sect ends of the continuum. The line between the left (or church) wing of Orthodoxy and the right wing of the Conservative movement is a very thin one. In fact, it is institutional loyalty far more than ideology which separates the two groups practically, though there are other, subtle distinctions, as well.

There are two alternative explanations for the differences among the Orthodox. The first argues that the two major categories of Orthodox—modern or church Orthodox and sectarian Orthodox—differ from one another in their degree of acculturation. It is true, as we shall show, that the sectarian Orthodox tend to be of lower income, poorer secular education, and more recent immigration than the modern Orthodox. (Sociologists of religion have noted that these tend to correlate with affinity to sect rather than church among Christians as well.) But the sectarians can boast their share of outwardly acculturated adherents; the leaders of the Association of Orthodox Jewish Scientists, to be discussed below, are far more sectarian than modern in terms of their concerns and orientations. And, most significantly, acculturation must be viewed as a dependent rather than an independent variable. The large number of American-born advanced yeshivah students who attend college at night to minimize interference with their Talmudic studies and value their secular education only for its vocational benefits have in a sense deliberately rejected acculturation because of their sectarian tendencies, rather than being sectarian because unacculturated.

A second explanation for the differences among the Orthodox distinguishes among them along a fundamentalism-liberalism scale. It argues that the sectarian Orthodox differ from the modern or church Orthodox by virtue of their beliefs concerning the Mosaic authorship of the Torah or the Sinaitic origin of the Oral Law. Although some modern Orthodox thinkers would consider Franz Rosenzweig's position,[4] for example, as within the framework of Orthodox belief, questions of actual dogma have not yet been broached among Orthodox leaders. When they are, as seems likely, there will be explosive consequences. Unquestionably there are Orthodox intellectuals who would like to raise the question, but with few exceptions neither they nor the fundamentalists have yet articulated exactly what they mean by Mosaic authorship or Sinaitic origin of the Oral Law.[5] It is fair to say that the entire belief

[4]Rosenzweig accepted the notion of a biblical Redactor, but saw the task of compiling the Bible as the human presentation of divine revelation. Rosenzweig's oft-quoted statement is that for him the symbol "R" does not stand for *Redactor* but for *Rabbenu* (our rabbi, our master).

[5]In one respect the argument that the written law (the Torah) and the oral law, which constitute the basis of halakhah, were given by God to Moses at Sinai requires no elaboration. It has always been an article of faith for the Orthodox Jew, and the meaning of the words and their historical referent seems simple enough. Biblical criticism has not challenged this belief; on the contrary, biblical criticism becomes meaningful only when this article of faith is denied. But it is this very article of faith in its plain meaning which has become "preposterous" to the modern mind. (This, of course, says nothing about the truth or falsity of the doctrine. A round world once also seemed preposterous.) That segment of American Orthodoxy which lives in the orbit of the *rashe yeshivot* does not find such a faith preposterous. It has no severe problem in reconciling its conception of God and human experience to its faith in the divine origin of Torah. That is not so for the more acculturated Orthodox Jew. The observer is perhaps forbidden to challenge a man's belief, but he is entitled to ask

structure of American Orthodoxy still finds verbal expression within the bounds of a rather narrow fundamentalism. Privately, the modern Orthodox admit that they simply interpret the same words to mean different things from what they mean to the sectarian Orthodox.[6] They have sought to keep the subject outside the area of controversy, making no serious effort, for example, to engage in biblical criticism, and thereby ruling out the development of any outstanding Orthodox biblical scholars in the United States. Modern Orthodoxy pays lip service to the notion that something ought to be done in this area and that aspects of biblical criticism can be incorporated into the Orthodox tradition, but no one is prepared to undertake or even encourage the work. It is sometimes acknowledged that some abandon Orthodoxy because their intellectual predispositions cannot be reconciled with traditional patterns of belief. But such losses, qualitatively important, are quantitatively insignificant. The main body of Orthodoxy in the United States appears at present to be doctrinally untroubled.

Institutions and Currents

Using the church-sect dichotomy, then, let us turn to a discussion of specific institutions and currents within Orthodoxy. . . . At one extreme are the *shtibl*-type synagogues. They meet in small rooms, where bearded men cover their heads with *tallitim* (prayer shawls) to pray, generally unheedful of the leader of the service, their bodies swaying. Women are separated from the men by a full-length wall in the rear, punctured by several peepholes through which a few can peer. At the other extreme are the modern edifices with spacious auditoriums. Here services are conducted by a cantor whose trained voice is carried to the ends of the hall by a microphone. Men and women are seated together, and the heart of the service is the rabbi's

whether the secularly acculturated Jew truly believes in *Torah min ha-shamayim* (Torah from heaven) when the entire structure of behavior and belief of that Jew seems inconsistent with this one article of faith. Inevitably efforts will be made to reinterpret the meaning of *Torah min ha-shamayim* in an effort to resolve the inconsistency. A variety of strategies are possible. One can begin by acknowledging this as a preposterous belief and proceed to a kind of Orthodox Jewish existentialism, with the events at Sinai being the object of some "leap of faith." One can maintain that the doctrine of *Torah min ha-shamayim* has metaphysical rather than physical referents and that we are dealing with two discrete levels of meaning. One can seek to reinterpret *Torah min ha-shamayim* as meaning something less than the entire written and oral law. These and other strategies of reinterpretation will undoubtedly be undertaken.

[6]The same is true of Conservative and Reform leaders among themselves with regard to the concept of revelation.

sermon. Although mixed seating and the use of a microphone on the Sabbath violate halakhah, the modern congregation considers itself as Orthodox and is in fact more likely to support many of the supracongregational institutions to be discussed below than the *shtibl*.

MODERN ORTHODOX

By modern Orthodox we mean those individuals and institutions among the committed Orthodox who tend toward the church end of the church-sect continuum. On the one hand, they seek to demonstrate the viability of the halakhah for contemporary life; on the other, they emphasize what they have in common with all other Jews rather than what separates them. Until recently they composed almost the entire upper-income, well-educated strata of the committed Orthodox. Many of the best-known Orthodox congregations in the United States, and most of the wealthy ones, are led by modern Orthodox rabbis.

Like the other groups within American Orthodoxy, the modern Orthodox have not produced any systematic statement of their ideology; in part, perhaps, because they shun the practical consequences of their philosophical or theological position, and in part because none has been sanctioned by eminent Talmudic scholars, still acknowledged as the arbiters of ideology. To the extent, however, that the modern Orthodox have produced an ideologist, it is probably Rabbi Emanuel Rackman, although his position is not representative of all modern Orthodox Jews. He is certainly the favorite target of the Orthodox right wing, notwithstanding the private concession of at least some of its members that he has brought more people into the Orthodox fold than any other person. Rackman has published widely on halakhah, Jewish values, and contemporary life.[7] His concern is with understanding the

[7]Essays from a variety of journals were reprinted in Emanuel Rackman, *Jewish Values for Modern Man* (New York: 1962). See also "Israel and God: Reflections on their Encounter," *Judaism*, Summer 1962, pp. 233–241; "Halachic Progress: Rabbi Moshe Feinstein's *Igrot Moshe* on *Even Ha-Ezer*," *Ibid.*, Summer 1964, pp. 366–373, and *Sabbaths and Festivals in the Modern Age*, in the "Studies in Torah Judaism" series (New York: 1961).

meaning of the halakhic injunctions in order to find contemporary applications. In the course of his efforts he has suggested what many feel to be a radical reinterpretation of the halakhah:

> The Halakhah is more than texts. It is life and experience. What made the Babylonian and not the Palestinian Talmud the great guide of Jewish life in the Diaspora was not a decree or a decision but *vox populi*. From Maimonides it would appear that it was the acceptance of the people who by custom and popular will constituted the authority. Can a Halakhic scholar lose himself in texts exclusively when the texts themselves bid him to see what practice "has become widespread among Jews," what is required socially "because of the precepts of peace," what will "keep the world aright," and many other social criteria? These standards are as much a part of the Torah as the texts themselves.[8]

Rackman is also prominently associated with the idea that Orthodox Jews, both individually and institutionally, must cooperate with the non-Orthodox. He is outspoken in his conviction that Orthodox rabbis should be free to associate with such groups as the New York Board of Rabbis (composed of Reform and Conservative as well as Orthodox rabbis) and that Orthodox groups should remain affiliated with the umbrella organization for all religious groups, the Synagogue Council of America.

Before considering the groups within which modern Orthodoxy is dominant, some comment on the sources of authority and unity within the Jewish community will be made. We will seek to demonstrate why the drive for unity, even within the organizations controlled by modern Orthodoxy, has been blunted in recent years, and what the Orthodox basis for unity has become.

Authority in the Jewish Community

There are four possible bases of authority within the Jewish community today: numbers, money, tradition, and person or charisma.

Authority of numbers is rarely exercised directly. Although organizations and institutions make some claim to authority on the basis of their numerical superiority, issues have rarely been resolved on this basis. There have been a few exceptions, the most noteworthy being the American Jewish Conference and particularly its 1943 meeting in which the sympathy of the masses of American

[8]Rackman, *Sabbaths and Festivals* . . ., p. 8.

Jews for the Zionist program was reflected in the division of votes. Today almost no Jewish organization lays claim to authority within the community by virtue of its size. In part this is because no organization has a generally accepted, trustworthy membership list. More significantly, it is because no mass organization in Jewish life can even pretend to be able to mobilize its membership behind one position or another.

The most potent claim for authority in Jewish life today is exercised by money. Perhaps this was always so, but until recently the claim was exercised in alliance with religious tradition. Tradition's loss of status has resulted in the dissolution of this alliance and today those who control the purse strings, alone, usually speak for the Jewish community and decide questions within it. Although the professionals and staff members of the various organizations generally initiate policy, their authority is often determined by their access to financial resources and particularly to the few big contributors. Orthodoxy cannot accept the authority of money because it contains neither a class of large contributors nor a group of professionals with access to large contributors. In this regard, the Conservative and Reform rabbinate are in a far better, though by no means ideal, position, as they confront the "secular" Jewish institutions. The potency of money in the rest of the community, therefore, has the effect of pressuring Orthodoxy to withdraw from the community. In other words, the rule of the game in the Jewish community is that "money talks the loudest." Because Orthodoxy only loses by these rules, there is a constant pressure from within for it to leave the game unless the rules are changed. Of course, the concessions and compromises made by the Orthodox in order to play the game become unnecessary when they withdraw from it and they then move to a more intransigent right-wing position.

Orthodoxy claims the right to preserve the unity of the Jewish community by invoking the authority of tradition and charisma. With regard to the first, it claims communal support for its essentially parochial schools on the ground that these are traditional schools which simply teach Judaism as it has always been taught (in terms of content, of course, not method). This claim to legitimacy has been challenged recently, most particularly by the Conservatives. The foregoing is not meant to imply that numbers or money have only recently become sources of authority, or that tradition has lost all its force. It does mean that the weight of the different bases of authority has changed, and that Orthodoxy's claim to its exclusive access to this authority has been challenged.

The fourth possible source of authority in the Jewish community is that of person, or charisma. Jews in the United States have never produced a charismatic leader for the entire community, although Louis Marshall, Judah Magnes, Stephen Wise, and Abba Hillel Silver came close to being such leaders.

The only group within Jewish life which lays claim to charismatic leaders today is the Orthodox. Preeminent among these for the modern Orthodox is Rabbi Joseph B. Soloveitchik. RCA's claim to leadership in the general Jewish community and its belief that it ought really to exercise this leadership rest almost entirely on the fact that Rabbi Soloveitchik is its leader. RCA members consider it enormously significant that the non-Orthodox Jewish community has accorded his opinions an increasing respect. Rabbi Soloveitchik, acknowledged by most Orthodox Jews as one of the world's leading Talmudic authorities, has become increasingly active in social and political life and is quite conscious of his role as a communal leader. As the descendant of the longest extant line of *gedolim*, rabbis who combined Talmudic and communal authority, this could hardly be otherwise.[9]

On the other hand, the more right-wing yeshivah world (to be discussed below) rests its claim to authority on the leadership of the outstanding *rashe yeshivot* who claim the mantle of traditional as well as charismatic authority.

We turn now to those organizations in which modern Orthodoxy holds a dominant position, stressing that in none of these groups is that position exclusive.

Rabbinical Council of America (RCA)

The Rabbinical Council of America is the largest and most influential Orthodox rabbinical body in the United States. It has 830

[9]His father, Rabbi Moses Soloveitchik, was one of the great Talmudic scholars in the United States in the last generation. His uncle, Reb Velvel Soloveitchik, was the *gedol ha-dor* ("the great man of his generation") of the last generation in Palestine. His grandfather, Reb Hayyim of Brisk, the famous Brisker Rav, was the leading Talmudic scholar of his time, and his great-grandfather, Rabbi Joseph Beer Soloveitchik, after whom he is named, was the *rosh yeshivah* of Volozhin, the greatest Talmudic academy of its time. For a biographical sketch of Rabbi Soloveitchik and a popularization of some elements of his thought see his son-in-law's article: Aaron Lichtenstein, "Joseph Soloveitchik," in Simon Noveck, ed., *Great Jewish Thinkers of the Twentieth Century* (Washington: 1963), pp. 281–297.

members, all ordained by recognized rabbinic authorities. About 600 are in the active rabbinate, and most of the rest are teachers and school administrators. About half of the active rabbis were ordained at Yeshiva University's Rabbi Isaac Elchanan Theological Seminary (RIETS), and another 15 percent at the Hebrew Theological College in Illinois. Both of these institutions represent a point of view different from that of other yeshivot in the United States which confer ordination. Another 20 to 25 percent of the RCA membership come from these other American yeshivot, and the remaining few are from Europe.

A major controversy within RCA has centered on the question of its relationship with non-Orthodox rabbinical groups, particularly the affiliation of its members with the New York Board of Rabbis. In 1955, 11 *rashe yeshivot,* the most influential leaders of all the large academies for advanced Talmudic study in the United States (except Yeshiva University and the Hebrew Theological College), issued an *issur* or prohibition against Orthodox rabbis joining organizations in which non-Orthodox rabbis were officially represented. Their position was phrased in halakhic terms as a *pesak din,* a juridical decision, but has been buttressed with the practical political argument that by officially recognizing the non-Orthodox rabbi as a rabbi, Orthodoxy accorded him a status to which he was not entitled under Jewish law and which cut the ground from under its own claim as the only legitimate bearer of the Torah tradition.

RCA referred the question to its own halakhah committee under the chairmanship of Rabbi Soloveitchik. At the end of 1964 the committee had not yet reported, and showed no disposition to do so as long as the *status quo* was maintained within the Jewish community.

Nevertheless, the political aspects of the question were raised on numerous occasions; in all instances the forces for separation in RCA, led by Rabbi David Hollander, were defeated, although there is a growing sympathy for the values which Hollander espouses. The opponents of separation have argued that by cooperating with the non-Orthodox they are able to restrain them from public violation of halakhah and are in a better position to help shape policy for the whole Jewish community. . . . Besides, they suspect that the vast majority of nominally Orthodox Jews do not see any sharp distinctions between Orthodoxy and other denominations, that a policy of separation would fail of general support, and that it would jeopardize the considerable support for Orthodox institutions that comes from non-Orthodox Jews.

Finally, and perhaps most importantly, they feel that RCA members do not view themselves as living in a community apart from the rest of American Jews. The Orthodox rabbi, particularly outside New York City, lives among and serves a non-observant constituency. In addition, he himself is likely to be American-born, a product of the American culture, which places a premium on compromise, sanctifies majority rule, and decries dogmatism. . . .

RCA looks for spiritual and, more recently, political leadership to Rabbi Soloveitchik, known affectionately to his followers as the Rov (Sephardi: Rav). One can almost distinguish a Jew's religious position by the manner in which he refers to Soloveitchik. The non-Orthodox are likely to call him Rabbi Soloveitchik; the RCA modern Orthodox call him the Rov; his own students, Rebbe; and the right wing, J.B., for the first two initials of his name.

RCA has moved to the right in recent years, though not as far to the right as its separatists would like. It has continued to concern itself with communal problems but has become increasingly outspoken and antagonistic toward other groups, both religious and secular, within Jewish life. This is a result of a number of factors. The younger rabbis, particularly those from Yeshiva University, are more right-wing today in both their practice and their communal outlook than their predecessors of a decade or more ago. Secondly, as the Orthodox community has grown in numbers and risen in income and status, the rabbi has attained greater personal security and confidence in the future of Orthodoxy and has become less compromising. Thirdly, the right wing within Orthodoxy has become more acculturated. This means that it is better able to communicate with the left wing and make an impact on it. . . .

RCA's move to the right has had the further effect of healing somewhat the breach between its modern Orthodox and sectarian elements on such questions as the development of halakhah, which is only indirectly related to the controversy over communal involvement. Rackman, as we have noted, is the leading advocate of radical halakhic development, but his viewpoint is almost totally isolated. Rackman elicits a sympathetic response from his colleagues when he demands that the rabbinic leaders grapple with contemporary problems and when he criticizes them for their "ivory tower" posture. But there is less sympathy with him on what the content of the response should be. As one observer put it, "The RCA rabbi doesn't want *hetterim* [lenient rulings], he only wants a good explanation for a *pesak* [a ruling]."

Union of Orthodox Jewish Congregations of America (UOJC)

Officially RCA is the rabbinical arm of the Union of Orthodox Jewish Congregations of America (UOJC), the major national congregational organization of Orthodox synagogues. . . .

The forum for the controversy over Orthodox participation in non-Orthodox roof organizations has shifted in the last two years from RCA, where the separatists have been defeated, to UOJC. At its 1964 convention a resolution by the separatists was defeated, but on the ground that withdrawal would be unwarranted unless a roof organization for all Orthodox groups was first established. Toward this end, Orthodox organizations like RCA, the Religious Zionists of America, the Rabbinical Alliance of America, and Agudath Israel were invited to submit position papers on their conditions for entering a unified Orthodox organization. Agudath Israel, whose position probably best reflects that of the sectarian Orthodox, stipulated two conditions for its participation: that all members of the proposed organization withdraw from anything more than *ad hoc* participation in non-Orthodox roof organizations, and that a council of Torah authorities, composed essentially of Agudath Israel leaders, be the arbiters of the new organization. It was unlikely that the modern Orthodox would meet either of these conditions.

For many years UOJC was led by a young, Americanized, modern Orthodox element without any real constituent base among the mass of Yiddish-speaking, immigrant synagogue members. In the past decade a closer relationship has developed between Orthodox synagogues and the parent synagogue body, and UOJC has grown considerably. This is because the synagogue leadership has become more acculturated; the UOJC leadership has moved to the right, away from modernism, and the success of Conservative and Reform parent congregational bodies, as well as of Young Israel, has shown the importance of a united Orthodox synagogue body. None the less, UOJC is still not as representative of Orthodox congregations as the United Synagogue is of Conservative, or UAHC [Union of American Hebrew Congregations] of Reform, congregations. . . .

UOJC congregations range from those with mixed seating to those which go beyond the letter of the law in observing halakhic standards. Individual members include Jews from all walks of life and with a variety of opinions. Conscious of its hybrid membership and anxious not to offend any group within it, UOJC has avoided policy formulation in areas of controversy affecting internal Orthodox Jewish life and has turned much of its attention toward the broader Jewish society and the general society. Thus its resolution of 1962, repudiating its long-standing opposition to Federal aid to education, can be taken to mean that the consensus that once existed in opposition to Federal aid is no longer present.

The changing temper within the Orthodox community—the increased emphasis on halakhic observance—is reflected within UOJC. Thus, whereas status once accrued to the leaders and rabbis of congregations without *mehitzot* (barriers separating the men's and women's sections of synagogues), and a certain contempt was evident toward those "old-fashioned" congregations which still had mehitzot or even separate seating for men and women, the situation today is reversed. Since 1955, according to a spokesman for UOJC, some 30 synagogues which formerly had mixed seating have installed mehitzot, the first break in a trend which had been moving in the opposite direction since the nineteenth century.

Association of Orthodox Jewish Scientists (AOJS)

Although affiliated with UOJC, the Association of Orthodox Jewish Scientists (AOJS) . . . does not belong under the rubric of modern Orthodox. It is far less oriented toward problems of Jewish society and hardly at all to problems of the general society. It is rather concerned with problems arising out of the individual Orthodox Jew's role in the secular and scientific world. In 1964 it claimed approximately 500 members and 12 local chapters in the United States and Canada. The overwhelming majority of its members, according to its 1962 directory, are natural scientists with universities or large corporations, rather than social scientists, whom the organization has also been anxious to attract.

AOJS is preoccupied with the problem of secular education. It has never thought it appropriate to adopt a position on some of the moral issues confronting American society or American scientists as a result of the new technology and its uses, but hardly a national meeting passes in which some discussion, and usually a major address, is not devoted to the subject of the study of science or secular education in the light of the halakhah. It is as if the membership has to keep reassuring itself or others that their vocation is a proper one for Orthodox Jews.

Members of AOJS include some distinguished intellects, but the organization has exhibited little critical concern with the nature of American or Jewish life. In general, the natural sciences have attracted more Orthodox Jewish graduate students than the social sciences or humanities. This may be because they offer preparation for more lucrative and prestigious professions today or because they raise fewer critical problems for Orthodox Jews. It is not difficult to dichotomize religious belief and scientific work, whereas the very assumptions of the social sciences are often thought to run counter to traditional Orthodox views. Whatever the reason, AOJS reflects the special concerns of the natural scientist and has failed to attract to its ranks the growing number of Orthodox Jews in the social sciences and the humanities who might be expected to adopt a broader and more critical approach to Jewish and general affairs.

Yavneh, National Religious Jewish Students' Association

In contrast to AOJS, Yavneh, one of the two national Orthodox collegiate bodies, exhibits great intellectual ferment and general communal concern. Founded in 1960, Yavneh had close to a thousand paid members in over 40 chapters in American colleges and universities by 1964. The founders of Yavneh were largely Yeshiva High School graduates who were dissatisfied with the complacency and lack of intellectual excitement in the Jewish community generally, and Orthodoxy particularly. A generation earlier most of them would no doubt have abandoned Orthodoxy completely. In the 1960's they chose instead to create a subcommunity within the Orthodox world that affirms the Jewish tradition but is concerned with its application to contemporary social and political problems.

Yavneh's founders were soon joined by a more conservative group of students who sought to move the organization along more traditional lines, both programmatically and organizationally; they favored, for example, abolishing mixed-swimming weekends. Yavneh chapters are usually dominated by one group or the other. All chapters, however, have attracted students from non-Orthodox homes who find in the high level of Yavneh's programs an alternative to accepting the deficiencies of the Jewish and general communities. On many campuses Yavneh has come into conflict with local Hillel groups because of its unwillingness to accept the latitudinarian *status quo*. . . .

Yavneh's attitude [toward halakhah] is that regardless of private individual practices, halakhah must continue to be the public standard at least. This halakhic commitment is interesting because it may portend a future direction for American Orthodoxy. Unlike left-wing Orthodoxy, it does not call for radical reinterpretation of halakhah. Unlike the right, it does not demand that every Jew live his life in accordance with the halakhic prescriptions of the rabbinical authorities. Rather, it calls for an understanding of what the halakhah is and then a decision by the individual. In many respects this is a revolutionary outlook for an Orthodox organization, Rosenzweigian in its implication that the ultimate criterion for an individual's observance is his own judgment. . . .

National Council of Young Israel

The Young Israel movement, with 95 synagogues and approximately 23,000 affiliated families, may be the largest single organization in American Orthodoxy. There are probably more families affiliated with the member synagogues of UOJC, but the relationship between UOJC's leadership and the members of its congregations is still so tenuous that it would be unreasonable to compare it with Young Israel, a large proportion of whose members identify closely with the movement and a few of whom are more intensely committed to the national movement than they are to their own synagogues. This is not to suggest that all or even most member families in the Young Israel are Orthodox in their personal behavior. But there is no question as to where the direction of the organization lies. In fact, only Sabbath observers are permitted to hold office in a Young Israel congregation, and synagogues remove their *mehitzot* only at the price of their charters.

Young Israel was formed in 1912 by a handful of Orthodox Americanized youth who felt themselves a part of American society, rejected many of the folkways and practices of their parents, but wished to remain Orthodox. . . . Until World War II, Young Israel was a lay movement, dominated by a lay leadership. It was led by native-born, middle-class, college-educated Orthodox Jews, who in their own rather disorganized fashion stood as a bridge between Orthodoxy and the rest of the Jewish community. With modern facilities, stress on decorum in worship, and an attractive social program, Young Israel brought thousands of Jewish young people into the synagogue, many of whom were encouraged to enroll in intensive study courses or to enter yeshivot. (Ironically, some of them emerged from yeshivot only to condemn Young Israel for not being sufficiently Orthodox.)

As late as World War II, Young Israel was looked upon as the least observant Orthodox group. This misconception was partly due to ignorance. In part, however, it reflected an awareness of Young Israel's deviations from Orthodoxy. In developing an attractive social program, for example, Young Israel had closed its eyes to such activities as mixed dancing, which few rabbinic authorities would sanction. Its lay leadership, which was not yeshivah-trained, refused to defer to an Orthodox rabbinate who, they felt, lacked secular training, sophistication, and community status comparable to theirs. Being church-oriented, it tended to lay less stress on matters of individual observance and more on Orthodoxy's role in the Jewish community. Young Israel was among the first Orthodox organizations to seek to raise the level and dignity of *kashrut* supervision, to work with the American chaplaincy, and to lend support to Zionism, youth, and collegiate work. . . .

Since World War II the nature of the Young Israel movement has changed. In the first place, the lay leadership has been challenged by the Council of Young Israel Rabbis, the rabbinical organization of Young Israel congregational rabbis. Native-born and acculturated, with increased sophistication and, most importantly, time and information, the postwar rabbi was able to compete with the lay leader. The very growth of the movement had created a need for greater professionalism. In addition, the expansion of membership brought a larger number of marginal affiliates, who recognized the rabbi, rather than the lay leader, as legitimate spokesman for Jewish religious values. With increasing power at the congregational level, the rabbis were in a position to determine the effectiveness of the national program, and their cooperation became essential. As the locus of money shifted to the congregation, the layman, who viewed himself as part of a national movement seeking a national impact, was replaced by the rabbi, whose interests were more local, and status accrued to the rabbi of the largest, wealthiest, and most observant synagogue.

Another factor accounting for the changes in Young Israel has been the general move to the right within Orthodoxy—the intensification of demands for halakhic observance, which means, almost by definition, the ascendancy of the Orthodox rabbi as the halakhic authority of the congregation. This has particular significance in the case of the Young Israel rabbi, who is not typical of most Orthodox American rabbis, either European-trained or the products of Yeshiva University. The European rabbi is often disadvantaged by his lack of acculturation, and even when he fancies himself as a communal or chief rabbi, he is conscious of his utter dependence on lay approval. Yeshiva University graduates are not all of the same mold; but at least until recently they tended to be church-oriented, communally involved, and very much aware of the necessity for compromise. Rabbis ordained by other American yeshivot, like Torah Vodaath, Rabbi Chaim Berlin, and Rabbi Jacob Joseph, on the other hand, reject the Yeshiva University model. These Americanized, non-Yeshiva University graduates tend to be more aggressive and less compromising. About half of Young Israel's congregational rabbis are just such men. . . .

Religious Zionists of America (RZA)

The Religious Zionists of America came into being as the result of a merger in 1957 of the two Orthodox Zionist adult male groups in the United States—Mizrachi and Hapoel Hamizrachi. The women's organization of each group, as well as their respective youth groups, Mizrachi Hatzair and Bnei Akiva, have remained separate. . . .

RZA attracts an Orthodox Jew similar to the Young Israel members, and there is a large overlapping membership. Its most active officers and members are themselves rabbis but they play little role in the organization as rabbis. Spiritually, RZA looks to Rabbi Soloveitchik for leadership, and, as in the RCA, his influence has increased in recent years as he has become more outspoken on contemporary issues. A measure of his influence in RZA is that although many of its leaders were embarrassed by his criticisms in 1963 of the State of Israel on the missionary question, none publicly expressed his misgivings. RZA gives political, social, and philanthropic support to Israel and to the Israeli National Religious party, with which it is affiliated. . . .

Yeshiva University

The one institution most prominently identified with modern Orthodoxy is Yeshiva University. Indeed, the very growth of the university bespeaks the increasing concern of Orthodoxy with problems of the non-Orthodox community, both Jewish and non-Jewish. Beginning as the Rabbi Isaac Elchanan Theological Seminary (RIETS), Yeshiva University has developed or acquired

17 schools and divisions including a new West Coast center in Los Angeles. This tremendous growth has occurred since 1940 under the leadership of its president, Samuel Belkin, who has remained singularly exempt from the public criticism directed against Yeshiva University by many in the Orthodox world. The university engages in a host of activities, including sponsorship of three Jewish periodicals and a semi-scholarly series of monographs in Judaica, "Studies in Torah Judaism." Among its other divisions are a Hebrew Teachers Institute for men and another for women, a liberal-arts college for men and one for women, graduate schools of education, social work and science, and a medical school. The relation of some of its division to Orthodoxy has, at best, become tenuous. Interestingly, however, the brunt of the right-wing Orthodox attack against the institution has not been against the secular divisions but rather against the college and the Jewish divisions associated with it.

Students at the all-male college (we are not discussing Stern College for Women) are required, in addition to their regular college program, to enroll in one of three Jewish study programs: RIETS, with almost exclusive stress on Talmud and preparation for entering the three-year *semikhah* (ordination) program upon completion of undergraduate studies; the Teachers Institute for Men, with heavy stress on Talmud but a varied curriculum of Bible, history, literature, etc., all taught in Hebrew; and a Jewish-studies program for students with little or no background in Jewish studies.

The last program has been the most dramatically successful. In 1964, in its ninth year, it admitted 100 freshman (the men's college has a total of about 750 students). The program is adapted to the needs of the students, most of whom are from non-Orthodox homes. It is led by a group of sympathetic and dedicated teachers, who produce, at the end of four years, reasonably well-educated (certainly by American Jewish standards), observant, committed Jews. Some graduates continue their studies in Hebrew and Talmud, transferring to RIETS or going on for further study in Israel. Even the severest critics of Yeshiva University have acclaimed the remarkable success of this program and are inclined to concede that no other institution within Orthodoxy is equipped to do a comparable job. The program's impact on American communities is only beginning to be felt, but inevitably its graduates will assume positions of responsibility. (In contrast to the Jewish-studies program is the Lubavitcher movement, which has also achieved a measure of success in winning youth to Orthodoxy but finds that these converts are often unable to reintegrate themselves effectively in the community from which they came.)

Contrary to popular opinion in the Orthodox world, neither the college nor RIETS espouses any particular philosophy or point of view within the Orthodox spectrum of opinion. RIETS, in particular, is almost a microcosm of the committed Orthodox world and includes among its instructors some who are out of sympathy with secular education. Both the strength and weakness of the institution, no doubt, derive from this eclectic philosophic attitude. Within its walls the whole constellation of Orthodox ideologies contend. . . .

As in RCA and RZA, the preeminent personality at Yeshiva University is Rabbi Soloveitchik, who teaches Talmud. At the university, however, his leadership in communal matters is not necessarily accepted by the other Talmud instructors, many of whom have also achieved eminence in the world of Talmud learning. Besides, President Belkin, a scholar in his own right, stands forth as an independent personality. Belkin, however, has been elevated above controversy in recent years and the students' image of him is somewhat hazy.

In addition to its purely educational functions, the university plays a major role in the Jewish community through its Community Service Division. The division is responsible for rabbinic and teacher placement, conducts adult-education and extension courses, provides educational services to many Talmud Torahs and youth groups, sponsors seminars for teenagers throughout the United States, and has had a hand, together with the Rabbinic Alumni Association, in sponsoring Camp Morasha, a summer camp which opened in 1964, patterned on the Conservative Ramah camps but with an Orthodox orientation. Powered by a large staff of experienced professionals, CSD has become increasingly important as a source of information and assistance for other Orthodox bodies. Its placement activities, in particular, have so strengthened the Rabbinic Alumni that rabbis from other Orthodox yeshivot have sought (and been granted) associate membership in that association. . . .

Sephardi Community

There are an estimated 25,000 Sephardim and 63 known Sephardi congregations—congregations which do not follow the Ashkenazi form of worship or are not of Ashkenazi descent—in the United States. They are largely of Spanish and Portuguese, Syrian, Greek, Egyptian, North African, and Yugoslav origin.

The Spanish and Portuguese, whose origin in the United States predates that of all other American Jews, are the most prestigious, and the leading Sephardi congregation is the famous Spanish and Portuguese Shearith Israel of New York. In 1963 the chief rabbi or *hakham* of the Sephardic community of the British Commonwealth, Rabbi Solomon Gaon, was also made a rabbi of Shearith Israel, and given the responsibility for the school and authority in all matters of religious law.

Unlike the members of the large Spanish and Portuguese congregations, like Shearith Israel and Mikveh Israel of Philadelphia, Pennsylvania, those of most other Sephardi congregations are predominantly first-generation Americans. All Sephardi congregations appear to share a strong sub-ethnic commitment to their form of worship (which differs from one group of congregations to the other), and a relative neglect of private ritual observance. (Thus, even the lay leadership of the Sephardi congregations tend to be quite lax in their religious practice. However, this has in no way affected the intensity of their desire to retain the traditional Sephardi public ritual.)

. . . as a minority within the American Jewish community, the Sephardi congregations face the problems of cultural dilution. Without facilities to train their own rabbis, and more importantly their own *hazzanim* (leaders of the religious service), they face danger of extinction. In 1962 they turned to Yeshiva University, which initiated a program (financed by the Sephardi community) to train religious leaders for them. . . . The Yeshiva University program is under the official direction of Rabbi Gaon. Its success depends to a large extent on its ability to recruit college-age students from within the Sephardi community.

SECTARIANS

Jewish sectarianism, unlike that of many Protestant groups, results not from the beliefs of the membership but mostly from a differing strategy as to the best way of maintaining the tradition. Thus, an organization such as Agudath Israel, which is essentially a sectarian group in the United States, was deeply involved in problems and activities of a Jewish and even a general political nature in Eastern Europe. In the United States, on the other hand, they have felt that communal participation with other Jewish groups would perforce involve a recognition of the legitimacy of non-Orthodox religious groups and institutions.

With few exceptions, the sectarian camp is of lower income, poorer education, and more recent immigration than the modern Orthodox.[10] The world of sectarian Orthodoxy is preeminently a yeshivah world, and its leaders are the *rashe yeshivot* and a few prominent hasidic rebbes. It is a mistake to think, as many even within Orthodoxy do, that the Orthodox world which has been created in this country is a replica of the European or even East European one. In fact, the *rashe yeshivot* have achieved a degree of authority in this country unparalleled in Eastern Europe, in good part because there is no counterweight to this authority here in the *shtot rov* or communal rabbi, as there was in Europe.

The years before and immediately after World War II brought to the United States an influx of Orthodox immigrants far more militant than those who had come earlier. They found in this country an Orthodox community largely composed of residual Orthodox and under the ostensible leadership of communal rabbis who seemed to be in despair about the future of Orthodoxy and convinced of the necessity for compromise. They found institutions such as *kashrut* in the hands of people whom they considered as unreliable or careless. They found a bare handful of day schools and a Yeshiva University or RCA ready to accommodate themselves to secular culture. They found almost no institutions with total

[10]There is a vast literature on the relationship between religious sectarianism and social class indicating that among religious groups low social class correlates with sectarianism. The classic study is H. Richard Niebuhr, *The Social Sources of Denominationalism* (New York: 1929; reprinted Hamden, Conn.: 1954). See also: Liston Pope, *Millhands and Preachers* (New Haven: 1942); Russell R. Dynes, "Church-Sect Typology and Socio-Economic Status," *American Sociological Review*, 1955, pp. 555–560; Donald O. Cowgill, "The Ecology of Religious Preference in Wichita," *Sociological Quarterly*, 1960, pp. 87–96; Nicholas J. Demerath, "Social Stratification and Church Involvement: The Church-Sect Distinction Applied to Individual Participation," *Review of Religious Research*, 1961, pp. 146–154, and Liston Pope, "Religion and Class Structure," *Annals of the American Academy of Political and Social Sciences*, 1948, pp. 84–91. Not all sects, however, are lower-class. Both Christian Science and the Oxford Movement were middle- and upper-class groups. See Yinger, *op. cit.*, p. 146.

commitment to the Torah life which had been their world.

They began by creating their own institutions or taking over the few existing ones which they found acceptable. The first step was the creation and expansion of yeshivot.

In 1941 Rabbi Aaron Kotler, *rosh yeshivah* of Kletzk in Polish Lithuania, famous as a Talmud scholar and Orthodox leader, arrived in the United States intending to spend a short time here and then move on to Palestine.[11] A handful of Orthodox Jews persuaded him to stay in the United States to build Torah institutions. Reb Aharon, as he was known in the Orthodox world, assembled 20 students, mostly graduates of American yeshivot, many already ordained as rabbis, and established the Beth Medrash Govoha of America, in Lakewood, New Jersey, now also known as the Rabbi Aaron Kotler Institute for Advanced Learning (the first *kolel* in the United States). His choice of site was a deliberate attempt to isolate his students from American life and facilitate total concentration on the study of Talmud. Within a few years he was joined by some former students from Europe; by 1946 registration had risen to 100, and by 1964 to over 200.

Reb Aharon's conviction was that Torah could grow and be "experienced" in America only through *lernen* ("learning"—in the parlance of the Orthodox world, studying Talmud). According to one of Reb Aharon's former students, only "sharing the experience of the halakhic process could enable the Jew to understand the heartbeat of Judaism." The student at Lakewood lived on a small subvention from the yeshivah and whatever other financial help he got from his family or wife. Students sat and learned for as long as they wished. When they felt ready to leave the yeshivah, they left. . . .

Reb Aharon, himself, did not confine his activity to Lakewood. He engaged in a multitude of activities where his point of view gained recognition. He served as a *rosh yeshivah* in Israel, became the head of Chinuch Atzmai (Hinnukh 'Atzmaï the independent, religious, Agudath Israel-oriented school system in Israel) upon its founding in 1952, leader of Agudath Israel in 1952, and chairman of the rabbinical administrative board of Torah Umesorah, the National Society for Hebrew Day Schools in the United States, in 1945. Though (interestingly enough) a poor fund raiser in contrast to some other *rashe yeshivot,* Reb Aharon elicited tremendous

[11]For a biographical sketch see Alex J. Goldman, *Giants of Faith; Great American Rabbis* (New York: 1964), pp. 257–273.

passion and dedication from those who came in contact with him. He brooked no compromise, nor did he ever question or seem to doubt his own path. He was a preeminently charismatic leader.

The influence of Reb Aharon and like thinkers extended to the higher yeshivot in the United States, except for Yeshiva University and the Hebrew Theological College. Thus, older institutions like Yeshivah Torah Vodaath, with its own famous *menahel* (principal) Shragai Mendlowitz,[12] or Yeshivah Rabbi Chaim Berlin under Rabbi Isaac Hutner, were caught up in the emphasis on *lernen* and separatism. In 1944 Rabbi Mendlowitz founded the Beth Medrosh Elyon in Monsey, New York, at first called *Esh Dat* ("Fire of Religion"), as a pilot institute for training Jewish educators to found and staff the day-school movement. Within a short period the original idea was abandoned and the institution was reorganized to make it similar to the one in Lakewood.

Advanced Yeshivot

At the heart of the sectarian Orthodox world are all the post-high-school yeshivot except Yeshiva University and the Hebrew Theological College. . . . Graduates of the sectarian yeshivot provide the major source of staff for the day-school movement. Many of these graduates, including those with ordination, avoid the rabbinate because they neither wish nor are able to serve predominantly non-observant Orthodox memberships. By choice and absence of alternative they enter the less prestigious and more poorly paid field of Jewish education. Students from Lakewood itself have established five institutions of intensive Jewish learning at the high-school level in different parts of the United States.

Yeshivah graduates who enter Jewish education frequently supplement their Talmudic training at college evening sessions, and some even take graduate courses in education. But contrary to their hopes and expectations, many of them are unprepared for the world they enter. Outside the walls of the yeshivah they meet new problems of both a secular and Jewish nature. Furthermore, there is no organization that speaks in their idiom, capable of providing help and direction for them. They continue to regard *lernen* as the

[12]Now known as Rabbi Mendlowitz, the former principal of Torah Vodaath used to refuse to use the title of Rav. His stress on the importance of Hebrew grammar and of pedagogy made him a unique figure in the yeshivah world.

highest end, but have no direction in living life short of that end. Of course this is a problem for all yeshivah graduates, not only those who choose Jewish education as their vocation. As true sectarians, they reject the communal Orthodox institutions surrounding them; their only source of leadership and guidance remains their *rosh yeshivah*.

Some yeshivah graduates do, of course, enter the rabbinate. This is a most dangerous course for a sectarian, and each has to make his own compromise with the world. A small proportion serve Reform congregations; more serve Conservative congregations, usually the smaller, less successful ones, which pay the smaller salaries. Of the majority who serve Orthodox congregations some make their peace with modern Orthodoxy, join RCA, associate themselves with the Yeshiva University Rabbinic Alumni, and are indistinguishable from Yeshiva University graduates. A few have chosen to remain isolated from the larger camp of Orthodox rabbis and are organized in the *Iggud Ha-rabbanim* (Rabbinical Alliance of America), to be discussed below.

We can consider now the institutions of the yeshivah or sectarian world, bearing in mind that the most sectarian (exclusive of the hasidim) are the least organized and simply continue to revolve in the orbit of their *rashe yeshivot*. We should also note that even the sectarian organizations' involvement in communal activity is not at all a reflection of the rank and file's interests or wishes.

K'hal Adath Jeshurun (Breuer Community)

Much of the preceding discussion does not apply to K'hal Adath Jeshurun. The Breuer community, in Washington Heights, named for its rabbinic leader, represents the continuation in the United States of the separatist Orthodox community in Frankfurt established in 1849 and led by Samson Raphael Hirsch after 1851. The establishment of Hirsch's separatist community is a fascinating story but not of direct concern here.[13] The New York community, established in 1940, now has over 700 affiliated families and 1,300 adult members, mostly of German origin, and provides a day school, high school, and advanced classes in Talmud for its graduates, who, in the German tradition, are encouraged to attend

[13]The best English-language account is Herman Schwab, *History of Orthodox Jewry in Germany*, trans. Irene R. Birnbaum (London: 1950).

college. The community sponsors a mikveh and provides rabbinical supervision for a host of butchers, bakers, and other food processors in the area. The leadership has maintained the strong anti-Zionism of the German period and is publicly identified with Agudath Israel.

Unlike the East Europeans, the German Orthodox separatists had already made a successful accommodation to western culture before emigrating to the new world; secular education was, indeed, a positive good in the Hirschian philosophy of Judaism. The leaders of the Breuer community might well have expected, that as the most acculturated and economically comfortable but also strictly observant and rigidly disciplined Orthodox institution in the United States, their point of view would sweep American Orthodoxy. Instead although the community has been quite successful in establishing its own institutions, it has won few converts to its particular ideological position of both communal separatism and a positive acceptance of secular culture. On the contrary, it is on the defensive against the more parochial elements of Orthodoxy.

In part, of course, this is a result of its own decision. As a tiny minority in this country it was faced with the choice of identifying itself communally with Yeshiva University, its neighbor in Washington Heights, and the world of modern Orthodoxy, or with the European yeshivah world with which it had been aligned in Europe. It chose the latter. But in Europe, boundaries and distances separated the followers of Hirsch from the world of the Mirrer or Telshe yeshivot where secular education was discouraged. Even so, there were signs just before the Nazi period that some of the best talent was attracted away from Germany by these and other Lithuanian-type yeshivot. In the United States this continues to be the problem. The Breuer community is forced to look outside its own ranks for educational staff, and some of its teachers and administrators have a negative attitude toward secular education. Its institutions are the envy of the Orthodox world, but its future as a doctrinal community is problematical. . . .

National Society for Hebrew Day Schools (Torah Umesorah)

Torah Umeshorah is the largest national body serving Orthodox day schools. . . . Although Torah Umesorah is staffed by one of the most competent groups of professionals in the Orthodox world, it is, nevertheless, a small body, which must operate within a framework created by *rashe yeshivot* who are somewhat disengaged from contemporary problems, a lay group of officials who tend to be rather uncritical, and a corps of teachers many of whom are untrained. A rabbinical administrative board, composed almost entirely of *rashe yeshivot,* officially dictates Torah Umesorah policy. . . .

[The number of day schools continues to grow but] a number of New York City schools are in neighborhoods of declining Jewish population. This has constricted enrollment and created severe financial problems. In many day schools outside New York, too, the financial problem is critical. Often this is the consequence of inadequate community support. Sometimes the Orthodox financial base is too narrow to support the schools independently, and the wider Jewish community, as represented by federations and non-Orthodox rabbis, often demands too great a voice in school policy to make its support acceptable. The situation differs from one community to another. In many areas, as long as the secular department of the day school functions well, community support is forthcoming.[14] But where the Orthodox base of a community is quite small, day schools find difficulty in pursuing a policy of intensive Orthodoxy within the institutions' walls while projecting the image of a broad Jewish communal institution deserving of non-Orthodox support from without. In addition, while the non-Orthodox parent may be indifferent to the ideological content of the day-school program, he is not indifferent to the general personality, characteristics, and attitudes of the day-school Hebrew teacher, who is himself often the product of an "other-worldly" environment and a yeshivah where secular education was downgraded.

Of course, not all Orthodox day schools are within the orbit of Torah Umesorah, nor are they all the same type. There are 28 hasidic day schools

> . . . found mostly in the well populated areas of New York City—notably Williamsburg and Crown Heights and Boro Park to a lesser extent—now predominantly inhabited by followers of the

[14]This situation may change with the growing antagonism of Conservative leaders toward the ideology of the Orthodox day schools, but to date the Conservatives themselves have been handicapped by their own rabbis' unwillingness to undertake the arduous task of building day schools that are potential competitors to their own synagogues and Hebrew schools for money and pupils. Even Orthodox rabbis have often been lax in the actual support of day schools. The difference, however, is that Orthodoxy contains a more dedicated and Jewishly impassioned laity, who bear much of the day-school burden without rabbinical assistance.

> leading Hassidic "Rebbeyim". . . . The major emphasis in these schools is upon preserving the distinct philosophy and way of living of the Hassidic group to which the pupils belong. Personal piety, with the particular and unique manner of observance of the Hassidic sect, is stressed. . . .Attention to general studies is secondary. Generally, these are studied only until the end of the compulsory school age.[15]

Within New York City, the language of instruction carries definite ideological overtones. Schools which stress Yiddish are primarily designed to prepare boys for advanced Talmud study, because Yiddish is generally the language of instruction in the advanced yeshivot. In addition, Rabbi Kotler is reported to have had particularly strong feelings for Yiddish and to have urged principals to abandon the use of Hebrew and substitute Yiddish instead. There are 31 elementary, non-hasidic, Yiddish-speaking schools in New York City and 19 such high schools, or a total of 50 Orthodox Yiddish day schools. The schools whose Jewish studies are in Hebrew are more likely to be of the modern Orthodox type, placing greater emphasis on Israel and some modern Hebrew literature. The current tendency is toward the use of the Sephardi (or rather, Israeli) pronunciation, although those traditional yeshivot which use Hebrew as a language of instruction, such as the Beth Jacob schools for girls, teach the Ashkenazi pronunciation. . . .

Rabbinical Alliance of America (RAA: Iggud Ha-rabbanim)

The Rabbinical Alliance of America, founded in 1944, is composed of graduates of sectarian American yeshivot who were unwilling to affiliate with the Yeshiva University-dominated RCA and either were excluded from membership in the Agudat Ha-rabbanim by its *semikhah* requirements, or themselves rejected the Agudat Ha-rabbanim image.* The first members of RAA were primarily from Torah Vodaath (with a few from Rabbi Jacob Joseph) and to this day placement for RAA rabbis is handled through Torah Vodaath under an arrangement reached in 1957–58, when RAA cut its formal ties with the yeshivah. . . .

[15]Joseph Kaminetsky, "Evaluating the Program and Effectiveness of the All-Day Jewish School," *Jewish Education*, Winter 1956–1957, p. 41. Part of the material in this section is drawn from the same article by Torah Umesorah's national director.

**Editor's Note:* In an earlier section not reproduced here the author analyzes the Union of Orthodox Rabbis of the United States [Agudat Ha-rabbanim] at length. Pointing out that it is the oldest organization of Orthodox rabbis in the United States he stresses that its influence has declined during recent decades.

Agudath Israel

Agudath Israel was organized in the United States in 1939 as part of a worldwide movement, founded in Europe in 1912, which represented the largest organized force in the European Orthodox world before the Nazi period. . . .

In the light of its history, one might well ask why the organization has not become a more potent force among the Orthodox in the United States. The number of members is difficult to estimate, but undoubtedly falls below 20,000, many of whom are indifferent to Agudist ideology but become members automatically by virtue of their affiliation with Agudath Israel synagogues.

All observers are of the opinion that Agudah sympathizers and potential members outnumber those presently enrolled in the organization. There are a number of reasons why the organization has not been able to reach them. First of all, Agudah arrived relatively late in the United States. An effort to establish the organization in 1922 had failed. However, the Zeirei Agudath Israel (Agudah youth) predated the parent body. It was established in 1921, and by 1940 had seven flourishing chapters in New York City,[16] one in Philadelphia, and one in Baltimore. Much of the potential leadership talent did not join the parent organization until 1949, when the adult group forced a resolution requiring that no one above the age of 28 or married could remain affiliated with the youth organization. The adult body, however, was never able to develop the *élan* and social program that were so attractive to the youth.

A second and more important reason for Agudah's weakness stems from the depoliticalization and sectarianism of the yeshivot. Reb Aharon and the other *rashe yeshivot* who were leaders in Agudah trained a younger generation to value only one activity, *lernen*. The result was a devaluation of and contempt for political and societal activity in the Jewish community. Thus, the yeshivah students who might have formed the nucleus for a revitalized Agudah never joined the organization; nor has the organization ever become an active communal force. Its youth organization, now firmly under the control of the parent organization, avoids controversial topics of communal concern within the Orthodox community and confines its local activities to *lernen*. This, however, is hardly an attractive program to young people who spend

[16]For a discussion of the history of the Zeirei Agudath Israel chapter in Williamsburg and the growth of the national organization, see George Kranzler, *Williamsburg: A Jewish Community in Transition* (New York: 1961), pp. 248–286.

most of their time in a yeshivah where the level of *lernen* is likely to be as high if not higher. . . .

Hasidim

As noted above, the original hasidim represented a sectarian element in Jewish life. A variety of factors contributed to the rise of hasidism in the eighteenth century, but a discussion of its early period and its doctrines and religious expressions lies beyond the scope of this paper. We note only that the enmity between the hasidim and their traditionalist Lithuanian opponents—*mitnaggedim*—was quite bitter. The hasidim, with their particular doctrinal stresses and their original deemphasis on Talmudic learning, were considered by many to lie perilously close to the outer limits of normative Judaism.

The rise of the Enlightenment, Jewish socialism, and secular Zionism occasioned a reinterpretation by the mitnaggedim of hasidic behavior as an aspect of piety rather than rebellion. By the twentieth century there were strong ties between the hasidim and mitnaggedim which resulted, finally, in the joint participation of many of their leaders in Agudath Israel.

In the United States a further blurring of ideological differences between hasidim and mitnaggedim has occurred because most hasidim retain little that makes them doctrinally unique among ultra-pious Jews. Although they cling tenaciously to some of their special customs and generally retain their traditional European dress, with few exceptions they cannot be distinguished ideologically from the *rashe yeshivot*. The one constant that remains is the notion of the *rebbe* or hasidic leader, to whom the followers attribute extraordinary qualities and around whom they cluster.

Habad, the Lubavitcher Movement

The best-known hasidim are, of course, the followers of the Lubavitcher Rebbe.[17] It is impossible to estimate their number

[17]A sympathetic portrayal of the Lubavitcher movement and a description of their rebbe and his followers is presented by a Reform rabbi in two articles: Herbert Weiner, "The Lubavitcher Movement," *Commentary*, March and April 1957. Descriptions of other hasidic groups in the United States and Israel, which attempt to capture the essence of their religious meaning and attraction, are found in other articles by Weiner. See, for example, his "Dead Hasidim," ibid., March and May 1961 and "Braslav in Brooklyn," *Judaism*, Summer 1964. There is a vast literature on hasidism and the Lubavitcher movement in particular by both observers and followers. See for example publications of their former Rebbe, Joseph I. Schneersohn, *Some Aspects of Chabad Chassidism* (New York: 1944) and *Outlines of the Social and Communal Work of Chassidism* (New York: 1953).

because, unlike other hasidic groups, they are not concentrated in any one area, organized formally, or affiliated with any one institution. The Lubavitcher movement is in many respects the least sectarian of Orthodox groups although doctrinally it is among the most faithful of all hasidic groups to the tenets of its founders. (It is also the most doctrinally sophisticated and intellectually organized of all hasidic groups.) Its unique texts are taught in its advanced yeshivot or in private groups, together with the standard sacred religious texts shared by all Orthodox Jews.

The relationship of its followers to the Lubavitcher movement may best be described as one of concentric circles around the Lubavitcher Rebbe, Rabbi Menahem Mendel Schneersohn, with the inner circle located predominantly, but not exclusively, in the Crown Heights section of Brooklyn, where the Rebbe lives and the headquarters of the movement is located.

Unlike other hasidic groups, the Lubavitcher have friends and sympathizers, estimated by some members of the movement to be as many as 150,000, who far outnumber the immediate coterie of followers. The overwhelming majority are said to be non-Orthodox. Many Jews seek the Rebbe's advice on personal matters and accept him as a religious guide, and he sees an estimated 3,000 people a year for personal interviews averaging 10 to 15 minutes in length. . . .

The phenomenon of non-Orthodox hasidim (President Zalman Shazar of Israel is the outstanding example) is troublesome to many in the Orthodox camp. They wonder how a presumably ultra-Orthodox leader can find such affinity with and arouse such sympathy among unobservant Jews, and whether he has not in fact compromised some essential demands of Orthodoxy in order to attract this great following. The Lubavitcher movement, however, can only be understood on its own terms, and it does in fact stand outside the Orthodox camp in many respects. The movement does not recognize political or religious distinctions within Judaism. It has refused to cooperate formally with any identifiable organization or institution. It recognizes only two types of Jew, the fully observant and devout Lubavitcher Jew and the potentially devout and observant Lubavitcher Jew. This statement is often cited as a charming aphorism. In fact, it has tremendous social and political consequences. In every Jew, it is claimed, a spark of the holy can be found. The function of the Lubavitcher emissaries who are sent over the world is to find that spark in each Jew and kindle it. From the performance of even a minor *mitzvah*, they argue, greater observance may follow. Thus, every Jew is recognized as sacred, but no Jew and certainly no institution outside the Lubavitcher movement is totally pure. Consequently the Lubavitcher movement can make use of allies for particular purposes without compromising its position. It can follow a policy of expediency because it never confers legitimacy on those with whom it cooperates.

One result is that sympathy for the Lubavitcher movement generally declines the further along the continuum of Orthodoxy one moves. The militantly Orthodox are continually disappointed by the independent policy which the movement pursues. This is partly due to the fact that the *rashe yeshivot* are from the tradition of the *mitnaggedim* who once bitterly opposed hasidism and viewed its doctrines as heretical. Since the Lubavitcher are the most doctrinally faithful hasidim, they would naturally encounter the greatest opposition. But in larger part, the antagonism is a result of the fact that Lubavitcher sectarianism is very different from other Orthodox sectarianism.

Judgment as to the success of the Lubavitcher movement depends on one's vantage point. It is indisputable that many Jews, previously untouched by Judaism, received their first appreciation of their religious faith through the missionary activity of Lubavitcher emissaries. Almost every week students from colleges all over the United States, totally removed from Judaism, visit the Central Lubavitcher Yeshiva in New York City under the prompting of a Lubavitcher representative who visited their campus. But some Orthodox observers question how many of these students who thus visit the yeshivah or pray with an *etrog* and *lulav* at the urging of a Lubavitcher representative, whom they encounter by chance on the street, in school, or in a hospital, are genuinely affected by their experience. Despite pride in its intellectual foundation, the Lubavitcher appeal today is almost exclusively emotional. More than any group in Orthodox and Jewish life, the movement offers solutions to individual problems arising not only from the Jewish condition but from man's societal condition. . . .

Satmar Hasidim and Their Allies

The Satmar community is of Hungarian origin and is the most sectarian of all Orthodox groups in the United States. By the nineteenth century Hungarian Orthodox Jews had gained a reputation as the most zealous opponents of the non-Orthodox and as sponsors of a school system which introduced more intensive study of Talmud, and at an earlier age, than even the traditional Lithuanian-mitnagged yeshivot. The community is governed by the Satmar Rebbe, Rabbi Joel Teitelbaum, head of the Central Rabbinical Congress and leader of religious and political communities which are not identical.

As rov of the religious *kehillah* (community), Rabbi Teitelbaum is final arbiter in all matters of religious law. The kehillah numbers about 1,200 families, located primarily in Williamsburg, with smaller branches in Boro Park and Crown Heights (all in Brooklyn). Many of these families lost their rebbes to the Nazis and turned to the Satmar Rebbe when they came to the United States. The kehillah provides a full complement of religious and social services to its members, including welfare institutions, schools, mikvaot, bakeries, supervision over a variety of processed foods, and, informally, insurance and even pensions. It requires a high degree of religious conformity from its adherents, extending even to matters of dress. . . .

As rebbe, political or societal arbiter, the Satmar's influence extends to a number of smaller hasidic groups of Hungarian origin, each with its own rov. These include such groups as the Tzehlemer, Szegeder, and Puper. The total, together with the Satmar's own kehillah, is conservatively estimated at 5,000 families.[18] The Satmar Rebbe is also recognized as religious leader of the ultrasectarian Netore Karta of Jerusalem. . . .

The long-range impact of the Satmar community should not be minimized. Standing outside the mainstream of the communications network of even the Orthodox Jewish community, isolated from almost all Orthodox groups, it is easily ignored except when it erupts in some demonstration, such as picketing the Israeli consulate, which brings it to the public's attention. . . .

Although its attitude toward secular education is negative, some degree of acculturation is inevitable. The community has recently opened lines of communication with some personalities in Agudat Ha-rabbanim and invited Rabbi Moses Feinstein to a conference of its rabbinic body. The Satmar Rebbe was one of the

[18]The lowest figure was provided by a Satmar representative. Among those interviewed for this report the Satmar group was the only one whose own membership and school-enrollment estimates were lower than those hazarded by rival observers.

half-dozen prominent sectarian leaders who delivered a eulogy at the funeral of Rabbi Kotler, while Rabbi Soloveitchik, who also attended, was not asked to speak. . . . If the kehillah is successful in retaining the enthusiasm of its youth, it will inevitably play a more prominent role in Jewish life, and increasing numbers of Jewish leaders will have to reckon with the Satmar Rebbe.

LEADERSHIP

Orthodox institutions, as essentially religious organizations, "must rely predominantly on normative powers [as distinct from coercive or remunerative powers] to attain both acceptance of their directives and the means required for their operation."[19] Religious authority has been traditionally exercised charismatically. That is, the religious leader has been one able to "exercise diffuse and intense influence over the normative orientations of the actors."[20] But according to the value system and traditional expectations of Orthodox Jews, charisma can inhere only in a Talmud scholar. Talmud scholarship is a necessary but not sufficient condition for the exercise of maximum religious leadership or for becoming a *gadol* (plural, *gedolim*). The nature of the *gedolim* has been defined as follows:

> In Jewish life we rely completely on the collective conscience of the people that it will intuitively recognize its leaders and accept their teachings. There surely was no formal vote that thrust the Chofetz Chaim or Reb Chaim Ozer into world leadership. They emerged naturally. . . .
>
> There may be many [who] are recognized Torah scholars and yet they don't attain this wide acclaim. There is some ingredient, that transcends scholarship alone or piety alone—that makes one a Godol. Obviously, these qualities of knowledge, erudition, and piety are basic. But, over and above these there is another that is crucial and that is

[19]Amitai Etzioni, *A Comparative Analysis of Complex Organizations* (New York: 1961), p. 41.

[20]*Ibid.*, p. 203.

> what we generally describe as "Daas Torah." . . . It assumes a special endowment or capacity to penetrate objective reality, recognize the facts as they "really" are, and apply the pertinent Halachic principles. It is a form of "Ruach Hakodesh," as it were, which borders if only remotely on the periphery of prophecy. . . . More often than not, the astute and knowledgeable community workers will see things differently and stand aghast with bewilderment at the action proposed by the "Godol." It is at this point that one is confronted with demonstrating faith in "Gedolim" and subduing his own alleged acumen in behalf of the Godol's judgment of the facts.[21]

The notion of *gedolim* is, however, becoming increasingly institutionalized, at least for the sectarian Orthodox camp. Its first formal manifestation was in the establishment by Agudath Israel of its worldwide Mo'etset Gedole Ha-torah (Council of Torah Authorities). Rabbi Aaron Kotler, until he died in 1962, was the preeminent *gedol ha-dor* (*gadol* of the generation) for the yeshivah world. The fact that he also led the *Mo'etsah* did not add to his luster. Many, even in the Mizrahi camp or in the ultrasectarian hasidic camp to the right of Agudath Israel, recognized his eminence. Besides serving as chairman of the *Mo'etsah,* he was chairman of Torah Umesorah's rabbinical administrative board and head of Chinuch Atzmai.

With Reb Aharon's death, the vacant posts had to be filled, putting the unity of the right-wing Orthodox world to the test. In the absence of a personality comparable to Reb Aharon's, would the successors to his offices inherit authority equal to or approximating his? Would, in other words, Reb Aharon's charisma of person pass to charisma of office? Could there be "routinized charisma," so essential to organizational equilibrium, at least among religious groups?

There are three potential successors to Reb Aharon's authority among the American *rashe yeshivot.* (Only *rashe yeshivot* would be eligible since only they possess the necessary qualification of Talmud scholarship.) The most prominent candidate is Rabbi Moses Feinstein, *rosh yeshivah* of Mesifta Tifereth Jerusalem, who was elected chairman of the *Mo'etsah* and head of Chinuch Atzmai in 1962, but only vice-chairman of Torah Umesorah's rabbinical administrative board. He is also one of five members of the Agudat

[21]Bernard Weinberger, "The Role of the Gedolim," *Jewish Observer,* October 1963, p. 11.

Ha-rabbanim's presidium. Reb Mosheh is, as we noted, the leading *posek* (halakhic authority) of his generation. Within the world of authoritative *posekim* he is also the most lenient. His decisions, in fact, have bordered on the radical in departure from halakhic precedents to meet contemporary needs. However, greatness as a *posek* has never by itself entitled a scholar to the highest reverence in the traditional world. Reb Mosheh is a retiring, modest, unassuming person, who, while acknowledging his role as a leader of Orthodox Judaism, nonetheless, unlike Reb Aharon, seeks a strong consensus on political and social questions (in contrast to religious-ritual-ethical questions) before acting. . . .

The characteristics of leadership in the modern Orthodox camp are similar to those of the sectarian Orthodox. The modern Orthodox counterpart to Reb Aharon is Rabbi Joseph Soloveitchik (the Rov), and as long as the Rov remains active he will maintain his dominant positions in such organizations as RCA, RZA, Yeshiva University Rabbinic Alumni, and to a lesser extent UOJC. The future leader of the modern Orthodox world is likely to be Rabbi Soloveitchik's successor to the chairmanship of RCA's halakhah commission, an office which the rabbi is endowing with charismatic authority. At one time Rabbi Soloveitchik might have achieved a comparable role as spiritual mentor in Young Israel, but he rejected their overtures. (Significantly, his brother, Rabbi Aaron Soloveitchik, also a renowned Talmudic scholar, has come closer to the Young Israel recently and may possibly emerge as their religious authority. . . .)

Unlike Reb Aharon, the Rov assumed his leadership position only gradually. Indeed, the sectarians often charge that he never really became a leader, but is simply a front for the modern Orthodox. If that was true at one time, it certainly is no longer so, although he has been thought to change his mind on enough issues to introduce a measure of uncertainty among his own followers as to where he stands on a number of matters.

To call the Rov the leader of modern Orthodoxy is not to imply that he is always comfortable in that camp or happy with that designation. Nevertheless, his position is sharply differentiated from the sectarian *rashe yeshivot* by his positive affirmation of many elements in Western civilization (he holds a Ph.D. in philosophy from the University of Berlin) and his willingness to operate in a modern Orthodox framework. But the Rov is also part of the traditional yeshivah world. Indeed, in recent years he has moved to the right and has become more outspoken in his criticism of certain aspects of life in Israel, in his own halakhic interpretations, and in his attitude toward rabbis serving synagogues with mixed seating. The Rov may be the leader of modern Orthodoxy but he is not really modern Orthodox. Modern Orthodoxy has yet to produce a leader from its own ranks because it still continues to acknowledge mastery of the Talmud as a qualification for leadership and yet has refused to endorse, even at Yeshiva University, a restructuring of Talmudic education that would encourage bright, inquisitive minds which lack the fundamentalist position of the *rashe yeshivot* to undertake the many years of dedicated and arduous learning required to become a Talmudic authority.

Day-to-day leadership of Orthodox organizations has been assumed by professionals, almost all of whom are rabbis. The role of the professional is growing in importance, but the tremendous charismatic authority invested in the spiritual leader has contained the professional's image and often constrained his initiative.

The lay leader is left in a rather unfortunate position. He commands neither the prestige of the Talmudic scholar nor the time and information of the professional. No one within the Orthodox camp really regards him very highly or takes him very seriously. Even among laymen (that is, nonprofessionals), possession of rabbinic ordination, or at least extensive Jewish education, is increasingly becoming a ticket of admission to the councils of decision-making.

The only other premium is that placed on the money the layman contributes or raises, but any effort to dictate how the money should be used is resisted. However, as long as the Orthodox community contains only few men of really substantial wealth, it is inevitable that these will occupy positions of status and prestige.[22] On the other hand the growth of yeshivot means that Orthodoxy is producing a growing number of Jewishly educated laymen, many of whom acquire a good secular education and economically comfortable positions. This group is only beginning to make an

[22]One of the few Orthodox leaders who would augment the role of the laymen and argues that non-halakhic policy decisions should be made by the practicing rabbinate and lay leadership, together with the "masters of halakhah," is Yeshiva University's president: Samuel Belkin, *Essays in Traditional Jewish Thought* (New York: 1956), pp. 150–151.

impact on both the Orthodox and non-Orthodox Jewish community. It seems inevitable that they will play a more prominent role in all aspects of Jewish life.

DIRECTIONS AND TENDENCIES

In essence, contemporary American Orthodoxy or at least committed Orthodoxy, whence springs the leadership and direction of the community, is characterized by the growth of institutions whose origins and spirit are sectarian and who are reacting against the churchlike direction of Orthodoxy in its pre-World War II period. Orthodoxy, in truth, might have been characterized in that earlier period as simply lower-class Conservative Judaism. That this is no longer the case is due to changes in both Conservatism and Orthodoxy. Orthodoxy today is defining its role in particular and differentiated terms and more than ever before sees itself as isolated from other Jews. The result has been an increased sympathy for its own sectarian wing. But the sectarians themselves have not withstood all change. As one sociologist has written, if a sect is to influence the world to change, "it must itself acquire or accept the characteristics of this world to a degree sufficient to accomplish this goal."[23] It must become "of this world" and in the process it changes its definitions of what is or is not acceptable. Thus, the sectarian institutions themselves are beginning to move in a churchlike direction. Strident opposition to Israel among all but the Satmar hasidim is a thing of the past. Coeducational day schools outside New York are formally disapproved of and tacitly accepted even by the *rashe yeshivot*. Yiddish, which Reb Aharon stressed as a vehicle for maintaining tradition, has been deemphasized ever since his death.

On the other hand, the entire community is more rigid in its halakhic observance. Mixed dancing, once practiced even among Agudath Israel youth, is a thing of the past in most committed Orthodox groups. The formalistic requirements of "feminine modesty," such as covering the hair, are stressed far more than ever

[23]Glenn M. Vernon, *Sociology of Religion* (New York: 1962), p. 167.

before. Observance of the laws of "family purity" and mikveh, which once seemed to be on the verge of total desuetude, is rising.[24] There are 177 public mikvaot in the United States—36 in the Greater New York area alone—and a number of private ones. There is even a Spero Foundation, which assists communities planning to build mikvaot with architectural plans, specifications, and suggestions. But if ritually the community is more observant, even the most sectarian groups are becoming churchlike or communally oriented in the problems they take cognizance of and their means of solution.[25]

Both camps, the modern Orthodox and sectarians, are growing, but the basic sources of their new-found strength are different. For the sectarians it is the young yeshivah graduates now at home in at least the superficial aspects of American culture and committed to tradition and the *rashe yeshivot.* They need not adjust completely to America because they are sufficiently well acquainted with it to be able to reject many of its manifestations. For the modern Orthodox it is the *ba'ale-teshuvah,* the penitents who were raised in nonobservant homes but find in Orthodoxy an emotional or intellectual fulfillment. The first group lacks the intellectual-philosophical perspective to broaden its appeal, but while it may not expand, it will survive. The second lacks halakhic leadership and sanction for much that it reads into Orthodoxy; it lives in a half-pagan, half-halakhic world, and the personal problems of its members are more serious.

A characteristic difference between religious life today and a few years ago, particularly among the modern Orthodox, is that problems have become far more personal. In other words, the personal significance of religion has assumed increased importance over its communal significance. This has fostered increased interest in sectarianism among the ostensibly modern Orthodox, as has the right wing's courage, conviction, and sincerity. Modern Or-

[24]The observance of mikveh, which requires that a married woman go to a lustral bath a week (generally) after menstruation, before which she is prohibited from having marital relations, is the best single measure for determining who is a committed Orthodox Jew. To the uncommitted, it is inconceivable that so personal a matter should be subject to ritual regulation. To the committed, it is inconceivable that an aspect of life so important as marital relations should not be subject to halakhic regulation.

[25]One example can be found in the pages of the *Jewish Press,* an Orthodox weekly whose editoral position is akin to the sectarian yeshivah world but whose pages devote an increasing proportion of space to news and features of general Jewish interest.

thodoxy's appeal is dulled by the lingering suspicion of its adherents that they themselves have suffered a loss for living in a half-pagan world. . . .

Whether the Orthodox community as such, however, can generate sufficient force to meet the intellectual stirrings and emotional quests in the American Jewish world remains to be seen. The non-Orthodox intellectual is not ready yet to embrace Torah and halakhah in their entirety. But two things have changed. First, the old antagonisms to the world of Orthodoxy are gone from many intellectuals furthest removed from Orthodox life. Second, there is a recognition and admiration for Orthodoxy as the only group which today contains within it a strength and will to live that may yet nourish all the Jewish world.

THE CONSERVATIVE MOVEMENT / ACHIEVEMENTS AND PROBLEMS

by MARSHALL SKLARE

INTRODUCTION

In the last half of the nineteenth century it appeared indisputable that the future Judaism of America's Jews would be Reform, inasmuch as this was the religious movement most attuned to the norms of American society. Many congregations composed of Jews from Western and Central European countries abolished traditional practices and evolved into Reform temples; others found themselves split between those who wanted to retain traditional patterns and those who wanted the congregation to join the Reform camp. In instances of congregational division it was generally the Reform element that was more powerful in numbers, status, and ideological conviction. A handful of aristocratic Sephardic congregations refused to join the trend to Reform, but the Sephardic group was not only numerically insignificant but its synagogues had lost their former importance. Furthermore, Sephardic Jews were generally not Orthodox in their personal lives.

There were of course the new congregations founded by East European Jews. While such congregations were Orthodox the established element assumed this to be a temporary phenomenon, believing that once the East Europeans loosened their ties to the old country and became Americanized they would inevitably turn to Reform Judaism. If the transition did not occur in the immigrant generation it would certainly take place in the second.

This prediction has proved incorrect. As we have seen Orthodoxy did not die—indeed a new committed Orthodox group was eventually to appear on the American scene. But the prediction also did not take into account the emergence of Conservative Judaism.

In the first quarter of the twentieth century the Reform elite interpreted the newly developing Conservative movement as a halfway house, apparently necessitated by the unfamiliarity of the East European Jew with Reform thought and practice. From this perspective Conservatism was seen as helpful in assuring the eventual triumph of Reform; it would assist the East European in making the larger transition from Orthodoxy to Reform. The early proponents of Conservatism, on the other hand, maintained that while most East-European-derived Jews would desert Orthodoxy they could never accept the radical break with Jewish thought and practice that Reform involved. They further maintained that since Conservative Judaism sought to integrate the most meaningful and enduring practices of Jewish tradition with the best of American thought and practice, it would become the most significant force in the Jewish community. Nevertheless, the fact that the upper class and the established element were so solidly Reform left even Conservative leaders with lingering doubts about the permanence of their movement. And if Reform was the wave of the future, as it seemed, then possibly they were doing nothing more than preparing recruits for its ranks.

As American Reform gradually shifted from "Classical Reform" to "Neo-Reform" it did indeed attract a significant segment of second- and third-generation East European Jews. But Reform never succeeded in achieving primacy in the Jewish community; it was overtaken by Conservative Judaism after World War II. While some Conservative-trained young people did join Reform congregations, on the whole Conservatism managed the crucially important task of retaining the loyalties of the children of its founding generation. Furthermore, Conservatism made many new recruits from the ranks of uncommitted and residual Orthodox families.

Charles Liebman suggests that the reason for Conservatism's rapid growth was that it was closest to the folk religion of the East European Jew. There is no doubt that Conservatism was very open to the desire for ethnic continuity under the umbrella of religion. However its success may be explained, by the 1960's it was clear that Conservatism had triumphed—numerically it constituted the most *powerful wing of American Judaism. There were even a handful of Jews of Reform lineage who had affiliated with Conservatism, highlighting the inaccuracy of the old supposition that Reform was the only form of Judaism acceptable to the American Jew.*

The Conservative movement proved to be even more successful than its partisans had hoped. Fears about its durability evaporated as hundreds of new suburban synagogues were built after World War II. Many of the largest and most successful of such synagogues were Conservative. Indeed in some cities the new Conservative synagogues were so magnificent in architectural conception and execution, and the buildings of Reform so modest by comparison, that the very structures seemed to convey that the old predictions about the inevitability of Reform were not only unfulfilled but that they were in the process of reversal.

Conservatism, however, has never been able to take full satisfaction in its unexpected rise to primacy. As the following article points out there are members of the Conservative elite who look upon the rise of their movement with mixed feelings. Developments outside of Conservatism as well as the fact that certain problems within the movement have defied solution, have made committed Conservative Jews less satisfied with Conservatism's growth and less certain of its future than its present success would seem to warrant.

M. S.

DURING RECENT YEARS more American Jews have come to consider themselves "Conservative" than either "Orthodox" or "Reform." The trend to Conservatism is particularly evident in cities of substantial Jewish population, especially cities located in the Northeast. For example, a survey conducted in 1965 in Boston found that 44 percent of the Jews of that community thought of themselves as Conservative, some 27 percent thought of themselves as Reform, and 14 percent as Orthodox.[1] In smaller cities in the same geographical area the triumph of Conservatism has been even more overwhelming. Thus a survey conducted in 1963 in Providence, Rhode Island, discovered that as many as 54 percent of the Jews of that community considered themselves Conservative, while only 21 percent thought of themselves as Reform and 20 percent as Orthodox.[2] Furthermore, Conservative strength has also become evident even in the Midwest, which has long been a center of Reform. In 1964 as many as 49 percent of Milwaukee Jews considered themselves Conservative, in contrast to only 24 percent who considered themselves Reform. . . .[3]

The new predominance of Conservatism is still imperfectly reflected in synagogal affiliation, for not every individual who describes himself as Conservative is affiliated with a synagogue. In Boston, for example, some 39 percent of those who describe themselves as Conservative are unaffiliated.[4] The problem of non-affiliation cuts across all groups; there are also unaffiliated Reform and, to a smaller degree, Orthodox Jews. But the presence of so many unaffiliated Conservative Jews is in one sense especially

[1]Morris Axelrod, Floyd J. Fowler, and Arnold Gurin, *A Community Survey for Long Range Planning* (Boston: Combined Jewish Philanthropies of Greater Boston, 1967), p. 119.

[2]Sidney Goldstein and Calvin Goldscheider, *Jewish Americans* (Englewood Cliffs, N.J.: Prentice-Hall, 1968), p. 177.

[3]Albert J. Mayer, *Milwaukee Jewish Population Study* (Milwaukee: Jewish Welfare Fund, 1965), p. 48.

[4]Axelrod *et al., op. cit.*, p. 143.

advantageous to Conservatism—it means that there is a large pool of individuals to draw upon for future expansion.

Conservatism has made good use of its reservoir of potential recruits. Before the late 1960's there was a noticeable increase in the number of Conservative synagogues, as well as a sharp rise in the membership of those Conservative synagogues located in areas of expanding Jewish population. Furthermore, the type of synagogue that the Conservative movement pioneered—the "synagogue center" offering social and recreational activities in addition to the classical functions of prayer and religious study, and which conceives of itself as the central Jewish address in the geographic area it serves—has become predominant on the American Jewish scene. As a consequence, Reform and Orthodoxy have come to look to Conservative models in fashioning their own religious institutions.[5]

The rising influence of Conservatism can be traced, in part, to the suburbanization that has occurred during the past two decades among Jews living in the largest cities. Suburbanization brought with it the problem of the maintenance of Jewish identity, and it was to the synagogue that the new Jewish suburbanite tended to look for identity-maintenance. The result was that the synagogue emerged in the 1950's and 1960's as the crucial institution in Jewish life. And Conservatism exemplified the type of synagogue that was most appealing to the new suburban Jew. . . .

Prior to the 1950's, the emerging strength of Conservative Judaism on the local level was not reflected on the national scene. While the United Synagogue of America—the union of Conservative congregations—had been established as early as 1913, it remained a paper organization for many years. The only group that visualized Conservatism in national terms was the rabbis, organized as the Rabbinical Assembly of America. However, in the past two decades a sharp change has occurred: the laity has transmuted their loyalty to local congregations into attachment to a national movement.

The rapid development of the United Synagogue, which now has a membership of 832 congregations, is an index to the new sense of constituting a movement. During the 1950's and 1960's, the United Synagogue emerged as an important Jewish agency. In contrast to its older status as a paper organization, the United

[5]On the American synagogue see Marshall Sklare, *America's Jews* (New York: Random House, 1971), pp. 126–135.

Synagogue currently maintains some seventeen field offices in addition to its national headquarters. The conventions of the United Synagogue, held every two years at the Concord Hotel, have grown in size to the point where they tax the facilities of what is the largest kosher hotel in the country. The United Synagogue would long have surpassed its Reform counterpart—the Union of American Hebrew Congregations established in 1873—but for the fact that it has been under the control of the Jewish Theological Seminary of America. Fearful of the centrist and left-wing influence of the laity and of many congregational rabbis, seminary officials—all of whom belong to Conservatism's right wing—have discouraged aggressive growth. Their influence over the United Synagogue is symbolized by the fact that the agency makes its national headquarters in the buildings of the Seminary. . . .

In summary, the recent development of Conservative Judaism is characterized by: 1) the emergence of Conservatism as the favored religious self-designation of the American Jew and its consequent achievement of primacy on the American Jewish religious scene; 2) the emergence of Conservative synagogues, particularly in suburban areas in the East, as the leading congregations in their communities; 3) the emergence of national agencies that reflect the strength of Conservatism on the local level; and 4) the emergence of a sense of constituting a movement—a sense of a shared Conservatism on the part of the Conservative laity.

These developments appear to portend a brilliant future for Conservatism. The continued growth of Conservative Judaism seems assured: in the large metropolitan centers there are significant numbers of unaffiliated Jews who identify themselves as "Conservative." All that seems necessary to further augment the primacy of Conservatism is that such individuals be induced to activate a commitment they already hold.

THE PROBLEM OF CONSERVATIVE MORALE

Despite brilliant achievements and excellent prospects for future growth, the morale of the Conservative movement is on the decline.

Seemingly, present-day Conservative leaders are less satisfied with their movement than they have a right to be; they are less sanguine about its future than the facts would appear to indicate. Paradoxically, during the period when the movement was overshadowed by Reform and Orthodoxy, Conservatism's élan was high. But when Conservatism came into its own, morale began to sag.

Doubts about the movement are most frequently expressed by the rabbis. As religious professionals, they have a heightened interest in Conservatism, a special sensitivity to its problems, and a sophisticated set of standards by which to judge its success. The following statement illustrates the doubts felt by some Conservative rabbis:

> During these past decades we have grown, we have prospered, we have become a powerful religious establishment. I am, however, haunted by the fear that somewhere along the way we have become lost; our direction is not clear, and the many promises we made to ourselves and to our people have not been fulfilled. We are in danger of not having anything significant to say to our congregants, to the best of our youth, to all those who are seeking a dynamic adventurous faith that can elicit sacrifice and that can transform lives.[6]

This statement emanates from an esteemed leader of Conservatism, Max Routtenberg. As the rabbi of the Kesher Zion Synagogue in Reading, Pennsylvania, from 1932 to 1948, Routtenberg helped to establish Conservatism in eastern Pennsylvania. After a period during which he served as a leading official of the seminary and Rabbinical Assembly, Rabbi Routtenberg went on to become the spiritual leader of B'nai Sholom of Rockville Center, New York. He was instrumental in developing B'nai Sholom into an important suburban synagogue in the prime area of Long Island. In 1964 Routtenberg was elected to the presidency of the Rabbinical Assembly. He was viewed by his colleagues as a kind of ideal Conservative Jew: he succeeded in combining the scientific methodology he had encountered as a student at the seminary with the approach to learning he had assimilated during his earlier years at a yeshiva. Furthermore, Routtenberg was a man of the world—he sought in his person to combine Jewish and western culture.

[6]Max J. Routtenberg in R.A. [Rabbinical Assembly of America], *Proceedings*, XXIX (1965), 23.

However, in his presidential address to the Rabbinical Assembly from which we have quoted, Rabbi Routtenberg spoke in accents far different from those that characterize the man of success.

Why this disparity between achievement and satisfaction? Why the decline in morale among Conservative leaders? The proper starting point for an analysis of these questions is the world of Orthodoxy. More specifically, it is the attitude of Conservatism toward Orthodoxy.

The founders of Conservatism believed that Orthodoxy was fated to disappear. While some Orthodox Jews might persist, Conservatism held that such individuals would be relatively few in number and insignificant in social status. The founders of Conservatism did not relish the passing of Orthodoxy: they had strong sentimental ties with their Orthodox childhood, they had friends and relatives who had remained Orthodox, and they admired Orthodoxy's persistence in the face of seemingly overwhelming odds. However, while conceding Orthodoxy's historic contribution, they were convinced that it had run its course. As Rabbi Routtenberg put it:

> I think back to the period when my fellow students and I, at the yeshivah, decided to make the break and become Conservative rabbis . . . We were breaking with our past, in some cases with our families who had deep roots in Orthodoxy. We broke with beloved teachers who felt betrayed when we left the yeshivah. It was a great wrench . . . but we had to make it. . . . We loved the Jewish people and its heritage, and as we saw both threatened we set out to save them. We saw the future of Judaism in the Conservative movement.[7]

Orthodoxy, then, was viewed as a kind of *moshav z'kenim*—a home for the aged, and for those old in spirit. Accordingly, Conservatism was destined to supplant Orthodoxy, Furthermore, Conservatism was seen as a contemporary expression of what was most vital and creative in the Orthodoxy of old—that is, in the Orthodoxy of the pre-modern era:

> In spite of the claims made in other quarters it is we [Conservative Jews] who are the authentic Jews of rabbinic Judaism. . . . Many of those who attack our movement as "deviationist"—a term totally repugnant to the authentic Jewish tradition—and who demand

[7] *Ibid.*

> unswerving adherence to the written letter of the Law are actually the Sadducees of the twentieth century. Had they lived in the days of Hillel, Rabbi Johanan ben Zakkai, Rabbi Akiba, Rabbi Meir, or Rabbi Judah Hanasi, they would have condemned every creative contribution that the Sages made to the living Judaism of their age.[8]

In a sense, then, Conservatism is conceived by its elite as twentieth-century Orthodoxy. Or, to put it another way, if Orthodoxy had retained the ability to change it would have evolved into Conservatism. . . .

In recent years it has become clear that Conservatism was incorrect in its diagnosis of Orthodoxy and especially in its prognosis of Orthodoxy's future. Unaccountably, Orthodoxy has refused to assume the role of invalid. Rather, it has transformed itself into a growing force in American Jewish life. It has reasserted its claim of being *the* authentic interpretation of Judaism.

Having achieved a new sense of élan, Orthodoxy has proceeded to implement a policy of strict non-cooperation with Conservatism. Orthodox policy has called for the rejection of all changes proposed by Conservatism—even changes that might be acceptable if they emanated from a different quarter. Furthermore, the tolerance of individual Orthodox rabbis toward Conservatism, characteristic of the 1920's and 1930's, has become only a dimming Conservative memory, especially on the Eastern seaboard. . . . Today's Orthodox leaders proceed on the assumption that Conservatism is a hollow shell—that its seemingly strong synagogues are peopled by weak Jews who are fated to assimilate. Only Orthodoxy will have the tenacity to survive the temptations of the open society.

The Orthodox offensive against Conservatism has been waged on two fronts simultaneously: Israel and the United States. Orthodox leaders in the United States have stimulated their colleagues in Israel to attack Conservatism. Inasmuch as Orthodox leaders in Israel are in firm control of their country's religious establishment, have considerable political leverage, and are not inhibited by a tradition of Church-State separation, they have been able to implement anti-Conservative policies inconceivable in the United States. Accordingly, Conservative rabbis have been disqualified from performing any rabbinic functions in Israel. The few Conservative institutions that have managed to gain a foothold in Israel are barely tolerated. The fugitive position occupied by

[8]Robert Gordis in R.A., *Proceedings*, XXIX (1965), 92–93.

Conservatism in Israel has been a particularly bitter blow for the American movement. To Conservative leaders it appears that, instead of being rewarded for its long history of support for the Zionist cause, Conservatism is being penalized. . . .

In summary, during the 1950's and 1960's the yeshivot multiplied in number, size, and fundamentalism; the Orthodox rabbis became ever more intransigent; the influence exercised by Orthodoxy in Israel became clearer; the Orthodox synagogues established themselves in upper-class and upper-middle-class areas. Even hasidism was transformed from an antediluvian curiosity into a movement which, it was said, had much to teach modern man. The net result was that the Conservative understanding of the American Jewish present, together with the Conservative expectation of the American Jewish future, became confounded. The ground was prepared for the development of a kind of Conservative anomie. The problem was particularly aggravated in the case of one segment of the Conservative elite—the rabbis. Many rabbis had a deep sympathy with Jewish traditionalism. Thus on the one hand they admired and identified with the Orthodox advance, but on the other hand, they were filled with dismay and hostility toward this totally unexpected development.

THE CRISIS IN CONSERVATIVE OBSERVANCE

While the renewal of Orthodoxy has been an important cause of the decline in Conservative morale, developments internal to the Conservative movement have also been an important influence. Conservatism is a religious movement. As such, it is subject to evaluation from the vantage point of suprasocial achievement. Thus, Conservative Jews may measure the progress of their movement in terms of its success in bringing man closer to God, or, as Rabbi Routtenberg phrases it, by its ability to "transform lives." Conservative Jews, if they are strong religionists, not only have this option but are impelled to embrace it. That is, they must give preference to suprasocial achievement and disregard, or even disvalue, such social achievements as monumental synagogue buildings and prosperous congregations.

All religious traditions have several yardsticks to measure suprasocial achievement, but each tends to stress a particular yardstick. The one that predominates in Judaism is that of the performance of the *mitzvot maasiyot,* the commandments of the Jewish sacred system. True to this thrust, Conservatism uses a ritualistic yardstick in gauging its effectiveness. While at times it has been attracted to the moralistic-ethical yardstick in measuring religious growth, it has nevertheless remained close to the sacramental approach of rabbinic Judaism.[9]

Conservative Judaism believes that it possesses a unique approach to the mitzvot, and especially to the problem of maintaining their observance. Conservatism holds that it is possible to advocate change in halakhah (Jewish law) and simultaneously to be loyal to halakhah. Change is seen as essential. From the Conservative standpoint, the maintenance of observance has been immensely complicated, if not rendered impossible, by what is regarded as Orthodoxy's ossification. While the modern Jew must be responsive to the requirements of halakhah, such loyalty cannot reasonably be expected unless halakhah is responsive to the needs of the modern Jew. Thus, in the Conservative view, Orthodox authorities who refuse to sanction change, much less to stimulate it, bear part of the responsibility for the lamentable decline of observance. As Rabbi Ralph Simon put it in a presidential address to the Rabbinical Assembly: "We have felt that Reform Judaism abandoned halakhah while Orthodoxy permitted halakhah to abandon us."[10]

As Conservatism sees it, certain mitzvot are outmoded or even offensive to the modern spirit. In the interest of promoting observance, as well as out of a desire for intellectual honesty, such mitzvot should be declared null and void. Furthermore, emphasis must be placed on the promotion of the essential requirements of the sacred system. Minutiae of the Jewish code can safely be disregarded. Mitzvot that are "fences around the Torah" rather than central to the Torah itself may be allowed to fall into disuse. Change can be effected by proper interpretation of the halakhic system, and, where necessary, by legislation.

The essence of the Conservative position, then, is liberaliza-

[9]On the problem such sacramentalism creates for the modern Jew, see Marshall Sklare and Joseph Greenblum, *Jewish Identity on the Suburban Frontier* (New York: Basic Books, 1967), pp. 45–48.

[10]R.A., *Proceedings,* XXXII (1968), 160.

tion. While Conservatism believes that liberalization is its own justification, it also holds that liberalization makes possible the promotion of observance. As religious authorities come to differentiate between major and minor—between what is required and what is elective, between what is in keeping with the modern temper and what is offensive to it, between what can be reinterpreted in the light of new needs and what is beyond rescue—the ground for a renewal of observance of the mitzvot is prepared. In addition to liberalization, the Conservative platform has two additional planks. One is "innovation," the development of new observances or procedures that are required when there is a need to substitute for, modify, or extend the traditional mitzvot. The other is "beautification," the requirement that the mitzvot be practiced in as esthetic a manner as possible—"the Jewish home beautiful." In sum, the Conservative position is that liberalization—in combination with innovation and beautification—will succeed in averting the evil decree of non-observance. . . .

The crucial aspect of the Conservative position on observance is . . . its success in promoting religious growth among the Conservative laity, and specifically in advancing their observance of the mitzvot. Judged from this vantage point, Conservatism has been an abysmal failure: there has been a steady erosion of observance among Conservative Jews. And despite a strong desire to encourage observance, Conservatism has not succeeded in arresting the decline in observance among its adherents, much less in increasing their level of conformity to the Jewish sacred system. The belief among Conservative leaders that the movement's approach to halakhah had the power to maintain observance, as well as to inspire its renewal, has proved illusory. . . .

Conservatism's defeat on the ritual front can be demonstrated in almost every area of Jewish observance. Sabbath observance is a case in point. After World War II there was a good deal of optimism in Conservatism with respect to Sabbath observance. The influences that seemed to portend a renewal included the rising prosperity of Conservative Jews and the increased popularity of the five-day workweek. The new life style of the suburban Jew, which stressed the building of a meaningful pattern of identity for one's children, constituted an additional factor. And the need for surcease from the increasingly hectic pace of life appeared to offer new justification for Judaism's stress on the sanctity of Sabbath rest.

Encouraged by these prospects, the Conservative rabbis

pushed for liberalization. In 1950 the Law Committee of the Rabbinical Assembly proceeded to make a daring innovation. On a split decision it voted to permit travel on the Sabbath—travel specifically for the purpose of attending services. It also voted to permit the use of electricity on the Sabbath.

What these decisions were saying was that the traditional concept of prohibited work was outmoded and counterproductive. Thus, driving an automobile was not intrinsically bad, and if the machine was employed to transport the individual from his home in the sprawl of suburbia to the synagogue on the Sabbath, it was a positive good. In any case the emphasis should be not on prohibitions as much as on positive acts that would promote the holiness of the seventh day: attending services, lighting candles, making *Kiddush,* reciting the blessing over bread, and serving special Sabbath meals. Furthermore, such an emphasis would inevitably lead the congregant to refrain from following his accustomed routine on the Sabbath. Thus the emphasis on positive acts constituted a more profitable approach to building Sabbath observance than would harping on a detailed list of prohibited activities.

In addition to the technique of liberalization, the Conservative approach to building Sabbath observance stressed the role of beautification. Thus the congregational gift shops conducted by the sisterhoods were stimulated to promote the sale of candlesticks, Kiddush cups, hallah covers, hallah knives, Sabbath napkins, and other such items. Finally, innovation was utilized. Innovation was in fact a long-standing Conservative tradition in respect to Sabbath observance—late Friday evening services had been one of the movement's most significant innovations.

The available evidence suggests that the Conservative strategy of liberalization, innovation, and beautification has been a failure; it underlies the fact that the majority of Conservative Jews do not follow even the most basic Sabbath observances. To cite the example of Conservative-dominated Providence, Rhode Island, only 12 percent of those who designate themselves as "Conservative" attend services once a week or more. And what is even more serious, attendance at Sabbath worship declines with each generation: while some 21 percent of the first generation attend, only 2 percent of the third do so.[11] The lighting of Sabbath candles

[11]Goldstein and Goldscheider, *op. cit.*, p. 194.

fares somewhat better, in part because the ritual is a female obligation. But despite the fact that lighting the candles is required of the Jewish woman, it is observed in only 40 percent of Conservative households. And while the ritual is observed in 52 percent of first-generation households, it is followed in only 32 percent of third-generation households.[12]

Kashrut is another area of observance that constitutes a problem for Conservative Jews. Only 37 percent of Conservative households in Providence buy kosher meat. Furthermore, in only 27 percent of the households are separate dishes utilized. And true to the pattern we have already encountered, observance declines in each generation: while 41 percent of the first generation maintain two sets of dishes, only 20 percent of the third generation do so. . . .[13]

For understandable reasons, the Conservative elite have avoided publicizing the painful evidence contained in congregational and communal surveys. Aware of how far its followers deviate from Conservative norms, the movement has felt in recent years that it can do little more than provide a source of information and inspiration for those who might somehow find their way back to the mitzvot.[14] While a "National Sabbath Observance Effort" was sponsored by the United Synagogue in the early 1950's when there was hope of a renewal of observance, the campaign has not been repeated.

In recent years it has become increasingly clear that the problem of observance constitutes a permanent crisis in Conservatism—that the religious derelictions of Conservative Jewry are much more than a temporary condition traceable to the trauma of

[12] *Ibid.*, p. 203. See Axelrod *et al.*, *op. cit.*, p. 131, for the somewhat higher figures in Boston.

[13] Second-generation Conservative Jews in Providence locate themselves between the relatively observant first generation and the highly unobservant third generation. However, the second generation tends to be positioned closer to the third generation than to the first.

[14] See, for example, the following publications of Conservatism's Burning Bush Press: Samuel H. Dresner, *The Jewish Dietary Laws*, and *The Sabbath* by the same author. Rabbi Dresner is singular in that he is a veteran Conservative leader of Reform background—he came to the seminary from Hebrew Union College, the Reform rabbinical school. Since he embraced the mitzvot by an act of will rather than by virtue of family inheritance, Dresner has been especially well qualified to provide information and inspiration to the exceptional individual in Conservatism who is interested in returning to the mitzvot.

removal from the closed society of the *shtetl* to the open society of the American metropolis. The elite are losing faith in their belief that through liberalization, innovation, and beautification the mass of Conservative Jews can be persuaded to return to the observance of the mitzvot. In lieu of a solution to the crisis, the movement has sought to insure the observance of the mitzvot in public: in the synagogue, at the Jewish Theological Seminary, at the Ramah camps, and during the tours and pilgrimages of the United Synagogue Youth. Although such conformity is gratifying to the elite—particularly to the older men who were reared in Orthodoxy and who have a strong need to justify their defection—it does not serve to erase the suspicion that the movement has been a failure. And Conservatism's failure in the area of the suprasocial is heightened by its brilliant achievements in the social arena: its success in building synagogues, in promoting organizational loyalty, and in achieving primacy on the American Jewish religious scene. . . .

THE NEXT CONSERVATIVE GENERATION

Although Conservative Judaism was not a creation of the young, its rise in the 1920–1950 era was closely connected with its appeal to young marrieds who were in the process of establishing independent households and developing a pattern of Jewish living that would be distinctive to their generation. Younger Jews who wished to retain continuity with their past and at the same time integrate with American middle-class culture found Conservative Judaism to be the perfect solution to their dilemma. Conservatism was traditional yet flexible, Jewish yet American. Its religious services were based on the Hebrew liturgy but also included prayers in English. Its rabbis appeared as authentic representatives of an age-old tradition yet were accepting of the culture of the larger environment. Conservatism stood for religious observance without rejecting the less observant.

The élan of Conservative Judaism during the period of its rise was in no small measure due to the fact that the elite of the movement felt their formula was precisely the one acceptable to younger age-groups in the Jewish population—groups whose connection with traditional Jewish culture was less firm than their own. In 1949 a leading Conservative layman in the Midwest, Julian Freeman, neatly summarized the appeal of Conservatism when he commented: "A generation ago the young architect, the young engineer, the young doctor, the young lawyer, the young businessman saw in Conservative Judaism a chance for religious self-expression integrated with the best of thinking in the world at large."[15]

The present-day Conservative elite, however, is no longer so confident that its formula will be attractive to the younger generation. There are two aspects to this crisis of confidence. One is the problem of Jewish continuity—the problem of whether the battle against assimilation can be won. This question, most commonly perceived in terms of the threat of intermarriage, began to preoccupy the Jewish community in the 1960's. . . .[16] It seemed to many that the very physical survival of the group was at stake. The threat inevitably spilled over into feelings about the prospects for Conservatism: if group continuity was in doubt, how much less was there a future for Conservative Judaism?

In addition to pessimism about whether the battle against intermarriage could be won, Conservatism in recent years has lost its older confidence of being in possession of a formula that can win the support of younger Jews. Despite interest in the shtetl and the East European milieu, many younger Jews—including those reared in Conservative congregations—have little connection with the Jewish culture of the immediate past. Inasmuch as Conservatism assumes some continuity with the East European past and some familiarity with Jewish culture generally, it has been deeply affected by such Jewish deculturation. If the mission of Conservatism has been to show how it was possible to practice selected aspects of Jewish culture in an American milieu, the result of Jewish deculturation has been that the movement no longer has its older foundation of Jewish culture on which to build its synagogual loyalties. . . .

Conservatism labors under the further doubt that it can prevail

[15]See *supra*, p. 90.

[16]On the rate of intermarriage and the Jewish response, see Sklare, *America's Jews*, *op. cit.*, pp. 180–206.

in its battle to win the loyalty of young people. The reason for Conservative pessimism resides in the disjunction between its cultural system and that of younger American Jews. Many Conservative young people not only lack Jewish culture, but they have been influenced by youth culture—some are card-carrying members of the Woodstock Nation, others are fellow travelers, and still others have inchoate sympathies with the counterculture. While the problem of enlisting the loyalty of such young people is encountered by all Jewish religious movements, the issue is a particularly knotty one for Conservatism, with its stress on cultural reconciliation and the blending of Jewish and general culture. Despite the fact that the so-called *havurot* (communal fellowships) originated among Conservative young people, Conservatism has not been notably successful in enlisting the loyalties of those who are part of the youth culture, who have little connection with East European culture, or who are antagonistic to the type of American culture on which the movement is based. . . .

Sensitive leaders in Conservatism are aware of how deeply the movement is rooted in an older American middle-class culture which is currently out of favor with a significant segment of Conservative youth. The problem was presented to the Rabbinical Assembly by Rabbi Edward Gershfield in an address which celebrated the organization's seventieth anniversary. According to Gershfield:

> Our services of readings in fine English, correct musical renditions by professional cantors and choirs, and decorous and dignified rabbis in elegant gowns arouse disdain and contempt in our young people. They want excitement and noise, improvisation and emotion, creativity and sensitivity, informality and spontaneity. On the other hand, they feel guilty about the spending of large sums of money for synagogue buildings rather than for social services (generally for non-Jews). And they are "turned off" by the very beauty and decorum which we have worked so hard to achieve.
>
> Of course, the youth do not wish to go into the reasons why these aspects of our life have been created. They are impatient with our explanations that most people are not dynamic and creative, and look to religious leaders for directions and instructions; that we who have managed to survive the rigors of youth appreciate regularity and stability in life, that we honestly want to endow our heritage with dignity and beauty, and that a congregation of a thousand persons cannot have a prayer service in a coffeehouse to the accompaniment

> of a guitar . . . we seem to be doomed to having to watch as our youth relive the same self-destructive impulses that we have seen long ago, and have thought could not happen again. Our appeals to reason and history . . . go right past them and we are for the most part helpless.[17]

. . . in summary, the immediate reasons for the drop in Conservative morale at the very zenith of Conservative influence include the emergence of Orthodoxy, the problem of Conservative observance, and the widespread alienation among Conservative young people from the American culture to which their movement has been strongly attached. But on a deeper level the Conservative crisis—if that be the word—represents a questioning of whether the Jewish people and its "chain of tradition" can long endure on the American continent. Since Conservatism's future is predicated upon such survival, its fears are understandable. *Yisrael v'oraitha had hu*: the Jewish people and its tradition are indissolubly linked. There cannot be an authentic Jewish people without the continuity of Jewish tradition, even as there cannot be meaningful continuity of Jewish tradition without the maintenance of the integrity of the Jewish group. It is to this momentous issue that the Conservative movement, in its present mature phase, has been moved to address itself.

[17]R.A., *Proceedings*, XXXIV (1970), 90–91.

REFORM IS A VERB

by LEONARD J. FEIN, ROBERT CHIN, JACK DAUBER,
BERNARD REISMAN, and HERZL SPIRO

INTRODUCTION

HISTORIANS have done considerable research into American Reform Judaism. The accessibility of Reform records and archives, the interest in Reform Judaism by students of American Jewish history, and the intellectual curiosity of members of the Reform elite have resulted in the accumulation of considerable knowledge about the origin and development of this movement.

Social scientists have come to the study of Reform Judaism independently of historians. Furthermore, their findings have centered on present-day Reform rather than on its historical development. Their work has also taken on a different emphasis from that of the historians, tending to highlight not the accomplishments of Reform but the relative poverty of "Jewishness" among present-day Reform Jews. Thus in the various community surveys conducted from the 1930's to the present, Reform Jews appear as highly secular. They practice very few Jewish rituals in the home and, except for a small group, their attendance at religious services is minimal. Furthermore, the more pious element in the movement does not appear to have been motivated by its Reform affiliation but by the fact of having been reared by parents who were uncommitted or residual Orthodox Jews.

Ritual deviance has been accompanied by attitudinal deviance: most social science research indicates that Reform Jews have a weaker Jewish identity than Orthodox or Conservative Jews. Part of this difference can be accounted for by the fact that Reform Jews generally exceed Conservative and Orthodox Jews in class level, secular education, and in the number of generations their families have been in the United States. There is also the fact that the designation "Reform" has functioned as a kind of catchall category. Thus in most studies "Reform" includes unaffiliated Jews who so designate themselves in response to a question such as: "Would you describe yourself as Orthodox, Conservative, Reform, or none of these?" Apparently a fair percentage of unaffiliated Jews of weak Jewish identity choose the rubric "Reform" because it corresponds more closely to their image of themselves than does "Conservative" or "Orthodox," or because they prefer to associate themselves with something positive—"none of these" suggests a lack of commitment.

In evaluating the findings of social scientists it is well to remember that there are two divergent interpretations of Reform. Both have been made in respect to Reform in Germany, where the movement originated, as well as in respect to Reform in America, where the movement grew much more rapidly than it did in European countries. The first interpretation is that Reform constitutes an effort to break with one's Jewish identity; since a sharp separation would threaten personality integration the individual looks for a way of remaining Jewish until such time as he (or his children) is ready to assimilate. According to this interpretation, Reform is a way of remaining Jewish for people who prefer to assimilate; its latent function is that of preparing the individual to separate himself from the Jewish community.

The second interpretation of Reform is that it serves precisely the opposite function—it constitutes a movement serving the individual who wants to remain Jewish but who feels that his Jewish identity is threatened. No longer able to conform to traditional patterns, such an individual becomes attracted to Reform because it offers him the possibility of remaining Jewish on terms which take into account his life situation, his extensive acculturation, and the pressures which he experiences living in a Gentile world.

It is apparent that the motivation of most present-day Reform Jews conforms more closely to the second interpretation than to the first. Most Jews who adhere to Reform do so because they wish to remain within the Jewish community—their Reform affiliation represents a desire to affiliate with the Jewish community rather than a desire to depart from it. Nevertheless, the identity pattern common to many Reform Jews suggests the possibility that, while they may wish to avoid assimilation, they may not prevail in their desire to remain Jewish. The social scientist must entertain the possibility that the Jewish identity of the Reform Jew, and particularly the identity of his children, is not sufficiently strong to resist further secularization or acculturation—for any additional secularization and acculturation would inevitably end in assimilation.

The communal studies sponsored by Jewish federations contain extensive data on Reform Jews. However, these studies are demographic in orientation. The problem of the Jewish identity of the Reform Jew was an important aspect of the Lakeville Study and is analyzed in Marshall Sklare and Joseph Greenblum: Jewish Identity on the Suburban Frontier: A Study of Group Survival in the Open Society. *Since Lakeville was heavily Reform—the first synagogue established in the community was Reform, and of the four synagogues subsequently founded, three were Reform and the fourth was Conservative—the identity of the Reform group necessarily constituted an important focus of the research.*

The Lakeville findings indicated a sharp contrast between the strong attachment to Jewish clique groups and the much weaker attachment to Jewish religious observance and to synagogue attendance. While most Lakeville Jews disapproved of intermarriage and were fearful that intermarriage might occur in their own families, they were prepared to adjust (as they put it) to "reality" should they be confronted with a son or daughter who insisted upon intermarrying. Furthermore, it became clear that for most Lakeville Jews the essential qualifications for being a "good Jew" were Jewish self-acceptance, moral excellence, good citizenship, and a kind of general acquaintance with the essentials of Judaism. Only a minority of Lakeville Jews viewed marrying within the Jewish group, contributing to Jewish philanthropies, or attending services on the High Holidays as essential to being a good Jew.

The concern of both Reform officials and lay leadership about the long-range viability of Reform resulted in the initiation of a research program under the auspices of the movement. One study, directed by Theodore I. Lenn, was published under the title Rabbi and Synagogue in Reform Judaism *(New York: Central Conference* of American Rabbis, 1972). A second study, named "The Pilot Project for Synagogue Change," was directed by Leonard J. Fein. It represented a collaboration among a political scientist, a psychologist specializing in group dynamics who was connected with a human relations center, an academician trained as a social worker, a group worker in the Jewish community-center field, and a psychiatrist specializing in the field of community mental health, and it resulted in Reform is a Verb: Notes on Reform and Reforming Jews (New York: Union of American Hebrew Congregations, 1972).

Both studies utilized self-administered questionnaires, as well as other techniques. Samples were drawn from a selected group of Reform temples. Respondents did not represent a cross-section of affiliated Reform Jews, however; they tended to be more highly committed to the Reform movement than other temple members and presumably their Jewish identity was stronger than is the norm among Reform Jews.

While the two studies proceeded independently their findings are similar in many respects. Observance of basic home rituals is far from universal, attendance at services is infrequent, a significant minority is not upset at the prospect of intermarriage, and the only two actions which a majority of adults endorse as being essential to being a good Jew are "Accept being a Jew and not try to hide it," and "Lead an ethical and moral life." Further, both studies came to the conclusion that the Jewish commitment of Reform youth is far less than that of Reform adults. Finally, it was found that even the committed Reform Jew lacks deep attachment to his temple. Instead of seeing his temple as an extension of himself he sees it as outside of himself—as a purveyor of services to be utilized when required. The committed Reform Jew leads his social life quite independently of his temple.

Since the Lenn study was commissioned by the Central Conference of American Rabbis, it not only includes material on the practices and attitudes of the Reform laity but devotes considerable attention to the state of the Reform rabbinate. The study discovered a relatively high level of rabbinical discontent—most rabbis dislike their seminary training, only 53 percent would choose the rabbinate if they had it to do over again, and 64 percent feel that their congregation is "undergoing a crisis of existence and commitment." The study concluded that if present trends continue an increasing number of rabbis will question the basic religious tenets of Reform Judaism.

A summary of the second project—"The Pilot Project for Synagogue Change"—is reprinted below. In addition to reporting on questionnaire findings the summary includes the results of a series of workshops utilizing an experiential and group-dynamics approach. The summary also includes an extensive section devoted to recommendations made to the sponsoring agency.

While the Synagogue Change team does not present the assumptions on which their recommendations are based, it is clear that they believe that Reform Judaism, as a belief-system, has come to a dead end. They proceed on the assumption that Reform's religious message not only lacks the power to attract the unaffiliated but that it is incapable of transforming the lives of its leaders and devoted followers. Thus they recommend that the movement look elsewhere for its salvation. Rather than calling for the adoption of a new belief-system, they suggest that the movement seek to serve the need for community among its adherents.

One irony of this recommendation is that Reform has been strongly influenced by the cathedral model—that is, by the concept of the large impersonal religious institution of imposing architecture, a structure in which diverse individuals assemble at periodic intervals to discharge their religious obligations. It might be assumed that given their diagnosis the Synagogue Change team would call for the destruction of Reform temples and the return to the old-style synagogue housing a small group of worshipers who know each other intimately and who are drawn together by a common ideological commitment if not by common occupation or place of origin. However, the Synagogue Change team calls neither for the elimination of the imposing "cathedral synagogues" erected decades ago or for the destruction of the more recently erected sprawling suburban-synagogues surrounded by acres of parking space.

The Synagogue Change team maintains that a feeling of community can be created in giant institutions and suggests, furthermore, that large size can be an advantage—since the congregants are so varied, only a large synagogue can offer the opportunity to meet others like oneself. The temple can facilitate the identification of peers and the formation of friendship groups—or what the sociologist would call cliques—through an experiential-workshop approach, the team maintains. This process would be guided by professionals skilled in the techniques of group-dynamics and capable of leading the group in exploring the *resources of the Jewish tradition, especially as these relate to the problem of overcoming alienation and leading a more satisfying life.*

Looked at from the perspectives developed in earlier readings in this volume, the approach of the Synagogue Change team is based upon the following premises: 1) the informal Jewish community is composed of a clique network which constitutes the basic foundation on which the institutional structure in the Jewish community rests; 2) the synagogue lacks vitality because it is insufficiently coordinated with this network; and 3) the synagogue can be revitalized if it can move its members away from their present cliques and integrate them into new cliques which are synagogue-based and directed.

The report of the Synagogue Change team is a significant example of a new type of policy research in the Jewish community, and the reception accorded to it is itself of interest. The report was received with enthusiasm by the sponsoring body—the Long Range Planning Committee of the Union of American Hebrew Congregations—which immediately sought approval to begin implementation of the report's recommendations. Even those critical of the report did not charge the research team with a lack of faith in the message of Reform Judaism but merely stressed the subjective nature of the team's recommendations and questioned the efficacy of the workshop strategy.

When Isaac Mayer Wise (1819–1900), the organizer of Reform in the United States, established the Union of American Hebrew Congregations in 1873, he was confident that Reform would become the Judaism of all American Jews. The truths which Reform taught, he believed, were irrefutable. A century later Wise's successors are unsure of the viability of their movement and even of its mission. Lacking his complete faith in the superiority of Reform they seem prepared to recommend a course of action which the founder would have considered at best indicative of a disbelief in Divine mercy and justice, at worst as heretical. In Wise's view man's greatest need was not for community but to be brought closer to Divine truth. Truth could only be discovered in encounter with God and in his holy Torah; it would never be discovered in encounter with people.

M. S.

PART I of this report ("The Actual Jew: A Research Report on Reform Jews and Their Temples") is based on the findings of a sample survey. Questionnaires were mailed to a randomly selected sample of the membership of twelve temples across the country as well as to college student "alumni" of those temples and to students in their confirmation classes. The overall response rate was a bit over 50 percent, providing a total of 1,643 completed questionnaires. . . . The adult respondents represent accurately the views of the more involved and identified half of the membership of Reform temples in metropolitan areas outside the South; the confirmation class sample is accurately representative of the total population of confirmation class students who are enrolled and actually attend class; the college sample, in all probability, is somewhat more positively biased than the other two groups. . . .

. . . in respect to the statistical profile of the respondents the single most striking finding is the extraordinary level of educational attainment among the adult respondents, 60 percent of whom have at least four years of college (compared to 11 percent of the total American adult population). On the basis of comparisons with other studies, the report argues that this high level of educational attainment is not unique to the sample but likely reflects the high educational level of Reform Jews in general.

The study also finds that only 34 percent of the adult respondents were raised in Reform households, that a majority have only a minimal Jewish education (44 percent report Sunday school only and 17 percent report no formal Jewish education at all), and, that while a majority are at least third-generation Americans, those who are second generation are overwhelmingly of East European (rather than Central European) origin.

[In respect to] the beliefs and practices of Reform Jews . . . the major finding is that there is enormous variety in both behavior and in belief, both among temples and within temples. While the large majority report that they take part in a Passover seder and light candles on Chanukah, 62 percent report having a mezuzah on their door (the high is 80 percent in one temple, the low 40 percent in another); 50 percent light Sabbath candles (the range among the temples is from a high of 68 percent to a low of 38 percent); 50 percent read some Jewish publication other than their temple bulletin (the range is from 71 percent to 31 percent); over a third belong to no Jewish organization other than their temple; 10 percent have Christmas trees in their homes (the range here is from 29 percent to 1 percent); 31 percent attend religious services only on the High Holy Days, while, at the other extreme, only 7 percent report weekly attendance and another 17 percent report attending "a few times a month."

Diversity of response increases as we move from the area of behavior to the area of belief. A large number of questions deal with the area of belief. . . . The most intriguing responses are to a set of questions dealing with the qualities of a "good Jew." These answers permit us to compare our respondents to respondents in earlier studies . . . and especially to the sample reported by Sklare and Greenblum in *Jewish Identity on the Suburban Frontier*. Compared to the earlier sample, we find a significant attrition in support of general humanistic, or liberal, positions, and, save for one major exception, no concomitant increase in support for specifically Jewish positions. The major exception is the dramatic increase in the centrality of the State of Israel. . . . The evidence does not support the notion that Jews are involved in a significant backlash on social issues; rather, it suggests an increase in confusion, a disillusionment with traditional liberal precepts.

Further, there is a substantial gap between old and young on every item of specifically Jewish interest. Thus, for example, while 32 percent of the adult respondents hold that it is essential, in order to be a good Jew, that one contribute to Jewish philanthropies, only 4 percent of the young respondents agree; while 75 percent of the adults hold it essential or, at least, desirable that one marry within the Jewish faith, only 43 percent of the youth agree.

The overall conclusion of the report concerning the data on these questions is that there is "a general uncertainty regarding the 'requirements,' or even the desiderata, of Judaism, an uncertainty that is quite evident among adults and still more striking—substantially more striking—among youth. . . ."

We find also that there is no apparent segregation of Jewish belief into "religious" and "cultural" components. Those respondents who displayed a relatively high interest in, and commitment to, Judaism tended to do so across the board rather than selecting out one or another of the major "approaches" to Judaism for endorsement. In this, as in other ways, the evidence supports the conclusion that erstwhile points of significant difference between Reform Jews and other American Jews are not now significant. . . .

The chapter on beliefs and practices also includes a report of the answers to two hypothetical questions—one dealing with the distribution of the respondent's charitable dollar, the other with his preferences among several summer camps to which he might send his child. The first shows a distinct preference among adults for Jewish charities and especially the UJA and the respondent's temple. Among young people, there is a dramatic increase in support for political, as distinguished from welfare, causes, although they, too, accord a major allocation to the UJA. . . . As to summer camps, all respondents indicate a clear preference for a cosmopolitan, intercultural camp setting or, as a second choice, a recreational camp, as distinguished from camps with a distinctive substantive Jewish orientation.

The chapter closes with the observation that the one area of overwhelming consensus among all respondents concerns the possibility of anti-Semitism in America. Respondents were asked whether they agreed that "anti-Semitism will never be a major problem for American Jews." Only 7 percent of the respondents (in both the youth and adult populations) agreed with the statement. Given the wording of the statement, disagreement does not necessarily reflect a lively anxiety concerning the possible imminence of serious anti-Semitism in this country. It does, however, suggest that awareness of the possibility of anti-Semitism remains a factor, perhaps an important factor, in shaping the Jewish understanding. . . .

With respect to intermarriage, the study reports a major gap between the generations. While a substantial minority of adults do not appear particularly concerned with intermarriage as a "problem," most express both ideological and personal concern. Young people are much less concerned ideologically. But, although the young appear, in the main, to hold that intermarriage is not an ideological problem (e.g., 61 percent do not agree that "intermarriage is bad for the Jewish people"), the large majority report that the religion of a prospective mate would be a matter of important personal concern. One-third of the young would not marry a non-Jew under any circumstances, or unless the non-Jew were to convert, and another 54 percent would consider such a marriage only if they were certain they themselves could remain Jewish. The report suggests that the apparent discrepancy between ideology and (prospective) behavior is an important area for concern and for educational investment.

With respect to Israel, the report finds that more adult respondents attach importance to the relationships between American Jews and Israel than to a number of other "problem" areas, such as Jewish education, intermarriage, or "theological confusion." Indeed, only the "alienation of Jewish youth," among the items in the survey, was regarded as more important by adult respondents. And among young people, relationships with Israel were deemed more important than any other single item.

Over four-fifths of adults and two-thirds of young people believe that in order to be a "good" Jew it is either essential or desirable that one support Israel. This is the single most heavily endorsed item of specifically Jewish content in the entire survey (except for the importance of "accepting one's Jewishness"). At the same time, endorsement of Zionism is much less common. The indication is that non-ideological support for Israel is at the very center of the Jewish understanding of contemporary Reform Jews, and that this represents a major shift over time, a point confirmed by comparison of the data to those reported in earlier studies.

Several series of questions were devoted to the views of respondents concerning their temples. The general finding is that the temple is not, for most of its members, an object of important emotional investment. The three major reasons people say they joined a particular temple are the quality of its rabbi, their belief in Reform ideology, and the quality of the religious school. A very striking finding here is that friendship patterns do not appear to play a leading part in the determination of temple membership. Indeed, 60 percent of all adult respondents report that they have few, if any, close friends among the members of their temple. It appears that the temple is perceived chiefly as the site of certain desired services, rather than as the site for significant communal experience.

Worship services are not viewed critically. Forty percent of the respondents "like them very much," and most of the rest are neutral rather than dissatisfied. A major difference between young people and adults, in this connection, is that almost half of the young felt the opportunity for participation in the worship service was inadequate while 80 percent of adults were satisfied with the level of congregational participation.

In examining the rabbinic role, the report reveals that the single most important qualification people seek in a rabbi is his capacity to relate to young people. This is followed by his abilities as an educator, as a family counselor, and as a giver of sermons. Other aspects of the rabbinic role, such as interfaith activities, scholarship, involvement in social action, administrative ability, and interest in socializing with temple members, are viewed as much less significant, at least by adult respondents. Young people are rather more interested in "where a rabbi stands" than in "what a rabbi can offer."

Part II of the report ("The Potential Jew: Innovations in Experiential Techniques") contains a description of eighteen weekend workshops—three in each of six temples—designed to encourage people to examine themselves as Jews, both actual and potential, and to develop support systems for an intensified commitment to Jewish experience. The workshop design rested on two assumptions: first, the necessary prior step to any proposed program of institutional renewal is a program of personal renewal. Before people can plausibly ask whether their institutions are functioning adequately, they must have a reasonably clear sense of what it is they want their institutions to do, and the development of such a sense depends upon knowing what it is the person wants, or needs, the institution to do for *him*. Second, a simple reminder of the discrepancy between where most people are as Jews, and where most would ideally like to be, would in itself have little impact on behavior. Such reminders are, after all, part of the regular fare of many Jews. What might, however, prove useful is the conscious pursuit of a system of interpersonal supports which would encourage people to join together to achieve fairly specific Judaic goals. . . .

Following from these assumptions, a series of workshops was designed. In the first workshop, a dozen members of the participating temple, each with some experience in human relations-oriented activities, were trained to act as "facilitators," para-professionals who would, together with the workshop leader, guide the subsequent workshop process. The subsequent weekends involved an additional fifty members of the temple who, together with the facilitators, engaged in a set of specifically designed experiential techniques intended to raise the following questions: What am I as a Jew? What would I like to be as a Jew? How do I move from what I am to what I would like to be? Does the temple, as it now exists, help or hinder me in that movement? How might it be more helpful?

In connection with Part II a detailed description of the 22 specific exercises that were developed for use in the workshops has been prepared. (This description, intended as a guide for future workshops, is available only to professionals engaged in such work. Experience shows that its use by non-professionals, though well intended, is often counterproductive.)

The report also includes data on the post-workshop evaluation by participants in the workshops. Of the 294 participants, 94 percent had a generally positive evaluation of the experience and over one-third found it an "extremely important personal experience." A number of spin-off groups resulted from the workshops and are still functioning today supporting the hope that the workshop impact is enduring rather than ephemeral.

IMPRESSIONS AND JUDGMENTS

Against the background of the findings which emerged from both the survey and workshops, those of us involved with the project have, inevitably, formed certain impressions regarding the present state and impending directions of Reform Judaism. In this last section of our report, we turn from specific findings and observations to personal impressions and judgments.

The Reform Jew. Through all of our work, no single conclusion registers so strongly as our sense that there is, among the people we have come to know, a powerful, perhaps even desperate, longing for community, a longing that is, apparently, not adequately addressed by any of the relevant institutions in most people's lives. It is possible, of course, that this need is unique to those who volunteered as participants in our workshops, that, indeed, this need is the reason they volunteered. Yet that is not our impression. So much other evidence is available to support the perception that

Americans in general, and middle- and upper-middle-class Americans in particular, have lost the sense of community, that we cannot believe that the problem is limited to those few whom we had the good fortune to meet and to work with. And so much of what we heard from them, about their neighbors, and their colleagues, and their fellow congregants, supports their own description of aloneness, that we feel safe in our generalization.

The need for community is not something people speak of easily. Most of us cope with our circumstances, take pleasure from the diverse symbols of our success, and recognize only a vague, though often pervasive, malaise, which we are reluctant either to analyze or to articulate. (Thus, at least, for adults; less for today's youth—here the generation gap is real.) In our own experience, people did not pour out poignant stories of loneliness. Such stories as were told came out in fragments, in bits and pieces of evidence that became a story only in retrospect. Our sense of the matter is that the need for community is so strong, and the prospect of community so weak, that people are reluctant to acknowledge the need, knowing, or believing, that it is not likely to be satisfied. Moreover, it is a sign of weakness, and hence of lack of success, to speak aloud of need. In the workshops that were developed for this project—that is, in a carefully designed and professionally directed process, in which hope emerges slowly, in which support and encouragement are offered freely—people do begin to talk about their own sense of human deprivation. And even then, not all do. Some, to be sure, are silent because they do not share the experience; others say nothing because they have so long been accustomed to segmented and superficial relationships that they can scarcely imagine the possibility of something different.

But the need is not less great for its being largely inarticulate. In the desperate search for warmth, many people are attracted to cultish, often bizarre groups that appear to offer some hope of intimacy. Still more, especially within the adult generation, simply accept the desperation, viewing it either as a necessary cost of modern times, or as a reflection of personal, rather than societal, incapacity. Whether the "solution" is frenetic cultism or quiet loneliness, large numbers of people never experience the warmth, the shared emotion, the sense of support, which community provides.

The need of which we speak here is obviously not specific to Jews, although it may be more keenly felt by those whose own memories go back to the life style of the organic folk-society which characterized the immigrant generation. It is not, in any case, a "Jewish" need, one whose satisfaction depends upon some agency or institution within the Jewish community. People who are prompted to seek more intimate, more open, more organic relationships may look to Jewish institutions for a response, or they may look elsewhere. Where they choose to look, if, indeed, they choose to look at all, depends in part on their tastes and predilections, but depends even more on where they sense the greatest likelihood of response.

In the next section, we shall have something to say about Reform Judaism's capacity to respond. Here, our focus is with the individual, and the point that wants making is that from the perspective of the individual Reform Jew, the Reform temple appears an unlikely site for the effort to create community. Our survey data show that most people are not disappointed in their temple; the demands and expectations they have of the temple are too minimal for them to experience disappointment, even when they experience alienation. The temple is assigned certain limited functions, notably with respect to the young, and it is judged in terms of its performance of these functions. The large majority of our respondents report very few close friends among their fellow temple members; over a third hold that the temple is a relatively unimportant institution in their lives; most attend the temple quite infrequently. The most important reasons our respondents give for joining a particular temple are its religious school and rabbi; among the least important is that their freinds or neighbors are members. And in our workshops, over and over, people spoke of joining, without belonging; they spoke of the "new member" problem, of the common lack of interest in making new members feel welcome; they spoke of the fact that the temple seems the "property" of a small handful of its most active members; they spoke of their own sense of nonpartnership in the temple.

To complaints such as these, there was usually a response that active membership was always welcome, that those who were infrequent visitors to the temple could hardly expect to find it a home, rather than merely a place to visit. More often than not, however, even the most active temple members among our participants were not prepared to argue that the temple was a warm and welcoming place; there was much to do, but even for those who did much, not much to feel. In fact, the word "cold" was not an uncommon description of the feel of the temple. Like Charles Silberman's classroom, the temple is a joyless place; the house of worship is not a home, except to a tiny few.

At a time, and with people for whom the experience of affective community is not natural, how does one set about creating it? Except as a temporary phenomenon, community happens when people share important experiences with one another, of which the most important is the experience of personal growth. But if the temple is not seen as a place where experiences are shared, is seen instead as a place where a limited number of services are consumed, then it appears an unlikely place for community to be pursued. And our data show that the primary expectation people have of their temple is that it will provide certain services, such as education, and a place to be on the High Holy Days, and a rabbi in time of personal need. Beyond these, people expect little; expecting little, that is what they get.

As we have noted, the need for shared community is not unique to Reform Jews. There is yet another respect in which Reform Jews are not unique. Like many, perhaps most Jews in America today, they are highly uncertain as to what it is that being Jewish implies, involves, demands. There was a time, not so very long ago, when Judaism was chaotic, a dozen ideologies and a hundred varieties of ideologies all clamoring for attention and competing for adherents. We have moved, it seems, from a chaotic Judaism to an inchoate Judaism, to a generation of Jews whose ties to Judaism, whether as faith or as peoplehood or as both, may be no weaker than the ties of their parents and grandparents, but whose "competence" as Jews is very shaky indeed.

In coming to this judgment, we are not adopting a specific normative stance. It is not that the views and beliefs of the Jews we encountered in the course of our work, whether through the survey data or through the workshop experiences, were different from our own. The problem, instead, is the prevalence of opinion as a substitute for belief, for any belief; the existence of belief, but the absence of belief systems. We are not at all convinced that there is a serious crisis in Jewish identity, at least among the people we encountered; there is a very clear crisis in Jewish ideology.

This ideological crisis is not, in the first instance, a question for theologians or philosophers. What we find is that people with very potent Jewish instincts feel that they have no way of supporting those instincts intellectually. Indeed, to the degree to which people have relatively coherent ideological tendencies, those tendencies often appear to contradict their Jewish instincts. This is a source of substantial personal distress, all the more so as it is extremely difficult to transmit instincts to the young when the justification for those instincts has been lost, or is uncertain. Nor is the question one of Jewish literacy alone. Jews may be more or less familiar with their history and their texts; it is the operational conclusions that may be derived from that history and from those texts that are inadequately perceived.

In former times, the question "Why be Jewish?" could not have arisen. There was no plausible alternative, even should one have been disposed to search for rationale. In modern times, the question not only arises, it is thrust upon us all, for we have become accustomed to demanding rational foundations for our commitments. For adults of this generation, the question, even if unanswered, is buried beneath enough Jewish memory and enough Jewish scar tissue so that it can, most often, be ignored. But when rich and private memory is replaced by a smattering of impersonal history, there is no defense against the question—which might be no matter, were the answers, whatever they be, more readily apparent.

We do not know whether the answers exist, or what they are; that is hardly our task. But we can attest that if they exist, and whatever they are, they are not widely known. Nor, for that matter, are the questions themselves widely discussed. Time and again in the course of the eighteen workshops (three in each of six temples) we conducted, the reaction to our initiation of serious discussions of Jewish values and beliefs was one of adventure and novelty; time and again we were told by participants how interesting it was to talk about such issues, and how rare.

So much entirely aside from normative commitment. We would be remiss were we not to add, from a more normative perspective, our very strong impression that in dealing with the matters raised above, the Reform movement has, in one important way, made them worse rather than better. Specifically: it is our view that there are inevitable tensions involved in being Jewish in the modern world. To be part of a religious brotherhood is necessarily to be a partner in mystery, in commitments that lie beyond rationality. And to be a Jew is not only to be a partner in a religious brotherhood, but also to be subject to the specific tension that arises from the Jewish situation, a situation in which the competing claims of particularism and universalism must continually be confronted. For Jews, that competition seems to us inevitable, difficult, and, potentially, productive.

A relatively common criticism of Reform Judaism is that it emphasizes Jewish universalism at the expense of Jewish particularism. And we did, in the course of our work, occasionally encounter people who have a clear ideological perspective that traces back to such early Reform understandings. Our sense of the matter, however, is that the specific, and more common, weakness of Reform in this connection is not with the way in which it proposes to resolve the tension, but rather that it often appears to deny that the tension exists at all. And, of course, by denying its existence, people are denied the opportunity to learn how to deal with it. But, since the tension is, if we are correct, an inevitable consequence of being Jewish, then the failure to prepare people for it is a failure of the first magnitude.

This is not, and does not try to be, an essay in theology. We do not say that the tensions which Judaism implies should be resolved in this way or in that. Basing our argument on a series of unusually open and extended encounters, we suggest that Reform Jews do, as a matter of fact, feel ill-equipped to cope with the perplexities of being Jewish, and still less well-equipped to help their children cope with them.

Having said all this, we should add that most of the people we met are coping, however ill-equipped they may be. We were dealing, after all, not only with members of Reform temples, but, in our workshops, with those members for whom the business of being Jewish was sufficiently interesting to warrant a serious investment of time. Nonetheless, by their own testimony, once serious discussion got under way, they were not satisfied with their success at sorting things out. We are persuaded that one powerful motive for the repeated effort to translate serious questions regarding personal behavior and intellectual belief into organizational issues—expanding the temple membership, reforming its committee structure—is the feeling, that however difficult the organizational questions, they are child's play compared to the difficulty of grappling with behavior and belief.

In short: the people we have dealt with call themselves Jews, and their Judaism matters to them. But they are vastly uncertain, in the main, regarding what calling oneself a Jew or caring about Judaism means or is supposed to mean; meanings seem rarely discussed, at least in ways that help. Consequently, the interest in meanings is repressed, sometimes lost entirely. And when, as in our experience, it is expressed, and the quest for meanings resumed, the paths that most people travel are unfamiliar, the maps they once were given of little use.

This strong impression is supported by our survey data as well. Those data show that Reform Jews, on the whole, no longer can be characterized as "partial" Jews, if ever they could be. Those who are most positively oriented toward Judaism-as-faith are generally also the most positively oriented toward Judaism-as-community. In this respect, Reform Judaism is clearly solidly in the mainstream of contemporary Jewish understandings and commitments. Nor are the responses of Reform Jews across a whole range of attitudes and beliefs markedly different from those of more diverse Jewish groupings, as comparison of our responses to those encountered in other studies of Jews shows. It is also the case, however, that this movement toward the mainstream is, evidently, a movement toward the confusions of the mainstream as well. As we note in our discussion of the survey data: "If there is an ideology of Reform Judaism, the evidence suggests that it is largely irrelevant as a shaper of the values and opinions of Reform Jews." Nor has a different ideology been substituted; there is commitment, intense commitment, but virtually no coherence, nor any substantial preparation or capacity to deal with the consequent ambiguity.

What makes the ideological ambiguity tolerable, as it is for most people, is the fact that it is not very salient. As we have already pointed out, most adult Jews of this generation have a rich enough set of Jewish memories that they can act out their Jewishness in a framework of memory and instinct, even where theory is wanting. For younger Jews, whose memories are less ample and whose instincts are more austere, the matter may be very different. This leads us to identify still another unmet need of Reform Jews, the need for affective stimulation.

We are concerned not only with a lack of capacity to deal with Judaism as serious intellectual inquiry, but also with the apparent lack of adequate opportunities for Judaism as expressive, even sensory, experience. Several of our experiential techniques dealt with early memories of Jewish experience, and the richness of those memories was in stark, and threatening, contrast to the present experiences our participants reported. . . . Even the most highly motivated of the participants report a peculiar inability to match their motives to their lives within the temple. If the most likely translation of Jewish commitment and interest is an invitation to serve on a temple committee, an imbalance between interest and opportunity exists. Yet that is precisely what we heard, and heard with disturbing frequency.

Some people, of course, try to go it alone, creating in their own homes, and, less often, within the temple, a corner that reflects their concern with Judaism, and not only with Jewish organization. More people, it seems, do not know where to begin, or are self-conscious about trying. They are, to be sure, not always aware that they are missing anything. It is perfectly possible to spend an extremely active Jewish life, going from meeting to meeting, from board to board, dealing with pressing matters of Jewish moment, without ever participating in a substantive Jewish experience, without ever relating oneself directly to the tradition, to the artifacts, to the sensations and the understandings that are the ostensible purpose of all the meetings and of all the boards.

There is, quite obviously, a limit to how long one can sustain a Judaism that cannot be expressed, whether because one does not know how to express it, or because the opportunity to express it is wanting, or because one is too busy with organizational needs to find time for expression. In one way or another, most of the people we met informed us that they had exceeded the limit, that they were themselves dissatisfied by the poverty of their Jewish experience. This was not an easy matter for many to acknowledge. Many of our participants were very active members of their temples, as well as of other Jewish organizations. For them to confess that something was wanting from their lives as Jews was no small thing. It was made still more difficult by the sense that most people had that little could be done about it, that the effort to create new capacities and new opportunities was not likely to succeed. Yet, withal, we report here not a wish of our own, but a clear conclusion of the five professionals who met with one or another of the temple groups. There was much holding back, and there were some who held back throughout; most came to speak of these matters, and, when they did, were often powerfully reassured that they were not alone in their concern. Indeed, it was precisely in this regard that the major support systems which the group process fostered were

Yet on the basis of our experience, we are not pessimistic about Reform Jews. Having said all that we have thus far said, this may appear a somewhat surprising conclusion, but, again, it is our unanimous judgment. We encountered far too many people of high motive and serious purpose to warrant a gloomy prognosis. To the degree to which motive and purpose normally tend to be suppressed, we believe, and our experience has shown, that intelligent professional intervention can encourage their expression, and can initiate the development of support systems which will forestall disappointment. Put differently: it is perfectly possible to initiate a revolution of rising Judaic aspirations. The question that arises is whether such a revolution is not bound to be, in the end, an experience in rising frustrations as well. The answer to this question begins with the provision of interpersonal support, which we think can be generated. But the ultimate answer, for most people, depends upon institutional capacities, and it is to an assessment of those capacities that we now turn.

The Reform Temple. In the preceding discussion, we noted three major needs of Reform Jews—the need for community, the need for an ideological foothold on Judaism, and the need for more direct Judaic experience. . . . The most glaring inadequacy of the temple is precisely in the area of greatest need of the congregant, the need for community. We have already reported that we were repeatedly told that new members are not made to feel welcome, and that old members relate to one another only superficially. Indeed, our own experience confirms this testimony, since, quite commonly, participants in our workshops would express surprise that others shared, or differed, with their own central beliefs about Judaism; although they had been worshiping or serving on committees together, sometimes for many years, issues such as these had rarely, if ever, been discussed.

Put most simply: the experience of temple membership is only rarely an experience in community. There are, as we see it, at least two major reasons why this should be so. The first is that few people, even among those who may actively pursue community, turn to the temple to find it. Our survey data, it will be recalled, show quite clearly that the temple is not based on close friendship among its members, nor, apparently, does it foster such friendship. The temple is, instead, a purveyor of services, the most important of which have to do with young people. A large number of our respondents state quite frankly that the temple is a relatively unimportant institution in their lives; while a still larger number count it as one among a number of important institutions, our sense of the matter is that even then, it is not the object of great psychological or emotional investment.

Most people, as we have said, do not invest great energy in the pursuit of community. If they sense its absence, they adjust to its absence, for most would scarcely know where to begin to look for it, or how. Thus it is not the case—and we believe this point to be critical—that the temple is seen as less promising a site for community to happen in than some other institution or agency. The gap is not filled by "competitors"; in the main, it is not filled at all. Which creates, of course, a most important opportunity for the temple. Insofar as it may develop a capability for meeting the widespread need for community, it may evoke a wholly new order of loyalty, of passion, of concern and commitment, than it has hitherto experienced.

This leads us to the second major reason why the temple has heretofore not been used by its members as a basis for the creation of community. The temple is, after all, an institution, an elaborate enterprise, and it takes very special skill to create community in an institutional setting. How can one, after all, infuse a necessarily bureaucratic structure with warmth, with joy, and with genuine human interaction? . . .

Anecdote: One of us, in the course of talking with a group of temple members in connection with the project, sought to illustrate the need for community by telling of a friend who had taken his own life. After the tragedy, a group who had known this poor man rather well came together, and tried to review his last weeks, to see whether there had been a hint that should have been noticed, some premonition that might have led his friends to offer help. There had been none, and, realizing this, the group realized as well how grotesque it is that a person in such massive distress does not find it possible to ask, somehow, for help, not from friends, not from family, not from professionals. And after this perception came the terrifying knowledge that among those who had come together, there was not one who felt that he would be able to ask for help were he in need.

To which a temple official replied that the story was interesting, but that no such problem existed in his temple, for it was blessed with a suicide prevention committee to deal with just such problems. A suicide prevention committee may, after all, be a very good thing, it may even be the best kind of thing a temple can do. It is a limited, bureaucratic response, and a decent, perhaps even helpful response. But it does not, for no committee can, help answer what it is about our lives that prevents us from asking for help, nor does it, for no committee can, offer love as its help.

This is hardly the place for a comprehensive critique of modern culture. We make the point, rather, in order to indicate that Reform Jews have very serious and very genuine needs which are, on the whole, unmet, and which it would be entirely appropriate for Reform temples to seek to meet. Insofar as temples find themselves able to provide the settings where such needs are met, it is entirely possible that they will move from the periphery of their members' consciousness and loyalty to the center. Save as they provide such settings, there is no reason whatever to suppose that they will have important meanings to more than a tiny minority. The only serious question, then, is whether the fulfillment of those needs is compatible with the necessarily institutional environment of the temple.

That, of course, must remain in some measure an open question. It will be difficult, to be sure, to break through the inhibitions of the members and the inertia of the institutions to create more vital and more humane interactions. But our judgment, based primarily on the workshop experience, is that though difficult, the task is not inherently undoable. . . . How, then, does one create a temple that is congenial to community, to which its members, therefore, turn for more important purposes than now attract them? The way to create community is not to set about to create community. The concept of community implies an organic relationship, rather than a contractual relationship. Let no committees be created that will "have charge" of fostering community; organic relationships grow out of organic experiences, or they do not grow.

In our judgment, the single best way for the temple to turn toward community would be for it to provide its members richer opportunities in the other two problem areas we earlier identified, the areas of intellectual, or cognitive, Judaism, and the area of experiential, or affective, Judaism. The process of sharing in intellectual and emotional growth is also, and inevitably, a process in community-building. Few, if any, people will respond if the temple announces as its goal for the next year the creation of a spirit of community; more will respond, and the spirit will follow, if more plausible, and more directly manageable goals, are announced.

That is a judgment which is based on our general professional experience, as well as on the specific experience of the workshops. It would be a mistake to exaggerate the significance of the workshops over the long haul; three weekends, or two, out of a person's time will have only marginal consequences for most, especially where there is no concerted follow-up activity that is encouraged within the temple. But it would also be a mistake to minimize their importance as the first step along the path to community, even though the creation of community was never the explicit goal. But when people come together in open search, and share in one another's search, the seeds of community are planted; if nurtured, they will grow. The search in which our participants joined was a search for Jewish meanings and for Jewish experiences. And that is exactly the search we propose be extended to include larger numbers, over a longer period of time. . . .

We view this as a central point. In the frenetic pursuit of community which some adults and many of the young seem now to be embarked upon, the rewards, such as they are, are typically ephemeral. The decision to "find" community is like the decision to fall in love; deciding doesn't make it so. Nor have the diverse matchmakers of community done much better; after the initial thrill, the real work begins, but by then the matchmaker is gone. Yet for Jews, as Jews, the problem should be simpler. The way into the affective living community, the community of shared emotion, shared experience, and shared support, that is needed may well be through more intensive exploration of the meanings of the historic, religious, sociological community that already exists. Jews are, after all, not strangers to one another; the task for them is not so much to create community as to extend its scope and to deepen its significance.

The experience of affective community is usually a small-group experience. The large temple, we suspect, cannot seek to become a single community; more likely, it must see itself as the place where a variety of communities are encouraged. In this regard, the fact that the large majority of our survey respondents thought that, ideally, their temples should be larger than they are is not necessarily distressing. It suggests what we have already observed, that most do not see community as one of the purposes of the temple. But the large temple is not necessarily the enemy of community, nor the small temple its friend. Indeed, the large temple, by permitting people of common interest to find each other, and to work together, may have an advantage. This follows from the fact that the threshold, beyond which a temple cannot expect to be a single affective community, is likely on the order of fifty families, at most. Once a temple grows beyond that number, it may well be better for it to grow a good deal beyond it, in order to enable each of its members to find a sufficient number of kindred spirits.

Now it might well be argued that the search for Jewish meanings and for Jewish experiences is precisely the search to which temples have traditionally been devoted, and which most members have traditionally been reluctant to join as active participants. If, as we have found, the temple is a peripheral institution to many of its members, perhaps that is because they want it kept at the periphery, and would resist its efforts to become more central. But it is also possible that the temple, by coming to devote so large a part of its and its members' attention to organizational ends, has trained its members to think of it as essentially an organization, and a set of services, rather than a set of interactions and experiences. We have found it possible to generate both interactions and experiences which quite diverse groups of people have, in large measure, found rewarding. While it is always somewhat hazardous to generalize from experimental results, the test of whether our experiments are, in fact, applicable on a larger and more institutionalized scale is easy enough to conduct.

What is wanted, we believe, is not so much a sudden transformation, as a gradual process of development of mutual confidence and testing of new roles. If the temple announces that it is anxious to promote interaction as well as to provide service, the announcement is likely to be greeted with initial skepticism, even by those who already acknowledge the desirability of interaction. Others will simply be perplexed, uncertain what this new departure is all about. And if people approach the temple as a home of interaction and humanity, those who have traditionally set the tone for the temple will find, with all the good will in the world, that this new demand is not easily met. Special skills may be required, skills not normally available, and exceptional tolerance, as people stumble to find a way, will surely be required. The process of reaching out is a fragile process; in the short run, it is surely safer to avoid it. In the short run, indeed, the temple is safer where it is, at the periphery. But the short run is very short, and, if the price of safety is irrelevance, that may be too high a price to pay even for a moment.

If there has been one central theme to our effort, it has been the direct involvement, in an open and supportive environment, of people themselves in the process of Judaic goal-setting. As we interpret the plea that the temple become more "relevant," relevance is not to be defined as related to current events, but rather as related to the real, if inarticulate, needs of people. The need for community cannot be satisfied by sitting as an audience to a religious service, much of which unfolds on a distant stage; active shared experience is required, and if a majority of our survey respondents find the level of participation in the present worship service adequate, it may well be because they do not expect the service to help create community. The need for intellectual understanding and ideological coherence cannot be met by an educational mode so superficial as the weekly sermon; more serious confrontation, and participation in the effort, are required, a level of participation beyond even that of the typical adult education program. And if a majority of our respondents hold sermonic ability to be among the most important qualifications a rabbi can have, that may be because they do not expect the temple to offer serious education. The need for stimulating Jewish experience cannot be satisfied by participation on a temple committee, nor the need for a richer Jewish idiom by an occasional visiting artist; more immediacy and intensity are wanted. In each case, the key is a more participatory mode. . . .

Temples, in their organizational parts, are sometimes fearful that to seek to deepen meanings and to broaden scope, to demand more of their members and of themselves as institutions, would drive people away. Large numbers of people, after all, seem to want no more (perhaps even less) than is currently offered; will a still more ambitious program attract, or further alienate? It is our judgment that people tailor their ambitions to fit their estimate of possibility. We cannot be sure that the potential constituency for a more intensive (i.e., more initimate, more inquisitive, more expressive) Judaism includes the large majority of present temple members, but we are convinced on the basis of our work, that there is at the very least a constituency of substantial size. That constituency, it appears to us, is not so much interested in "more" as it is interested in "different," in the development of congregational styles that touch them and challenge them in ways they do not now feel either touched or challenged. We suspect, moreover, that were that constituency to be encouraged, were its needs to find

JEWISH EDUCATION

JEWISH EDUCATION IN THE UNITED STATES

by LLOYD P. GARTNER

INTRODUCTION

LLOYD P. GARTNER'S survey of Jewish education in the United States ranges from the earliest schools established by Spanish and Portuguese Jews to the recent growth of Jewish day-school education. Gartner's wide knowledge of American as well as of American Jewish history enables him to place the development of American Jewish schools in perspective and provide the reader with a new understanding of familiar institutions.

The crucial development which determined the direction American Jewish education was to take was the acceptance by Jews of the public school as the basic educational institution for their children. Gartner points out that as soon as public education achieved a modicum of quality and, furthermore, eliminated the grossest forms of Protestant indoctrination, German Jews were quick to endorse the new system. It was a matter of principle to them that Jewish children be enrolled in the new public schools. This occurred despite the fact that the wealthiest German-Jewish families seldom practiced what they preached, preferring to send their own children to private schools.

German-Jewish enthusiasm for public education was shared by later arrivals—if anything the newly-settled East Europeans were more devoted to public education than were the established element. Yet Jewish zeal for public education is surprising—if any group should have insisted on the primacy of "parochial" education it was the Jews. As Gartner emphasizes at the beginning of his analysis, for millennia religious study was not only an obligation of Jewish males but was actually an integral part of the Jewish cultural pattern. While the precise attitude of Jews toward secular study differed from age to age and from region to region, the study of sacred literature was always considered to have priority.

The dynamics of the process by which Jews transformed themselves from a group which gave primacy to sacred learning into one which gave primacy to secular learning is still inadequately understood. Whether the process was initiated overseas and completed in the United States, or whether it was entirely a result of the encounter with American culture, remains a matter for debate. There is no question, however, that the transformation took place free of any demand by Jews that their support of public education be reciprocated by having the public schools assume the task of educating the Jewish child in his heritage. This was true even in places like the New York metropolitan area where by the 1930's Jewish teachers and administrators (and later Jewish union officials as well) were not only common but were qualifying for crucial positions in the educational system.

Gartner supplies the reason for Jewish apathy, if not antipathy, toward Jewish education under public auspices. He emphasizes that Jews viewed the public school ". . . as the symbol and guarantee of Jewish equality and full opportunity in America." In the Jewish mind equality and full opportunity meant that the public school would take no notice of the existence of religious or ethnic differences—any recognition of such differences raised the possibility of discord and ultimately the specter of discrimination, and would also inhibit the healthy mingling of children of diverse background. (In practice there were few non-Jews to mingle with in the large urban centers with concentrations of Jews in single school districts, and until Jews reached suburbia those who were available were seldom models that Jewish parents would want their children to emulate.)

It is clear that at times Jews were forced into positions that violated what they believed the public schools stood for. Thus in some cities they reluctantly participated in "released-time"—a plan whereby children who wished religious instruction were to be excused from school at an earlier hour. It was difficult to reject such a plan without appearing to be anti-religious. Jews also reluctantly agreed to Chanukah celebrations in the schools after it became evident that it was well-nigh impossible to implement a policy forbidding Christmas celebrations. In some cities Jewish communal bodies supported the request that high schools with large Jewish enrollments be permitted to introduce Hebrew language instruction. However, even today when ethnic studies are commonplace in public elementary and secondary schools, Jews are wary of encouraging the teaching of Jewish studies.

The Jewish view of the function of public education had as its correlate the following: that in the privacy of the ethnic and religious enclave any group had the freedom to make whatever institutional arrangement it deemed appropriate to induct its young into its culture. In practice this meant that it was the obligation of the Jewish parent to provide his child with a Jewish education. Indeed the history of Jewish education in America can be looked upon as the search for a viable arrangement whereby children whose prime learning experience was in the public sector could be afforded the benefit of an encounter with the culture of their group. Gartner analyzes the evolution of each of these arrangements: the Jewish Sunday School, copied from Protestant models; the engaging of melamdim *(tutors) by parents and the opening of* hedarim *(elementary schools), both copied from European models; the communal Talmud Torah; the* folkshul*; the congregational Hebrew school.*

All of these institutional arrangements began in high hope; each was thought by its protagonists to be the key to the educational needs of the hour as well as the true fulfillment of the injunction to raise up the child in the way of his fathers. And each form has proved to be a disappointment—frequently more of a disappointment to its supporters than to those outside. Since the last century a considerable literature has accumulated about the shortcomings of elementary Jewish education, the deplorable conditions of secondary Jewish education, and the meager accomplishments of adult Jewish education. Perhaps the most withering criticism has come from the educators themselves—knowing the shortcomings of the schools at firsthand they have been in the best position to expose their inadequacies.

The focus of the more sophisticated type of criticism of the American Jewish school has been the inadequacy of the school in attaining the very goals which it has set for itself. With the possible exception of radical folkshuln and melamdim who confined themselves to Bar Mitzvah preparation, all of the schools have sought in one way or another to continue the classical objective of Jewish education: to inculcate a knowledge of sacred texts. While their approach to the text may be untraditional, while they may prefer to focus on particular texts which they find congenial and neglect others no less sacred, and while they may introduce new subjects in the curriculum, at a minimum the schools have paid lip service to traditional ideals.

Among the many factors which have militated against the achievement of their objectives have been the scarce time and resources at the command of the schools and the attraction of students to the outside culture. Generally speaking the schools have been able to succeed only with outstanding students coming from above-average homes. The language problem has been a central difficulty. For many laymen and professionals connected with the schools the teaching of Hebrew has been essential—because it is the language of the sacred texts, because it is the language of prayer, or because it is the language of the Zionist movement and the State of Israel; whatever the motivation, the results have been seen as disappointing.

If the American Jewish school has not succeeded in producing literate Jews it has also been charged with failing to produce "identified" Jews. The charge is surprising in the sense that Jewish education has never pretended to create identification, proceeding instead on the assumption that the child comes to the school with a firm Jewish identity. The task of creating Jewish identification has been imposed upon the school by parents, who wish the school to create a countervailing force to the child's "Gentile" identity which emerges from his exposure to public education, to the mass media, to the general milieu, and most recently to what has come to be known as "youth culture."

The need for such a countervailing force has long been felt by American Jews, but in recent years it has taken on a new urgency. Forces as diverse as pride in the State of Israel, the threat of intermarriage, and fear of the consequences of suburbanization have all had a role in stimulating new support for Jewish education and new directions in the field. These changes have included informal education, especially summer camping; a shift in Hebrew-language teaching from classical to more up-to-date methods; study of Israel and summer programs including travel to the Jewish state; and a new attention to Jewish education for students of high-school age. As Gartner points out there has even been support in the Jewish community for the introduction of Jewish studies into the American university.

Gartner completes his analysis by pointing to what has indeed been a radical change in American Jewish education—the rapid growth of the Jewish day school. Crushed in the nineteenth century by the Jewish zeal for public education, in the past two decades the day school has undergone a remarkable resurrection and development. Some regard its growth as a function of socially conservative and anti-integrationist sentiment among Jews, while others see it as resulting from disillusionment with the achievements of public education in the 1960's and 1970's. From a Jewish perspective the rise of the day schools can also be seen as resulting from the determination of ultra-Orthodox elements in the Jewish community and from disillusionment with the accomplishments of the supplementary school—whether this be the Hebrew School, the Talmud Torah, the Sunday School, or some other arrangement. It is still too early to know whether the day school will succeed where other schools are said to have failed—whether it will produce both literate and "identified" Jews. But it has the distinction of viewing the problem of American Jewish education in radical terms—terms which are at once new and very old in the millennial history of Jewish education.

M. S.

SCRIPTURE commands the Jew to "impress upon your children" the revealed Divine teaching, and to think and speak of it day and night. In ancient times, the verses in Deuteronomy which contained this enjoinder became liturgy, to be pronounced daily with devotion by every worshiper. Actual education in biblical times had been conducted largely in priestly circles, but later, during the Second Commonwealth, universal schooling for all males became the ideal and, to a considerable extent, the rule. Every member of God's unique people had to be imbued with the Bible and with the oral traditions later committed to writing as the Talmud, which were also regarded as Divine in origin. Lifelong study and contemplation of the Torah became essential in the Jewish paideia. During Talmudic times and after, the Jew was enjoined to make a living which left him time not only for religious devotion but also for systematic study of the sacred literature. Honor and deference were due to the master student, even when he was poor or bashful. Social prestige and religious merit were thus intimately linked in Judaism with intellectual effort.

In Talmudic and medieval Jewry, and to the present day in some communities, scholarship was not only abstract erudition but a quite practical matter. Centuries of Jewish autonomous life were lived largely governed by this Divine law, which required legal responsa and judicial decisions.

Nowhere did the zeal for pious study exceed the intensity it attained in Poland and Lithuania, the areas from which the greatest masses of Jews came to America in the nineteenth and twentieth centuries. One law code widespread in Central and Eastern Europe summarizes the obligation to study:

> It is a positive commandment of the Torah to study the Torah . . . therefore every Jewish person is so obligated, whether rich or poor, healthy or sickly, youthful or venerable; even a door-to-door beggar or a husband and father. He must fix a time for Torah study, day or night . . . and one who is completely incapable of study shall assist others who do study and it will be reckoned for him as though he himself had studied.

> Until when is a man obligated to study? Until the day he dies. . . . (*Hayyey Adam*, Section 10, Parts 1 and 2.)

The main content of all this study was law, as discussed in the tractates of the Talmud—civil, criminal, moral, ritual. The Talmud seldom lays down the law, but discusses and disputes it back and forth within accepted categories of reasoning along with a great deal of seasoning: tales, aphorisms, biblical commentary, speculative theology. It is not necessarily true, of course, that the techniques or content of Torah study can be transferred to other realms of study. In secular terms, however, the legacy from two millennia of intellectuality is indeed imposing. Education as a universal lifelong obligation, skill at critical and abstract thought, honor to the intellectually distinguished, could outlast the environment in which they first arose. From the onset of modern times in Jewish history—approximately the eighteenth century in Central Europe and the nineteenth century in Eastern Europe—the tradition of intellectuality became diffused among many branches of the arts and sciences. Our present interest, however, lies in the fate of the tradition of Jewish education itself in the open, emancipated, untraditional American society.

Educational ideals and intellectual tone were rather definite, but a consistent Jewish school system was quite rare. The educational institutions of the Jewish community as such were for advanced students. The biblical obligation was understood as that of overseeing the primary education which parents had to provide for their children, and of directly educating only the indigent, orphaned, or neglected. The parent, upon whom the obligation lay in the first instance, generally hired a *melammed* (tutor) for his child. This melammed was often a wandering student, an impoverished tradesman, or some elderly factotum who kept a *heder* (one-room school). His figure has come down to us in an aura of pity and mockery, as one who failed in the main arenas of life. However, the melammed who taught Talmud to an older boy was a respected person. The Jewish community provided higher studies for the talented after these parental responsibilities had been fulfilled. Often it did so by engaging a renowned scholar as its rabbi, providing stipends even for strangers who came to join the townsmen in studying with him. A *bet midrash* (house of study) was found everywhere in which young and old might occupy themselves with individual or group study of the Talmud and other works of the sacred literature. Artisans and Jewish guilds might periodically study or hear learned discourses as part of their program. More than the synagogue, the bet midrash was the meeting place where pious study and social life could be carried on. The capstone was the yeshiva academy for advanced, nonprofessional study of Talmud. During the nineteenth century, the small, locally supported yeshivot were overshadowed by new, regional institutions, several of which—such as Volozhin, Mir, and Slobodka—became world famous. The heder, bet midrash, and yeshiva have all appeared in America.

These institutions of Central and Eastern European Jewry dealt exclusively with textual study and exposition. The culture and language of the surrounding society found no place, nor did any vocational or scientific or physical training. The aim was to produce religiously devout and learned men whose worldly requirements could be attended to by induction into a parental business or by an advantageous marriage.

The first major Jewish strain to arrive in America, the Sefardim —Jews of Spanish and Portuguese stock—came, to a considerable extent, from backgrounds quite different from those just described. Their glorious centuries on the Iberian peninsula had fostered an educational ideal of the cultivated Jewish gentleman, rather than the intense pietist of Northern and Eastern Europe. Sefardic education was given in Spanish and included loving attention to Bible, Hebrew language and poetry, and perhaps some rationalist Jewish philosophizing. During the tragic decline before the expulsion of Spanish Jewry in 1492, mystical and redemptionist thinking overshadowed but did not eradicate the earlier ideal. Most of the Sefardim who came to the New World were not cultivated persons, and their Marrano past did not prepare them for polite learning, much less for urbane skepticism. But they were modern in the limited but important sense that the Jewish and the secular managed to coexist within them.

The first Jewish children in America were born to these Sefardim. The education of the American Jewish child before 1800 was rather hit or miss. In the little colonial synagogues whose membership was pretty much coterminous with the local Jewish communities, the ministers' duties included the instruction of youngsters in the rudiments of the ancestral religion and necessary secular knowledge. Three to five years spent in learning to read Hebrew and more or less understand selected biblical and liturgical passages, and becoming acquainted with the main headings of practical Jewish observance like holidays, synagogue procedures, and customs, was the basic Jewish learning. The minister-teacher also drilled his pupils in English, reading, writing, arithmetic, and sometimes also in Spanish, which was still used in some homes and synagogues. Little more was expected by parents who were mostly small merchants and craftsmen. Only in Charleston, where a Jewish bourgeoisie became established at a relatively early period, were the graces of polite society inculcated. Some specimens of parental injunctions to children have survived, and they emphasize the maxims of diligence, honesty, and filial devotion.

It was the absence of schools other than Christian which compelled Jews thus to arrange for the entire education of their young. An agreement between Philadelphia Jews and Ezekiel Levy, dated July 18, 1776, requires that his services to the congregation include "to teach six children the art of Hebrew reading." These six were poor; others had to make private arrangements with Levy for pay. Such tutoring was rarely superseded by actual schools. One appears to have been founded in 1755 under the aegis of New York's Shearith Israel (the "Spanish and Portuguese") congregation and existed until 1776, when New York Jewry was disrupted by the British occupation. The curriculum resembled that of the private tutors—Hebrew and some Spanish, Bible, and the three R's. The same congregation opened a second school in 1808, known as the Polonies Talmud Torah, which lasted intermittently as a day school until 1821. (It still exists as the congregation's afternoon school.) In this and similar little schools maintained at various times in Philadelphia and Charleston, Jewish studies consisted for the most part of reading and translation of portions of the Bible and prayerbook, laws and customs of the religion, and perhaps some instruction in the Hebrew language and a smattering of rabbinic literature. They differed little from what a Jewish child would be taught in Western Europe. The novelty lay in instruction being given as a matter of course in general secular subjects during the eighteenth century. Such a practice was barely known in Central and Eastern Europe, and stirred bitter controversy wherever it was introduced.

During the first decades of the Federal Union, Jews still played little cultural or political role. Two changes faintly discernible during the 1820's became more noticeable during the 1830's and 1840's. At the Hebrew Sunday School of Philadelphia, founded by Rebecca Gratz in 1839 for children of the poor, the catechetical teaching of Judaism was introduced. Some of the very few educated native Jews, including Mordecai M. Noah, Daniel L. M. Peixotto, and Isaac Harby, began to think of the means to raise the pious, cultivated American Jewish gentleman. Their suggestive but rather nebulous ideas rapidly became antiquated, however, as a new immigration commenced, far greater than any earlier one. These were Jews from German lands. Few of the earlier German newcomers were of learned stock, and their Judaism was still essentially that of venerable tradition. (Later arrivals were fully Germanized.) They brought to America, or soon begot here, enough children to make large-scale Jewish schooling feasible and necessary. Some of the German Jews manifested dissatisfaction with the Jewish education they found, and from their midst came the numerous attempts between the 1830's and the 1850's to found Jewish day schools.

Mid-nineteenth-century Jewish immigrants stood out especially among the early settlers of the new cities of the Middle West—Chicago, Cleveland, Cincinnati, Milwaukee, St. Louis, and elsewhere. In these cities, extensive Jewish settlement preceded sometimes by decades the founding of a satisfactory public school system. Jewish parents in the early days founded private schools under synagogal sponsorship, such as Cincinnati's Talmid Yelodim Institute, and often collaborated with liberal local Germans in opening "German-English Academies."

The three decades during which Jewish day schools sprouted were not necessarily informed by zeal for Jewish education. Actually, their underlying *raison d'être* was the absence or poverty of public schools, or the Protestant sectarian tone of those which did exist. The definitive establishment of public schools without such sectarian features as prayers, Bible and especially New Testament readings and moralizing, and strongly Christian holiday observance, was the death knell of the Jewish schools. A new ideology regarded the tax-supported, religiously neutral, universal public school as the indispensable training ground for American citizenship. This outlook was enthusiastically adopted by the Jews. As they soon came to believe, Jewish children could best become loyal and fully accepted Americans by mingling freely in public school with children of all religions and social classes. Sectarian

Jewish education suggested undesirable, even dangerous separatism. Obviously also, Jews as taxpayers should use tax-supported institutions. Only here and there did Jewish voices question the view that Jewish children should on principle be enrolled in the new public schools. The Philadelphian, the Reverend Isaac Leeser, a traditionalist leader, stressed the inevitably Christian influence of public schooling where virtually all teachers and most pupils were Christians. Bernard Felsenthal, a Chicago Reform rabbi, urged the need for Jewish schools to raise an American Jewish intellectual class comparable to that of European Jewry. These views were little regarded and virtually forgotten. After 1860, scarcely any private Jewish schools remained in the United States. Wealthy Jewish families, however, often educated their children at private, non-Jewish institutions.

The triumphant growth of the public school and the spread of its ideology occurred when Reform Judaism was fast becoming the dominant mode of Judaism in America. Reform Judaism and the public school complemented each other admirably in American Jewish thinking. Fundamental to Reform Judaism was its conception of the Jews as fully integrated citizens of the modern secular state, differentiated only by religion. All rules of Jewish religious tradition to the contrary had to be discarded. State-sponsored, universal, religiously neutral schools were a blessing and a necessity, for they were a microcosm of the society in which Jewish children would find a place as adults. . . . The public school was viewed as the symbol and guarantee of Jewish equality and full opportunity in America. This deep American Jewish affinity for the public school lasted a full century, and turned to disenchantment only in places subjected to urban school crises in the 1950's and 1960's.

From the time the public school took over general education, Jewish education became solely Jewish in content. The millennial conception of a detailed, holy law as the object of meticulous observance was discarded, and also the ideal of its reverent study from childhood on. Judaism, interpreted by Reform mainly as a universal moral code, turned the content of Jewish education into moral didacticism derived from biblical exemplars. Study as such was no longer a paramount value. The Sunday School, derived from Protestant models, became the regnant institution for transmitting Judaism to Jewish children. Its curriculum included history (actually Bible stories) and religion taught catechistically, with a few Hebrew verses used in worship generally included. The Sunday School usually met on Saturday and Sunday mornings in rooms within the synagogue under the direction of the rabbi who served as "Superintendent," with volunteer teachers taking the classes. Textbooks appeared, written mainly by Superintendent rabbis, which were mostly manuals or catechisms of religious belief and of biblical history. The program was generally of three years' duration, and culminated in the newly introduced ceremony of Confirmation, when the graduating class of boys and girls were "confirmed" in their religion around the age of thirteen. In addition to Confirmation, some more traditional-Reform congregations also permitted the old-style individual Bar Mitzvah for boys. . . .

The once- or twice-weekly schools "caught on" very quickly. By 1880, the Sunday School was almost synonymous with organized Jewish education, among traditionalists as well as Reformers. Families who belonged to Reform temples invariably sent their children to Sunday School, and many an unaffiliated family did likewise. To this day it remains the most widely attended form of Jewish schooling in America.

The year 1880 marks the great divide in the history of American Jewry, as unprecedented numbers of Jewish immigrants began to pour into the United States. With few exceptions they came from Eastern Europe. Thanks to these arrivals, the approximately 280,000 Jews of 1880 increased to about 1,000,000 in 1900, 3,500,000 in 1915, and were 4,500,000 when mass immigration was shut off in 1925. The Jews who had come earlier from German lands were possessed of some or at times a great deal of modern culture, usually in German garb, but those from Russia and Poland or Romania and Galicia were generally of traditional, fully Jewish culture, with little from the surrounding environment. However, the modern secular culture which was seeping into East European Jewish life overwhelmed the immigrant in America, where he indeed expected and wanted to enter the modern world while preserving something of the traditional culture. It is truly remarkable with what ease and alacrity immigrant Jewish children were despatched by their parents to the government's compulsory public schools. Attempts to require this in Eastern Europe had been bitterly resisted, but America was indeed different. The Jewish affinity to the American public school, which by the early twentieth century included the high school, was at its closest during these decades of East European Jewish mass immigration. The rapid social ascent of American Jews was in large measure owing to their zeal for education, for centuries the high road to honor and religious merit in the Jewish community.

During the first decades of this mass immigration, Jewish education among the immigrants expressed the determination, such as there was, to maintain the old ways rather than adapt to the new. Children were taught after public school hours in a heder kept by a melammed in his dwelling somewhere in the immigrant slums. *Hadarim* (pl.) existed in the hundreds. The content of their teaching, with rare exceptions, was rudimentary Hebrew reading and perhaps some Pentateuch and synagogal rules and customs. The melammed seldom taught a class but tutored each child in turn amid the clatter of the others. It was a poor system by any standard, whether that of the old learning or of the public schools the children had just come from. The heder, however, was familiar to immigrants, who came overwhelmingly from the poor, working classes of East European Jewry. To them it symbolized ethnic continuity in the ways of their fathers, especially yearned for when neither the fathers nor their ways were to be seen. The American heder also taught Yiddish, often giving the revealing reason of preparing children to "write a letter to grandparents." Only in terms of generational loyalty can the persistence of the heder in the 1940's be explained.

Surveys taken in various immigrant Jewish communities demonstrated that a majority of children attended no heder nor any other Jewish school. Not only the immigrant faithful but native Jews also were disturbed by these findings which seemed closely connected with the attractions of socialism and atheism, and the appearance of criminality in the immigrant districts. In most larger cities, native Jewish organizations like the National Council of Jewish Women established Sunday Schools and community houses for the children of immigrants. These educational institutions grew out of the prevalent desire to divest immigrants of their particular character and culture and remake them as "Americans." New York's Educational Alliance, founded as the Jewish People's Institute, for years typified this outlook. The persistent refusal to regard immigrants except as people to be made over into the philanthropic sponsors' conception of an American caused sharp intramural friction and limited the usefulness of these institutions. The combination of heder and settlement house Sunday School bestowed by "uptown" Jews set the Jewish educational pattern "downtown" until the turn of the twentieth century. Some immigrant synagogues or societies did maintain schools, but these were little more than several hadarim under one roof with the usual inadequate melamdim.

Higher Jewish studies began in America during the late nineteenth century as rabbinical training. After several unsuccessful beginnings, Isaac M. Wise, the Reform leader, founded the Hebrew Union College as a rabbinical school in Cincinnati in 1875. The traditionalist Jewish Theological Seminary and Yeshivath Etz Chaim both opened in New York in 1886. . . . [Etz Chaim] transplanted the East European Talmudic academy, and was the germ of today's Yeshiva University. Of these three schools only Hebrew Union College was firmly established by 1900. None then possessed the caliber either of major American colleges or of European Jewish models.

The major phase in American Jewish education began early in the twentieth century, when a theory and practice of Jewish education developed which has remained basic ever since. This new educational vigor owed much to the example of public education, which during the 1890's and 1900's underwent its most searching examination since the time of Horace Mann. The disciplinary severity and rigid rote learning, as well as the inadequacies of teachers and supervisors, came under sharp and well-informed criticism. The outlook of American philosophers of education during this period, above all John Dewey, became influential in finding American foundations for Jewish education. Two of their principles were especially important for Jewish education and invite further examination: cultural pluralism and the nexus between school and society.

The early goal in educating immigrant children had been "Americanization" in the native American mold. As seen above, native Jews fully concurred in this aim, which found room for Judaism as an American faith. The newer idea of the "melting pot" meant a modification of this doctrine; the term itself originated in a play by Israel Zangwill, an English-Jewish author and Zionist. In this view, the historic culture of the United States was to "melt" in the American social crucible along with the many immigrant strains, and ultimately a single, new American cultural amalgam would be produced. In its assumption that patriotic immigrants and natives should help a uniform American culture to emerge, the melting-pot idea did not really differ from the doctrine of Anglo-Saxonism. Much further-reaching was the doctrine of cultural pluralism, which came forth during the second decade of the century. It proposed the radically contrary view that Jews and all other groups best fulfilled their duty as Americans by fostering their distinctive ancestral heritage in all its forms—language, art, literature, and ethos in general. Cultural pluralists insisted that if the schools and other public institutions held the immigrant and his background in greater respect, and if children did not sense the constant disdain for parental ways, many a family fabric would remain unbroken and youth not go astray. Not only this psychological argument was employed. Cultural pluralists presented a critique of existing American culture as narrow and provincial, and prescribed a tonic of European immigrant inheritances to lend it depth and variety.

Cultural pluralism received its first full statement in Horace M. Kallen's essay of 1915, *Culture and Democracy in the United States*. The theory and particularly its implications for Jewish education were brilliantly expounded five years later in Isaac B. Berkson's *Theories of Americanization: A Critical Study with Special Reference to the Jewish Group*. It is probable that much of the basic thinking, which came from young American Jews, derived indirectly from the intellectual ferment of East European Jewry, especially the Hebraist intellectual Asher Ginzberg (pseud. Ahad Ha-Am, 1856–1927) and the historian Simon Dubnow (1860–1941). Ahad Ha-Am's cultural nationalism, focused on Palestine rebuilt, and Dubnow's doctrine of national minority rights were translated and adapted for America by the Polish-born Israel Friedlander (1876–1920), Professor of Bible at the Jewish Theological Seminary. Friedlander and several associates influential in Jewish public life proposed an American Jewish educational theory resting on the cultural pluralists' view of the duty of Jews as Americans to continue to be Jews. As scholars and Zionists, they envisioned Judaism modernized along the lines of Hebraic, humanistic, religious ethnic life. The Jewish school would be the laboratory where citizens of this new American Jewish community would be trained—a most interesting application of Deweyan thought.

Cultural pluralism began its career in Jewish education as new institutions were introducing far-reaching changes. In several dozen large new afternoon schools, the reviving Hebrew language became the vehicle of the "natural method," *Ivrit be-Ivrit.* Under this system, children first learned Hebrew and, having mastered its rudiments, proceeded to the study of Bible and other subjects, all taught in Hebrew. It is hard to overstress the meaning of the Hebrew tongue for the new educators. To them, the "natural method" was no mere pedagogical tool. Hebrew was the language and the symbol of the modern Jewish culture which they dreamed of implanting in newborn Palestine and fostering in America. As to the Yiddish of the immigrant plebs, it was considered culturally inferior and neither worthy nor likely to outlive the immigrant generation. The Hebraic modernists tended to shy away from religion as such. Among them were secularists who, like the mentors Ahad Ha-Am and Dubnow, viewed the Jewish religion as the shell, not the kernel, of Judaism. Most of the Hebraic modernists were quite Orthodox, however, and most Orthodox parents sent their children to the Hebraist afternoon schools. Parental and communal expectations ensured that whatever the private leanings of some Hebrew educators, their schools would be religious. One whose outlook was greatly influenced by association with the Hebraic modernists, Mordecai M. Kaplan (1881–   ), took Hebraism, Zionism, and cultural pluralism as bases for the new American Judaism which he promulgated, called Reconstructionism.

The new spirit in Jewish education of the early twentieth century became institutionalized in the Talmud Torah. This communal school was typically found in the densely settled working- and lower-middle-class Jewish neighborhoods in large cities. Talmud Torahs* were rarely found in more prosperous districts, where synagogue-affiliated schools tended to be the rule. In addition to tuition fees—$20 to $25 per annum seems to have been average during the 1920's—the school derived its support from synagogue and neighborhood appeals. Support in several cities also came from the federations of Jewish charities. To most of these federations, however, it was a controversial question whether the charity and social services they provided for needy Jews ought to be extended to hard-pressed Jewish schools. The choice before the Jewish charity federations was complicated not only by financial

*The grammatically correct Hebrew plural is Talmudei Torah, but the common usage is employed here.

considerations but by the qualms, ranging from polite reservations to disdainful antagonism, felt by federation directors toward the Hebrew, rather Orthodox, nationalistic schools.

The Talmud Torah usually offered a five-year course, seven to ten hours weekly. With Hebrew the principal medium and content of instruction, the pupils were led into Bible, Jewish history, literature, religious customs, and ceremonies. Even Mishnah and Talmud were studied in some of the best schools. The curriculum was rounded out by Hebrew songs, games, holiday parties, and a junior congregation. This was indeed an exacting course of study, made more so by coming after a full day at public school. The Talmud Torah's intellectual zeal and content were impressive on paper, but its realities were less appealing. For in fact, although the educators built Hebrew schools with burning devotion, they never really converted the mass of Jewish parents to their outlook. Hardly different from heder days, two or three years in Talmud Torah were considered quite sufficient. No Hebrew school really counted on boys attending beyond their Bar Mitzvah, and preparations for that event, so despised by the pedagogues, had to be provided to satisfy a virtually unanimous parental demand. On the other hand, girls were taken as pupils equally with boys. Because they had no Bar Mitzvah preoccupations, families were usually better motivated in sending their daughters, who therefore made better pupils.

The Talmud Torah was voluntary and depended directly upon parental support, while the Sunday School had the institutional force of the temple behind it. Indeed some advocates of the Sunday School argued that seven years of consistent attendance, which well-run Sunday Schools secured, equaled two to three years of indifferent enrollment at a Hebrew school and produced more positive Jewish attitudes. Two hours daily after school, and Sunday morning, was a large dose of schooling indeed. Not surprisingly, classroom discipline was a frequent Talmud Torah problem.

Talmud Torah education became the foundation of Jewish education as a profession. Its pioneer teachers arrived mostly in the decade preceding the outbreak of World War I, and were augmented by a still larger postbellum immigration. In intellectual attainment these teachers formed quite a notable group, differing radically from the rather motley teaching corps of the earlier Jewish schools. They included Hebrew essayists and poets, some of high standing, as well as scholars and modernist Orthodox rabbis. Many had taught in the modern, intensive Hebrew schools of Eastern

Europe and Palestine, and they turned to Hebraic education with missionary zeal. In 1911 they founded the Hebrew Teachers Union, which exhibited real power from the 1920's as a militant trade union. Their main struggle lay in establishing professional standards of Hebrew education, which in turn provided the basis for their own employment at the relatively high salaries of $1,000 and even $1,200 yearly. Until 1929, the Hebrew Teachers Union enjoyed modest success in establishing pedagogical professionalism and security of tenure and improved salaries.

From Hebraist educational circles also came the drive to establish local educational systems. The pioneer of the new pedagogy and educational structure was Dr. Samson Benderly (1876–1944), a Palestine-born physician who abandoned medicine for Jewish education during his internship at the Johns Hopkins Hospital. He became the first head of the Bureau of Jewish Education of the Kehillah (Jewish Community) of New York City, the city-wide communal organism founded in 1910. He was backed morally and financially, even if with reservations, by leading "uptown" Jews disturbed at some of the social ills of the immigrant East Side. Rejecting the hadarim as hopeless and the Sunday Schools as alien to its East European clientele, the Bureau of Jewish Education federated and supported the afternoon Hebrew schools, provided in-service training to acculturate their teachers, wrote the first modern textbooks, and vigorously recruited pupils. A corps of zealous young college students collected school tuition from house to house and educated parents in the process. Benderly and his staff had flair and inventiveness, and generated excitement never known before. "Benderly's boys" became the leaders in the field after Benderly's personal importance declined around 1920.

Other communities followed New York Jewry's lead. During the 1920's, men like A. H. Friedland in Cleveland, Bernard Isaacs in Detroit, Louis Hourwich in Boston, and Dr. George Gordon, a practicing physician in Minneapolis, led Hebrew schooling in their cities, federating the schools and raising standards. With far smaller and more cohesive Jewish communities than in New York, it was a good deal easier to found bureaus of Jewish education and adjust educational facilities to local needs. Moreover, the local federations of Jewish philanthropies proved somewhat more amenable to assisting Jewish education.

The intellectual movement which helped to create Hebrew education in America also produced a contrary movement—secularist, left-wing Yiddish education. The devotion of Yiddish socialists and laborites to Jewish education came late, for their movement which began in the 1880's originally had no such interest. For decades, it aimed to prepare Yiddish-speaking workers for absorption into the American labor movement in anticipation of the social revolution sooner or later to come. The use of Yiddish was merely regarded as an unavoidable expedient until linguistic assimilation was complete. Although many older leaders continued to hold this view, time brought its own changes. Around 1910, an impressive Yiddish social, cultural, and trade union environment existed, and the doctrine of absorption into the larger American entity was put aside. Indeed, as linguistic assimilation progressed speedily, especially among the young, the desire grew to preserve the Yiddish language and its new secular milieu. A considerable immigration of writers and intellectuals arrived who added depth and color to Yiddish, and a new outlook defined "the language of the Jewish masses," Yiddish, as the true Jewish tongue, rather than Hebrew with its implications of intellectual aristocracy and traditional religion. One major intellectual, Chaim Zhitlovsky (1865–1943), contributed to a Yiddish, secular reinterpretation of Judaism. The Yiddishists sought a Judaism divorced from its millennial religious anchorage, and like the Hebraists they regarded American cultural pluralism as the basis for their educational program. Unlike the Hebraist educators, however, the Yiddishists' educational efforts were ridden with political factionalism which split their school systems. From the founding of the first schools about 1910, there was a schism between the Socialist Zionists and the anti-Zionist majority which regarded the plans for Palestine as delusive or a diversion from the main business of building Yiddish and socialism throughout the world. After the Bolshevik revolution, the split between Communists and their opponents became a savage feud which reached into the schools.

By the mid-1920's, at the peak of Yiddish secular education, some 10,000 to 12,000 youngsters attended the folkshuln where the study of Yiddish was the main business. Modern Yiddish literature and songs held a place of prominence; Zionist folkshuln added some Hebrew. A "usable past" was fashioned by recasting the Bible and Jewish holidays in secular, humanistic terms, and the struggle for labor's rights and socialism had its part in the curriculum. An early influence came from contemporary "Socialist Sunday Schools," where children of socialist parents were taught socialism and labor brotherhood and inoculated against the biases implanted by the government's public schools. Yet even with the lively and inventive Yiddish curriculum, underlying problems remained. The Yiddish schools did not become part of the general Jewish educational scene, and tended to be somewhat sectarian. To the disgust of Yiddish secular educators, they had to accommodate themselves to the insistence on the Bar Mitzvah of parents who could not be satisfied by the "secular" Bar Mitzvah which the folkshuln contrived. Yiddish education's terms of reference remained Jewish, and the general socialist, humanistic elements were always secondary. Above all, the Yiddish language never succeeded in transcending its character as an immigrant tongue, discarded in the process of acculturation. Hebrew, although diffused in much smaller circles than Yiddish, had profound historic roots and its devotees with increasing frequency could cite the shining example of growing, Hebrew-speaking Palestine. Yiddish had the stamp of the Lower East Side, and this identification proved a crippling handicap.

Secondary and especially higher Jewish education slowly became significant after 1910 as the rabbinical schools expanded and schools for Hebrew educators were attached to them. The Jewish Theological Seminary in New York City was refounded as a modernist traditional institution, headed by Solomon Schechter (1847–1915), and quickly rose to prominence and scholarly eminence. Hebrew Union College, disadvantaged by its location in provincial Cincinnati while population and movements focused in the Northeast, grew at a slower pace and continued to be a religious and intellectual focus for Reform Jewry. Stephen S. Wise founded the Jewish Institute of Religion in 1925 as a rabbinical school of Zionist, Hebraic orientation, generally Reform in religion; in 1948 it united with Hebrew Union College. The Rabbi Isaac Elhanan Yeshiva was not a professional school resembling these, for it long continued in the East European manner as an institution for pure Talmudic learning, not formal rabbinic ordination. Gradually, however, it sponsored secular studies by opening a high school and, in 1929, the liberal arts Yeshiva College under the direction of Bernard Revel (1885–1940). The Orthodox institution's ambition, only slightly realized in practice, to synthesize Jewish sacred learning with the modern arts and sciences, was a fighting matter for many years. To some high Orthodox, a college alongside a yeshiva was religiously unacceptable. More revealing, however, was the widespread Jewish antagonism to a college under Jewish (especially Orthodox) auspices. This was viewed as a "return to the ghetto" and to "parochialism" opposed to true higher education which had to liberate young Jews. Hebrew Union College and the Jewish Theological Seminary were readily accepted and supported as professional schools, but the path of Yeshiva College (later University) was a hard one, intellectually and financially. Outside these schools, Jewish learning itself had no place in American universities save some chairs of Semitic languages and The Dropsie College, a small graduate school of Hebrew and Semitic studies in Philadelphia which opened in 1910.

The new Hebrew teachers institutes were an interesting genre. Aside from those linked with the rabbinical schools, there were independent institutions—Herzliah in New York City, and in Boston, Philadelphia, Baltimore, and Chicago. They were generally of high academic quality. Their hallmark, however, was less pedagogical preparation than whole-souled Hebraism and cultural Zionism. The Yiddish schools had the analogous Jewish Teachers Seminary and People's University, the latter title reflecting their populism.

Several after-school Hebrew high schools were established after 1910, as well as a Yiddish *mittelshul.* New York City's Marshalliah Hebrew High School network offered curricula which basically continued that of the Talmud Torahs. For several thousand willing young students an educational progression thus existed, from a Talmud Torah to Hebrew high school, to one of the Hebrew teachers institutes. Hebrew as a modern language could also be studied in many high schools in New York City and elsewhere, beginning in the 1930's.

At the close of the 1920's the Jewish educational picture included Hebraic, traditionalist Talmud Torahs and their Yiddish counterparts; Sunday Schools, typical of Reform and widespread among Conservatives and even some Orthodox; a few all-day schools, called yeshivot, whose growth lay ahead. Many larger cities had bureaus of Jewish education supported by Jewish communal philanthropies.

Jewish education was badly mauled by the Great Depression of the 1930's. The social class differences between the varieties of Jewish schools were glaringly revealed: it was the poorer Jewish population who tended to prefer the more costly forms of education. As incomes fell and unemployment and business failures rose steeply, tuition revenue in the Talmud Torahs—not to mention day schools where each pupil had two full-time teachers—plummeted. A very large proportion of children was carried on the rolls without charge. The local Jewish philanthropic federations, to whom Jewish education was usually of marginal interest, found their income severely pinched and had to devote it primarily to material relief. In many communities, federation support of schools was eliminated. Often, Talmud Torahs and day schools stayed open only because their hapless teachers allowed themselves to be owed months of pay. Sunday School staff were part time and usually taught in the public schools. On account of this, and thanks to the better financial condition of the Reform and Conservative temples, the 1930's proved hard but not catastrophic. The same may be said of the Jewish Theological Seminary and Hebrew Union College. On the other hand, Yeshiva College suffered even worse than the Talmud Torahs.

It is interesting to note that the great surge of American trade unionism late in the 1930's included militant activity in the miniscule sector of the Hebrew Teachers Union. The 1940's arrived before this proletarized intelligentsia again found steady work and money on pay day.

While the Depression still dominated Jewish education as it did American life, deep emotional forces were astir. Germany's turn to Nazism and its undreamed-of treatment of the Jews horrified and shook American Jews. Disturbing manifestations of anti-Semitism appeared throughout the world, even in America. Only the growth of Palestine radiated hope. During the 1930's Jewish self-identification and solidarity greatly increased and a new kind of Jewish bond began to be discernible, replacing that which had grown from the earlier common immigrant experience. As Yiddish faded and economic distinctiveness became blurred, and the Jewish neighborhood began to look like any other, a new unity was forged by concern over the fate of Jews overseas—the lot of the Jews under Nazi rule and then the founding of the State of Israel. A half-articulate search began for a Judaism removed from East European and immigrant ways, yet retaining something of the forbears' traditions and fervor. The profound educational consequences of all this were delayed, however, until World War II ended.

The effect of world Jewish events was emotionally overpowering, but American Jewish education was overtly shaped by the social and cultural development of American Jewry after 1945. Thus, extensive suburbanization focused Jewish communal life in the new synagogue buildings and weakened older organizational interests. The Hebrew schools which nearly all these synagogues sponsored kept shorter hours than the urban Talmud Torahs, meeting Sunday and twice weekly, and had less ambitious curricula. They were financially more stable, paying their teachers better and on time. Also, they generally managed to hold their pupils for four or five years by establishing this period as prerequisite for the still universally desired Bar Mitzvah. Most Talmud Torahs, situated in declining urban areas, diminished steadily. Some which boasted enrollments of 700 and even higher during the 1930's had to close during the 1950's. However, a number reestablished themselves in newer neighborhoods with congregational affiliation.

Of all demographic changes the birthrate proved the most influential. Like Americans generally, Jews had their "baby boom" during the late 1940's and 1950's which filled to overflowing Jewish school classrooms eight or nine years later. The form of school preferred by parents was that which functioned as an arm of a usually Conservative congregation. The advantage of a school within a congregational establishment was a ready flow of pupils, financial backing, and good facilities in the hundreds of new synagogues being built. Ideologists of the congregational school pointed out that since Judaism was above all a religion, it was fitting and necessary that Jewish education and the religious institution par excellence be linked. The real and alleged secularist tendencies of the earlier Hebraic Talmud Torah came under their sharp criticism. Congregational Jewish education was not by any means wholly advantageous, however. The widespread habit of tying children's schooling to parental synagogue membership and building fund contributions irritated many. The school was subordinate to the policies of the congregation, its board and rabbi, even though autonomy was usually extensive. The tendency could be noted in some schools to stress narrower synagogal concerns over broader Jewish interests.

Generally, their curriculum inherited the Talmud Torah's,

concentrating on Hebrew and Bible, and Jewish religious and synagogal practice. The Conservative approach to Judaism in terms of the historic, collective religious experience of the Jewish people justified all these elements of the modern Hebraic curriculum. However, Conservative educators sought increasingly to inculcate a religious synagogue-centered outlook. The teaching of religious observance was more latitudinarian than that of the Orthodox, since the Conservatives did not feel strictly bound to the full ritual in the tradition. On the other hand, the ideal of study was honored, albeit in modernized form and content, and some young people were inducted into it. At the elementary level, however, beyond which few students advanced, Hebrew become greatly attenuated. Time was too limited, and moreover, the reality of Hebrew as the actual language of the State of Israel proved a less alluring educational ideal than it had been when only a dream. The general decline of instruction in foreign languages in American schools probably affected Hebrew, which by the 1950's could count on little of the old piety toward the sacred tongue. Yet with all its weaknesses, the synagogue school produced some distinguished specimens in places as diverse as Milwaukee, Detroit, Brooklyn, Philadelphia, and Albany.

Vigorous efforts by congregations to retain adolescent youngsters attained some success. The social and cultural activities of synagogues drew many youths and "Hebrew High Schools" sprouted, but usually of a standard far beneath genuine secondary education. A contribution of utmost value came from the Hebraic summer camps operated by the Teachers Institute of the Jewish Theological Seminary, Massad Camps, and others. The link between Jewish education and the house of worship was no novelty in Reform Judaism, where the Sunday School was always connected with the temple. While the Conservatives virtually abolished Sunday Schools except for the youngest children, the Reformers tended to add one or sometimes two days of weekday instruction. The curriculum shifted away from the old moralizing Bible stories to a new concentration on Jewish existence in the non-Jewish world as a moral individual and as a Jew. Greater interest in Jewish tradition, widespread in Reform Judaism from the 1930's, also became manifest in the curriculum.

It was during the 1950's that the first adequate nation-wide statistical surveys were taken. They revealed that the number of children enrolled in Jewish schools, which stood at an estimated

200,000 in 1935 and 268,000 in 1950, skyrocketed to 488,000 in 1956 and 589,000 in 1962. Yiddish schooling and communal Talmud Torahs dwindled to insignificance as some 88 percent of total enrollment was to be found in synagogally affiliated schools (1958). A most suggestive statistic indicates the rise of day school enrollment from barely 10,000 in 1945 to above 50,000 in 1962. While the total for all schools has leveled off in the low 600,000's since the latter year, the day schools at the time of writing reach 80,000.

This large-scale growth of private institutions giving both Hebrew and general education is probably the most significant Jewish educational movement since the 1940's. Until Conservatives began entering the field in the 1960's the movers were almost all Orthodox Jews; there were also a few secularists. Day schools (widely called *yeshivot ketanot*—elementary academies) had actually existed since early in the twentieth century. Most of them were not only Orthodox but Hebrew and modernist. Their abundant hours of Jewish studies, from about 8:30 A.M. to noon daily, permitted the full implementation of what was only an ambition in the contemporary Talmud Torah. The day schools generally drew their pupils from pious and sometimes learned families. Several schools cultivated intensive piety and taught in Yiddish, opposing the modern trends. All shared the Orthodox conception that the totality of Jewish law was sacred and binding, and that the main function of Jewish education was to induct the child into this personal and communal religious life. The ideal of sacred study held an important place. Secular American culture was recognized and accepted more or less willingly, yet the Orthodox hoped also to raise up learned Jews of the traditional type.

The yeshiva day schools stirred more controversy then any form of Jewish education. Questions were raised regarding the adequacy of their secular studies, their lengthy hours, and physical facilities. The real issue, however, lay deeper: the day school contravened the venerable American Jewish alliance with the public school. As noted above, that was no marriage of convenience but the wholehearted acceptance of an ideology, which Jewish day schools now seemed by implication to question. When the issue was thus perceived, it was no wonder that feelings could run strong against these institutions. None of the Jewish philanthropic federations would grant them support, and regnant philosophies of Jewish education also regarded them dubiously.

That acculturated American Jews sent their children in sharply increasing proportions to Jewish day schools requires explanation. For many parents, prosperity made private schooling financially feasible and could betoken higher social status. Much more prevalent, however, were strong Jewish convictions and the desire to bestow upon children a comprehensive Jewish education, together with reluctance to send them to a second (and usually superficial) school after the public school day. The most menacing cause appeared around 1960—the decline of the urban public schools and the racial turmoil within them. In areas seriously affected by these problems, Jewish parents especially sought out Jewish and other private schools. Most of their doubts about the adequacy of secular studies were dispelled by the impressive performance of graduates in secondary and higher education. At the same time, spokesmen presented the day schools not only in simple terms of intensive Jewish education but also as an alternative to the educational bias of the public school. The yeshivot, as they saw them, inculcated esteem for intellectual achievement and moral responsibility, in both of which public schools failed. In terms of American Jewish communal needs, day school graduates were expected to become the sorely lacking educated leadership.

A significant feature of the day school movement was the rise not only of yeshiva high schools but of yeshivot for advanced students. Most of them were founded by refugee rabbinic scholars during and after World War II. The curriculum was exclusively Talmudic, and the general outlook was transplanted from nineteenth-century Eastern Europe. Several thousand young men, mostly of American birth, deferred or abandoned college study to enter into the yeshiva regimen of intense piety and Talmud study.

Jewish day schools suffered constant financial troubles, basically because each child required two teachers' services. Early in the 1960's tuition ranged between $500 and $1,000 yearly, a heavy burden for families with several children. Rarely was a teacher paid as much as $6,000 yearly; most of the staff also taught in afternoon congregational schools to make an adequate living. However, except for the day schools, the financial position of Jewish education as a whole measurably improved. This was a consequence not only of prosperity but also of increased communal support. Several dozen local Jewish communities added Jewish education as a beneficiary to their annual campaigns for hospitals and social services, community relations, overseas relief, and aid to

Israel. A superstructure of nationwide bodies was added during the 1940's— the American Association for Jewish Education, concerned with educational publicity, research, and statistics; the National Council for Jewish Education, consisting of upper-level professional educators; the National Society for Jewish Day Schools (Torah Umesorah), an Orthodox group; and denominational bodies like the United Synagogue (Conservative) Commission on Jewish Education.

Considerable improvement was thus to be seen in the enrollment, financial position, facilities, and regard for Jewish education. Yet the most serious problem, the shortage of teachers, showed no improvement. The European-trained generation of learned, profoundly committed pedagogues was dying out and new arrivals could not be expected. Young American Jews, with all professions open, were most unlikely to choose Jewish education as a career. The Hebrew teachers colleges had modest enrollments, and few in their graduating classes became—and remained—professional educators. A highly diverse group took up the slack—Israeli students, part-time rabbis, upper yeshiva students, and partially trained housewives. The salary and conditions of Hebrew teachers improved, but the professionally trained pedagogue on the staff of the Jewish school was the exception. Despite widespread awareness that the shortage was more serious than that in the public schools, it only grew worse.

Higher Jewish education also enjoyed an impressive growth from the 1940's. The Orthodox yeshivot have been mentioned, and the rabbinical schools enhanced their stature and renown. Yeshiva College remained firm in its Orthodoxy, and became a university granting degrees in many fields of the arts and sciences. A new institution, Brandeis University, was Jewish in sponsorship. A significant trend of the later 1950's and 1960's was the founding of chairs of Jewish studies at many universities, some of highest academic quality. This development was generally greeted in the Jewish community with enthusiasm, with little critical discussion whether one or two "Jewish courses" a Jewish student might take in college properly realized the goals of Jewish education.

The Jewish educational philosophy formulated after 1910, which reached its widest diffusion during the 1920's and 1930's, unquestionably exhibited signs of obsolescence. A tide of objection rose against the old Hebraism, arguing that Hebrew study in the stringently limited school hours required too much time and produced too meager results. Better, it was urged, use the few years to learn Bible, Jewish history, and religious principles and practices in English with a patina of Hebrew terms and verses. Orthodox day schools, which did not lack the class time, were for their part influenced by the sometimes anti-Hebraic pietistic surge of the 1950's and early 1960's. They tended to turn in many cases toward religious devotionalism. During these years, attempts were made to find a new educational vision, the most distinctive of which came from the Melton Research Center at the Jewish Theological Seminary, directed by Seymour Fox. Their ambitious, carefully articulated program proposed to combine modern behavioral science with the findings of contemporary biblical and historical scholarship to reach rather traditional Jewish educational goals. The end purpose, as the Melton group formulated it, was to produce a personally moral, socially responsible traditional Jew, in whom the synthesis between the secular and the Jewish had begun from the elementary level of his education. Similar curricular reexaminations were undertaken in other circles, but with less comprehensiveness and intellectual power.

Jewish education was better established and financed during the 1950's and 1960's than ever before. At the same time, the level of Jewish knowledge among American Jews lagged further and further beneath their general educational attainment as study, that ancient Jewish cynosure, inspired young Jews in almost every field except that in which it originated. By the standards of centuries, American Jews were indeed functionally illiterate as Jews. By the standards of American life, however, an ethno-religious community which founded and sustained a network of schools attended at some time by most of its youth possessed a great resource to assure its own future and enrich the fabric of American life.

THE PRESENT MOMENT IN JEWISH EDUCATION

by WALTER I. ACKERMAN

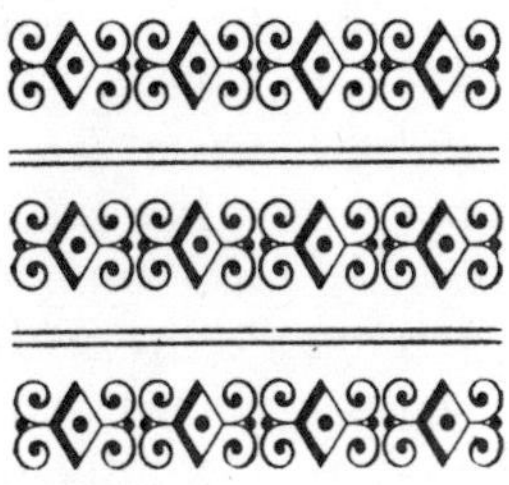

INTRODUCTION

CHANGES in American Jewish education result from a variety of influences: new demands upon the schools, disillusionment with the results of traditional forms of American Jewish education, and the impact of developments in general education. These changes are analyzed by Walter Ackerman, a leading professor of Jewish education who has had considerable experience as a teacher and principal in American Jewish schools. Ackerman's analysis also draws on a wide knowledge of the field of general education and the numerous proposals which have been made in recent years to restructure the American school.

In a previous study published in the American Jewish Year Book, *Vol. 70 (1969), Ackerman presented a detailed analysis of the shortcomings of Jewish education in the United States. In the present article he turns his attention to some recent efforts to effect radical changes in the American Jewish school. Ackerman emphasizes the emergence of a group of new-style Jewish educators who matured during the years of the counter-culture and whose perspective differs from that of the previous generation. Where earlier Jewish educators sought to develop schools which would compare favorably with the models they knew from public education, new-style Jewish educators deem such models worthless,* a bankrupt and even harmful system of education. Ackerman is sympathetic to their proposals but he is also concerned with the conservation of traditional values; he warns that changes must prove their worth before existing ways of educating the young are discarded.

What is the central idea of the new-style educators? It is that the task of the Jewish school is to help the child realize himself as a Jew. In pursuit of this objective the child must be transformed from a passive recipient of the wisdom of the past to an active seeker after whatever will result in self-realization. Thus it follows that Jewish education must emphasize the creation of an environment where the child may experiment with a variety of materials and media in his attempt to achieve self-realization. For the older youngster the emphasis is on the school as a community in which a variety of Jewish experiences and activities are available.

Although Ackerman realizes how far this approach diverges from the text-centered approach of the traditional Jewish school, he maintains that it should be given a hearing—at least it has the advantage of making the child an active participant in his own education, and therefore may facilitate learning. An earlier generation of educators, too, had maintained that the child had a role to play in his own education, but Ackerman believes that whatever willingness they displayed to modify the traditional curriculum was based on adult-centered needs and on their appraisal of the limitations of the American Jewish school.

Self-realization aside, Ackerman emphasizes that all Jewish educators—whether old-style or new-style—have had to assume central responsibility for the building of the child's Jewish identity, and he questions whether the full implications of this have been understood. Building identity may call for restructuring the curriculum. New importance may have to be given to the crucial years of adolescence. Indeed the objective of building Jewish identity may involve a deemphasis of the classroom; it may be that experiences outside the classroom are crucial to the realization of the objectives of the Jewish school.

Ackerman is sympathetic to the need for affective experience in building identity, but he is concerned about the values which may be lost when the traditional stress of the Jewish school on the mastery of subject matter and on intellectual skills is disregarded. He is hesitant to go the way of the counter-culture with its emphasis on the primacy of inner experience; apparently he believes a middle way can be found.

Ackerman approves of certain other aspects of the approach of new-style Jewish educators. While old-style Jewish educators—whether Reform, Conservative, or Orthodox (or even Hebraist or Yiddishist)—emphasized that being a good Jew and being a good American were mutually reinforcing, new-style educators emphasize the confrontation between Judaism and the American consensus. Ackerman implies that such confrontation is healthy; he states that there is a "justified distance" between "Americanism" and Judaism.

Like Gartner, Ackerman is impressed with the growth of the most intensive form of Jewish education—the day schools. New-style Jewish educators have said very little about such institutions. Rather, they have concentrated their attention on the shortcomings of the Sunday and Hebrew schools. Ackerman—at one time a principal of a day school—believes that day schools have problems of their own. He is troubled by the division of the school into two curricula with a resulting double standard and compartmentalization. He notes that even in Conservative day schools only limited attempts have been made to develop an integrated curriculum. He quotes the principal of an Orthodox day high school to the effect that in the general curriculum the student is taught to develop his critical faculties and to question authority, whereas in the Jewish curriculum he is taught that what is written in sacred literature must be accepted.

Ackerman concludes with a brief analysis of the introduction of Jewish studies into the American university. He views this development favorably and feels that it may have salutary effects, although he draws a distinction between Jewish education and Jewish studies. The academic study of Jewish culture is neither a panacea which will remedy all of the defects of elementary and secondary Jewish education, nor a solution to the problem of building Jewish identity and commitment.

M. S.

JEWISH EDUCATION in recent years has been accorded an unaccustomed place of priority in discussions of communal policies and programs. Journals of Jewish concern, national membership organizations, synagogue groups, and welfare funds—the panoply of Jewish life in this country—have all devoted space and time to an examination and critique of the workings of the Jewish school in the United States. The reasons for the current spate of interest are varied, but taken together they reflect the concerns of the American Jewish community at this moment in its history.

The rhythm of attention given by a society to schools and other institutions engaged in the education and training of the young is very often a reliable barometer of its sense of the present and hopes for the future. A case can be made, I think, for a reading of the relationship between society and its schools in the following terms: pious platitudes about the ennobling effects of schooling generally reflect a society which is calm, self-satisfied, and confident; serious talk and analysis of the purposes and effects of schooling signal a sensitivity to change and an awareness of tension and strain; substantial inputs of *new* effort, money, and time for education denote a society in crisis. These differentiated levels of concern all share the often naïve assumption that complex social movements originate in schools and are significantly susceptible to the influences of formal schooling—a view which looks upon education as both cause and cure.

There is no need here to detail the fact that many American Jews no longer feel calm, self-satisfied, or confident. What is important to note, however, is that an increasing number of American Jews are today talking seriously about Jewish education. Individuals and groups that heretofore had displayed little or no interest in Jewish schools are asking themselves and others questions about what these schools do and do not do and what they should and should not do. The talk may lack the rigor of sophisticated analysis and the grandeur of philosophical design but it does reveal a painful anxiety about the quality of Jewish life and a perturbed diffidence for the future of the Jewish community.

The cadence of discussion in Jewish circles takes its beat from the events which racked America in the decade of the sixties. The clash of cultures echoes to Jewish accents. The older generation looks to the Jewish school for solutions to the manifestations of alienation and indifference, intermarriage, anti-Israel postures, drug abuse, and sexual permissiveness which dot the Jewish youth scene. At the same time young Jewish activists whose "radicalism" is directed toward the Jewish community taunt the Establishment with accusations of hypocrisy and cant, shallowness and indifference to traditional values and institutions, and demand increased and more generous support of Jewish education.

Community interest in schools is, of course, at least one step removed from the actual work of the schools themselves. While the interest and support of the community are vital if schools are to achieve their maximum effectiveness—and we really do not know to what degree and in what ways Jewish schools can be effective—the actual outcome of the activities which take place in a school depend, in the final analysis, on those who work there. Jewish schools, or any other kind, for that matter, can never be any better than their personnel.

I

Three generations of educational administrators presently influence the course of Jewish education in this country. First from the point of view of age, experience, and service are those men who, guided by Samson Benderly and his work in the development of the Bureau of Education of the New York Kehillah during the first two decades of this century, laid the foundation of Jewish education in the United States. Most of these men are no longer living, and those who are, are no longer actively engaged in the conduct of schools or other educational agencies. Their presence, however, is felt in a variety of ways. As respected members of the community, their advice is often sought by communal leaders and agencies interested in education; some of them continue to write and publish; others are still active in professional organizations and help shape policy. Most important, however, is the fact that the institutions they created and maintained are still normative in Jewish education.

The administration of the overwhelming majority of Jewish

elementary and secondary schools, Bureaus of Jewish Education, and teacher-training schools is today in the hands of a younger group of men, and in some instances, women. This second generation of professional Jewish educators, most of whose members are American-born and trained, began to move into positions of responsibility in the years immediately after World War II. Its principal sphere of activity has been the congregational elementary school. Indeed this is the group of men and women who have given that school its present shape and form. The detailed shortcomings of that institution which characterize current criticism of Jewish education are in effect a scathing indictment—not always justified—of two decades of effort.

Several salient characteristics of this group of educators are worth noting. Its psychology was formed by immigrant parents, the Depression, service in the armed forces during World War II, the Holocaust, and the creation of the State of Israel. In most instances the decision for a career in Jewish education was deliberate and willful—a sharp contrast to the maligned melamed of an earlier day who often taught only because there was nothing else he could do. The work of this generation is marked more by administrative finesse than by intellectual sophistication. Its efforts have been directed more toward consolidating, firming up, and smoothing out the rough edges of the plans and programs of predecessors than toward innovation and change. Its dominant stance has been *how* rather than *why*. Finally the men and women of whom we are here speaking were already into middle age during those years of the 1960's which brought such far-reaching changes in values and life styles. They had spent a good part of their lives working in a vacuum of indifference to much of what they stood for and then found themselves faulted for having failed to inculcate their students with deep commitments to traditional Jewish concerns. Small wonder then that their posture today is sometimes edged with a mixture of futility and despair.

Yet another group active today in the work of Jewish schools deserves attention. The presence of this third generation was first felt some five years or so ago. Some of these young men, and a greater number of women than has heretofore been the case, have come to Jewish education along a route which, beginning in a congregational school, led to deep involvement in summer camp programs and synagogue youth organizations, and brought them to Jewish teacher-training schools and rabbinical seminaries as preparation for their careers. These are the "good kids." Others traveled a more circuitous road which finally arrived at Jews and Judaism through a newly found ethnic and religious sensitivity developed less by planned programs of Jewish education than by events on college campuses and in America at large.

While this group does not yet hold positions of dominating influence, it has aroused an interest in its views and activities which is greater than its numbers and limited professional experience would ordinarily warrant. There are among these young people some who are prolific and sometimes even eloquent writers. The mushrooming of the "underground" Jewish student press has provided them with a ready forum attended to by a circle which is wider than the intended audience. Several experiments in education, most notably the Havurot in Boston and New York,[1] are quite properly identified as the design and style of a younger generation of Jews and have attracted considerable notice. The frenetic and sometimes fawning response of the organized Jewish community to the "youth revolution" has brought invitations to young educators, who are supposedly more "with it" than their older colleagues, to address Federation meetings, to participate in national conferences of professional organizations, and to take part in workshops and colloquia, all of which provide them with opportunities for expression not always available to an earlier generation. Basic, however, to the hearing—not always sympathetic, by the way— these young men and women are receiving, is the sense that they are an instance of something having gone right. They are loyal and committed Jews and one wants to listen to them in the hope of discovering what went into making them what they are—what worked with them might work with others.

An understanding of the educational stance of this younger generation of educators must begin with an appreciation of its location in time and place. It is a generation born into an affluent society permeated by the spirit of modernism.[2] The Depression, World War II, the Holocaust, the events which shaped the world

[1]Stephen C. Lerner, "The Havurot," *Conservative Judaism*, Vol. XXIV, No. 3, Spring 1970, pp. 2–15.

[2]For a discussion of the relationship between modernism and Jewish Education see Leonard J. Fein, "Suggestions Toward the Reform of Jewish Education in America," *Midstream*, February 1972, pp. 41–50.

they inherited, speak to them only through the filter of an older generation's memories. The State of Israel, born at almost the same time, is a commonplace of life stripped of the romance of the struggle for independence. Anti-Semitism is more a datum of sociological research than a burden of searing personal experience. Theirs is a time which eschewed the embracive ideologies of an earlier day and sought its definition in the specifics of the civil rights movement and the detailed turmoil of anti-war demonstrations. They are Jewish and they are American and they are of the world in a new and complicated mixture.

The everyday world of the Jewish schools in which these people work carries the mark of their presence. The translation of their own experience into an educational strategy introduces a vocabulary heretofore only rarely used in Jewish education:

> The major objective of the Hebrew High School in America should be the creation of an authentic Jewish community. This community would be defined as a group of Jews identified with "Klal Yisroel" who are ready and willing to share feelings, ideas, perceptions, questions, and insights into who they are, from where they have come, what they are doing, and in what direction they are going. In short, they will be both experiencing and examining together the content of their lives in terms of ultimate meaning and purpose. . . .
>
> Given such an objective, the role of the Hebrew High School must be somewhat changed from the limited concept of the conventional school, that of imparting book knowledge in classrooms according to an ordered and prearranged scheme. The school if it is to be truly meaningful and significant, has to focus on real life challenges.
>
> It ought to become a community and cultural center open to and fostering all kinds of relevant experiences, including formal classes, social organizations, special interest groups, religious functions, interschool activities, and many other experiences not even envisioned yet. . . .
>
> School ought to become the kind of place where each person in the school community "can do his own thing." This implies providing a super-rich environment of options, a potpourri of experiences laden with educational value, and a collection of diverse, talented, and concerned people who are teenagers, teachers, specialists, artists, rabbis, scholars, community leaders, and parents.[3]

[3]Efraim Warshaw, *Jewish Education and Ecstasy: Toward a Theory of Instruction and Curriculum* (Temple Israel of Great Neck: Hebrew High School, n.d.).

I have quoted the foregoing because it seems to me to state and imply much of what is the approach of the group under discussion. This includes a high degree of student involvement and participation in all phases of planning and execution, a heightened emphasis on the affective, and attention to interpersonal relationships, a readiness to move beyond the framework of prescribed forms and structures, and a willingness to admit to the legitimacy of a wide variety of views and patterns of personal expression. It is a conception of learning which affords place to traditional modes and methods of study but finds them lacking when used in isolation from broader and more encompassing experiences. The task of the educator then is not to direct a school or to inculcate a point of view but rather to create an environment in which the student is free to experiment in a variety of settings and with an assortment of materials and media in an encouraged attempt to define a pattern which suits his needs.

This sketch of an educational posture acquires more pronounced shading when it is lined by attention to several attitudes which are of a more general nature than those cited above. The acknowledgment of the centrality of mitzvot in Judaism is accompanied by a view of religion as a continued search for self-realization rather than as a closed system of pre-ordained imperatives. Religious practice, as a consequence, is a highly personal and individualistic matter and even though its communal aspect is significant, the final determinant of the student's religious behavior is his position of the moment. This conception of religion and religious behavior obviously requires a curriculum and methodology radically different from that which obtains in most Jewish schools at present. The legitimacy of Jewish nationalism finds expression and support in identification and commitment to the State of Israel and a recognition of its crucial role in the Jewish future. At the same time the Jewish community of the United States is accorded a place of primacy alongside the *Yishuv*. Those Jews who find fulfillment in *Aliyah* are granted the rightness of their position—for themselves; those Jews who choose to remain in the United States are equally rightminded and need not suffer guilt and self-recrimination for their decision. The teaching of Israel, a subject whose parameters are today only vaguely perceived, is perforce a dialectic in which the student is asked to measure the weight of various alternatives in attempting to place the locale of his life. The relationship of Jews to America is tempered by the critique of American society and culture which characterizes the "counter-culture." There is, I believe, a substantive difference in both tone and content between the statements of synagogal educational commissions and those of young "radical" Jewish educators when they try to limn the connections between Jews and Judaism and the Jewish community and America.

Contrast statement *a* which is from a Conservative document, statement *b* which is from an Orthodox document, and statement *c* which is from a Reform document, with *d* which is from a volume by radical Jews:

> a) The curriculum should be constructed in accordance with the following goals:
>
> . . . *To explore the teachings of Judaism and the ideals of American democracy for the reciprocal influence they should have on each other,* especially during the study of American Jewish history and the Bible, when the biblical roots and spiritual values of American democratic ideals and of some American holidays should be pointed out.
>
> b) Talmud Torah should convey the sense of the large bond of unity with all people believing in God and living the right life. It should inspire an intense patriotism for the Jewish people together with a ready acceptance of *dina di malkhuta* (the law of the land) and of the unity of all men created in the image of God.
>
> c) To inculcate in children and youth the universal ideals of Israel's prophets and sages, leading toward dynamic involvement in service for freedom, brotherhood, and peace.[4]
>
> d) . . . demonstrations of Judaism's compatibility with American life are pathetically uninteresting because increasing numbers of Jewish teenagers are themselves uncomfortable with their governmental, cultural, and economic surroundings. . . . [The] Jewish tradition would share youths' critique without supporting everything kids have

[4]The quotations are from the following: a) "Objectives and Standards for the Congregational School," United Synagogue Commission on Jewish Education; b) "Model Program for the Talmud Torah," Union of Orthodox Jewish Congregations; c) "Curriculum for Jewish Religious Schools: Guiding Principles and General Aims," Union of American Hebrew Congregations. The statements of curricular aims and objectives may be found in their entirety in Alexander M. Dushkin and Uriah Z. Engelman, *Jewish Education in the United States* (New York: American Association for Jewish Education, 1959), pp. 35–38. While it is true that the specific statements I have quoted date from the decade of the fifties, I doubt that a reworking today of those particular sections would result in any substantial change.

> done (or have been duped into doing) as a result of the critique. It offers examples of constructive alternatives. . . . Jewish education for these young people will have to build its own supportive community of actions and shared ritual because the existing organized Jewish community is little more than a collection of mimeograph machines and pooled nostalgia. The Jewish school must not be a set of classrooms, but a tentative community which provides hints of viable cultural, spiritual, and interpersonal alternatives to the emptiness of students' current pressured, cram-packed, instrumental, goal-oriented, and fragmented lives. . . . The Jewish community in history has represented an arena in which . . . a joyful passing on of fundamental affirmations from old to young—and back—was felt. I am suggesting that if the Jewish community is to remain such an arena, it may have to alienate itself from, and be increasingly critical of, the general drift of American society.[5]

A curriculum consistent with statement *d* would mark a significant turn of direction for Jewish education in the United States. Among other things it would move the school from teachings which attempt to convince that there is no essential conflict between "Americanism" and Judaism, an underlying motif of current practice which frequently borders on the apologetic, to honest confrontations and justified distance between the two.

Now it may be argued that I have dwelled inordinately on the views of what is after all only a small group of educators who have yet to prove themselves over the long and often lonely haul of Jewish education. One may also point out that the ideas I have presented as theirs are really not all that new and at best are derived from the style and rhetoric of the current crop of American educational romantics and reformers. The criticism is correct if not entirely valid. The worth of an idea cannot be determined by its origin.

[5]James Sleeper, "Authenticity and Responsiveness in Jewish Education," *The New Jews* (New York: Random House, Vintage Books, 1971), pp. 124, 135, 138, 140. My understanding of the young educators I have been describing is drawn, in part, from my reading of *The New Jews*, the quarterly *Response* and a variety of papers and magazines which they and their colleagues publish, or edit, or use as vehicles for the expression of their views. A listing of these publications may be found in Ann Rothstein, ed., *A Guide to Jewish Student Groups* (New York: North American Jewish Students' Network, 1971), p. 63 ff. The proliferation of newspapers and journals is a fascinating phenomenon and merits consideration in any evaluation of Jewish life in America today. For an analysis of the student press see Bill Novak and Robert Goldman, "The Rise of the Jewish Student Press," *Conservative Judaism*, Vol. XXV, No. 2, Winter 1971, 5–19.

There is little in the theory and method of modern Jewish education that is not derivative and while that may be one of the root causes of the failures of Jewish schooling, the fact is that until Jews succeed in developing a powerful and generative theory of education which is drawn from our tradition and responsive to our needs and purposes we shall be dependent on the work of others. The real question, then, is not whether or not we borrow, for borrow we must, but whether or not a theory which arose out of a particular set of circumstances and was designed to solve a specific type of problem is sufficiently generalizable to permit its application to another setting. The answer will almost always have to be empirical—e.g., we shall never know whether or not the "open classroom" is appropriate for Jewish schools until Jewish schools begin to experiment with the open classroom.

There is a striking similarity between the young men and women of our time who have made a commitment to Jewish education and that handful of men who some forty and fifty years ago undertook to develop a system of Jewish schools suited to the needs of a new time and place. Both reflect the regnant educational philosophies of the period—in the earlier instance the predominant influence was that of John Dewey and his disciples at Teachers College and there is a direct line of thought which connects the two in more ways than are immediately apparent. The "new" voices today meet the same kind of resistance as that which greeted their predecessors. Hopefully we are now a little more sophisticated and will afford our younger colleagues a wider latitude in the exercise of their inspiration. Indeed the hospitality withheld or extended to ideas which are somewhat different from accepted practice may serve as an index of the future vitality of Jewish education in this country—we will simply not attract able, dedicated, and well-trained young men and women if they do not see in Jewish education a wide-ranging opportunity for the full expression of their talent and ideas.

II

A profound dissatisfaction with the current state of Jewish education, a discontent common to lay supporters, communal agencies, parents, children, and educators alike, coupled with a sense of urgency born of the temper of the times has stimulated a shift in the foci of educational effort. That is not to say that the majority of Jewish schools in the country have become something other than what they have been in recent memory. It is rather to note that here and there one can discern changes in style and emphasis which for all their distance from a really new conception of what Jewish education ought be, do significantly affect the character of existing institutions.

The pattern of educational practice touched upon above may best be understood when described in terms of elements common to all schools and all programs of formal education—the student, the teacher, subject matter, and society. The distinguishing characteristics of an educational theory are found in its comprehension of each of these commonplace elements, the place it sets for each in the hierarchy of emphasis and importance, and the role it assigns to each in the process of teaching and learning. Each element obviously stands in a delicate relationship to the others; the contours of their interaction with all their modifying consequences are determined by the authority attributed to each.

Now what about the student? It is no exaggeration to state that the traditional modes of Jewish education, both in their classical European forms and the more modern American styles, view the student as object. The archetypical curricular statement of *Aboth* (5:24): "*Scriptures* at age five; *Mishna* at ten; *Gemara* at fifteen" can hardly be construed as "child-centered." We have here a predetermined course of study which all but ignores the student's abilities, needs, and interests. Such questions of pedagogy as did concern previous generations of teachers were by and large restricted to figuring out how one might teach the prescribed subject matter rather than to asking whether it was appropriate or not. That the student himself might have a say in the determination of his course of studies was, of course, beyond the realm of admission. In fairness one must add that this stance was not peculiar to Jews alone; indeed it was, and in many instances still remains, the dominant posture of most of the world's educational systems.

Even more recent curricular formulations do not grant the student an active role in the development of school programs. A case in point is the *Curriculum Outline for the Congregational*

School published by the United Synagogue Commission on Jewish Education. The introduction to that statement declares, "Of primary considerations are the requirements of the growing Jewish child within the evolving American Jewish community. Our concern does not lie in a curriculum determined exclusively either by child interests or by adult considerations. Both factors should determine the nature of instruction. As set forth herein, the two elements must be viewed as complementary in the real life situation.

"To insure the vitality of Judaism in the American environment, the Jewish community must transmit its rich cultural heritage to the child. It is imperative that the child acquire the knowledge and experience essential to Jewish living. The Jewish school program also must provide a foundation of basic content and skills that will foster the leadership so essential to the continued growth and development of the Jewish way of life in the United States. . . .

"Accordingly, this curriculum attempts a twin focus—on the child as child and on the child as a future adult. A curriculum which is in the main adult-centered . . . defeats itself; it ignores the vital factors of child interest and level of maturity in selecting, grading, and presenting content at any particular age level. The pupil is a child as well as a potential Jewish adult: he has his own needs and interests, as essential to his well-being as group survival is to the community. The elements of child interest and level of maturity are therefore basic and constant factors determining the selection of content and the way in which it is presented at each grade level."[6]

Whether or not this curriculum achieves its stated purpose is beside the point here. What is germane is the palpable discrepancy between the detail of its program and its professed concern for the child. For all its "modern" terminology it is, in its own way, as prescribed, predetermined, and inflexible as its predecessors. The division into strict subject matter categories, the allocation of time calculated in some instances in minutes, and the overriding concern with the past hardly bespeak attention to "elements of child interest and levels of maturity." The plain fact is that this is a

[6]Louis L. Ruffman, *Curriculum Outline for the Congregational School* (New York: United Synagogue Commission on Jewish Education, 1959), pp. 4–5.

curriculum which is grounded in the rhetoric of conclusion; its structure reflects categories of adult thought and its ideas of childrens' interests are drawn from the minds of adults. Fairness once again dictates the observation that most curricula of the time, Jewish and non-Jewish alike, are couched in similar terms.

There is, I believe, a substantial difference between the examples I have cited above and a number of recent projects in curriculum development and classroom instruction. The latter offer clear evidence of serious attempts to use expressed student interests and concerns as a basis for courses of study and to allow the student an active role in the determination of the school program. The most ambitious undertaking of this sort is the current curriculum development program of the Commission on Jewish Education of the Central Conference of American Rabbis—Union of American Hebrew Congregations.[7] The conceptual framework of the proposed curriculum rests on the assumption that ". . . educators must be receptive to the problems and needs of the students and attempt to create a synthesis between traditional values and present concerns. The two focal points of curriculum are both what the learner *wants* to learn and what he *ought* to learn." Student inputs were delivered through "a national survey . . . conducted to determine the interests, concerns, and problems of students on all age levels. The most prevalent concerns and issues were then tabulated and organized into several broad categories. . . ." This proposal for a curriculum is only the first step in a complicated process and any judgment as to the program's effectiveness must await the development of specific courses, materials, and educational procedures. There is no question, however, that the program devolves from a fundamental commitment to student interests as perceived by the student himself.

While not as elaborate in design nor as potentially far-reaching in impact as the program described above, the experiences of several congregational high schools, by their very limited nature, may help sharpen our understanding of the issue at hand. One educational director reports the following, ". . . our students have [an] unstructured program. They learn in their own way. We set it up so that they could learn what they feel *they* need. The majority of the students fit into an exciting game approach. In the future

[7]Jack D. Spiro, "Toward a Conceptual Framework for Reform Jewish Education," *Compass* (Commission of Jewish Education CCAR-UAHC), No. 13, January-February 1971.

something different may work better. The basic principle here is that we are working with the students and their needs. For example, we weren't teaching Hebrew in any intensive way. And about a dozen students came to us and said, 'We would like to learn more Hebrew,' so we made it possible. They are now learning it on overtime, because they feel they are not getting enough twice a week. Now more kids have said they want the program so I have to get another teacher. The main thing is that the kids want to learn. I don't think you can teach something to kids who don't want to learn."[8] Another school principal describes a similar approach in this way, ". . . The first level is that of uncovering the thoughts and feelings of the kids themselves, not on a specific issue, but rather in a free-wheeling, open-ended way. This should allow the kids to bring in their own experiences with very little intervention on the part of the teacher. . . . The kids made . . . choice(s) before the summer, so that I could spend part of my summer preparing materials for the fall. Their choice was among . . . five or six areas. And they presented this choice in terms of questions: What is my relationship with X? Who am I, what can I be in terms of X? They hopefully made their choice in terms of real needs, needs they felt and which became responses to religious questions, to existential questions. Now I hadn't planned out each of these six curricula in detail. I decided not to do that but wait and see how the kids respond."[9]

The commitment to the child and his crucial role in determining the work of the school presently finds its most complete expression in the "open-school" movement. The influence of the open-school movement has already been felt in Jewish education in a variety of ways.[10] The experience of an enthusiastic young teacher who applied the principles of the open school to an afternoon Hebrew school is illustrative of the approach:

[8]Richard Goldman in *Report of Work Conference on Current Concerns in Jewish Education* (American Jewish Committee and American Association for Jewish Education), Jewish Communal Affairs Dept., American Jewish Committee, September 1970, p. 15.

[9]Burt Jacobson in *Report of Work Conference on Current Concerns in Jewish Education*, pp. 45, 47.

[10]*Opening the Classroom and Individualizing Instruction* (New York: Dept. of Teaching Methods and Materials, National Curriculum Institute of the American Association for Jewish Education), May 1972.

This year in an attempt to create a microcosm of Jewish community in the classroom, as well as to provide a better environment for learning, I have decentralized the room, providing an open flexible space which is divided into functional areas. I have constructed an environment rich in learning resources—concrete materials as well as books and other material. The children are free to explore this room as well as the hall, the stairwell, the library, and the sanctuary, individually or in groups and to choose their own activities. As for the teachers, my aides and I work most of the time with individual children or two or three, rarely presenting the same material to everyone or to the class as a whole. . . .

Our day usually starts with an *asepha*—a gathering of teachers and students on our large multi-colored rug. Originally this was a time for announcements or a description of something new in the room. Lately, I've begun to use this fifteen minutes to introduce new Hebrew vocabulary or new ideas and concepts to the class as a whole. In the past few weeks we've learned how to count to 1,000. Now that they've learned numbers, the children want to be able to tell time, so that will be their next project.

After the *asepha* the children are free to choose their own activities for the day. I use the first forty-five minutes to work with three or four small groups on Hebrew while my assistant helps the others to plan their day. And each day is different because each child uses the room differently according to his own interests, concerns, and feelings on that particular day.

For example, let's take a typically "untypical" day. Michael and David are decorating the Holy Ark (which we made out of heavy tri-wall cardboard) with a picture of Jerusalem. Their crayons are strewn out on one side of them and their Hebrew books open on the other, and they're practicing their *B'yad Ha'Lashon* dialogue while they color.

In the meantime, Karen and Sharon are taking a more conventional approach. They are listening to the tapes of the dialogues in the language lab. This structure was also built out of the tri-wall material and is equipped with two cassette tape recorders and four earplugs.

David and Chuck, curled up on the large overstuffed chairs in the library, are immersed in their books. David is reading about the Baal Shem Tov, whom he calls Rabbi Israel. During an *asepha,* I had read a story from *Classic Hassidic Tales,* by Meyer Levin. When I had finished, David borrowed the book and for two weeks was oblivious to everything until he had finished it. At a later *asepha,* he told the class some of the tales he had read. So many others wanted to read the book that I had to find another copy. Now David is reading a biography and another book of legends about the Baal Shem Tov. Every once in a while he asks a question like "What is a Tzaddik," or "Why do these people dress this way" which will either start a long discussion or will send us to the school library looking for more information.

Chuck's topic is a more sober one—the Holocaust. One day he was looking through some material about the menu Soviet Jews are fed in forced labor camps. He became curious as to what Jews ate in Nazi concentration camps, and his research led him to many sources which he began reading in greater depth.

One day he told me he'd built a model of a concentration camp at home and began asking me questions which resulted from his reading. "Cherie, is it true that if babies were born on transport trains they were thrown out the door?" And, "Cherie, I don't understand why they picked on the Jews."

Needless to say, these were difficult questions to answer in the middle of a demanding class, but the open structure gives teachers more freedom. So for over an hour, we struggled with the problems which Chuck had raised. Soon a whole group gathered around to join in the discussion.

The next day, I brought him my copy of *Night* which he devoured in one sitting. Today, he is re-reading it so that he can answer some questions I posed to him. On his own, he's started what he calls a concentration camp folder to collect material and keep track of things he's learned. The story of *Night* attracted one of the other boys who was looking over Chuck's shoulder, and now he, too, is reading Wiesel's book.

Some children have set more concrete goals for themselves. They want to develop their Hebrew skills. On this particular day, my assistant is standing at the chalk board surrounded by two children. They are trying to write words on the board that she can't read and she's trying to stump them, too. Two other boys are working with the Hebrew "printing press" (letters and stamp pad) first making words and then sentences. Still another child is in the corner typing the alphabet and simple words on the Hebrew typewriter.

A couple of girls came to me asking for a subject for a play. We found a book about Jewish women and they picked the story of the ill-fated Marianne, wife of Herod. Each of them wanted to be Marianne, but I suggested to them that when they found out how she died they might not be so eager to play that role. Unfortunately, the story did not tell them precisely how she died, so it was up to the library and the Jewish Encyclopedia for the answer. By this time, their appetite for playmaking was gone and they went looking for something else to do.

Not everyone works all the time, of course. There is the inevitable wanderer who will walk around the whole period looking over shoulders and re-arranging books on the shelf. On this particular day,

I noticed a pair of girls doing little else but giggling like only ten-year-olds can. As I approached, I noticed that they were exchanging phone numbers and that gave me an idea. After reviewing the numbers one through ten with them, I suggested that they go around and tell everyone what their phone number would be in Hebrew—a task they joyfully undertook.

Our day ends with a prayer session during which we teach new prayers. We emphasize meanings and types of prayers, and we try to show the children how to become involved personally in prayer. Then in the last moments we clean up the rooms and the children mark down their day's activities on a file card which serves as an on-going record of their activities.[11]

The examples cited above, and they are but a few of the many which are available, support the contention that there is in Jewish education today a recognizable tendency to address students as active participants in the determination of their school programs rather than to view them as passive recipients of predistilled truth. The roots of this turn of emphasis are not difficult to uncover—they are to be found in the writings of the radical school reformers,[12] in the more temperate critique of American education of Silberman,[13] in the influence of Piagetian psychology in teacher-training programs and graduate schools of education, in the ambience of American colleges and universities which permit students a significant role in governance, and in the general permissiveness which pervades American society. It is as yet too soon, both in general and Jewish education, to know the ultimate effects of this approach. Final judgment must await the development and application of rigorous techniques of evaluation. In the meantime, however, several observations do seem in order.

It is, I believe, more than passingly significant that much of the material and programs from which the foregoing analysis of the

[11]Cherie Koller, "A Time for Joy: The Open Classroom and the Jewish School," *Response*, No. 12, Winter 1971–72, pp. 43–50.

[12]The best known of these are probably Edgar Z. Friedenberg, the late Paul Goodman, John Holt, and Ivan Illich. Their books, articles in mass-circulation magazines, and lectures have reached audiences generally beyond the reach of educators. These "stars" of school reform are surrounded by lesser lights who publish in a variety of "little magazines." The best of them is probably the Canadian quarterly *This Magazine is About Schools.*

[13]Charles E. Silberman, *Crisis in the Classroom* (New York: Random House, 1970).

student's role is drawn is directed toward and based upon experiences with young people of high-school age. One can argue, of course, that a student-centered approach is more effective when applied to pupils who have already mastered the basic skills and bring a self-conscious motivation to their studies. Whatever the truth of that assertion, it appears buttressed by the feeling that the Jewish elementary school, the level on which most of Jewish education in this country operates in its present form, is at worst a dismal failure and at best altogether inadequate to the task of providing the young Jew with the skills, knowledge, and attitudes he must have if his Jewishness in his later years is to be something more than a matter of casual identification. Many Jewish educators, depressed by the seeming futility of elementary education and its minimal achievements, would readily support the notion that, "If we could have our young people in a Jewish school from the ages of 13 to 17 with the proper motivation and interest, these four years, even without any previous Jewish education, would bring us far greater dividends than having children from the preschool years until 13."[14]

If this trend toward greater emphasis on adolescents and high-school education is to assume significant proportions, a massive retooling of American Jewish education will be required. The individual efforts of single congregations must be supported and supplemented by new programs of teacher training, Bureaus of Jewish Education equipped to deal with the problems peculiar to the adolescent, more rational patterns of school organization, continuing development of methods and materials geared to the affective and cognitive maturational levels of the high-school student, and policies of funding which assign high priority to secondary education.

The machinery of education, no matter how refined, can have little momentum, however, unless it is propelled by the guiding force of an overarching purpose. The day-to-day work of the school derives its ultimate significance from its relationship to some clearly stated formulation of goals. The programs we have been discussing here offer no such clarity of aims. The attention given to the student

[14]Dr. Louis L. Kaplan as quoted in Judah Pilch, "The National Curriculum Research Institute," *Jewish Education*, Vol. 37, No. 4, p. 155. A penetrating discussion of the period in a child's life most appropriate for formal education may be found in William D. Rohwer, Jr., "Prime Time for Education: Early Childhood or Adolescence," *Harvard Educational Review*, Vol. 41, No. 3, August 1971, pp. 316–341.

and the opportunities afforded him for involvement in the matters affecting his life in school are largely motivational techniques unrelated to an encompassing philosophy. Indeed the emphasis on the person of the student, with all its anti-institutional overtones, permits an easy avoidance of the difficult task of articulating purpose. The school as an expression of a unifying concept of Judaism is thus replaced by a cluster of hopefully significant moments and issues determined by highly personalized choice.

III

And what about subject matter? The hallmark of traditional Jewish education is in its view of knowledge, the concomitant place of intellectual activity in the learning process, and their relationship to behavior. The Jewish school, even in its most watered-down American form, has always acted on the assumption that knowledge was the key to proper conduct. The dictum of the Rabbis that an ignoramus cannot be pious, and the observation of Maimonides, "All the evils which men cause to each other because of certain intentions, desires, opinions, or religious principles . . . originate in ignorance, which is absence of wisdom . . . if men possessed wisdom . . . they would not cause any injury to themselves or to others; for the knowledge of truth removes hatred and quarrels and prevents mutual injuries"[15]—to cite only two examples—were more than casual homilies. They were in fact the epistemological ground of a theory and practice of Jewish education which accorded intellect primacy of place.

Current opinion, by contrast, swings in an arc which ranges from a denigration of intellect altogether to the more moderate assertion that knowledge alone is hardly a sufficient condition for the inducement of specific behavior. This position, it must be stated, is not without precedent in the history of Jewish education. The *musar* movement, which in its time was an educational reform of significant consequence, was sparked in part by the Salanter's question, "How does it happen that people of great intellectual power who are past masters in human wisdom and in the knowledge

[15]Maimonides, *Guide to the Perplexed* (tr. I. Friedlander), (New York: Hebrew Publishing Co., n.d.), pt. 3, ch. 11, p. 36.

of Torah are from a moral-religious point of view, idiots or weakminded?"

The de-emphasis of intellect and the consequent criticism of a curriculum which is text-centered is the result of a concatenation of circumstances. A partial explanation may surely be found in the distressing fact that most Jewish schools in the United States have neither succeeded in imparting any kind of Jewish knowledge to their students nor have been able to develop even the minimum of intellectual competencies required of the literate Jew.[16] The seeming impossibility of transmitting the ideal of *lamdanut*, Jewish erudition, and the consequent disappearance of the *talmid hacham* as an accessible model have forced some Jewish educators to consider the affective at least as important as the cognitive in the weaving of that fabric of attitudes and feelings which is the underpinning of meaningful Jewish life. As one educator put it, "In our hot pursuit of relevance through the intellect, we are ignoring that relevance which comes through feeling and empathizing. . . . This sense of emotional relevance is most effectively imparted through the creation of an all-pervading, multicolored environment."[17]

One must hasten to add, however, that the questioning of the effectiveness of the traditional text-centered curriculum is not restricted to those whose work is in the afternoon- or one-day-a-week school—institutions which even under the best of circumstances would be hard put to recreate the ideal of Jewish learning. Even among day-school personnel, those who have stubbornly maintained a deep commitment to *Torah l'Shma* and rightfully take pride in the scholastic achievements of their students, one discerns a note of anxiety. One participant in a recent symposium on the day school declared that among "the most serious shortcomings of the day school" one must include "education confined to the classroom. Too many of our schools are satisfied with formal education, conducted in and around the classroom. If our goal of

[16]For a discussion of the achievement levels of Jewish schooling in the United States see my "Jewish Education—For What?" (New York and Philadelphia: *American Jewish Year Book*, American Jewish Committee and the Jewish Publication Society, Vol. 70, 1969), pp. 3–36. See also my "An Analysis of Selected Courses of Study of Conservative Congregational Schools," *Jewish Education*, Vol. 40, No. 1, March 1970, pp. 7–23; Vol. 40, No. 2, Summer 1970, p. 37–48.

[17]Philip Arian, "Emotional Relevance in Jewish Education," *Conservative Judaism*, Vol. XXIII, No. 1, Fall 1968, pp. 50–51.

commitment is to be a realistic one we must look for opportunities for students to act out the values and life style we are teaching . . . students will 'learn' more about the plight of Soviet Jewry in two hours devoted to neighborhood campaigning for signatures on a petition they have formulated than in two weeks of classes on Soviet-Jewish problems. . . . Students must be encouraged to participate in protests and demonstrations even at the risk of using school time (*bitul Torah* included) (sic!). The underlying assumption is that the student will learn more by doing something constructive outside the classroom than by sitting in the classroom. . . ."[18]

The treatment of subject matter in the day school is complicated by the fact that the general studies curriculum and the program of Jewish studies are two separate tracks which rarely converge. Attempts at developing an integrated curriculum, even in Conservative day schools, have seldom gone beyond sporadic units dealing with isolated themes; the more Orthodox day schools, anxious to maintain the exclusivity of the two worlds of *halakha* and secular studies, eschew the very notion of integration. One Orthodox schoolman pinpoints the problem:

> We educate our student in two opposite directions—philosophically and psychologically. On one hand we guide our students in the belief that Torah is a way of life which encompasses every phase of life. On the other hand, we expose them in the humanities department to a secular way of life influenced by the sciences, history, and world literature, with an entirely different approach to life. From our point of view, we teach our students the importance of authority in that we have to accept the rulings of the Sages and of the *poskim* (codifiers). Whatever is written in the Torah cannot be questioned. No criticism may be directed against our tradition; but we also teach literature, history, and science in which any authority may be challenged. Every part of science, literature, and history is open to criticism.
>
> We inform our students that any problem in life must be solved according to halakha. This means a definite follow-up of *Chazal* permitting no critical views. And at the same time we teach them that in political and social problems they may follow their own point of view—be it the Democratic or the Republican way—both of which

[18]Haskel Lookstein in "The Jewish Day School: A Symposium," *Tradition*, Vol. 13, No. 1, Summer 1972, pp. 113–114.

> philosophies have nothing to do with *Da'at Torah* (Torah outlook upon life). Thus we create a figure with a split personality within a compartmentalized mind, and in most cases working in two opposite directions.[19]

It would be incorrect, however, to assume that the emphasis on the feelings of the student and the role they play in the assimilation of subject matter is the result solely of the internal problems of the Jewish school. The talk of emotions, experience, and the like is derived, in part, from the language of the counter culture and its dethronement of the Western intellectual tradition. At the same time one can find here the impact of research in the behavioral sciences and its practical application in the "human potential" movement—T-groups, encounter groups, sensitivity training, etc. Taken together these various strands of influence have given Jewish education a tone which is not always in harmony with the traditional motifs of learning.

In its classical formulation Jewish education is nothing less than a religious imperative. The study of the sacred texts is a form of worship and the acquisition of knowledge the key to human perfectibility. The vicissitudes of Jewish life and the secularization of Western culture have contributed noteworthy permutations of the original concept. Zionist thought viewed education as the means of fostering national pride. The Jewish socialist movement and its network of Yiddish schools stressed the importance of education in the development of class consciousness and its contribution to the achievement of the classless society. Jewish education in pre-World War II America, heavily influenced by the work of Kurt Lewin and the mental hygiene movement, was regarded as a means of avoiding social marginality and an important line of defense in the struggle against anti-Semitism.

In our time the core idea which seems dominant in thinking about Jewish education is that of identity-formation. As conceived by Erik Erikson, the psychoanalyst who has provided us with the most sophisticated formulation of the notion of identity and its manifold adumbrations, identity-formation is the process whereby the young person determines "what he should believe in and who he shall—or,

[19]David Eliach in "The Jewish Day School: A Symposium," pp. 100–101.

indeed, might—be or become."[20] Identity then is a "pattern of observable or inferable attributes 'identifying' a person to himself and others."[21] Within the context of the identity-concept the relative significance, or possibly more correctly the relative power, of the affective and the cognitive may be more sharply delineated. One must draw a distinction between the "educated Jew" and the "identified Jew" and perhaps even be prepared to acknowledge that where identity is the goal, formal education may not be the most effective means. Indeed "the goal of identity-formation is probably better cultivated outside the classroom than inside—a trip to Israel, summer camping, the Havurah, the youth movement, retreat, the 'happening,' the demonstration."[22]

Jews of previous generations had no problems concerning their identity. The home, the community and its institutions, the regimen of religious observance, and an intricate pattern of social relationships all attributed to the definition of the growing child's self and his place in space and time. He was deeply conscious of the interdependence of all Jews and understood that "whatever happened to Jews *qua* Jews anywhere had implications for Jews everywhere."[23]

The Jewish child of today, by contrast, grows up in a fragmented society which lacks the supportive ambience of an enveloping Jewish milieu. A Jewish community desirous of an existence beyond the present must look to the school and its activities, or some educational equivalent, as the arena in which the fidelity of the young is formed. To assume, however, that formal education or any other kind of educational program for that matter, is an adequate substitute for the impact of a total culture is to stretch the parameters of identity-formation beyond reasonable limits. The best that Jewish schools and other educational institutions can hope to do, therefore, is to attempt to identify those aspects of identity which seem susceptible to their influence—not an easy task by any means —and design their programs accordingly.

Where content and conventional modes of learning still remain

[20]Erik H. Erikson, *Childhood and Society,* second edition, (New York: W. W. Norton and Company, 1963), p. 279.

[21]Simon Herman, *Israelis and Jews* (New York: Random House, 1970), p. 18.

[22]Marshall Sklare in "Colloquium for Jewish Education," Philip W. Lown Graduate Center for Contemporary Jewish Studies, Brandeis University and The American Jewish Committee, June 1971, p. 3.

[23]Simon Herman, *Israelis and Jews,* p. 17.

desiderata, the goal of identity and its corollary of commitment color the treatment of traditional subject matter. Text material is chosen not because this or that book of the Bible is thought to be a necessary part of the vocabulary of an educated Jew but rather because of the evocative power of a particular selection. The criterion for the choice of subject matter is its power to evoke "appreciation," "empathy," "involvement," "sensitivity," etc. Mastery of the text can be a valid goal, therefore, only as it leads to the discovery of values and their application to problems of current concern.

Now this approach suffers from several obvious shortcomings. While it is specious to quarrel with the criterion of choice—all curriculum is, after all, selective—and somewhat pedantic to cavil at selections which have emotional resonance—a curriculum need not, after all, be chosen for its dullness—it is pertinent to argue that without some rigorous standard of intellectual analysis the treatment of text all too often degenerates into aimless "shmooze." Far more serious, however, is the fact that the stress on feeling as the determinant of values neglects the crucial role of intellect in the shaping of value judgments. Applying values to a particular set of circumstances, resolving equally valid but seemingly irreconcilable principles, translating "felt" goods into formulated precepts, amending values in the light of new circumstances, and anticipating the consequences of acting upon a specific value—all necessary steps in judgments of value—are intellectual skills and the school which fails to train its students in their use can hardly lay claim to a value-oriented program.[24]

An interesting attempt to meld the affective and the cognitive aspects of learning is to be found in an experiment in "confluent education" currently being conducted by the Rhea Hirsch School of Education of the Hebrew Union College–Jewish Institute of Religion in Los Angeles.

The project is an adaptation in the setting of the Jewish school of work done at the Esalen Institute and the University of California at Santa Barbara. As described by one of its major theoreticians "confluent education is the term for the integration or flowing

[24]Burton Cohen and Joseph J. Schwab, "Practical Logic: Problems of Ethical Decision," *American Behavioral Scientist,* Vol. VIII, No. 8, April 1965, pp. 23–27.

together of the affective and cognitive elements in individual and group learning . . . affective refers to the feeling or emotional aspects of experience and learning . . . cognitive refers to the activity of the mind in knowing an object . . . whenever one learns intellectually there is an inseparable accompanying emotional dimension. The relationship between intellect and affect is indestructibly symbiotic."[25] To date the experiment to which we refer has concentrated on the training of teachers in the correct belief that changes in the student's style of learning can come about only as the result of changes in the teacher's behavior. The statement of the goals and purposes of the Jewishly oriented Laboratory in Confluent Education notes the following:

> We are concerned with difficulties in combining the emotional presence of the teacher and student with the more academic and cognitive goals of education. Curriculum planners often either focus on specific behavioral objectives which over-determine what a child receives, or are too concerned with presenting factual material and not with whether the child learns. In addition, education today finds itself on the threshold of a great technological revolution through which mechanical equipment will alter radically our teaching techniques.
>
> While not opposed to teaching with behavioral objectives in mind, and certainly not to technology, it is our belief that 1) a teacher cannot teach values nor indeed cognitive data without himself undergoing basic changes as a teacher; 2) values and data come best through the emotional experience of the child; 3) values are best learned when there is a climate of support present in the class; values cannot be conveyed as if a classroom had a homogeneous composition; 4) students will derive different values from the same experience and the teacher must be equipped to deal with that multiplicity of values; 5) technology can only be the handmaiden of human beings, and not the reverse; 6) the greatest lesson for a Jewish teacher, a religious leader, or any teacher for that matter is to take personal risks and responsibility for those risks![26]

The training of teachers, the first and crucial step in the development of any instructional program, took place over five intensive weekend sessions conducted first in a camp setting,

[25]George I. Brown, *Human Teaching for Human Learning* (New York: Viking, 1971), pp. 3, 10, 11.

[26]William Cutter and Jack Dauber, *Confluent Education in the Jewish Setting* (Los Angeles: Rhea Hirsch School of Education, Hebrew Union College–Jewish Institute of Religion, n.d.), pp. 4–5.

followed by three such weekends in the city, and concluded by a final weekend in camp. The training sessions were devoted to the following:

> 1) Specific personal growth and sensory exercises. A special emphasis on the identity of the teacher and group worker emerged and produced some of the most fruitful sessions.
> 2) Personal growth exercises of the individual as teacher. Personal growth exercises of the individual as Jew.
> 3) Developing of lesson plans and designs which incorporated insights from the above two items and drew upon Jewish knowledge. . . .
> 4) Exercises relating to contact between teacher and administrator.
> 5) Group discussions of theoretical and practical nature.
> 6) Monthly report sessions as to how the experience had affected the teacher's work in his setting. . . .[27]

Teachers who participated in the laboratory experience reported that they felt themselves clearly affected by the experience. Evaluation of the classroom effects of the teacher's training is unfortunately restricted to anecdotal reports, e.g.:

> In religious school during the study of Abraham, I had the students become Abraham and physically smash idols made of plaster of Paris. Then each student told the class how he felt. I also broke the class into diads and one person became Abraham and the other Abraham's father. Abraham had to explain to his father why he did what he did. Then the roles were reversed. The students also got a chance to stand up in front of the class and try to convince idol worshipers (the rest of the class) why they should become monotheists. This was an opportunity as well to learn about "iconoclasm" in more general terms.[28]

It is difficult to determine whether or not any of the long-range purposes of the program were achieved. Has learning indeed been made more effective and meaningful because of the attention paid to the emotional aspects of subject matter? Does a student feel more "Jewish" because he was given the opportunity to "act out" or imagine certain Jewish predicaments? How long-lasting are the

[27] *Ibid.*, pp. 6-7.

[28] *Ibid.*, p. 12.

effects of the training and the school experience when for all their recreating of reality they must remain just that, a pale imitation of the real thing refracted through the artificial setting of the classroom?

Whatever the answers to these questions and many others, there are several serious objections to confluent education and its many variations which should give pause to those whose techniques for teaching focus on the affective domain and who would use emotions and feelings as subject matter. A classroom procedure which encourages the free play of the student's emotions requires a teacher who by training and temperament is equipped to deal with the consequences. Moral issues aside—do teachers have the right to ask their students to act out feelings—the instructor in this sort of setting assumes a role which is all too often beyond his capabilities. Further, the planned arousal of emotion unchecked by intelligent control and patient guidance sets the stage for unbridled narcissism and subjectivism which block the possibility of rational and objective evaluation of experience. The notion that self-expression is the beginning and end of creativity ignores the potent fact that true art requires the restraint of disciplined craftsmanship.

The issue is not whether or not emotions play a role in learning—the commonsense of experience and the insights of the behavioral sciences provide clear and unequivocal answers. We must rather ask what is it that schools and teachers must do in order to provide students with the maximum benefits to be derived from an understanding of the complicated interaction of mind and heart. Many would share the observation that "Affective education is not and cannot be an end in itself. In life, feelings are intricately and complicatedly embedded in reflection, problem-solving, and action. The emotions emerge incidentally but essentially."[29]

Some educators eschew the classroom entirely in their attempts to capture the hearts and imagination of their students. A new prominence has been given the youth group and its program of informal education. More striking, however, is the use of camps as the setting for educational activities. In many places around the country classroom sessions, particularly for adolescents, have been replaced by weekend retreats in camp locations. The pattern varies—one weekend a month in camp instead of four Sunday

[29]Geoffrey Summerfield in a review of *Human Teaching For Human Learning* in *Harvard Educational Review*, Vol. XLII, No. 2, May 1972, p. 294.

mornings in school; a camp experience as the culminating event of a particular project; periodic programs in camp as a means of providing experiences and opportunities not easily generated within the limited time and space available to the school. These variegated approaches share a common doubt regarding the sufficiency of the school as the sole agency of Jewish education.

Camping has long been a part of the activities of the organized Jewish community. Despite the fact that intensively Jewish camps—Massad, Yavneh, Ramah, Zionist youth camps, some Jewish-center camps—have an enviable record of successful achievement in the development of commitment and loyalty, those whose work is primarily in formal education have only recently begun to appreciate the educational possibilities of camping. The summer camp in particular offers opportunities not easily vouchsafed other educational institutions. The camp is a total milieu; it can provide for all age groups—from infant to grandparent—at the same time and thereby becomes a community of shared experience; the intimacy of the camp setting serves as backdrop for unparalleled opportunities for self-discovery and interpersonal relationships; in a camp significant models are easily accessible; the time spent in camp is a significant slice of the camper's annual life span and is more rooted in reality than most other efforts which seek to involve the child; a camp staff embraces a wider variety of talents and abilities than is possible in even the most richly endowed school; and finally, the freedom a camp enjoys in its programming, even where formal study is a significant aspect of camp life, permits experimentation not always possible in the necessarily more limited confines of a school. Camping may not take the place of the school, but it is difficult to imagine, or condone, a school program which does not avail itself of the resources of camping.

To acknowledge the importance of camping, however, is not necessarily to agree with those who view the camp as an alternative to the school. Just as there are programs and activities which are best conducted in a camp environment, some aspects of the educational process are most properly located in a school setting. The mastery of specific intellectual skills—acquisition of information, logical analysis, problem-solving techniques, generalization and discrimination, use of symbolic language—requires the careful attention of a sequential progression that only a well-organized school curriculum can provide. The enthusiasm for camping and the solution it seems to offer to the problems of Jewish education tends to divert cogent analysis of the strengths and shortcomings of the Jewish school. The traditional subject matter of the curriculum of the Jewish school is in a sense neutral; its impact depends in no small measure on the purposes it is intended to serve, the manner in which it is presented, and its relationship to other aspects of the school experience. The careful ordering of these elements is the essence of curriculum. The Jewish school has not particularly distinguished itself in matters of curriculum and only rarely has it adhered to commonly accepted principles of curriculum design: a) determining the precise boundaries of the educational unit to be treated; b) identifying the subject matter which is to be dealt with within that unit; c) the embodiment of subject matter in material form such as text, materials, and learning aids; d) preparing teachers in the use of the new subject matter and material; e) evaluation.[30] There is surely something quixotic about the abandonment of an institution whose potential has hardly been plumbed.

IV

Whether or not the trends we have been here discussing become the dominant pattern in Jewish education in the United States, it is clear that the role of the teacher has been deeply affected. The day of the teacher who arbitrarily imposed his will on a classroom of docile youngsters has passed over the border of acceptance. Proponents of a different style of teaching can find ample support in much of the literature of education in our time. Not all the teachers in Jewish schools may be prepared for the changes required of them, but both parents and children alike are no longer willing to tolerate the antics of the authoritarian teacher.

The source of a teacher's authority in the more traditional models of educational practice is variously located in his position as a representative of the adult society, in his ability to resort to punitive measures, in his prestige, in his charisma, or in a combination of all or some of these variables. Common to all these conceptions is the view of the teacher-pupil relationship as one of

[30]Jerrold R. Zacharias and Stephen White, "Requirements for Major Curriculum Revisions," in Robert W. Heath, *New Curricula* (New York: Harper & Row, 1964), p. 69.

subject to object. The inherently demeaning character of such a relationship creates serious obstacles to the development of that moral and intellectual autonomy of the pupil which must be the ultimate goal of the educative process.

A more constructive approach to the question of the teacher's authority results from the idea of the school as a social institution whose primary purpose is to aid students in the solution of problems and the fulfillment of needs. The teacher is the proximate representative of the school in this process. This view of the school and its teachers locates the source of the teacher's authority not in the fact of his appointment to a particular post but rather in the knowledge, experience, and skills which enable him to mediate between the students and their goals. The teacher as expert encourages the development of that mutual relationship which invites the student to full partnership in the problem-solving process.[31]

Jewish teacher-training institutions have generally addressed themselves to only one aspect of the teacher's role as conceived here. Their programs emphasize the transmission of knowledge and provide relatively limited opportunity for the development of those skills and attitudes which are a necessary adjunct to competence in subject matter. The teacher as mediator is, like his pupils, a participant in a joint effort to create a community of learning which should serve as prologue to the induction of the young into the broader arena of Jewish communal life. The preparation of teachers capable of working in this fashion must allow for the growth of those sensibilities and insights which are the necessary condition for the application of specific techniques of teaching. Hebrew teachers colleges and other institutions involved in the training of teachers for the Jewish school must assume a larger share of the responsibility for the reshaping of the institutions they purport to serve.

Whatever the form Jewish education in this country takes, it cannot remain indifferent to the larger social scene in which it functions. Jewish life cannot but react and be affected by the ebb and flow of events in America and that reaction must find its echo in education. Schools and other educational agencies must, however, avoid the easy escape into hastily conceived programs designed to

[31]This discussion of the teacher's authority is mainly drawn from Kenneth D. Benne, "Authority in Education," *Harvard Educational Review*, Vol. 40, No. 3, August 1970, pp. 385–410.

satisfy some vaguely defined and ephemeral notion of relevance. The issues which affect Jews today are really not all that new and we could do worse than provide our students with the historical perspective which is the genius of traditional Jewish learning.

V

No survey of what is happening in Jewish education in the United States at present would be complete without reference to the unprecedented growth of Jewish Studies programs in colleges and universities.[32] While the number of Jewish students involved in these programs is but a fraction of the total number of Jewish college students, course enrollments across the country exceed anything imagined possible a decade ago. While it is still too early to assess the significance of the phenomenon it is clear that the availability of these programs in colleges and universities has given Jewish studies a new status and prestige. The fact that instructors are by and large American-born and trained and have won their place as respected members of the academic community has contributed much to a changed image of the Jewish scholar. Many of these courses and programs resulted from student demands and their involvement is a welcome turn of activism to matters of Jewish concern. Communal anxiety for the college-age student has stimulated Federation support for programs on the campus and will hopefully produce some spin-off for Jewish education on the secondary and elementary levels.

The response of many sections of the Jewish community to the establishment of Jewish Studies programs in colleges and universities seems, however, to be a mixed blessing. The attempts of Federation and other agencies to "get on the bandwagon" of an area long neglected has elicited a note of caution from academicians. ". . . the growing involvement of the American Jewish community, with its labyrinthine superstructure of interlocking agencies,

[32]See Arnold J. Band, "Jewish Studies in American Liberal Arts Colleges and Universities," *American Jewish Year Book,* Vol. 67, 1966, pp. 4–30; Leon Jick, ed., *The Teaching of Judaica in American Universities,* Association for Jewish Studies and Ktav Publishing House, 1970; Alfred Jospe, *Jewish Studies in American Colleges and Universities,* second edition (Washington, D. C.: B'nai B'rith Hillel Foundations, n.d.).

with its rabbis and educators, and its competitive synagogue movements, presents serious problems to the proper development of the field of Jewish studies in higher education. Simply stated, the danger is that the limited perspectives, the lack of professionalism, and the classic misjudgments relative to the educational process on the primary and secondary levels will now be transferred bodily to the colleges and universities."[33]

Despite the strictures noted above the fact that many of the programs of Jewish Studies found their first funding, and continuing financial support as well, in the Jewish community does permit several questions. No one can reasonably object to the growing place of Jewish Studies as a recognized academic discipline; it is a welcome development and long overdue. The limited communal resources available for Jewish education do, however, force questions of priorities of investment. How should funds be divided between elementary, secondary, and higher Jewish education? What should be the ratio of allocations between programs for college-age students conducted by Jewish institutions and academic programs within the context of general colleges and universities? Answers to these questions depend in large measure on whether or not we can determine how crucial the college-age is in the development of Jewish identification and identity and if the disinterested teaching and research of the academician is the most effective tool in the attainment of that goal.

I have not touched on a number of areas which today concern educators and laymen alike—the decline in school enrollments, the continuing shortage of teachers and administrators in many parts of the country, rising costs and increasing difficulties in meeting school budgets, particularly in the day school, the pathetic lack of proper textbooks and other learning aids, the complicated role of Israel in the school curriculum, etc. While these are surely matters of importance they seem to me to be secondary to the themes I have discussed. The practical aspects of school management, the day-to-day conduct of the school, and even the development of specific curricular units cannot mean much unless they are informed by a wider vision.

[33]Baruch A. Levine, "Issues and Perspectives in Jewish Studies," *Jewish Studies: History and Perspectives* (Waltham, Mass.: Brandeis University, 1972), p. 2.

THE JEWISH COMMUNITY AND THE GENERAL SOCIETY

THE AMERICAN JEWISH LIBERAL TRADITION

by LUCY S. DAWIDOWICZ
and LEON S. GOLDSTEIN

INTRODUCTION

JEWISH POLITICAL behavior must be viewed in the context of Jewish-Gentile relations, and constitutes an aspect of the orientation of Jews to the general society. The characteristic political stance of Jews in modern times has been liberalism. In fact liberalism has been so common among East European derived Jews in the United States that an American Jewish liberal tradition has been established that has not only influenced Jewish behavior but has attracted the intense interest of politicians as well as of commentators on the political scene.

The origins and character of the Jewish liberal tradition are intriguing subjects for investigation. Some have traced it back to the European past when the left stood for a social order in which Jews would be given equality, while the right not only espoused a position which would perpetuate Jewish subordination but at times even fanned the flames of anti-Semitism. Other analysts believe that the origins of the Jewish liberal tradition can be found in Jewish values—values which have their ultimate source in Jewish religious beliefs. According to this view Jews support liberalism not so much because it is in their interest to do so but because they are attracted by liberalism's emphasis on compassion and justice—values which parallel those found in their own tradition.

The survival power of Jewish liberalism has also provoked interest and speculation. Some analysts have taken the position that Jewish liberalism is fated to die; conceding that it may be temporarily perpetuated by a lag between the class and status positions occupied by Jews, they stress that as anti-Jewish discrimination declines so will Jewish liberalism. Others have reasoned that Jewish liberalism will expire as Jews complete the move from cities to suburbs, where they will feel greater pressure to conform to Gentile patterns.

In the early 1960's Lucy S. Dawidowicz and Leon J. Goldstein presented a cogent analysis of the American Jewish liberal tradition. At the conclusion of their analysis they too speculated about the survival power of the tradition. They wondered whether Jewish liberalism could survive the acculturation process. More specifically, could Jewish liberalism endure if Jews were fully accepted by their conservative Gentile peers?

Dawidowicz and Goldstein could not have foreseen current threats to Jewish liberalism, which seem to come from an opposite direction altogether—from the impact on American society of racial issues (including the demands of blacks for group rights and community control) and the vexed issue of support for the State of Israel (including such recent developments as the hostility to Israel of many radicals and the increasingly lukewarm attitude of some liberals). The Jewish commitment to liberalism seems to some observers to have been undermined less by the process of Jewish acculturation to Gentile society as by the increasing polarization and fragmentation of American society as a whole.

Yet it is clear that although Jews have given greater support in recent elections to conservative candidates, the Jewish liberal tradition has persisted longer than anyone expected, and this fact renders the Dawidowicz-Goldstein analysis of more than historical interest. For, as Mark R. Levy and Michael S. Kramer demonstrated in The Ethnic Factor *(1972), the Jewish move toward the right has not proceeded at anything like the predicted speed. As a consequence the study of the Jewish liberal tradition remains essential to the sociological understanding of American Jewry.*

M. S.

THE CONSISTENT liberalism of American Jews has been noted time and again by scholars and politicians. Jews tend to be equally liberal on political, economic and social matters, whereas workers, for example, tend to be liberal only on economic issues, the educated on political subjects like freedom of speech but not on economic questions, and Negroes on civil rights but not on foreign affairs.[1]

Most Jewish voters in the United States regard themselves as political independents. But in practice Jews during the last forty years or so have tended to vote Democratic rather than Republican. This voting behavior has appeared aberrant, particularly in the last two decades, because other Americans in the same socio-economic position have voted mostly Republican.

American Jews today are predominantly native. Their incomes are mostly in the middle and upper-middle range; many have college degrees and are self-employed businessmen, proprietors, professionals, or managers. More and more of them are adopting a suburban style of life, even though most still live within city limits. In occupation and income, they most nearly resemble Presbyterians and Episcopalians, upper-status Protestant denominations. Similarly situated Protestants and Catholics vote Republican in considerable numbers, and by all the rules, Jewish support of the Democratic party should have declined and withered away. True, during their upward socio-economic passage Jews have trimmed their vote on the Democratic line—witness Great Neck in Long Island and Highland Park outside Chicago. But what is striking is not that Jews in Great Neck vote only 60 percent Democratic; it is that they vote only 40 percent Republican.

This display of party loyalty seems to contradict the popular

[1]Cf. Gerhard Lenski, *The Religious Factor* (Garden City, N.Y.: Doubleday & Co., 1961), pp. 121–153; Samuel A. Stouffer, *Communism, Conformity and Civil Liberties* (Garden City, N.Y.: Doubleday & Co., 1955), p. 143 *et passim*. The same phenomenon has been observed among Jews in Amsterdam, England, Australia, Canada, and pre-Nazi Vienna. Cf. Seymour Martin Lipset, *Political Man* (Garden City, N.Y.: Doubleday & Co., 1960), pp. 242–244.

notion that Jews will vote for a Jewish candidate regardless of party—or Catholics for a Catholic, Italians for an Italian, Negroes for a Negro, and so forth. Actually, this kind of voting reflects the striving of the group for status in society and its need for political recognition.[2] Nearly every ethnic, religious, and social group in America, in its drive for power and prestige in the community, has sought public office for its members as tangible evidence of its place in the political body. The more the group needs such recognition, the more likely are its members to vote for "one of their own"—a circumstance to which politicians have traditionally responded with "balanced" tickets. Such political contests among groups, for prestige and sometimes for control of the political machine, occur most frequently in local politics, though occasionally they erupt also on a national scale, the notable example being the presidential elections of 1928 and 1960.

As issues have grown increasingly complex, many voters have grown more sophisticated and have learned to vote not necessarily for one of their own, but for the candidate who, regardless of faith, color, or ethnic origin, seems likeliest to serve their individual, class, and group interests.[3] Jews have been especially apt in absorbing this political lesson, and other groups seem to be learning it too.

Jewish voters are probably more influenced by the political stance of a candidate than by his ancestry or religion—at any rate in national elections—because they view politics more ideologically than other groups. Even in municipal elections, where voting for "one of our own" is most common, Jewish voters usually support the Democrat who is not a Jew over the Republican who is, at least in places where they are not hungry for political prestige. For example, in New York's mayoral primary in 1961, 63 percent of the voters in 23 predominantly Jewish election districts in Brooklyn voted for the reform Democrat, Robert F. Wagner, a Catholic of German-Irish background, while only 37 percent voted for his

[2]See Moses Rischin, "*Our Own Kind*": *Voting by Race, Creed or National Origin* (Santa Barbara, Calif.: Center for the Study of Democratic Institutions, 1960), pp. 3–12.

[3]Cf. John Slawson, "Guidelines," [American Jewish] *Committee Reporter*, October 1960, p. 7: "Each voter is the judge of his own interests and if he believes these include religious, racial, or ethnic factors, as well as a host of others, his vote may reflect that belief. It is no less legitimate to vote as an American of Greek origin interested in liberalizing the immigration quota for Greece, than as an importer interested in lowering the tariff on foreign textiles."

Jewish opponent, Arthur Levitt, the regular Democrat.[4] In the election proper, Jewish voters once again backed Wagner substantially against the Republican and Jew, Louis J. Lefkowitz.

Another example was the mayoralty election of 1945, when Jewish voters overwhelmingly backed William O'Dwyer, an Irish Catholic Democrat, against his Republican opponent, Jonah J. Goldstein. This has been a recurrent pattern in New York City since 1903, when Jewish voters failed to support Cyrus L. Sulzberger, running for Borough President of Manhattan on a Republican-Fusion (reform) ticket, and voted instead for his Democratic opponent John S. Ahearn, not a Jew.

The untypical character of Jewish voting has been the subject of considerable analysis and speculation among politicians and students of politics. In 1948 a study of voting among eight religious groups (Baptists, Lutherans, Methodists, Episcopalians, Presbyterians, Congregationalists, Roman Catholics, and Jews) showed that on politico-economic questions, groups low in class and status were liberal and groups high in class and status conservative. But the Jews were an exception: though high in class, they nevertheless remained politically liberal. In spite of their economic interests, their feelings as Jews seemed to have determined the way they voted. The authors speculated that Jews felt insecure because they were not fully accepted by high-class ingroups, and that this insecurity forced them to identify with outgroups, that is, low-class groups.[5]

A more elaborate interpretation along these lines was based on the political experience of a Philadelphia Jewish banker who had made his fortune in real estate.[6] Early in his career he associated himself with the Republican party and at the 1928 Republican National Convention seconded the nomination of Herbert Hoover. Shortly thereafter, in the crash of 1929, the bankers of Philadelphia—Republicans all—banded together to meet the crisis, but failed to include the Jewish banker and even denied him help. After that he turned to the Democratic party. This experience in the early

[4]"The Mayoralty Primary in New York City, September 1961," unpublished memorandum, The American Jewish Committee, 27 September 1961.

[5]Wesley and Beverly Allinsmith, "Religious Affiliation and Politico-Economic Attitude: A Study of Eight Major U.S. Religious Groups," *Public Opinion Quarterly*, XII (1948), pp. 386–388.

[6]James Reichley, *The Art of Government: Reform and Organization Politics in Philadelphia* (New York: The Fund for the Republic, 1959), pp. 72–75.

1930's was summed up as an example of the position of Jews in politics:

> . . . The Jews, as a commercial class, could never hope for better than second-best out of an alliance with the commercial and financial class of old-family businessmen or with the political party that they dominated. The trouble with the Republican party for the Jews . . . is that the front benches are already taken. . . . Under such circumstances, why not ally himself with the party of the industrial wage earners, the small-time politicians, the uneducated toilers? For abandoning the party of a class that in any case will not have him, he is rewarded with front seats on the bandwagon of the "party of the little man" when it rolls into power.[7]

A more ideological interpretation of the Jews' political position is that "Jewish liberalism" took shape when Franklin D. Roosevelt began to formulate the New Deal. In the light of their European experience, this theory holds, Jews saw in the New Deal a liberalism which they construed as the political opposite of the right, whose extreme was fascism.[8]

Still another explanation is that traditional Jewish values, rooted in the religious culture, have affected political behavior. *Tsedakah* (charity), love of learning, and rejection of asceticism are thought to have molded the political outlook of Jews, as has their constant sense of identification with persecuted minorities.[9]

Undoubtedly all these factors have played larger or smaller roles in making Jews politically liberal. Their European heritage and their political experiences in the pursuit of emancipation, which Werner Cohn analyzes in some detail, may have been the most significant. With the French Revolution, when the attainment of political equality became the goal of enlightened Jews, support of Jewish enfranchisement became part of the program of non-Jewish liberals and revolutionaries throughout western Europe. As Jews gradually won their political rights in western countries, they found that the liberals and radicals who sought to change society were their allies, whereas the conservatives and reactionaries who wanted

[7] *Ibid.*, p. 74.

[8] Werner Cohn, "The Politics of American Jews," in Marshall Sklare, ed., *The Jews: Social Patterns of an American Group* (Glencoe, Ill.: Free Press, 1958), pp. 622–626.

[9] Lawrence H. Fuchs, *The Political Behavior of American Jews* (Glencoe, Ill.: Free Press, 1956), pp. 175–200 *et passim*.

to keep the system of caste and privilege—the nobility, the landed gentry, the established churches—were their enemies. In England, for example, it was the Archbishop of Canterbury who rallied the House of Lords to prevent seating a Jew in Parliament and thus to preserve the Christian character of the state. The constant opposition of the conservatives to Jewish equality drove the Jews into the opposite camp. Disraeli long ago said that "the persecution of the Jewish race has deprived European society of an important conservative element."[10]

As the struggle for emancipation moved eastward it became more intense, because social, political, and economic conditions in the Hapsburg empire and in Czarist Russia were more desperate than in western Europe. Russia was the outstanding example of despotism, autocracy, and oppression. Most of Europe's Jews suffered under the rule of the Czars, and most of the Jewish immigrants who began to come to America in large numbers during the 1880's were from the Czarist empire. The political concepts they brought with them molded their political views in America, and the explicitly ideological attitude of many Jews toward American politics may be a product of that European experience and outlook. It was an ethnocentric outlook, to be sure, common to most minorities; good and bad in political life were assessed largely in terms of the different parties' attitudes toward Jews. As outcasts of Czarist society, they considered themselves a people apart from the Russians, and wherever they had the vote they favored Jewish parties, which addressed themselves primarily to the situation of Jews rather than the country's general problems.

The Jewish experience in the Russian and Austro-Hungarian empires established even more emphatically what Jews had learned in western Europe: that the political right was at best conservative, avowedly Christian, and committed to the preservation of ancient privileges; it could, and often did, become reactionary and anti-Semitic. The left was either moderate—favorable to change in the established order, opposed to anti-Semitism and often neutral in matters of religion—or revolutionary, anti-clerical, and committed to the overthrow of the social and economic system that had brought little besides poverty and persecution to Jews.

Small wonder, then, that many Russian Jews sympathized with

[10]Benjamin Disraeli, *Lord George Bentinck: A Political Biography* (New York: E. P. Dutton, 1905), p. 324.

the opponents of the Czarist regime. Certainly their position in Czarist society seemed so hopeless that only a truly radical change could redeem them: general revolution or total emigration, whether to the golden land of America or to Palestine.[11] Thus Jews, moderate and conservative in operating their own communal institutions, came to sympathize with the non-Jewish liberals and radicals who wanted not merely to reform the political order in Russia but to remake it. The situation was clear to all who could see it. In 1903 Pahlen, the governor of Vilna, wrote in a confidential memoir about the Bund, the Jewish Social-Democratic organization:

> . . . this political movement is undoubtedly a result of the abnormal position of the Jews, legal and economic, which has been created by our legislation. A revision of the laws concerning the Jews is absolutely urgent, and every postponement of it is pregnant with most dangerous consequences.[12]

Jews, then, supported the left, not primarily because they were exploited as workers or oppressed like peasants, but because they were a persecuted minority. This political outlook was characteristically East European. The German-Jewish immigrants of the previous generation had had a somewhat different political experience. They had come to America during the reaction that followed the 1848 revolution. In Germany the struggle for emancipation had seemed possible within the framework of the existing society, and Jews by and large had felt committed to that society, provided it made room for them. In the revolution Jewish leaders had fought for the individual rights of Jews as German citizens differing from their neighbors only in religion—a matter which they felt ought to make no difference to their civic status. This opinion was shared by many of the German liberals who played leading roles in the 1848 revolution.

Disappointed by the reaction after 1848, German Jews migrated to America together with other German liberals and followed the

[11]In his autobiography, *Trial and Error* (New York: Harper & Brothers, 1949), p. 13, Chaim Weizmann writes about his pious mother, to whom the various modern Jewish ideologies were quite alien: "She would say: 'Whatever happens, I shall be well off. If Shemuel [the revolutionary son] is right, we shall all be happy in Russia; and if Chaim is right, then I shall go to live in Palestine.'"

[12]Quoted in Paul Miliukov, *Russia and Its Crisis* (New York: Collier Books, 1962), p. 364.

German pattern of settlement in the Middle Atlantic states, the Middle West, and the West. Active participants in the German immigrant community, they often shared the political outlook of their Christian compatriots. The liberalism of Lincoln's Republican party attracted them though comparatively few Jews were passionate abolitionists. Even Isaac Mayer Wise, who was to become a Copperhead and Democrat, at first was sufficiently interested in the Republican party to attend its Ohio organizing meeting. He withdrew because non-Jewish German atheists in Cincinnati were too closely identified with the party for his taste.[13] Despite his sympathy for the Confederacy he came to be one of the numerous Jews who admired and loved Lincoln not only for his acts on behalf of Jews but also for his great qualities of heart and mind. This admiration for Lincoln was what enabled many Jews to remain Republican and vote for General Grant in 1868, despite well-founded charges of anti-Semitism against him.[14]

In time, the German-Jewish immigrants flourished; many who had started as peddlers became prosperous businessmen and some even merchant princes. They remained almost uniformly loyal to the party because of its business outlook and its conservative fiscal and tariff policies. There was, in fact, hardly any other choice for the politically liberal middle-class voter in the second half of the nineteenth century. The Democratic party, at that time, could not have appealed to him; even when not actually split, as it often was, it was riddled with factions—torn between economic radicalism and conservatism, pulled apart by regional differences among the agrarian populists in the Midwest and West, the agricultural conservatives in the South, and the immigrant groups in the East.

To the East European immigrants, streaming into the squalid ghettos of the industrial cities, the Democratic party looked quite different. They viewed it from their position among the poorest, most sweated, exploited, and submerged proletariat of the rapidly expanding industrial system. True, the competition between Democrats and Republicans did not fit their old-country concept of a left-vs.-right polarity. That ideological outlook found expression instead in radical parties, largely transplantations from Europe, which occasionally attracted a significant proportion of the Jewish

[13]Bertram Wallace Korn, *American Jewry and the Civil War* (Philadelphia: Jewish Publication Society of America, 1951), p. 256.

[14]*Ibid.*, pp. 128–137.

immigrants' vote. But the Democratic party performed a vital function for the immigrant: however corrupt and greedy, it was often the chief mediator between him and the larger society. The ward heeler and the local boss could help in misunderstandings or disputes with the police, the landlord, the "authorities."[15] All the party wanted in return was a vote, and immigrant Jews were among those who provided the votes. Morris Hillquit describes an area inhabited almost entirely by Jewish immigrants from Russia—the 9th Congressional District on New York's East Side, where he ran unsuccessfully as the Socialist candidate for Congress in 1906: "Geographically it is located in the slums; industrially it belongs to the sweating system; politically it is a dependency of Tammany Hall."[16]

If Jews tended to vote mostly Democratic in those early days, it was not merely out of mistaken loyalty to the local machine. The Democrats were also the pro-immigration party, and immigration was a subject of considerable interest to Jews. In the last decades of the century, the Republican party was essentially nativist, favoring restrictions on the admission of aliens.[17] Later, when even the Democrats could no longer resist restrictionist pressure, the Republicans clamored still more loudly for closing America's gates.

There were exceptions to this voting pattern, however. If a Republican candidate was clearly pro-Jewish or responsive to some Jewish need, the immigrants gave him their votes.[18] For example, Jews supported Theodore Roosevelt in 1904, no doubt because in 1902 his Secretary of State, John Hay, had issued a strong note to Rumania condemning mistreatment of Rumanian Jews, and the following year both Hay and Roosevelt himself had denounced the Kishinev pogrom.

The third parties—Socialist, Socialist-Labor, and Progressive

[15]Richard Hofstadter, *The Age of Reform: From Bryan to F.D.R.* (New York: Vintage Books, 1960), pp. 182–185.

[16]Morris Hillquit, *Loose Leaves from a Busy Life* (New York: Rand School Press, 1934), p. 108.

[17]John Higham, *Strangers in the Land* (New Brunswick, N.J.: Rutgers University Press, 1955), pp. 97–105; Maldwyn Allen Jones, *American Immigration* (Chicago: University of Chicago Press, 1960), pp. 261–262.

[18]At the turn of the century the middle-class response to the "shame of the cities" expressed itself in the municipal reform movement. Largely drawn from the ranks of Republicans, the movement was often able to attract high-minded Democrats, too, appalled by the corruption of local Democratic machines. An outstanding example was Cyrus L. Sulzberger.

—attracted substantial numbers (though never a majority) of Jewish voters when the major-party choice was between an agrarian populist Democrat and a conservative Republican, a choice without meaning for the Jewish industrial proletariat, whose estimate of social justice was based on how Jews and urban workers were treated. Among Socialist candidates, the voters distinguished between those who identified themselves with their interests and those who did not.[19]

The ideological, as against the pragmatic, attraction of the Democratic party for Jewish voters all over the nation emerged with Alfred E. Smith's candidacy in 1928. Usually this attraction is thought to have been created by Franklin D. Roosevelt, first with the New Deal and later with anti-Nazism. But in actual fact Roosevelt seems to have merely reinforced an attachment which had been in the making throughout Smith's four terms as Governor of New York (1919–20, 1923–28).

Smith has been called the first Democratic candidate to speak on behalf of the workers in an industrial society.[20] Brought up in a New York slum, trained in politics in the state legislature and the Tammany machine, he rounded out his education by confronting the explosive problems of industrial urban life. He saw that Tammany's Christmas baskets and Fourth of July picnics were no answer to child labor or to disasters like the fire at the Triangle Shirtwaist factory. He was quick to learn from social workers and investigating commissions, and became a pioneer in social legislation.

When Smith was Governor of New York, more than half of America's Jews lived in New York City. Mostly factory workers and small businessmen, they were increasingly drawn to the Democratic party by its growing concern with the social and economic evils of industrial society. In Al Smith they saw not merely the practical social legislator but also the social conscience, the spokesman for the underprivileged and the downtrodden. He fitted into the European concept of the liberal leader who seeks to change the *status quo* peacefully in ways that will help the Jews. Moreover, though he was not of their religion and ethnic background, the Jews

[19]Cf. Arthur Gorenstein, "A Portrait of Ethnic Politics: The Socialists and the 1908 and 1910 Congressional Elections on the East Side," *Publication of the American Jewish Historical Society*, L (1960), pp. 202–238.

[20]Arthur M. Schlesinger, Jr., *The Age of Roosevelt*, Vol. I: *The Crisis of the Old Order: 1919–1923* (Boston: Houghton-Mifflin, 1957), pp. 95–100.

of New York looked upon Smith as a symbol of embattled minorities, including their own—a symbol with which they could identify.

By 1928, when he finally won the Democratic presidential nomination, Smith's attractiveness to urban industrial workers and to religious, ethnic, and racial minorities was unmistakable. The old Democrats were not pleased. One wrote that Smith obviously intended to appeal

> to the aliens, who feel that the older America, the America of the Anglo-Saxon stock, is a hateful thing which must be overturned and humiliated; to the northern Negroes, who lust for social equality and racial dominance; to the Catholics who have been made to believe that they are entitled to the White House, and to the Jews who likewise are to be instilled with the feeling that this is the time for God's chosen people to chastise America yesteryear [sic].[21]

The campaign of 1928 succeeded in tying the Jewish voters even more closely to Smith than might have been foreseen. The vicious anti-Catholic propaganda deeply reinforced Jewish loyalty to Smith in a way that class interest could not have done. The Rev. John Haynes Holmes, minister of the Community Church in New York, commented:

> What I had in mind about the Jews in this campaign is the fact, which I hold not to their discredit but to their honor, that their hearts leap out in sympathy for a man like Gov. Smith who is suffering under the stripes of persecution which the Jews have borne for centuries, and in admiration for this man's courage in defying bigotry and vindicating liberty.[22]

In all large cities, Jews voted overwhelmingly for Smith.[23] Because Smith spoke unmistakably for the industrial worker in the big city (he broke the Republican hold on the Northern cities, carrying 122 previously Republican counties[24]), and because Jews were largely industrial workers, their support of the Democratic

[21]George Fort Milton of Tennessee to W. G. McAdoo, July 1928, *ibid.*, pp. 126–127.

[22]*Jewish Daily Bulletin*, 30 October 1928.

[23]Fuchs, *op. cit.*, pp. 66–67.

[24]Samuel Lubell, *The Future of American Politics* (New York: Harper & Brothers, 1952) pp. 34–35.

ticket was generally assumed to be based essentially on class interest. Actually, with this election the modern liberal voting tradition among American Jews emerged, in which the class point of view was subordinated to a larger political outlook.

There is no precise way of knowing how much a voter's perception of his situation as a Jew affects his political behavior. It is doubtful whether most Jews consciously think of themselves as Jews when they act politically. Perhaps only the most ethnocentric do so. Most Jewish voters who support a liberal party or candidate probably justify their position intellectually by explaining that a liberal program extends more benefits to more people than a conservative program, and is more likely to lead to a good society where it is individual merit rather than family, race, or religion that counts. But who can say to what extent these voters explicitly calculate that such a society is inevitably good for Jews, or that in such a society Jews will not be scapegoats? Studies of political behavior are not yet refined enough to tell us how much and in what way submerged or subconscious insecurities affect rational political decisions and color political motivations. In any event, this widespread feeling about the good society which we have come to identify as Jewish liberalism first began to express itself in the support for Al Smith in 1928.

With Roosevelt's accession and his New Deal program, American politics took on a character which Jews had no difficulty in recognizing as distinctly European. The New Deal reforms made the image of the Democratic party created by Smith appear ideologically even more appealing. Left and right were now clearly discernible. In addition, Jews were particularly susceptible to Roosevelt's charisma—witness Republican Judge Jonah J. Goldstein's pun: "The Jews have three *velten* [worlds]: *di velt, yene velt* [this world, the next world], and Roosevelt."

In 1940, when fears of intervention in Europe's war stirred isolationism and oppostion to Roosevelt, Jewish voters became even more firmly rooted in the Democratic party. On the eve of the election, one report to Roosevelt stated that in New York only the Jews were solidly for him.[25] By 1944, when America was deeply involved in the war, political alignments were shifting decisively and the Roosevelt coalition began to break up; but the Jews stood firm.

[25]James MacGregor Burns, *Roosevelt: The Lion and the Fox* (New York: Harcourt, Brace, 1956), p. 453.

They remained Democratic even in 1948, except for a modest defection to Henry A. Wallace, the Progressive candidate.

Jewish voting since 1928 has paralleled the pattern of voting in industrial urban areas where working-class immigrants and their children have predominated. But in the 1930's the occupational composition of American Jews began to undergo substantial changes. The second generation, better educated than their immigrant parents, were then taking on white-collar jobs, entering government service, and becoming professionals,[26] though widespread unemployment and the prevailing poverty of the Depression partially obscured the extent of the occupational transformation. Observers during this period erroneously took economic factors to be the main reason why Jews supported the Democratic party. A few cited influences other than economic, but on the wrong evidence: they suggested that Roosevelt had solidified the Jews' Democratic loyalties by his appeal as an anti-Nazi. Actually, Roosevelt was far from being a political or ideological pioneer of anti-Nazism; he followed a policy of utmost caution until the tide of public sympathy following the Battle of Britain in 1940 swept him into the interventionist camp.[27] Most Jews did indeed see Roosevelt as an ardent anti-Nazi even in the early days, but in their intense admiration they were attributing their own feelings and views to him.

After World War II, the economic and occupational metamorphosis of American Jews became unmistakably apparent. They had shared in the country's rising prosperity. At the start of the 1950's most Jews were in business, white-collar occupations, and the professions. Their socio-economic structure now increasingly resembled that of high-status groups who voted Republican, and their continued preference for the Democratic party appeared ever more idiosyncratic. In the 1952 presidential election, the Democratic candidate received about 75 percent of the votes cast by Jews.[28] No other group in the population—trade unionists, Negroes, or young people—supported the party so solidly and consistently. And

[26]Nathan Glazer, "Social Characteristics of American Jews, 1654–1954," *American Jewish Year Book*, LVI (1955), pp. 20–24.

[27]Burns, *op. cit.*, pp. 262–263, 397–404.

[28]According to the 1952 post-election surveys by the American Institute of Public Opinion (Gallup), the figure was 77 percent; the National Opinion Research Center (Roper) found it was 74 percent and the Survey Research Center of the University of Michigan found it was 73 percent.

in 1956, when many Democratic voters shifted to Eisenhower, the Gallup poll found that 75 percent of Jewish voters still remained firmly entrenched in the accustomed column.

In the absence of firm data, we can only speculate about the reasons. Jews were greatly attracted to Adlai E. Stevenson, in part because the qualities of urbanity, education, and culture which he personified have always appealed to them. But, more important, Stevenson's popularity with Jews was deeply rooted in their political—in fact, ideological—outlook on McCarthyism. Stevenson had been a target of Senator Joseph R. McCarthy's "anti-Communist" campaigns, which neither the Republican presidential candidate nor the Republican party leadership had repudiated. The images McCarthy conjured up among Jews were frightening: visions of storm troopers goosestepping down Broadway, of an America taken over by a red, white, and blue reincarnation of Hitler's Brown and Black Shirts. The Senator from Wisconsin seemed to symbolize that "it could happen here." However exaggerated their fears, most Jews recognized McCarthy as a demagogue bent on exploiting for his own aggrandizement the nation's abhorrence of Communism and anxiety over Russia. They sensed in McCarthy's anti-Communism qualities similar to Hitler's, though he was not anti-Semitic and even tried to show his philo-Semitism. They feared his cynical opposition to liberalism and his contempt for due process. Many felt threatened in their security not only as American citizens but also as Jews, associating McCarthy with anti-Semitism. Most believed instinctively that no good could come to them from this quarter.

The depth of hostility against McCarthy among Jews has been measured in various surveys. A Gallup poll in June 1954 found intense disapproval among 65 percent of Jews interviewed, as compared with 31 percent of Protestants, 38 percent of Democrats and 45 percent of college graduates. In March 1957 a Roper poll gauged attitudes toward McCarthy by index numbers; the index for the Jewish group stood at -46, while the group next in line, consisting of executives and professionals, rated only -18.

McCarthy may have pushed Jews toward the Democratic party as much as Stevenson pulled them. Stevenson did not actually hold all the views which many Jews imputed to him. He was for instance, not an enthusiastic supporter of Israel in the Arab-Israel conflict, though most Jews seem to have taken it for granted that he was. Nor was he as prolabor as Jews and liberals believed. In 1952, as a generation earlier, the political or ideological, more than the economic, differences between the Republican and Democratic parties determined how most Jews voted. The same was true in 1956 and 1960, when Nixon incurred a good deal of the suspicion Jews had felt about McCarthy. To be sure, the hostility was less intense, yet Nixon's association with ideologically rightist anti-Communism again raised the question, however unwarranted, of anti-Semitism.

Political traditions brought from Europe (particularly Eastern Europe), economic experiences among the urban proletariat, and insecurities about anti-Semitism have combined to shape a middle-class American Jewish liberalism that has usually expressed itself at the polls in Democratic voting. This liberalism has become so pervasive that many descendants of German-Jewish immigrants, whose fathers and grandfathers were Republicans, have come to vote Democratic in the last two or three decades. By now liberal voting may have become part of a family group tradition—a habit and custom difficult to shed, particularly at that final moment in the voting booth when what Paul Lazarsfeld once called "terminal horror" assails the voter, preventing him from pulling the unaccustomed lever.

Today American Jewish liberalism seems to be sustained largely by this family and group tradition. Its earlier formative elements apparently are fading. European experiences antedating World War I are remote and unfamiliar to the three-fourths of American Jews who are native-born. Even the recent past of Nazi Germany and World War II is a matter of book learning for a new generation. Memories of unemployment and poverty may still linger among the many American Jews who experienced the Depression of the 1930's or witnessed the economic hardships of immigrant parents; but such recollections, too, are increasingly becoming part of a distant and even irrelevant past. The decline of overt anti-Semitism, the growing acceptance of Jews in nearly all occupations and at nearly all levels, will also probably affect the political behavior of Jews. If Jews find themselves wholeheartedly accepted, socially as well as professionally, by Gentiles whose class and status have made them Republican, the Jewish political style may change. The identification of the political right with anti-Semitism—an identification based almost exclusively on European politics—may then lose its meaning. Acculturation and full acceptance by Christians may in time deaden or at least dull Jewish sensitivity and feelings of insecurity. When this happens, class interests will probably affect voting more than Jewish group identity. But that time is still in the future.

THE NEW LEFT AND THE JEWS

by NATHAN GLAZER

INTRODUCTION

THE AMERICAN JEWISH liberal tradition has not only included participation in conventional liberal politics—it has also involved membership in and contact with a wide variety of radical movements. Whether pursued by immigrants at the turn of the century who resided on the Lower East Side, or in more recent decades by members of the second generation in more prestigious neighborhoods, Jewish radicalism of the older variety was not viewed by its practitioners as a threat to their Jewish identification; the typical Jewish member of the Old Left did not feel any less a Jew because of his leftism.

Since a significant proportion of the Old Left was Jewish, radicalism could be pursued in a Jewish setting. Furthermore, in the immigrant era it was common for radical groups to organize Jewish affiliates. These affiliates were meant to utilize the cohesion of the informal Jewish community to strengthen the radical cause. It was understood that members of such Jewish affiliates would develop strong interpersonal relationships with each other, but such bonds would be with fellow radicals and thus would become indivisible with loyalty to the "cause." The Jewish affiliate had the advantage to the party that it could address the Jew in his own language and idiom. In addition, the recruit was under no compulsion to modify his culture as the price of joining the cause; he could continue to speak Yiddish and follow other Jewish cultural patterns. His way of life was not disturbed.

If the party leaders of the Old Left exploited Jewish identity and culture and the existence of an informal Jewish community, they offered something in return. The Old Left addressed itself to Jewish grievances. It took a stand against anti-Jewish discrimination. It also took a stand against anti-Jewish prejudice and held out to its Jewish followers the vision of a new society in which bigotry would come to an end.

While the Old Left formed Jewish affiliates that sponsored activities of interest specifically to Jews, a number of acculturated Jews preferred the party itself to the Jewish affiliates. But such Jews were also appealed to in terms of their Jewish interests. Leaders of the Communist Party, or its numerous front organizations, stressed that in the USSR anti-Semitism was a crime against the State; that Soviet Jews had achieved high positions in the party, at the universities, in the State bureaucracy, and even in the Red Army; and that Birobidzhan had been established as an autonomous Jewish region. The implication was clear: the position of the Jew in Soviet society was in sharp contrast with the prejudice, discrimination, and pogroms that had been the lot of the Jews under the Czarist regime. To be sure, not all Jewish radicals were prepared to accept such claims at face value. But many felt that the Jewish position in Russia had improved considerably and some maintained that the Soviet Union was in the process of becoming a model society for Jews.

Yet whatever the position of Jews in a new radical society would be, Jewish radicals who were rigorous in their thinking understood that unless radicalism were combined with Zionism or with some other form of Jewish nationalism such a society would not lend itself to the perpetuation of Jewish identity. However, most Jews in the Old Left did not face the issue squarely. They felt that they were being good Jews by working for the cause. Their relationships with Jewish kin, Jewish neighbors, and Jewish friends proceeded as usual. Some Jewish radicals even established schools to afford their children the advantage of a Jewish education. (While there were radical Jewish families where children intermarried or no longer regarded themselves as Jewish, such occurrences did not create great alarm in Jewish radical circles.)

Jewish radicalism is as fascinating a subject as Jewish liberalism. Nathan Glazer, a sociologist of extraordinary scope and competence who has advanced our understanding of many aspects of American society, has been a long-time student of Jewish radicalism; in The Social Basis of American Communism, *Glazer explored the approach of the Communist Party to the Jews as well as to other minorities. In the following article he analyzes the approach of the New Left to the Jews.*

Glazer finds a striking contrast between the Old Left and the New Left. Instead of seeking to demonstrate the identity of Jewish interests and radical interests so characteristic of the Old Left, the New Left has disregarded Jewish interests. Whether in respect to Israel or to job or educational opportunities, the New Left has taken positions which contravene Jewish interests. The result is that the New Left has had quite a different meaning for its Jewish followers than was the case with the Old Left, for it has involved a considerably greater degree of alienation from the Jewish community. And ideology aside, the New Left has afforded an avenue of assimilation that was missing from the Old Left. Jews active in the New Left have lacked the Jewish culture of those who participated in the Old Left, the New Left includes a higher percentage of Gentiles than did the Old Left, and there are no separate Jewish affiliates in New Left organizations. Finally, the New Left has been influenced by youth culture with its stress on a style that anyone can adopt regardless of his religious or ethnic background.

While it is commonly felt that the New Left is on the decline it is still too early to assess the ultimate impact of New Left activity on the identity of Jews active in the movement. Since the New Left has characteristically been a youth movement, it remains to be seen whether its adherents will become integrated into the informal and formal Jewish community as mature adults. What we do know is that some young Jews have broken with the New Left over its indifference and hostility to Jewish interests and have formed radical groups of their own. The emphasis of these "Radical Jews" has been on criticizing the Jewish Establishment, experimenting with communal living arrangements, and defending Israel against its detractors.

M. S.

THE NEW LEFT in the United States has origins before 1962—the peace movement and the movement to ban nuclear testing (itself strongly influenced by the stronger English movements, such as the Aldermaston marches), the rise of new interest in Marxist thought in the late 1950's (expressed in such magazines as the *New Left Review* in England, *Studies on the Left,* and *New University Thought* in the United States), the concern over slum clearance in the late 1950's, and the rise of interest in community organizing of the Saul Alinsky type as a means of altering it, are all earlier developments that played a role in creating the New Left. Far more significant than any of these early movements contributing to the New Left was the civil rights revolution, which moved into a new stage of activism with the involvement of Negro youth in the sit-ins of 1960. But 1962 appears to me to be the date—others will choose others—of the beginning of that shifting, amorphous, and amazingly successful movement of protest, rebellion, and perhaps shortly now revolution, the New Left, or simply, the Movement. For that is the year in which the nascent Students for a Democratic Society, then still the student branch of the democratic socialist League for Industrial Democracy, met at Port Huron, Michigan, and adopted the Port Huron statement, which in its clear humanism, its refusal to use old radical or even liberal language, its emphasis on a pragmatic effort to involve people in the solution of their own problems, appears to me to be the founding document of the New Left.

In the spring of 1969, the SDS grew to become the largest and most powerful student movement in American history, with a membership of 70,000, according to the *New York Times,*[1] on 350 campuses. But more significant than its membership, which is shifting, undisciplined, and poorly defined, is its actual power—to disrupt and close campuses, to change the shape of American higher education, to place issues on the national agenda, to draw hundreds of thousands of students to its issues, to arouse the anger of a score of state legislatures, and conceivably—this is in the

[1]*New York Times,* 5 May 1969, "S.D.S. Scores Big Gains but Faces Many Problems," p. 1.

future—to arouse a reactionary and repressive movement that will be far more serious than McCarthyism. . . .

. . . just what is the "New Left"? It is more, on the one hand, than the Students for a Democratic Society—though that is its heart. It is less, on the other hand, than the civil rights movement, which has involved so many Americans since the early 1960's, and less than the anti-Vietnam war movement, which had also involved large parts of the population. . . .

. . . To define the New Left precisely: the New Left—I do not know the origin of the term—means "New" in two specific senses; in one sense, it is "New" simply because there was hardly any Left at all in the 1950's, before the New Left rose. There were liberals, of course. The Communist Party was half legal and in any case almost non-existent, its Trotskyite and Socialist opponents barely maintained life, and whether because of McCarthyism or of a prevailing conviction that most American domestic problems were or could be easily solved—see the rhetoric of the two Stevenson campaigns and even the first John Kennedy campaign—few people thought themselves to be of the revolutionary left, or even of the reformist left. This was a time when *Dissent*, edited by Irving Howe and Lewis Coser, seemed to be *the* Left in America—it now staunchly opposes (and is opposed by) the New Left. This was the age when everyone spoke of campus conformity and conservatism, when the Far Right made a greater appeal to youth than the Far Left, when a religious revival was believed to be in process on the campuses, and when religious speakers drew larger audiences than the occasional representatives of the Left. But more significantly, the New Left was new in that its members consciously dissociated themselves from the Old Left (by which they meant the Communist Party), and its Marxist critics of Left and Right, the Socialists and the Trotskyites. . . .

Its main interests, in addition to the civil rights movement, were American military and foreign policy—the role of the military in the society and in shaping foreign policy, and the emphasis in foreign policy on anti-Communism—and the poor whites as well as blacks. Underlying all the specific areas of concern was a common outlook which emphasized resistance to large bureaucratic institutions—to urban renewal agencies clearing slums, to public housing agencies administering housing for the poor, to welfare agencies distributing aid, to chain stores and local merchants. . . .

Obviously, a great deal has happened since [the 1960's]. The slum organizing work, after a few hard years, was largely abandoned—it was taken over by foundation- and later government-supported community action agencies. In part it was discredited in SDS as having been "co-opted" by the power structure. In a later stage, with the rapid rise of Black Power, New Left adherents began to feel that the work in the Negro slums and to a lesser extent among Negroes in the South should be left to Negroes (and even if they did not think so, Negroes soon pushed almost all whites out of such work). SDS continued to work in some poor white areas, particularly one in Chicago. But the main change in the locus of SDS activity came after the Berkely explosion of 1964, when it concentrated its activities on the campus. . . .

What has been the Jewish role in all this? If we list some people who have come to some prominence through their role in creating or developing the New Left—Tom Hayden, Carl Oglesby, Rennie Davis, Mario Savio, Mark Rudd, Abby Hoffman, Jerry Rubin, and others come to mind—we will not find an overwhelming predominance of Jews. In fact, perhaps Jews are *less* obvious among the leaders of the New Left than they were in the leadership of the Old Left. Among the troops—the students who follow these leaders, who are aroused by the issues that the New Left has exploited, and in particular the issues surrounding the Vietnam war (the teach-ins, opposition to the draft and to military and industrial recruiting on campus, the Reserve Officers' Training Corps program on campus, the issues of university complicity with government and war research, etc.)—Jews are numerous. Statistics are not easy to get; the membership of SDS is itself a shifting one, and defines itself as much by action as by formal affiliation. In the case of certain major campus actions (involvement in the Free Speech Movement in Berkeley and the movement against reporting class rank to draft authorities in Chicago), we have studies and they tend to show that more Jews participate in student activist movements than their proportion on campus.[2]

Other studies are underway, and there will be more information on this point. I have discussed in another article, though largely in speculative fashion,[3] the prominence of Jews in the New Left and the reasons for it. Some writers emphasize the conflict between

[2]Robert Somers in S. M. Lipset and S. Wolin, eds., *The Berkeley Student Revolt* (New York: 1965), p. 547; Richard Flacks, "Liberated Generation: An Exploration of the Roots of Student Protest," in the *Journal of Social Issues*, Vol. 23, July 1967, p. 65.

[3]See Nathan Glazer, "The Jewish Role in Student Activism," *Fortune*, January 1969.

permissive, liberal, child-centered, idea-oriented environments, such as are to be found in parts of the prosperous middle classes, and the rigid bureaucratic environments the children of these classes find in the high schools and colleges[4]. They point out that such a clash between an enlightened childhood and restrictive organizations—and to a child whose opinion has been taken seriously, whose wishes have helped determine the actions of adults around him and the nature of his environment, a university with its rules may be seen as such a restrictive organization—may be a factor in encouraging Left attitudes in young people, whose experience will appear to them to contradict the claims of the society to be free and open. These types of childhood would characterize the professional classes, and are certainly more likely to be found in Jewish than in non-Jewish families, owing to the occupational and economic characteristics of American Jews.

As against this social-psychological explanation, I myself tend to emphasize historical factors in explaining the tendency of Jews to find the New Left more attractive. These historical factors date back to the Emancipation. At that time, the Right was identified with romanticism, monarchy, hierarchy, tradition, nationalism, and generally anti-Semitism. The Left—and by this I mean liberals as well as radicals of various kinds—emphasized rationality and science, parliamentary democracy, social equality, internationalism, and of course freedom and equality for the Jews. There was a tendency to anti-Semitism in parts of the Left too, and this has been explored in particular by Z. Szajkowski, in articles in *Jewish Social Studies* and elsewhere. Still, there seemed little question that Jews were better off with the Left than the Right in Europe, particularly when the Left was liberal rather than radical.

This political bias was carried over to the United States. German Jews identified with the Republicans for a while in the North, when this was in certain ways the more "liberal" party—it opposed slavery. Eastern European Jews, who became the dominant part of American Jewry after 1880, were often Socialists, of one outlook or another. Many others were enrolled in the Democratic machines of the large cities. But even when they were not Socialist, they were more liberal than other Democrats, on such key indices as internationalism, higher government expenditure for public purposes, and government control of business to assist

[4]See Flacks, *op. cit.*; and Kenneth Keniston, *The Young Radicals* (New York: 1968).

workers and trade unions. It can be argued that Jews, in taking these positions, were defending their self-interest; and in part they were. Certainly, since so many Jews were overseas in countries in which Jews were threatened, it seemed in the Jewish self-interest to defend a more active and internationalist foreign policy. Jewish attitudes in defense of workers' interests seemed understandable enough as long as Jews were workers—in the thirties and forties, the proportion of Jewish workers dropped rapidly while the proportion of Jews in business and the professions (always substantial) increased rapidly. Yet as their economic position rose, the Jews continued to hold liberal domestic political attitudes, breaking the American pattern whereby increased wealth leads to identification with Republicans. Despite some contradictions between the Jewish economic position—predominantly now in business and the professions—and the economic orientation of the Democratic Party (which is the party of heavier taxes, heavier public spending, stronger restrictions on business, and stronger support for organized labor) the non-economic interest of Jews, their interest in a government tolerant and understanding of the non-Protestant minorities, seems to outweigh their purely economic interests.[5]

Jewish identification with the Left today I believe stems in large measure from the fact that the parents of Jews are generally liberals, and many of them were radicals in their youth. If these fathers are liberals, young Jews very often share with them disillusionment with recent political developments, and carry this disillusionment further. Young Jews are not insulated against radical and Marxist thinking by a childhood in which these were considered mad, immoral, or criminal—as is true in so many American homes. This means they do not become radical by reacting against their parents—rather they become radical by seeing themselves as willing to carry the thinking of their parents to its logical conclusion, unhampered by inhibition, caution, or concern for position and family. In their minds they overcome the hypocrisy of their parents, whose thinking is not carried out in action.

If their parents were once radicals, the children often see themselves as carrying out the heritage from which their own parents were deflected by fear, or lack of sufficient strength. Let us

[5]See Nathan Glazer, *The Social Basis of American Communism* (New York: 1962); Lawrence Fuchs, *The Political Behavior of American Jews* (Glencoe, Ill.: 1956); and for recent evidence that this historic bent among Jews still prevails, see Milton Himmelfarb, "Is American Jewry in Crisis?", *Commentary,* March 1969.

not underestimate the significance of this heritage. Perhaps half of the American Communist Party in the 1950's and 1960's was Jewish. While the party never had much more than about 50,000 members, the turnover was so rapid that perhaps ten times that number or more were party members. This makes a substantial reservoir of present-day parents for whose children to be radical is not something shocking and strange but may well be seen as a means of fulfilling the best drives of their parents. To parents who were Communist, we must add an equal or larger number who were Socialists of one kind or another.

Despite this historical background, there is one striking aspect of the Left position held by many young Jews today: today, for the first time in some decades, to be Left is to contradict some strongly held Jewish interests. To be Jewish and Socialist was understandable—the Socialists were against bigotry, persecution, and dictatorship. To be Jewish and even Communist, whatever the contradictions, was also understandable up to the early 1950's. The Communists claimed to be for an ultimate universal freedom. They were certainly against fascism, the mortal enemy of Jews; they too has suffered heavy losses from Hitler Germany. To escape to Russia from Nazi Germany, whatever the hardships that later followed, was to live rather than die. The Communists also made a special appeal to Jews. In the thirties and forties, they pointed to the opportunities for Yiddish and Yiddish culture in the Soviet Union. They pointed to the attempt to establish a Jewish autonomous region in Birobidzhan. Whatever the reality of increasing persecution of Jews in post-war Russia, Communists concealed and denied it.

What is striking today in contrast is the open contradiction between certain Jewish interests and New Left positions. In particular, Israel is seen almost everywhere on the Left—and here Russia, China, and Cuba are united—as the enemy of Arab national aspirations and the ally of the Imperialist West. The bloody and near-genocidal proclamations of the Arab states and guerrillas are defended within the New Left. In contradictory fashion, the New Left applauds the justice of every nation's interest in maintaining its independence—except for Israel. Black identity is seen as something that requires every possible support and encouragement. Even groups that are scarcely subject to any substantial degree of prejudice and discrimination in the United States—such as Chinese and Japanese Americans—are seen as being in need of independent cultural institutions so as to escape the blighting effect of schools and mass media which impose on them white middle-class standards. Oddly enough, Jewish Leftists see little need for such activity for Jews. This is not true of the entire Jewish Left—small groups of Jewish Leftists are now claiming for Jews what they claim for Negroes, without giving up an inch of their insistence that they are as revolutionary and as antagonistic to American state and society as any member of the New Left.

Other orientations of the New Left are also in opposition to Jewish interests, but here the argument is not so clear. Thus, the New Left opposition to bureaucracies of all kinds, as well as institutions in which one succeeds through merit, challenges the specific personal interest of many Jews, who have flourished in a society in which rationally determined talents are rewarded. The New Left generally supports the fight of many Negroes in New York City for a reorganization of the school system in which the teachers in public employ (largely Jews) would lose some of their privileges and perhaps their jobs. It supports the demands of Black students—raised most sharply at the City College of New York, which has for sixty years or more had a majority of Jewish students in a student body admitted only on the basis of merit—that colleges should admit Black students without regard to academic qualifications. Jewish advocates of the New Left either see no contradiction to Jewish interests in supporting such demands, or they are indifferent to them, or perhaps—another possibility—they take some actual pleasure in supporting positions that will hurt members of the Jewish group. Perhaps this is an expression of self-hatred; perhaps it is an expression of some degree of masochism, justified by the argument that some must suffer to help others; perhaps they do not feel *they* are affected because Jewish New Leftists are generally from the elite colleges, and from affluent and well-to-do families, and have no fear for *their* future, which will not depend on the protection offered by civil service regulations and admission tests. It is the Jewish working- and lower-middle classes who are most affected by the weakening of the civil service and of admission to college by academic qualification—and it is revealing that Jews of lower socio-economic status tend to be much more poorly represented in the New Left than Jews of higher socio-economic status.

But there is one final contradiction between New Left attitudes and Jewish interests that may affect, in the end, even the children of affluence who form the main Jewish contingent to the New Left. This is the substantial encouragement to domestic violence that has been given by the rise of the New Left. This encouragement of violence has a double character—on the one hand, the disruptions of universities by the favored youth of the country encourages violence by the authorities; the latter are supported generally by the working- and lower-middle classes who are outraged by the radical students' attack on values they cherish. We have seen this violence spread, particularly in the form of police attacks on student demonstrators, on and off the campus. We had feared for a long time that it would intensify to become even more dangerous, vigilante-type, community violence against students, of the kind which has been so common in the South to keep Negroes down. Fortunately there has been almost none of this up to now. It is scarcely possible to believe, if the disruptions which have been so massive in the year 1968–69 continue, that this will not come. Certainly George Wallace's 1968 campaign suggested it would not be hard to raise community (vigilante) violence against radical students.

This violence also increasingly comes from the students themselves; it was first directed against buildings, but later against fellow students, occasionally against university officials, and more frequently against police. While Black students have been more forward in such acts of violence than white, white radical students, in their sycophancy—and in any case since the philosophy of Fanon, Mao, and Ché plays such a substantial role among them—will not be far behind, and are not.

And obviously one kind of violence encourages the other, and we are in a spiral of increasing violence now.

Can anyone doubt that if regular procedures of government and the maintenance of order through legislatures, elected officials, courts, and police break down, that inevitably minorities, against which a substantial reservoir of dislike already exists, will in the end have to suffer? Jews have never been among those who have glorified violence, even when, as in Israel today, they must be prepared to exercise it at any moment. Thus we find another major contradiction between the New Left and Jewish interests. The question is whether Jewish supporters of the New Left will come to see it.

INTERGROUP RELATIONS / THE CHANGING SITUATION OF AMERICAN JEWRY

by SEYMOUR MARTIN LIPSET

INTRODUCTION

ALL MINORITY GROUPS must seek an accommodation with the groups that dominate the societies in which they live. A given pattern of accommodation is the result of many factors, not the least of which is the expectations a minority group harbors. For much of Diaspora Jewish history—the medieval period in Europe being the characteristic example—Jewish expectations were modest. The best that Jews could hope for was that anti-Semitism would be held in check—that the ruling class would guarantee physical survival by making it clear to the populace that the molesting of Jews would not be tolerated. Furthermore, Jews hoped that the ruling class would see to it that their opportunities to achieve a livelihood would not be unduly circumscribed. In essence, then, Jews believed that anti-Semitism was a "normal" phenomenon; the best that could be expected was a regime that would limit anti-Semitism to tolerable levels.

In modern times Jews have approached the problem of accommodation in ways different from those of their medieval ancestors. Zionists have held to the inevitability of anti-Semitism but have discarded the old faith in benign sovereigns and regimes, seeing in the establishment of a homeland a refuge that would place Jews out of the reach of anti-Semitism. Others, viewing the Diaspora as a permanent arrangement, have nevertheless come to conceive the possibility of an end to anti-Semitism. This, they believe, will occur not at the messianic "end of days" through Divine intervention, but will result from the improvement of the social order, whether peacefully in a liberal version or violently in a radical version.

The absence of a medieval past in United States history and the constant recurrence of the theme of human equality have lent force to the idea of anti-Semitism as a transient feature of the social order. The Jewish affinity to liberalism, analyzed in the previous articles, has not been unconnected with the fact that in many Jewish minds liberalism was sure to triumph and would inevitably bring in its wake the eradication of anti-Semitism. In the 1930's, the rise of Hitlerism together with its domestic reverberations delivered a jolt to this view, but the subsequent defeat of Nazi Germany, the decline in discrimination in the United States during and after World War II, and the status seemingly accorded Judaism in the 1940's and 1950's as one of the three major faiths served to reinstate it in full vigor.

The belief in the emergence of a society free of anti-Semitism has taken many forms, most conspicuously the various national defense agencies like the American Jewish Committee or the Anti-Defamation League, as well as the scores of local Jewish community relations councils. The agencies betray a characteristic American activism. Rather than passively waiting for the "end of days" they propound the idea that Jews are obliged to promote the cause of improving intergroup relations.

At periodic intervals the AJC, the ADL, and the local community relations councils (and other interested agencies) federated in the National Jewish Community Relations Advisory Council, have sought to take stock of their assets and liabilities, to estimate how far they have gone and have yet to go. The excerpt which follows is taken from one such inventory: the report of a "task force" on intergroup relations convoked by the AJC in 1969.

The statement introducing the task force report by its chairman, Morton K. Blaustein, is of more than casual interest. According to Blaustein: "Believing that the seventies would present the Jewish community with new and complex problems which could be dealt with successfully only through a process of long-range planning, the Committee's Board of Governors created a

Task Force Policy Committee for the purpose of planning such a program." Blaustein's statement can be taken to suggest that hopes for a society free of anti-Semitism are premature. His tone suggests that the "end of days" is not in sight; not only that, but there are signs that the gains of the post-war years can erode if strenuous efforts are not made to conserve them.

That the climate of intergroup relations had unexpectedly changed was suggested by the fact that in the late 1960's a new Jewish organization rose to prominence: the Jewish Defense League. The JDL was based on the premise that the gains of the post-war years were imperiled. The maintenance of Jewish status and Jewish security, the JDL suggested, demanded the implementation of the most militant tactics which Jews could muster—tactics which went much further than customary procedures and included illegal activity. While all of the national as well as the local Jewish intergroup-relations agencies condemned the JDL in the strongest terms, the organization made explicit what others hesitated to verbalize: that American Jewry was far less secure than its prosperity, prominence, and seeming influence suggested.

The AJC's selection of Seymour Martin Lipset to direct its task force on intergroup relations was appropriate. A social scientist of eminence, Lipset exhibited a much stronger sympathy for Jewish concerns than most of his colleagues. (His observations about Jewish social scientists and his implied criticism of those who would separate themselves from the Jewish community are noted in The Jew in American Society, pp. 255–288.) Of equal importance was the fact that Lipset was not a "new" or radical sociologist bent on promoting disaffection with American institutions, and his findings therefore would not be the product of an imagination in search of evidence of social malignancy.

Lipset and his associates did indeed discern sharp changes in the Jewish position in American society—changes which they felt were cause for deep concern. Jewish advance in the past had been predicated upon the success of liberalism, and upon the alliances which gave liberalism its vitality. Now there was a gradual erosion of such alliances. To many the old liberalism seemed bankrupt. It had not paid off on its promises; it had produced disaffection among such diverse groups as blacks, students, and "hard hats." A new liberalism, as well as a New Left, had come into being to replace the old liberalism and the Old Left. These new versions of familiar ideologies held new implications for Jews: they did not invariably support Jewish interests, nor were Jewish interests invariably advanced as a result of new liberal victories.

The demand for group rights dramatized the radical changes which had occurred. The old liberalism had demanded individual rights, and it was through the implementation of such rights that Jewish advance had proceeded. However, the new liberalism (as well as the new militancy of deprived minority groups) stressed group rights. It was apparent that group rights might not only be objectionable in theory but could be deleterious in practice—they could undercut gains which Jews had so painfully won as they sought to move up out of the working class.

The crisis of the old liberalism and the policies of the new liberalism had the effect of producing what Lipset called ". . . the tension between Jewish liberalism and Jewish interests." Such tension produced the dilemma of ". . . whether to opt for universalistic liberal and radical principles at the expense of Jewishness, or for particularistic Jewish identity at the cost of involvement in liberal or radical politics." The result of the dilemma was a cleavage in the Jewish community—an uncharacteristic split between well-off Jews and poorer Jews, between the well-educated and the less well-educated, between the strongly committed and those with weaker Jewish identification. The larger the income, the higher the education, and the weaker the Jewish identification, the greater the tendency to opt for universalistic principles at the expense of Jewishness.

Lipset and his task force colleagues went beyond diagnosis; they presented the AJC with recommendations as well. We do not reproduce all of their recommendations in the extract below, but we can summarize their approach. The task force was not sure that the fight for meritocracy and individual rights could be won. Furthermore, it inferred that even if the fight were successful social cleavages might result which would ultimately threaten Jewish interests. Thus the task force recommended that a new balance be sought between individual rights and group rights.

The task force stopped short of recommending quota systems on behalf of aspiring groups. Pointing out the strong objections to quotas, it accepted an intermediate position—what has come to be known as "affirmative action."

The task force also recommended large-scale projects to improve the position of the disadvantaged, and advocated the passage by Congress of an economic bill of rights. The hope here *was that efforts like these might diminish alienation and undercut the militant rhetoric on all sides. An expansionist economy would minimize competition for jobs and for advancement opportunities.*

American Jewry was also counseled by the task force to seek to renew the old liberal coalition. It was suggested that Jews modify some of their old-style liberalism in the interest of building (or rebuilding) bridges to other groups. Lipset made clear that the need for allies was much more than a desire for a sentimental reunion with old comrades. Allies were imperative, he felt, because the tide of events placed all American institutions and traditions in a position of extreme fragility, and made it mandatory to assume that "the Jewish community is threatened by a revival of anti-Semitism after a quarter of a century of quiescence in the wake of the Holocaust."

Even those members of the task force who dissented from recommendations formulated by Lipset on behalf of the group found it difficult to believe in the speedy arrival of the "end of days"—a society free of anti-Semitism where Jewish security and acceptance could be taken for granted.

M. S.

UNITY IN THE POST-WAR ERA

THE POST-WAR PERIOD (1945–1965) must be clearly demarcated from the periods that immediately preceded and followed it. . . . The two decades following World War II saw growing affluence, domestic tranquility, and heightened intergroup rapport. With increased commitment to civil rights and integration for the black population, Jewish communal organizations gradually shifted their emphasis from a concern with defense of Jewish rights and opposition to anti-Semitism, to cooperation with, and assistance to, groups involved in the struggle for civil rights and equality for blacks. Jews also became an ever more important component of the general liberal political movement, bringing to it needed assistance in the form of membership and financial support from a well-educated and relatively well-to-do population. The liberal movement and organizations, in turn, continued to support matters of particular Jewish concern, which in these decades largely meant aid to Israel, first in its struggle for independence and later for its survival.

Perhaps the general trend most relevant to the role of the Jews in intergroup relations before the mid-1960's was the decline in ethnicity and the growth of ecumenism. Many sociologists categorically predicted that ethnic identifications would vanish, that World War II had intensified the American belief in a melting pot which would dissolve group ties. Thus Lloyd Warner stated at the end of the war that "it is likely that [ethnic groups] . . . will be quickly absorbed." A few years later, Robert MacIver, in his famed report on the future of Jewish organizations, agreed; he argued that if the Gentile community was to understand efforts to preserve Jewish communal organizations, they must be linked to religious identification rather than to secular ethnicity. Writing in the mid-1950's from within the Jewish community, Will Herberg, in his *Protestant, Catholic, Jew,* elaborated on the MacIver generalization, arguing anew the thesis that America basically contained three melting pots in the form of the three great religious traditions, and that hyphenated old-country identifications were becoming un-American.

The deemphasis of ethnicity in the post-war era was accompanied by a growing commitment to religion. The Gallup Poll and others attested to increased church attendance, to an almost universal expression of faith in God. Yet, as Herberg further noted, the commitment was to an American version of religion, with a minimal set of beliefs and ritual requirements. The literature made reference to the growth of an American church or religion, which had three cooperating branches: Protestantism, Catholicism, and Judaism. And the opinion surveys on prejudice seemed to bear this out. They indicated a decline in disagreement over variations in religious background, increased acceptance of interfaith marriage, exchange of pastors, and the like. Apparently, America was beginning a stage in its development that would change it to resemble the socially homogenous nations of Scandinavia.

The period saw a more widespread adherence to values associated with conservative eras, especially an emphasis on meritocracy. Jews, particularly, gained from the general acceptance of the thesis that individuals should be considered solely on their merits, which, in an increasingly bureaucratic and science-based economy, meant educational achievements. The decline of religious and nativist bigotry, at the end of the war, brought with it an end to restrictions within academe. Jews poured into the socially and intellectually elite universities and professional schools, the very ones which had maintained a *numerus clausus* before 1945. By the 1950's, Jews constituted a major segment of the student body and faculty of Ivy League schools. And after graduation from the best colleges in America, they went on to participate in many areas of the private economy which once had barred them. The Jew now stood out as a symbol of the import of the democratic American system: its willingness to take the accomplished scions of European immigrants into any position for which they qualified.

The group sharing least in this new abundance and mobility was, of course, the black community. Clearly, Negroes were still at the bottom of the ladder economically. Yet those looking at America with optimism equated them to the most recent "immigrant" peasant group: they were now entering urban America handicapped, as were all earlier peasant immigrants, by inadequate education and a lack of urban skills, but would soon follow the upward path of their predecessors. The optimists could point to a variety of indicators of black progress. Opinion polls showed steady improvement in white attitudes regarding Negro rights and abilities.

Institutions which had once barred them—ranging from professional baseball to hotels and restaurants—opened their doors. And the positive changes were capped by the Supreme Court's 1954 school desegregation decision implying an end to deprivation in education. Fair employment practices acts and other legislation designed to extend Negro rights in housing, education, and other fields were passed in many states and cities in the North.

Yet, in the many efforts to explain and understand these trends, including the increase in ecumenism and the decline in ethnic identification, one stood out which, if valid, might have suggested perilous implications for the future: that these trends were in part, cold-war phenomena; that they reflected a commitment to national unity and patriotism directed against the Communist enemy, at home and abroad.

The decline in ethnicity and the rise in religiousness and the concomitant generalized patriotism seemingly paralleled or reinforced conservative philosophy and politics. A prolonged period of international conflict, first against fascism and later against Stalinism, reduced domestic tensions. Intellectuals (in twentieth century America, usually of the left), occupationally disposed to be sharply critical of domestic institutions, also felt the need to defend American democratic institutions against Communist attack. They continued for a short period their wartime-born support of America, thus helping to reduce potential discontent.

BREAKDOWN IN CONSENSUS

The political consensus and sense of liberal egalitarian progress of the post-war era, that were both celebrated and condemned by different groups, broke down in the mid-1960's. The breakdown manifested itself chiefly in increased resort to extreme forms of militancy and even violence by ghetto blacks and the growth of a powerful and ultimately quite alienated movement of resistance to the Vietnam war, which drew its main sustenance from groups and individuals, who were once the backbone of the more liberal and pro-Israel wings of the old New Deal-Great Society coalition within the Democratic party. The new disunity showed itself most dramatically in ghetto riots, in campus sit-ins, and in the emergence of a mass radical movement around the symbolic concept of a New Left, uncorrupted and uninhibited by ties to earlier radical movements and existing leftist governments, and trying to break with traditional establishment life styles by participation in the bohemian "counter culture."

Of course, the change did not begin in 1965. Ethnic groups, radical movements, and intellectuals were strongly affected by two earlier decisive developments: on the international scene the removal of the threat of an expansionist, monolithic Stalinist power, and at home, the Supreme Court school desegregation decision, a high point in domestic affairs. . . .

Racial Equality and Black Militancy

Racial equality was the best possible issue around which the new criticism of America could develop. The adult population outside the South, particularly the elite, agreed that Negro inequality was wrong, that efforts to change the situation should be supported. The movements which mainly conducted the struggle—the NAACP, the National Urban League, Congress of Racial Equality (CORE), Student Non-Violent Coordinating Committee (SNCC), Southern Christian Leadership Conference (SCLC), and others—initially were far from radical; some were not even very militant tactically.

Resistance to these groups initially in the South and later in the North intensified their militancy and, ultimately, their radicalism. The refusal of Southern authority to accept the law convinced the active supporters of civil rights, both black and white students, that normal, peaceful democratic methods would not work, and they resorted to civil-disobedience tactics, which ultimately spread throughout the country, to the campuses and other areas of American life.

Black militancy, supported by white student activism, in alliance with more conventional civil-rights supporters, secured more government measures for the improvement of the lot of the black masses than had been enacted since the Civil War. The hope of opportunities for steady jobs in a prosperous economy encouraged large-scale migration of Southern blacks to cities in the North. But these developments did not bring racial peace; extreme militancy among blacks increased.

In response to increased political militancy and fear of continued ghetto riots, and in harmony with traditional American ideals, the Kerner Commission and a Southern-born President put the nation on record as seeking to do everything possible to wipe out white racism. Mainstream America—churches, the National Alliance of Businessmen, foundations, schools and universities, social welfare agencies—picked up the white-racism theme. The Urban Coalition was formed under the leadership of major businessmen around the country; business started hiring (or at least publicly talked of hiring) large numbers of blacks. The civil-rights law of 1964 was as extensive a law as any ever proposed. As Joseph Rauh, former head of the Americans for Democratic Action, pointed out, the 1948 platform of the Democratic party, which resulted in a Dixiecrat walkout and which, in any case was not translated into law, had promised much less. Various laws proposed in 1948 by the left wing of the Democratic party had now been enacted, but in stronger form than had been thought possible in the then foreseeable future.

But despite strong federal civil-rights legislation, and even broader laws in many Northern states, the social and economic reality of the American Negro remained brutal. As he finally sought to enter American society, with the government and other powerful institutions seemingly strongly behind him, he found the labor-market situation changed by an ironic—perhaps the better word is cruel—twist of fate. The economy of the 1960's had more room at the top than at the bottom. There was an increasing need of educated, trained people. And, although many unskilled jobs were still available, the enormously expanded welfare program in the North undermined their value. They were not only lowly regarded within the urban occupational structure; more importantly, they paid less than the worker's wife and children could secure from welfare. Thus government policy in effect undermined the value of work. Since World War II, upward mobility in an expanding economy and a more demanding society increasingly has required a good education or a high level of skills, or both. But cultural residues of slavery, inadequate education in bad schools, and what was essentially the "peasant" background of those reared in the rural South, prevented many blacks from securing such mobility. In a real sense, and apart from race, the migrating blacks who came to Northern cities from the South, were in the same situation as the hordes of peasants who came to America's cities from Europe before World War I. They came seeking work, and though many faced discrimination in employment, they were encouraged to take unskilled jobs, which were an improvement over alternatives in the old country. As pre-World War I surveys indicated, most of these immigrants did not benefit much from education; the average Sicilian dropped out of school after two years. It took three generations for the offspring of Southern European peasants to begin to achieve anything approximating parity in school attendance, and their occupational attainments suffered as a result.

Faced with such difficulties, the contemporary black migrant found that he had been given a false promise; that the civil-rights legislation did little to improve his opportunities. Muscle-power was no longer enough, and few blacks were sufficiently trained to fill positions as engineers, highly skilled technicians, computer programmers, or teachers. Thus, while the civil-rights movement had won almost all the political victories it ever hoped to win, unemployment among blacks was higher than in the nation as a whole, and almost all urban blacks lived in crowded ghettos. It is easy to understand why this contrast between great promise and little visible positive results produced increasing bitterness, increasing alienation, greater violence, and greater lawlessness, particularly among the unemployed and the young.

The growth in black militancy was to have a deep effect on the general issue of ethnicity in America, for the frustrations led many Negro leaders in the 1960's to turn from the fight for equal rights to pressing for black power: community control of various institutions, including schools, separate black organizations, and separate cultural identification. In other words, segments of the black population, which was defined as a racial group solely by the unwillingness of white Americans to grant it equality, now began to insist that it was an ethnic group with a common African cultural heritage. As a distinct ethno-cultural group, blacks demanded their own institutions, much as those of the Jews, Chinese, Irish, and other ethnic groups. They began to insist that organizations for the defense of black rights be composed of Afro-Americans, just as the membership of the American Jewish Committee or the Anti-Defamation League is Jewish. They insisted that white America accept, and cooperate with, their demand for separate and equal cultural institutions and study programs, both outside and within the public education system.

These demands took white America by surprise. The more

tolerant wanted to treat the blacks as they thought the Jews and other initially deprived ethno-religious minorities had been treated by liberal America: as full equals who, in time, would become as American, as accepted as anyone else.

Of course, the growing black militancy affected the various parts of white America in sharply different ways. The central-city population reacted along class lines to the high crime rate rooted in the ghetto, as well as to demands for school integration. Affluent whites moved to the suburbs or sent their children to private schools, "understood" the crime rates, and accepted with quiet regret the black insistence on separation. Working-class and poorer whites living in urban areas adjacent to black ghettos, or pressured to bus their children to achieve school integration, tended to support politicians who sought to capitalize on law-and-order and school issues. But few challenged as a legitimate aspect of American life the revival of ethnic separateness subsumed in the concept of the "black community," with its own quite distinct culture-sustaining institutions.

Demand for Group Rights

The demand of black militant groups that they be accorded rights as a *group*, in addition to rights as *individuals*, had extraordinary consequences for general conceptions of equal rights in America, and for the position of the Jews in particular. Historically, minority groups which had suffered discrimination, institutionalized prejudice, or handicap, with respect to skills and education, had demanded the elimination of barriers denying *individuals* access to opportunity. Jews, Orientals, and Italians objected to the *numerus clausus* established by institutions of higher learning against qualified members of their ethnic groups. They opposed policies designed to increase the advantages enjoyed by members of majority groups. The Irish, who had been rebuffed by signs reading "No Irish need apply," looked for political and economic fields in which they could qualify. Except for Catholic proposals for state support of parochial schools, which were almost invariably rejected as "un-American," no minority group had demanded significant special-group advantages.

Liberal and Socialist opinion had always assumed that the egalitarian creed meant advocacy of a universalistic rule of meritocracy, enabling all to secure positions for which they qualified in open, fair competition. . . . This traditional liberal-left position, implicit in the American creed's emphasis on equality of opportunity, broke down with the demand of blacks that they be given "equality of results" which meant special group advantage in the form of quotas which would bring their number up to their proportion in the population in university admissions, various occupations, and trade unions which control access to jobs. And, as the affluent sector of the liberal-left community, including the intelligentsia, has come to accept this principle, other disadvantaged groups—Chicanos, Puerto Ricans, American Indians, women—have, not unnaturally, taken up the same demands for *group* rather than *individual* rights and for *group* mobility, as a way of bypassing the historic process of upward mobility of the individual through the acquisition of skills.

Compliance with these demands for special quotas means denial to others of positions for which they are qualified, or which they now have. It means that other minority groups which have been particularly successful in certain fields are now being asked to give up their gains. This is true of such groups as the Jews, Japanese, and Chinese, that have concentrated on education as a means of mobility. More universalistic than other job markets, the civil service has always been a special arena for mobility for disadvantaged groups doing well in school and in examinations. Other immigrant minority groups have used different skills, which they brought from Europe, to gain a special advantage in different job markets. Given the diverse cultural backgrounds of the American ethnic groups, it is not surprising that their occupational distribution also varies. Relatively few Jews are found among the farm population or in the executive suites of banks and major industrial corporations. If the concept of positive group-discrimination is accepted, as it has begun to be, America will have accepted a version of the principle of *ascription*, or hereditary placement, to advance equal opportunity.

Since this development not only revolutionizes traditional basic values, but also challenges existing distribution of reward, it is not surprising that it has upset the relations among different minority ethnic groups. Those who "made it" under the more or less meritocratic rules have strongly resented the efforts to deprive them of their gains. And around the country, concrete proposals to this end have pitted some Jews, white ethnics (Catholics), and Chinese against blacks, Chicanos, Puerto Ricans, and their affluent liberal allies.

Anti-War and Other Protests

The tensions arising from black militancy and white reaction have run parallel with and have been reinforced by those caused by the initially intellectual and liberal opposition to the Vietnam war. Vietnam became the symbol of incompatibility of American actions and basic American beliefs, chiefly anti-imperialism, and of the politically weak peoples' right to self-determination. As the war continued, the growing sense that we were involved in an oppressive war seeking to impose our will on another people undermined the very legitimacy of the American polity in the eyes of the more liberal, particularly the intellectual, segment of the community. It had considerable impact on the content of the mass media, as well as on the character of the widespread student activism initially dedicated to ending the Vietnam war but later also toward widening the egalitarian promise of America. In effect, the liberal intelligentsia (including a large segment of the Jewish community) found itself in conflict with society-at-large when its college-student children insisted that the principles preached by their parents and teachers should be practiced, *now*. . . .

White Ethnicity Revitalized

As we have seen, rising extremism, and black militancy in particular, helped relegitimate "tribalism" among the less privileged whites in the inner cities. While each group emphasizes its uniqueness, the ethnics have discovered common concerns in maintaining a stable pattern of urban life, neighborhood safety, and good schools. In their quest for solutions of these problems and for the defense of the rights of groups other than blacks, the Jews, the proto-ethnic group, also rediscovered ethnicity. Jewish leadership's awareness of these changes, and the need to find coalition allies among the diverse groups in dealing with the situation is reflected in the work of the National Project on Ethnic America. As each group discovered that it had its own particularistic interests, it became more sympathetic to the concerns of the others. These groups came to recognize that politics in a nation bitterly divided over ideological issues also involved catering to self-interests. As a result, the lower middle-class and working-class whites, who felt that the liberal clergy and the WASP and Jewish "suburban elites" were interested solely in the plight of the blacks, were impelled to create a new leadership structure defined and perceived as ethnic.

In a way, the revitalization of organized ethnicity largely has been a class response by organized white workers to certain institutions which no longer seemed to support their class interests. The very commitment of a large segment of the Democratic Party leadership and various Protestant and Catholic clergy to "cosmopolitan" positions on issues of changes in morality, patriotism, law and order, education, and black rights, and their lack of concern during the 1960's over income policies affecting the regularly employed, left a void which ethnic leaders have filled in part.

An indicator of the breakdown of traditional forms of symbolic and actual representation late in the decade is the considerable support initially given to George Wallace, who exploited the sense of isolation of the "forgotten workingman" (over 25 percent of workers supported him a month before the 1968 election).

Overriding all changes, as they affected the "majority" American, was the threat to the pride and identity of the nation itself. The United States, which had come out of World War II as the leader of the alliance which thoroughly defeated its enemies, as the wealthiest and most powerful nation on earth, which alone possessed atomic weapons, found itself, 25 years later, unable to defeat militarily a small Communist opponent. By the beginning of the 70's the American military forces were also suffering a serious failure of nerve, with large numbers of West Point graduates resigning their commissions. This was the situation after two decades of international setbacks, the loss of China to the Communists, the stalemate in the Korean war, the victory of the Castro revolution in Cuba, and the weakening of the American economy, which was unable to compete effectively with nations whose economic revival had been made possible by American aid. . . .

CRISIS OF LIBERALISM AND POLITICAL SITUATION OF AMERICAN JEWRY

. . . there can be little doubt that liberalism is in a state of crisis, pointed up by the government's failures in dealing with the situation of the blacks and the Vietnam war. In its most extreme form, the crisis is apparent in the overt rejection of liberalism by some intellectuals and their fellow travelers—university students, the principal media voices, the clergy of the more liberal denominations, and a large segment of the Jewish community, who have grown pessimistic about the ability of liberal governments to solve "problems" through public action. After some forty years of liberal rule, with two major political parties accepting the principles of Keynesian economics and the welfare state, the country is troubled by problems created by an inadequate welfare system, by an inflation difficult to control, and a higher rate of unemployment than it has known for years. The rise of urban problems and crime rates have created a clear sense that cities have become ungovernable. The failures of the nation's best publicized example of a sophisticated, charismatic, liberal mayor, aided by all the consultative knowledge money can buy, demonstrate how little can be done on that level.

Most recently, the liberal and national psyche has suffered another blow in the breakdown of America's post-war commitment to extensive development-aid to the less developed countries, to "free trade," and to reduced tariffs, designed to encourage both prosperity and international peace. Whatever the underlying economic consequences to diverse interests at home and abroad, liberal America did favor an internationalist foreign policy for what it thought were idealistic reasons. Perhaps more important than the collapse of the liberal economic policies toward other countries has been the erosion of the belief that collective security alliances are the way to prevent international war. Vietnam was most responsible for this change in mood, but assorted other events, including relations with some of our allies, have contributed.

Increasingly, liberal spokesmen now admit, more often in private but sometimes in public, and particularly in discussing foreign policy, that they have little faith in their own, or anyone else's, ability to manage the society, much less international relations. Social scientists on whom liberalism has relied are equally pessimistic, confessing they do not know how the situation could be significantly improved. Many are concerned about "unanticipated consequences" of purposive action, and call for more research.

This answer only serves to frustrate and embitter those who insist on action *now*, particularly the more idealistic young and the more militant among the racial minorities. They will not take seriously in looking for new solutions the opinions of those confessing to past failure; they will see their statements as acknowledgements that their system has failed and as acquiescence in the radical's proposition that the only solution is revolutionary action.

The crisis of liberalism, its failure of nerve, and its change of "line," has special implications for intergroup relations strategy and Jewish communal activities. Both the general politics of the Jewish community and its efforts in the intergroup relations field have been closely related to the condition of American liberalism. American Jewry has been heavily liberal in its ideology and organizational strategies. And organized liberalism has cooperated closely with Jewry on issues of Jewish rights, anti-Semitism, assistance to the State of Israel, and support for the rights of other deprived minorities. The change in liberal foreign policy affects Israel. The dismay over the inefficacy of applying traditional universalistic and integrationist principles to the condition of the blacks challenges norms and institutions which Jews have long regarded essential for their own security. And the Jews, confused by the same sense of inadequacy which upsets the liberals, are divided on what is to be done, as they have not been since the rise of Nazism.

Declining Jewish Political Influence?

These various changes have led a number of observers to suggest a considerable weakening of the ability of the Jews to affect the course of American life, to cope with their own group concerns, and to further universalistic liberal objectives. Earl Raab has argued strongly that Jews have indeed lost much of their political influence and therefore will be increasingly ignored by other elements in the society. As out-and-out bargaining among different groups has followed loss of faith in liberal solutions to the race problem, some segments of the dominant WASP elite, including the liberals, have been ready to part with the universalistic principles of meritocracy and return to an emphasis on ascriptive traits, on ancestral background, as a means of assigning "quotas" to minorities. Thus liberalism is no longer a bridge for the Jews to other groups in society; it may soon become a barrier, particularly since liberals no longer see Jews as an oppressed minority in need of assistance.

Others see the Jews retaining, if not enhancing, their influence and bargaining power through their involvement in the Democratic party. Evidence of this is a considerable increase in the election of

Jews to public office, including Democratic district leaderships in New York City. They are said to have "*ousted* the Catholics" from their long-held positions of power in the late 1960's. In 1969, for the first time in history, Jews won a majority on the Board of Estimate, holding two of the three top posts. Elsewhere, as the 1970's begin, there are Jewish governors in Pennsylvania, Rhode Island, and Maryland; a Jewish mayor in a major Southern city, Atlanta, and a myriad of other Jewish public officials. There appear to be few states in the Union where Jews have not, or could not get a major party nomination (usually Democratic) for the most important posts. Also, since Jews now participate in politics more vigorously than other groups, and since those who have political resources, intellectual talent, and money often are extremely generous in donating them in campaigns, Jews appear in high places close to many major non-Jewish politicians, particularly if they are Democrats. Though Jews less commonly wield influence among Republicans a number are in high posts close to the President: Henry Kissinger, Leonard Garment, Herbert Stein, and Arthur Burns. And Republican Senator Jacob Javits has accumulated enough seniority to be the ranking (and thus the most powerful) minority party member of important Senate committees.

Surveys of the power resources of American Jews outside the realm of politics point to their high income level, as compared to that of other ethnic and religious groups, and their special position in opinion-forming institutions, particularly the media and the universities. Findings of the extensive Carnegie Commission on Higher Education survey of the American professorate indicate that the proportion of Jews in academe increases with scholarly quality and status of the institution. They constitute fully a quarter of the faculties of Ivy League colleges, where they are much more heavily represented in the politically relevant social sciences than in most of the humanities and natural sciences. The most dramatic change, in recent years, in the participation of Jews in the intellectual elite has been their appointment to university presidencies. Until 1965, Jews were almost entirely absent from these posts; since then, they have been chosen to head many major institutions, including Buffalo, Chicago, Cincinnati, the City College of New York, Dartmouth, Massachusetts Institute of Technology, Pennsylvania, and Rutgers. As for the broadcast media, Jews not only have considerable representation among their top officers; a survey conducted by the Harris Poll of the "critic" in all forms of intellectual endeavor in the mass media concludes that if "he is in a large metropolitan center and very well known . . . he is probably Jewish or unaffiliated with any religious group."

Those who believe the gradual erosion of the liberal alliance is weakening the position of the Jews point to a quite different set of social processes as compounding their political difficulties. They suggest that reaction to the Holocaust not only led many Christians to adopt a philo-Semitic posture immediately after World War II as a means of compensating for the failures of Christendom; it also served to repress overt expressions of ordinary anti-Semitism, which has existed in the West for two millennia. After the revelations of the mass murders committed by the Nazis, attacking Jews became an unspeakable act. But it is unlikely that this meant that one of the most stubborn cultural conventions of Western civilization had disappeared so quickly. Various earlier conscious efforts following liberal and leftist revolutions had failed to root it out.

Cultural anti-Semitism, transmitted from generation to generation, is best understood as a kind of collective consciousness almost irradicably built into our literature, our language, our most general cultural myths. Although the memory and significance of the Holocaust inhibited the use of anti-Semitism, it still persisted. Now that the events of 1939–45 have entered history, the chances increase as time goes by, that cultural anti-Semitism, folk anti-Semitism, may be revived and used for political purposes. Many, who would find it unthinkable to use anti-Semitism themselves, may no longer regard its use by others as an expression of dangerous views to be vigorously countered, but rather as somewhat peculiar beliefs, which may be tolerated, particularly if they come from representatives of the "oppressed" or uneducated; much the same reaction existed in Czarist Russia among student revolutionaries with respect to peasant anti-Semitism.

Attitudes toward the Jews have been affected by the change in the image of American Jewry and of Israel. American Jewry no longer evokes sympathy as an oppressed "minority" nor does Israel, as a poor, militarily weak state surrounded by powerful enemies. Interested Americans cannot help but realize that the Jews are a prosperous and influential group, very capable of defending their rights. Liberals of all backgrounds, and the Jews among them, see the Jews as belonging to the privileged of the society. A recent article by Michael Novak, a philosopher of Slavic origin, who seeks to speak for the East European ethnics, points out that "Polish feelings do not go easily into the idiom of happy America, the America of the Anglo-Saxons and , yes, in the arts, the Jews." The image of a WASP-Jewish elite, with fewer poorer Jews than WASPS, exists among many, including Jews and WASPS. And this rise in position has lent itself to anti-Semitic reactions, especially among the less educated and economically underprivileged. Surveys of New York residents indicate that the poorest and most recent groups of ethnic settlers, the Puerto Ricans and blacks, are most apt to be anti-Semitic in voicing resentment at Jewish business, and the position of Jews in civil service and politics.

Of more immediate impact on public opinion regarding Israel and the Jews, was the Six-Day War. Up to that point, Israel and the Jews of the world had retained much of their historic identity as victims, as the oppressed. But with its rapid and decisive victory, Israel ceased being an underdog nation. Many, particularly on the left, regard it as a strong and wealthy nation, backed by the power, influence, and financial resources of world Jewry, and by the United States, itself strongly influenced by Jews, while the Arabs are seen as weak, underdeveloped, and poor. And liberal and leftist egalitarian values, as well as Christian religious sentiments, tend to make common cause with the weak against the more powerful.

Jews and Blacks. In recent years, the rise in political consciousness and militancy, first and foremost among blacks and to a lesser extent, among other ethnic groups, also has undercut the position of Jews. Ironically, the split between the Jews and the blacks initially came about because Jews had been so involved in the civil-rights movement. Up to the mid-1960's many interracial civil-rights organizations were led and financed by whites, and the majority of their white members were Jews. The integrationist movement was largely an alliance between affluent Negroes and Jews (who, actually dominated it to a considerable extent). Insofar as the rising black consciousness led to efforts to break loose from involvement with whites, from domination by white liberals of the civil-rights struggle, this meant in fact a break with the Jews. An early explicit statement of this problem was made by a militant black, Harold Cruse, in his book, *The Crisis of the Negro Intellectual.*

However, more important for the relationship between Jews and blacks was the conflict inherent in the historical fact that poor blacks in the North usually moved into former Jewish neighborhoods, such as Harlem, Bedford-Stuyvesant, and Roxbury. This was also true of Watts in Los Angeles, as well as Jewish districts in Washington, Chicago, Philadelphia, and many other cities. This pattern of ethnic succession attests to the fact that Jews reacted to blacks moving into their neighborhoods much less violently than did other white communities. It meant, however, that, though Jews eventually moved out as residents, some of them remained as landlords and storeowners, and many blacks came to see Jews not as neighbors, but as economic oppressors.

The consequences of ecological succession have been reinforced by another factor. During the 1930's, many able Jews found that they could get jobs only in government service, as teachers, social workers, and other professionals. Thirty to forty years later, many of these same Jews, now in their fifties and sixties, are at the top of the civil service hierarchy, as school principals, division heads, and the like. And as blacks follow the Jews into civil service, they often find Jewish directors in units operating in black areas. Thus the demand that blacks be given top jobs in such organizations often has been tantamount to a demand that Jews be removed from positions which they had obtained through merit and seniority.

In the late 1960's black demands at odds with Jewish interests and Arab demands of Israel increasingly put American Jewish communal groups and supporters of Israel in conflict with the pro-black and anti-American imperialism stance of the left and, increasingly, also, of liberal elements in the United States. The blatantly anti-Semitic statements of top leaders of such groups as the Black Panthers, SNCC, and others, did not stop many liberals and leftists from supporting what seemed to be the black cause in such conflicts as the New York City teachers' strike. The attitude toward Israel has been strongly affected by the radicalism which emerged in the struggle against the Vietnam war. For many in that movement, the United States became the epitome of international reaction, the stronghold of all that is evil. And, any government which has the strong backing of the United States appears almost as wicked by association. Conversely, people opposed by the United States must be good, or at least better. The support of the Arab cause by American black nationalists strengthened the stance, since many white liberals and leftists take their cues from the black militants. Among many, who have not been as convinced of the immorality of the Vietnam war, the disaster of American policy in Vietnam, together with other evidence of the failure of a broad internationalist foreign policy, has led to a revival of isolationist sentiment: that the United States should withdraw from most of its foreign commitments; that other governments must stand on their own. This position, too, implies opposition to continued American support for Israel.

Jews and Conservatives. But if Jews have been under fire from groups with whom they have traditionally been allied, they have been gaining increasing support for their positions and "interests" from groups with whom they have not been accustomed to work. Conservative, fundamentalist, or evangelical Protestants are much more disposed to back Israel than are other, less Bible-oriented Protestants. The liberal WASP elite almost invariably backs what seems to be the black side on issues affecting Jewish (or white ethnic) interests, such as the principle of meritocracy in university admissions, job placement, and elsewhere. In contrast, Jews find conservative and Republican leaders strongly defending that principle. As a group which has an historic memory of populist pogroms; which has learned that respect for law and order, for due process, for civility in political conflicts serves to protect unpopular minority groups, Jews are confused at the denigration of constitutional guarantees by blacks, liberals, and leftists, and the seeming support of their protections by conservatives.

These conclusions, based on an analysis of the public positions of the diverse groups, are reinforced by the findings of survey research: that the disillusionment of American opinion with foreign involvements over the past few years has brought an unwillingness to support militarily *any* foreign country; that even support for giving economic and other forms of aid short of armed intervention has declined. There is a general attitude set that favors assistance to *all* potential anti-Communitst allies, or to *none*. Israel is backed by the interventionists and opposed by those more pacifistically inclined. Beyond this, Israel receives somewhat less support from blacks than from other Americans. New York State surveys find Puerto Ricans more prejudiced than other ethnic groups toward blacks and Jews. Blacks are more disposed to expressing negative feelings about Jews than various white groups. Such expressions of bigotry, however, represent minority opinion among both blacks and Puerto Ricans. They reflect the bitterness, deprivation, and lesser education and cosmopolitanism of the most recent arrivals to urban America, and perhaps also an effort to identify with the dominant WASP segment by looking down on those who are religiously or racially different.

This description of current relationships between Jewish

positions and assorted political forces suggests that the political weakness of the Jews, discussed by Raab, is not caused by a lack of potential allies. It rather follows from the fact that most politically conscious Jews still respond to the motto, "No enemies on our left," although it is no longer easy to find support for the matters concerning Jews as Jews from the liberal-to-left segments of the polity. The vast majority of American Jews remain committed to liberal political positions (including advocacy of rights and special privileges for blacks and opposition to the Vietnam war), and large numbers identify with the most liberal leaders in the Democratic party. In or out of organized politics, they find it difficult to be consistent on major political issues while also defending identifiable Jewish interests.

Cleavages in the Jewish Community. Torn between traditional liberal loyalties and Jewish concerns, the American Jewish community is beginning to break up politically. The situation is epitomized by the fact that though Senator Henry Jackson had been the most consistent supporter of Israel's international position among the presidential candidates, he was opposed as a "rightist" by the most liberal wing of the party because of his position on Vietnam, before he withdrew from the primaries. Senator Hubert Humphrey, whose record on Israel is almost comparable to Jackson's, moved from second to first place on the list of disliked potential nominees among the left-wing of the party. Strong isolationist-oriented candidates have run successfully against pro-Vietnam *and* pro-Israel congressmen in some constituencies with large Jewish electorates. Some of the most pro-Israel senators are among the most conservative Republicans in Congress, among them James Buckley, Barry Goldwater, and John Tower. These men, however, have found it difficult to get Jewish groups to give them a platform from which to express their views, or to distribute their statements criticizing American policy, so fearful are even some Zionist groups to be linked to conservative politics. . . .

The tension between Jewish liberalism and Jewish interests has perhaps been most vividly manifested in recent New York municipal politics. As a committed liberal of elite WASP origin, John Lindsay backed the demands of the more militant black separatists for community control of the public schools, even though this placed him in conflict with the efforts to defend meritocratic selection procedures and seniority in the school system's employment policies, positions strongly supported by the Teacher's Union in the interests of its predominantly Jewish membership. The ensuing struggle, which culminated in a city-wide teachers' strike, was widely viewed as one between black elements abetted by the mayor, and white liberals and the union supported by the Jews and white conservatives. John Marchi, Republican-Conservative candidate in the municipal elections that followed, had a record of strong support for Jewish requests as state senator and chairman of the New York City Committee of the State Senate. The Democratic nominee, Mario Procaccino, made strong overtures to the Jewish community by defending meritocracy throughout the school system, including the City University.

The Jewish vote in this election illustrates the breakdown of any one Jewish position when political values and interests are at variance. The mayor received only 42 percent of the Jewish vote, which was, however, more than he secured from any other ethnic group, except for the blacks, Puerto Ricans, and Manhattan WASPs. The Jewish vote split along age, income, educational, and religious-identification lines. Lindsay was backed by the more liberal Jews, who were also younger, better educated, wealthier and less religious than those who voted for his two rivals. When forced to choose, Jews who are more identified with liberalism than with Jewishness in effect remain with the liberal community. The more Jewishly identified, also poorer and more likely to be affected adversely by limitations on meritocracy and by urban tensions, are ready to work with more conservative groupings, including other white ethnics. Comparable cleavages occurred within the Jewish communities of Los Angeles and Philadelphia in recent city elections. Yorty and Rizzo received large Jewish votes from the same strata who backed Lindsay's opponents in New York City. These divisions in the Jewish community were also evident in the 1972 presidential primaries. George McGovern clearly appealed to the younger, better educated, more affluent, "less Jewish" Jews, while Hubert Humphrey was backed by those more involved in, and committed to communal institutions and Jewish interests. A similar basis of division within the Jewish elite is suggested by a survey of Jewish professors, which found that the more successful in scholarly output and prestigious institutional employment are both less committed to Judaism and more liberal-to-left politically.

It would appear that there is no conflict between the two interpretations of what is happening to Jewish influence, and that both are partially valid. As noted, Jews, as individuals, are increasingly found in high and influential places, both in government and elsewhere. But this does not imply that the Jewish community is more powerful, since the issues which concern Jews as a community have divided that community in a way not experienced in many decades. It has, in effect, pressed Jews, both young and old, to opt for universalistic liberal and radical principles at the expense of their Jewishness, or for particularistic Jewish identity at the cost of their involvement in liberal or radical politics. This division is strikingly pronounced on the college campuses, which have experienced both a significant increase in undergraduate involvement in Jewish groups of various kinds, and heavy participation by Jews in assorted left-liberal political campaigns. While these are not rigid alternatives, they tended, in the late 1960's, to divide Jewish students and to separate the more Jewishly identified among them from universalistic liberals and radicals.

It is obviously impossible to predict what will eliminate this division. It could be reduced by a new crisis affecting Jewry at home, abroad, or in Israel, much as the Six-Day War brought about near unanimity. It is possible to see ways in which social policies dedicated to achieve liberal objectives, the reduction of racism and of poverty, i.e., a revived commitment to egalitarianism, could reunite the different strands of Jewry, much as they were joined in the New Deal-Fair Deal coalitions of bygone days. In fact, this alternative is not as utopian as it might first appear, for just as the white ethnics continue to support the basic objectives of that coalition, so do the vast majority of American Jews. Perhaps the one enduring domestic set of issues which divides Jews, and also affects the loyalty of other ethnic groups, is their response to certain black demands. Programs to further black rights which do not appear to undermine economic security and community structure of other ethnic groups could reduce much of the present differences among the ethnics, including Jews and blacks. The foreign policy divisions too, are not eternal. Stemming from the Vietnam war, some of them may decline, once the war is over and some of the bitterness engendered by it has been reduced, hopefully forgotten. . . .

Jewish Interest in Meritocracy

Achievement versus ascription, or affirmative action versus quotas is a broad national issue. Yet, it clearly is a "Jewish" issue as well, for

Jews have benefited considerably from the American emphasis on meritocracy. Jews, particularly, consider the educational system as offering them the best opportunity for advancement, and many of them seek a career in it. The percentage of Jews of college age in institutions of higher learning (80) is twice that in the general population, as against 25 percent for the blacks. As indicated before, close to one-tenth of American college faculty are Jews; the proportion rises considerably for the more distinguished schools. Jews also are found in considerable numbers in various other professions requiring graduate degrees. Significant achievement in some of these professions requires attendance at one of a small number of prestigious institutions which have considerably more qualified applicants than can be admitted. Yet despite the relative economic success of Jews, as a group, it also is true that about one-fifth of them have low incomes; that many hundreds of thousands of them are manual workers. A significant number of Jews are in white-collar civil service jobs, employment which they secured on the basis of high marks in competitive examinations. Surveys conducted during the 1950's suggested that they chose civil service as an alternative to various other white-collar occupations, in part because of the continuation of considerable discrimination against Jews. Relatively few Jews hold high executive positions in major non-Jewish firms.

Any emphasis on quotas in the field of education or civil service is likely to affect Jews adversely even if no slight is intended to them, as a group. Although Jews are identifiable members of an historically disadvantaged group, they are considered to be in the same category as WASPs by the Department of Health, Education and Welfare and other government agencies concerned with minority-group employment. Actions that reduce opportunity for Jews must, therefore, be a matter of Jewish community concern. But the sharpened competition provided by legitimate affirmative action programs, which follow the reasonable guidelines suggested, is a fact of life which Jews will have to sustain, along with other whites. Affirmative action is an obligation and a necessary ingredient of the health of our society, which is of utmost importance also to the Jews. These considerations obviously strengthen the argument . . . that Jews must have a special interest in an expansionist American economy, especially in public-service fields where "collisions" are most likely to occur.

Jews must also be very much concerned that the line between

affirmative action and the increasingly used ascriptive action be firmly drawn in each instance. An ascriptive society is a society without spiritual growth, without equal opportunity, without freedom—one inimical to the values and security of the American Jew.

Conclusion

As America moves into the 1970's, it has yet to find tentative working answers to the age-old problem of how people of diverse cultural, religious, and racial backgrounds can live together. Troubled times have turned many inward; they seek a sense of belonging to an entity that is smaller than the nation. Ethnicity seemingly has become a source of stability for the larger society. Yet it is important to recognize, as we have argued in the body of this report, that a free society must respect the primacy of the individual. Although politics and collective bargaining can work only through the conflicts and alliances of diverse groups, the outcome of such conflicts, particularly as they are resolved by government, must be to guarantee and enhance the equality and rights of the individual. Whether a group, ethnic or other, preserves or extends itself must be the voluntary action of its members, never the action of the larger society. . . .

JEWISH-GENTILE RELATIONS IN LAKEVILLE
by BENJAMIN B. RINGER

INTRODUCTION

As was emphasized in the introduction to the previous article, during many periods of Diaspora Jewish history the expectations which Jews had of Gentiles were modest—Jews sought physical security and hoped that the dominant group would grant them at least a modicum of economic opportunity. It was assumed that contact between the two groups would be largely confined to the formal level, and would revolve around necessary economic activities. The Jewish view was that primary relationships should be confined to other Jews—only with other Jews did one share a common way of life. The Jewish way of life was prized—it was infinitely preferable to the Gentile way of life. And despite the fact that Christianity was all-powerful, the Church was constantly fearful of Judaizing. Together with the State, it sought to keep Jewish-Gentile interaction to minimal levels. The existence of ghettos during some periods in some nations has come to symbolize this pattern of interaction.

One important emphasis in the recent work of historians of European Jewry has been to demonstrate that the barriers between the two groups were not as high in practice as they were in theory. There was more interaction between Gentile and Jew, and consequently more cross-fertilization, than the theory of Jewish-Gentile relations (whether from a Jewish or Christian perspective) would suggest. In any case, with the coming of the modern era, the theory of Jewish-Gentile relations underwent change. Particularly for some Jews there emerged a vision of a society free of anti-Semitism. Brought about by man himself rather than through Divine intervention, such a society would not only involve a revolution in Gentile attitudes toward the Jew but would also require a radical shift in Jewish attitudes toward the Gentile. The old separatism, and the old enforced or voluntary segregation of the Jews, would have to disappear. A new world of meaningful interaction between Jew and Gentile would take its place.

Some Jews saw the new integrated society as one which would involve their assimilation. However, the dominant response of American Jews who were attracted to the ideal of an integrated society has been to pursue this ideal while at the same time seeking to preserve Jewish identity. In their view Jewish-Gentile "integration" (the term used in the following article) constitutes the ideal pattern of Jewish adjustment: it allows for the preservation of Jewish identity but not at the price of isolation from the larger community. The following article by Benjamin B. Ringer analyzes Jewish integrationist sentiment in a specific community called "Lakeville." It also analyzes the response of Gentiles in Lakeville to the Jewish presence.

In our analysis of the friendship pattern of the Lakeville Jew (see pp. 28–36) we emphasized that Lakeville had a reputation as an elite Gentile community. This reputation, in combination with its tradition as a suburb open to Jews, served to attract upper-class German Jews (who are now considered old-timers to the community). They were followed by prosperous and highly educated East European Jews, most of whom are considered newcomers.

Lakeville was particularly attractive to Jews who valued integration. The decision to move into an established and prestigious suburb meant that they were attracted to such a way of life, and had no intention of "taking over" the community. Although some Gentiles interpreted Jewish behavior as being extremely aggressive, Jews did not wish to make Lakeville into an all-Jewish community; on the contrary. Jews who were less committed to integration in fact tended to settle in several of the newer suburbs of Lake City, especially suburbs where the established Gentile community was small in numbers and inferior in social status. While Lakeville became one-third Jewish after more than three decades of the Jewish settlement, other suburbs became heavily Jewish within the space of a few years. In some of these suburbs the percentage of Jews achieved the same high level which had prevailed in the old Jewish neighborhoods of Lake City.

When asked about the kind of neighborhood they prefer only 1 percent of Lakeville Jews respond with a preference for an all-Jewish neighborhood and only 20 percent prefer a Jewish majority in their neighborhood. Ringer finds that the most common response (totaling 50 percent) is for a neighborhood which has equal proportions of Jews and Gentiles. The magnitude of the "parity response" (as well as the presence of a group that prefers a Jewish majority) is quite remarkable if we consider the relatively high degree of integrationist sentiment in the community. Thus, despite integrationist inclinations most Lakeville Jews reject the idea of a neighborhood that would reflect their percentage in the national population or even in the Lake City population. Apparently they wish to avoid being an insignificant minority—if the neighborhood reflected the composition of the national or the local population they would constitute a group well under 10 percent.

How is this choice to be understood? It can be interpreted as a fear of the Gentile world, or as a feeling of insecurity which stems from unfamiliarity with its ways. Ringer interprets the preference for parity as being an aspect of the desire of Lakeville Jews to preserve their Jewish identity. This explanation is undoubtedly correct. However, as the responses which he quotes suggest, the seemingly simple question of neighborhood preference not only evokes the question of the preservation of Jewish identity but involves many other feelings: reactions to minority status, reactions to the tragic history of Jewish-Gentile relations, and dreams of a better tomorrow for oneself and particularly for one's children. The quotations suggest that many Lakeville Jews wish simultaneously to realize the solidarity, cohesion, and freedom from the tyranny of the majority which are the features of a self-segregated neighborhood, with the peace, harmony, and conformity to the ideal of brotherhood which, in theory, are the features of an integrated neighborhood.

Whatever their preference in respect to neighborhood composition, Jews are self-conscious about their intergroup behavior. This attitude is not paralleled among Gentiles: constituting the majority in Lakeville and in the nation-at-large they are less self-conscious toward Jews than Jews are toward Gentiles. Furthermore, Gentiles have no commitment to integration paralleling that of Jews. To the Jew integration is a value: it expresses the desire to be in the mainstream of American life and to overcome the age-old enmity between Gentile and Jew. The end of the matter is that Lakeville Jews are motivated to live with Gentiles but Lakeville Gentiles have no strong motivation to live with Jews. Indeed there have been Gentiles who have left Lakeville and settled in nearby communities. It is generally believed that at least some of these moves represent a reaction to the Jewish influx of the 1950's.

The Jewish influx has made clear to Gentiles that they are being asked to do more than tolerate individual Jews, as had been the case when the first Jews moved into Lakeville. Rather, the Jewish influx is of sufficient magnitude and visibility to make it apparent that Lakeville contains a Jewish subcommunity. Such a subcommunity, no matter how strongly it conforms to dominant life style, is an entity unto itself. As we have seen, it establishes a network of clique associations that constitute an informal community, and it later develops a formal institutional structure. The structure includes educational facilities designed to retain the adherence of the young and thereby to insure group continuity. The subcommunity evokes loyalty on the part of its members; it must be reckoned with in the decision-making process.

Ringer concludes that most Gentiles in Lakeville are unwilling to legitimate the existence of a Jewish subcommunity. They are unwilling to concede that they live in a pluralistic community. There are even some Jewish old-timers who prefer the days before the present Jewish subcommunity came into being. Ringer concludes that until the existence of the Jewish subcommunity is legitimated, there will be an aura of unreality about Jewish-Gentile relations in Lakeville.

M. S.

THE MIXED NEIGHBORHOOD: THE COMMON BASIS OF INTEGRATION

Our findings indicate that integration is a central value among the Jews of Lakeville. Despite the trait of clannishness that is attributed to him, the Jewish newcomer is as likely to be convinced as the older residents that he should not confine his social interests and associations to Jews and to the Jewish community. The emphasis placed by both newcomers and longtimers on becoming part of the larger society is reflected by the fact that two out of three of our respondents say that to be a "good Jew" one must promote civic improvement in the community. Of the remaining Jewish respondents, all but 4 percent consider civic involvement to be a desirable, if not essential, aspect of Jewishness. Along with participation in general community affairs, the good Jew, according to the majority opinion, is also obliged to build good personal relations with Gentiles, particularly those who are his neighbors, and to win their respect.

Positive relations with Gentile neighbors require their presence in the immediate environment. The mixed neighborhood is also part of the ideology of the Lakeville Jew. All but 1 percent of our respondents want a substantial number of Gentiles in their neighborhood: indeed, half of them would prefer to live in a neighborhood that is 50 percent Gentile. This figure is even more striking when we realize that 60 percent of those who choose it live in a neighborhood where Jews are presently a majority, while only 15 percent live in a dominantly Gentile neighborhood.[1] Moreover,

[1]While there are well-defined community areas in Lakeville, the lack of a grid system or other uniform pattern and the presence of hills and other distinct topographical features in certain parts of the town made the use of the term "street" or "neighborhood" in the conventional sense unrealistic. We therefore developed an arbitrary definition of "neighborhood" that could be applied uniformly to all respondents but would still be rooted in the realities of the local situation. After a preliminary investigation, we decided upon the twenty houses nearest to the respondent. Thus, we asked our Jewish respondents: "Let's consider the twenty houses nearest to yours . . . about how many are occupied by Gentile families"? (If the respondent said that fewer than twenty houses were in the area, he was asked for the relevant figures.) Gentile respondents were asked a similar question, except that the word "Jewish" was substituted for "Gentile."

only 6 percent of our Jewish respondents say that they are indifferent to the ethnic composition of their neighborhood.[2]

The desire of our respondents to have a substantial proportion of Gentile neighbors represents a decisive break from the world of their ancestors. While few Jews in past historical eras preferred enforced segregation, they had a definite preference for a Jewish neighborhood. In fact, the Jew whose occupation required him to live among Gentiles felt himself to be in a kind of double Diaspora, and was regarded so by other Jews. Not only was safety and security a factor in choosing a neighborhood, area, or town populated predominantly by Jews, but the choice was preferable on other grounds as well. A Jewish neighborhood afforded the Jew easy access to Jewish facilities. Even more important, it facilitated the preservation of his way of life. Finally, since the Jew assumed that his way of life was not only different but superior, to live among Gentiles did not confer distinction upon him.

On the other hand, in explaining why he wants 50 percent of his neighbors to be Gentile, the typical Lakeville Jew reveals the strong attraction of the world outside the Jewish community. It is an attraction, however, that is more often primarily of the "head" rather than of the "heart." Approximately 60 percent of those who prefer a parity of Jewish and Gentile neighbors are mainly interested in the benefits of social learning, while the rest are mainly motivated by the desire for more direct and personal relations with Gentiles. . . .

Speaking of the educational benefits of such a neighborhood, a young high school teacher, who grew up in a predominantly Jewish neighborhood, explains, "I suppose I don't want to be too insular. It limits you in outlook. You become narrow and prejudiced." A young mother of three children who was active in interfaith activities at Ohio State similarly observes: "I feel this figure [a 50–50 neighborhood] can give our children and ourselves a better viewpoint toward living, a more true viewpoint, a more wholesome view into what life is." "I am a woman of the world, not only a Jew," says an accomplished painter who is troubled by the constraint between Jews and Gentiles in her predominantly Jewish neighborhood. "As a result, I feel I'd like to know Gentile people more, because they have different attitudes and ways of thinking and I would like to incorporate that into my way of life." Along with

[2]The extent of concern among Jews about the composition of their neighborhood is further suggested by the fact that 43 percent of our Gentile respondents claim to be indifferent about the ratio of Jews to Gentiles in their immediate environment.

freeing oneself from a narrow, ethnocentric perspective and developing new social and moral awareness, some respondents also see a positive gain in group relations. A young used-car dealer who has lived in Lakeville for three years sums up the matter in these words:

> I feel that I'd like for my own personal feelings to get rid of the sense of difference. It's important to be in contact with other faiths without losing your identity. Specifically, it's important for Jewish people to dispel the stereotype notions of Jews held by Gentiles and to get a broader outlook.

The general value of Jews and Gentiles learning to live with each other in a mixed neighborhood is frequently affirmed by those respondents who are conscious of the divisiveness that exists in Lakeville. "You learn to get along better with other people," observes a housewife who has also recently moved to Lakeville. "And when they get to know you, their prejudices lessen. I know the woman next door was very worried when she learned Jews were moving in, but now she is very happy." Or again, another newcomer who has had little to do with Jews until now remarks: "I think it's a better community, better for both. People might then get together and get to know each other's beliefs and learn to respect each other." As well as reducing intergroup tensions, such a neighborhood also answers to the democratic dream that continues to have a powerful appeal to Jews as one of the more recent immigrant groups. A parity of Jews and Gentiles is "certainly democratic," says a woman active in liberal politics. Or as another woman who devotes her free time to ORT "because I am Jewish" and to the League of Women Voters "because I am a citizen," puts it, "I feel this percentage is important for democratic integration."

The mixed neighborhood is particularly desirable to respondents who are interested not only in their own integration and acculturation but in that of their children. Indeed, a number of respondents, such as a middle-aged engineer, say that "it's primarily because of the children that I'd want this percentage." As this respondent goes on to remark, "I'd like them to have contact with the problems they'll face in later life, but as an adult I'd prefer an all-Jewish neighborhood." Whether as an education in the realities of ethnic differences or in the possibilities of democratic pluralism, the open and balanced community is felt to be the best type of milieu for the Jewish child. One respondent speaks of an "interchange of habits, values, ideas"; another of mutual "understanding and respect"; another of a "more rational idea of what the world is like"; another of "preparation for the bumps they'll get." "Even a high-class ghetto I wouldn't like," says a salesman who grew up in a non-Jewish neighborhood and who wants his children "to develop an understanding of other people and other religions." In many such responses, it is clear that one of the chief advantages which the Jewish parent is anxious to bestow on his child is the experience of living among Gentiles and relating freely to them. The wife of a manufacturer speaks on this point in the following manner:

> I like this figure [50 percent] for the simple reason that children should be raised in a neighborhood where there are Jews and Gentiles. When they get out into the business world, they will find that there are many Gentiles, and I'm afraid they won't all be kind. If my children are going to be called a "Dirty Jew," I would like it to be when they are young and it can be explained. I know that when I was of high school age, I was sent away to a private school where another girl and myself were the only Jews in a class of about sixty. We really were pushed around; I remember the pins being knocked out from under me; I almost think it left me with a complex about Gentiles. Sometimes I think I must be prejudiced against Gentiles.

It is worth noting that the preference for parity of numbers and cultures frequently expresses the respondent's wish to protect the security and integrity of his children as Jews as well as to introduce them to the mixed society in which they will live. In other words, a 50–50 neighborhood provides for pluralism while guarding against assimilation. A self-made man who regards himself as an atheist still speaks for many of our respondents when he says, "I think this percentage provides a healthy atmosphere. It meets the purpose we had in mind when we moved here. We feel that the child should know his origins but should also know differences as well." Or as a lawyer whose teenage son dates Gentile as well as Jewish girls puts it: "It's just that I feel that I want my son to know both; not, in other words, to be afraid to understand them, and yet not to forget his own people." Or again, another lawyer who grew up in Russia provides a more extended statement of the same attitude:

> My child should be exposed to the experience of meeting with Gentiles for we are a minority in this country and one could get an erroneous

idea of the role of a minority group if one didn't live with Gentiles. In school, if the pupils were all Jewish, it wouldn't be best for my child. Yet, if she were the only Jewish child with all Gentiles, it would be equally bad; she might not have a sense of belonging or might become assimilated. I don't want to have that. I want her to have a feeling of Jewishness too.

It is thus apparent that the 50 percent figure has assumed a deep symbolic significance for a majority of Lakeville Jews. It expresses their view of a model community, one which guarantees the best opportunities for social learning while preserving the opportunities for Jewish identity. In other words, it envisions a solid middle ground of pluralism that lies between ethnocentrism on the one hand, and assimilation on the other.

The other 44 percent of Lakeville's Jews who express a preference do not find this magical potency in parity of numbers and instead favor a majority—minority arrangement in their neighborhoods. They split almost evenly, however, over which group should be in the majority. Approximately one out of four Jews in Lakeville wishes Gentiles to be the preponderant group. Accordingly, slightly less than half of these respondents (46 percent) prefer to have more Gentiles than are presently in their respective neighborhoods, 43 percent want the same proportion that currently exists, and only 11 percent want fewer Gentile neighbors.

Though their notions of a favorable imbalance range from 60 to 90 percent, the respondents who prefer a majority of Gentiles usually offer much the same explanations. They are more committed to the experience of adaptation than are those who prefer parity, for they wish their neighborhoods to reflect the fact that Jews are a minority in Lakeville and in the society at large. A native of Lakeville who elects a 60–40 split remarks: "As a minority group [Jews] should realize that there are certain inherent disadvantages when a minority group nationally becomes a majority group locally. Accordingly, I'd like to see, other features being equal, the Jews remain a minority group in Lakeville." A manufacturer dislikes the "parochialism" of his Jewish neighborhood and prefers a neighborhood that is 90 percent Gentile: "I'd like the proportion to resemble a cross section of the country in order to acquaint my children with all kinds of people." "I feel that [70 percent] is more representative of the distribution of the population," says a civil engineer who is active in his temple but is disappointed by the fact that most of his neighbors are Jewish. "It's better for the children. You want kids to be used to the majority to face up to the world as it is. I don't like the tendency for Jews to congregate in certain localities. It is no good for the Jewish community."

What tends to distinguish this group from the respondents who want a neighborhood closer to parity is a more marked interest in developing personal relationships with Gentiles. Approximately 60 percent say that they are primarily interested in the social relations rather than the social education of living among Gentiles. (This priority is reversed by nearly the same percentage among those who prefer a balanced neighborhood.) "I like it as it is—75 percent non-Jewish," says the young wife of a realtor. "I feel that I'd like to be friendly with non-Jews and also that I'd like my children to know both. We'd get a little too clannish and cliquish if it were more Jewish."

Most respondents in this group, however, do not wish the percentage of Jews in their midst to drop to the point where they would comprise a scanty and isolated minority. Their model neighborhood in the matter of religious-ethnic distribution is much closer to the Lakeville of today than to the prewar community in which Jewish residents made up a small marginal group. According to several of our respondents—who are satisfied with being in a minority of 25 or 30 percent—a smaller percentage would create a misleading image of modern society, or separate the two groups and weaken the ground for friendly relations, or foster an undue amount of assimilation. An executive who grew up mainly among Gentiles expresses this attitude as follows:

> I don't want Jews to be the majority nor only 5 percent of the population either. I want enough to give my children some security so that they can understand, for example, that those who celebrate Hanukkah are different from those who celebrate Christmas and that the latter are the majority. I want, in other words, enough Jews for collective security but not enough for a majority.

Indeed, there is often a certain ambiguity in the responses of this group which results from a desire to maintain a security in numbers and at the same time avoid an unrepresentative cluster of Jewish residents that smacks of a "ghetto." This tension is expressed by a housewife who wants her neighborhood to be 40 percent Jewish. "I want to create a proportion akin to that in the world. On the other hand, I want enough Jews to create an atmosphere where I have my own identity. We should also have Catholic friends too."

The desire for the reassurance of numbers is much more pronounced among the Lakeville Jews—20 percent of the total—who prefer a Jewish majority in their neighborhood. So, too, is their preference for social relations with other Jews. As an accountant who comes from an immigrant Jewish background remarks: "For security, comfort, and ease I'd want mostly Jews. A stranger who is Jewish can't be the same kind of threat that a stranger who is non-Jewish can be." An attorney who grew up among Gentiles agrees: "It's more comfortable and more pleasant with more Jews around."

However, only 26 percent of this group want fewer Gentiles than actually reside in their neighborhood. And an even smaller proportion—1 percent of the total Jewish respondents—would be content with an all-Jewish neighborhood. The rest are convinced that they want a significant minority of Gentiles. Three out of five are satisfied with the *status quo* in their neighborhoods, and another 14 percent desire more Gentiles than are presently living there.

By far the prevailing reason for this choice is the benefit of social learning that will accrue to their children. As with the other Jewish respondents, those who prefer a majority of their coreligionists as neighbors are mindful of the need to educate their children in the realities of a mixed society. For example, a wealthy young housewife who is active in the Girl Scouts observes: "It's good for children to come into contact with non-Jews and to see the differences and to know the differences and not to think too much of them. They'll have to face such matters all their lives because they'll never live in a world of all Jews." It is evident, then, that the general acceptance of integration leads our respondents to believe that they ought to live in some sort of mixed environment. The issue is the relative proportions of such a mixture. . . .

AN OVERVIEW OF JEWISH–GENTILE RELATIONS IN LAKEVILLE

We have attempted to study the relations between Jews and Gentiles in an established, traditionally Protestant community where Jews now form a significant part of the social environment. . . . We have tried to keep two basic questions directly in view: *First,* what are the main sources of conflict and comity between Jews and Gentiles in Lakeville? *Second,* what are the chief forces and situations in the lives of individual Jews and Gentiles that bring them together, and how frequent and significant are these contacts?

Probably the single most important factor in Jewish-Gentile relations in Lakeville has been the recent influx of Jewish residents. This has shifted as well as expanded the population base, affected the traditional character of the community, and introduced immediate problems of municipal growth. Consequently it has placed the Jewish newcomer in a particularly vulnerable position. He is the main scapegoat of the residents who disapprove of the cultural and political changes in Lakeville as well as of those who simply disapprove of Jews. The common image of the newcomers has been that of an aggressive and ethnocentric band of Jews who have only recently achieved the status which they seek to display and to confirm by living in Lakeville. Thus they are accused of trying to wield their newly obtained wealth to acquire social and even political power in the community. At the same time they are accused of clannishness, of lacking dignity and taste, of not knowing how to use their money, and of exaggerating its importance in their own lives and in their relations with others.

This image does not accurately represent the kind of Jew who has moved into Lakeville in recent years, since he is likely to be better educated and acculturated and to possess much more modest circumstances and status drives than the image implies; but it does serve important functions for different segments of the Gentile community. Those who appear to feel most threatened by the influx are longtime residents of moderate and low income. They worry that the traditions of Lakeville as a Christian community will be undermined, that the Jews will become politically potent in contrast to their own sense of powerlessness, and that the free-spending newcomers will continue to raise taxes, force up standards of living, and create new norms of status and conduct. Such complaints by this group of Gentiles take on a particular urgency because of their beliefs that their children are being exposed to the precocious *nouveau riche* behavior of the newcomers' children and will seek to emulate it. Thus the influence of the Jews will undermine the habits of modesty, frugality, and sobriety that they have sought to inculcate in their children. The main sphere of this danger is the local high school, since teenagers are felt to be the most susceptible to the deviant manners and values of their peers. The wealthier old-guard Lakeville residents who have not followed many of their peers in moving out of the community are also disturbed by the waning of the genteel traditions of Lakeville which they attribute to the influence of new "Jewish" money and manners.

If the only Jews in Lakeville were newcomers and if all the newcomers were Jews, it seems likely that these concerns would increase the tensions between Jew and Gentile and result in a more openly expressed antagonism than we have observed. What modifies this situation is that some newcomers are Gentiles, who tend to look more favorably on the changes in the community and more favorably on the Jews as enlightened, energetic, and civic-minded agents of progress in Lakeville.

The potential sharpness of the group conflict has also been modified by the presence of the longtime Jewish residents, who are viewed as an acceptable, even exemplary, group by their Gentile counterparts. Their image is that of a solidly established social and economic elite which has developed a style of life that is modest, tasteful, and proper. By virtue of his roots in the community and his adaptation to its prevailing mores and manners, the longtime Jewish resident is perceived to be a model of tact and deference who is willing to play a responsible role in the community without seeking to undermine its Christian traditions.

Thus there are three fairly distinct images of the Lakeville Jew, two of which are definitely positive in content. This diversity, however, is of small comfort to the Jewish newcomer, who is aware of the distaste, enmity, and invidious comparisons that he has evoked. He feels that he is being attacked from all sides, that his contribution to the community is not being given its due weight, and that his sensibilities are not being respected. Despite the justness of this reaction, which much of our data confirms, it is also apparent that the Jewish newcomer benefits from the fact that he has moved into a community where a small group of Jews was firmly established prior to his arrival. Thus he need not be a pioneer in making a place for himself in Lakeville. There are pathways of adjustment and acculturation that he can follow in adapting his behavior and values to the norms of the community and in aligning his identity as a Jew with his new situation as a mobile, middle-class suburbanite. That many of the Jewish newcomers are strongly motivated to follow these paths toward greater acceptance is suggested by their own life style as well as by their strong desire to dissociate themselves from behavior patterns which could be construed as aggressive, indecorous, clannish, or defensive.

Style of Life: Similarities and Differences

One of the major pathways of acculturation that Lakeville Jews—both newcomers and old-timers—have taken is clearly revealed in their leisure interests and activities. They have been particularly attracted to a model of leisure that reflects Lakeville's history as a summer colony of an elite Gentile group. Their favorite sport is golf; they are widely committed to the performing arts and are among the most avid supporters of Lakeville's own cultural traditions; and one of their favorite pastimes is playing bridge. So widely diffused are these preferences and interests among Jews that even those of moderate and low income, particularly among the women, have adopted them. Only the activities of men in the low-income bracket depart significantly from this model.

Among the Gentiles, however, this elite model tends to be confined to those of high income. And even in this stratum, the men show a marked attraction to another traditional model of leisure: that which reflects Lakeville's past as a home-centered small town in which a person, usually of relatively modest means, spends his leisure time in tinkering around the house and garden or in hunting and fishing.

Just as Jews and Gentiles differ in their attraction to the leisure traditions of Lakeville, so do they differ in the range of activities in which they become involved: Gentiles tend to specialize in their activities and Jews tend to generalize them. In other words, the average Gentile is intensively involved in a relatively few hobbies, games, or groups, while the average Jew extends his participation over a greater variety of them. For example, Jews typically participate in more sports and play more of the different games of cards than do Gentiles. This is due, in part, to the desire of the Jews to participate in a sport or card game (such as golf or bridge) that is characteristic of the community norms as well as in one more or less indigenous to their own background (such as handball and gin rummy). We have found a similar pattern in their organizational affiliations. The average Jew has many more affiliations than the average Gentile, though he does not devote appreciably more time to working in them. Thus, while youth-serving and health-welfare organizations are popular among both Jewish and Gentile women, only the former are likely to belong to both concurrently; the Gentile woman tends to move from one to the other in a sequence that follows her family cycle. Similarly, Jewish men are much more likely to belong to both occupational and fraternal groups than are Gentile men.

Finally, in keeping with these generalized and specialized patterns, we have observed that Jews are more likely than Gentiles to engage in activities regardless of whether they are personally interested in them. This is true of their participation in sports or in cultural activities such as concert-going. Similarly, Jews are more likely than Gentiles to belong to organizations that they do not participate in.

Why these seemingly consistent ethnic differences in the use of leisure recur is open to speculation. In part, they may be less a function of uniquely Jewish or Gentile group differences as such than of the composition of the two subcommunities. As we have already noted, the Jews of Lakeville are much more homogeneous than the Gentiles in age, income, and education. Given these similarities, we would expect greater consensus among Jews in their tastes and interests. In addition, many of them are relatively new to the community and are anxious to belong to it, which provides a further incentive for them to conform to the elite leisure mode even though they may not have a personal interest in its activities. Inversely, the Gentiles who are established at one strata or another in the community experience less pressure to adapt to the elite model and are therefore more likely to do what they want to with their leisure time rather than what they perceive will gain them acceptance. All of which suggests that the distinctive orientation of the Jews, as well as their socio-economic composition, contributes to their patterns of leisure use. As we have further observed, Lakeville Jews in their twofold desire for integration on the one hand, and for maintaining group ties and interests on the other, are likely to involve themselves in both sectarian and nonsectarian activities and associations. Thus for this reason also they tend to distribute their affiliations over a broader range than Gentiles do. Though they may be unable to participate fully in more than a few of these groups, their membership in the others allows them to be identified with the two communities.

In sum, the extensiveness of the Jews' activities suggests that they are attracted more by certain extrinsic functions which these activities serve than by the activities themselves. Thus playing golf and bridge, for example, are likely to be viewed as a good way of getting together with people and of establishing one's claim to a desirable status in the community.

Climate of Opinion and Mutual Acceptance

Despite the many underlying differences and difficulties that mark Jewish—Gentile relations in Lakeville, overt group conflict is quite rare, and the general social atmosphere is usually characterized by tranquillity and tolerance. In part this is due to the passing of sufficient time for the initial impact of the population change to have spent itself, and for the municipal measures adopted to accommodate it to take effect. Also, in the intervening years the more bitterly hostile residents, particularly among the elite, have moved out of the community. At the same time, their need and desire to adapt to the prevailing social norms of the community and to participate in its daily life have made the Jewish newcomers more sophisticated in Lakeville terms; their presence has become less visible and objectionable. Some five years after the main influx, Jews and Gentiles in Lakeville today share many of the same interests in their homes, neighborhoods, schools, leisure activities, and so forth. Such common interests make the remaining differences between them less manifest and contribute to the tranquil surface of Lakeville society.

This process of "settling in" has also been abetted by the prevailing value systems of the Jewish and Gentile communities. Among Jews the basis of these values is clearly their strong desire for integration. Accordingly, few of them are willing to restrict their commitments and associations to their coreligionists and to the Jewish community. They are motivated to gear their behavior to Gentile standards, and though some of the newcomers may be willing to provoke group conflict in a matter such as Christmas celebrations in the schools, the general tendency is to avoid giving offense in the interests of being accepted.

Lakeville's Gentiles, of course, are in a different social position. Because of their dominance in the community and in the general society, they have little motivation to win the favor of the Jews. Consequently, their behavior is determined by how willing they are to accept Jews. In Lakeville, four out of five Gentiles say they are willing to live among Jews, though the degree and grounds of their tolerance vary in several respects. Some 23 percent would prefer to have only a minority of Jews: the figure they give averages just over 20 percent of the neighborhood population. A smaller group would allow at least as many Jews as Gentiles. The rest, the substantial minority of 43 percent, say they "don't care" how many Jews live in their neighborhood. By using our findings on the extent to which Jews, as a group, are perceived to be different from Gentiles, on the positive or negative evaluation of these differences, and on the number of Jews who are believed to exhibit these traits, we were able to classify the variety of Gentile attitudes into four general categories: the "exclusionist," the "exemptionist," the "pluralist," and the "egalitarian."

The Contexts and Limits of Friendliness

Much of the interfaith tolerance in Lakeville is of the passive "live and let live" variety. It is unlikely, then, that Jewish-Gentile relations would develop much personal content without the community institutions and the individual pursuits that bring members of the two faiths together in some meaningful way. In the course of their daily lives Jews and Gentiles frequently find themselves in some sort of functional relationship where it is to their mutual advantage to work together amicably. Such functional relationships do more than cause Jew and Gentile to meet; they also provide a continuing context for them to get to know each other, to become friendly, and possibly to develop the strong ties of friendship. What is more, the separation of these functional relations from the more private spheres of life allows Jew and Gentile to participate in them without the usual inhibitions of class and ethnic factors.

Thus the necessity of making a living involves most Lakeville men in some economic or work relationship with people of the other faith. Such relationships often entail some social entertainment to promote business transactions or to improve cooperation within a work group or firm. Since these quasi-social arrangements have become widespread in the business and professional world, there is abundant opportunity for Jewish and Gentile men to get together in social situations.

In such situations each party understands that the motive of self-interest has brought them together, and therefore each takes in stride whatever socializing that ensues as part of the rules and requirements of the economic game. But in the course of their transactions they may get to know a bit more about each other and to like each other as individuals, so that the original relationship is transformed into personal friendship.

Indeed, the business and professional world is one of the most fertile grounds for our Jewish and Gentile respondents to cultivate significant interfaith relationships. Another is the organizations within Lakeville. Those organizations that provide most opportunities for Jews and Gentiles to come into friendly and meaningful contact are the youth-serving, neighborhood-community, and vocational groups—in other words, those designed to serve an "instrumental" rather than an "expressive" function.

The friendliness of the instrumental organizations derives from the personal relevance of the community of interests and needs that Jew and Gentile share. These extend beyond the organization itself and reflect the fact that many of Lakeville's Jews and Gentiles perform similar social roles and face similar problems in childrearing, home-ownership, and their professional lives. In addition, the instrumental groups designed to serve these common interests and needs do not impinge upon the more private spheres of life. Thus relationships between Jew and Gentile in these associations do not compete directly with existing networks of friendship and do not involve status factors, both of which often inhibit Jews and Gentiles from relating to each other.

For our purposes, one of the significant features of these instrumental associations is that they provide a variety of opportunities for members to work together in small groups where they are joined by a specific common purpose and where the potential for personal contact and cooperative spirit is high. Thus committee work and the like provide settings where both parties can approach and work with each other as individuals and not merely as members of a group.

Once a basis of mutual acceptance and friendliness is derived from such contacts, it is unlikely that the relationship will be confined to these settings and functions. Instead it will usually take on more personal overtones and give rise to activities such as entertaining at home, sharing outside social engagements, and following other leisure activities that enable the relationship to develop a character of its own and to be sustained by the individuals themselves.

The third major ground of Jewish-Gentile contact in Lakeville is the neighborhood, and we have found that the neighborhood which best serves this purpose is the one where Gentiles remain in the majority. This finding is explained partly by the influence of certain demographic factors and group affiliations that affect the relative frequency and suitability of interfaith contacts. In a Gentile neighborhood, for example, the tendency of Jews to belong to the PTA makes more of them available in this organization than in the neighborhood itself and thereby enhances the effectiveness of the organization in bringing Jews and Gentiles together. In a Jewish neighborhood the PTA is less effective in this respect, because the selective recruitment to the organization makes it even more Jewish than the neighborhood is and reduces the possibility of Gentile participation. In addition, the age differences between Jews and Gentiles, which are relatively uniform in the various neighborhoods, create the probability that more of the younger Jews will find Gentile peers in a Gentile neighborhood rather than a Jewish one. Finally, we have observed that the neighborhood in which the Gentile occupies the majority status and the Jew the minority one more naturally fits the psychological orientation of each group toward the other, and thereby facilitates social intercourse.

So pervasive are the opportunities in Lakeville for Jews and Gentiles to come into contact with each other and to cultivate practical, cooperative relationships that the great majority of them report they have developed an identifiable friendship with at least one person of the other faith. In measuring the character and quality of this relationship, we found that it rarely matches in warmth, intimacy, interest, spontaneity, and trust the friendliest relationship that respondents have developed with someone of their own faith. Still, the best interfaith relationships are not casual or chance acquaintanceships, but have considerable personal content and significance. The level of intimacy they achieve tends to resemble that of the relations Gentiles and Jews develop with the friendliest neighbor of their own faith. However, few respondents who have both such relationships establish the same level of personal commitment in both; that is, they are more confiding and engaged with their friend than their neighbor, or vice versa. This finding indicates that the two relationships may be functional substitutes for each other.

To attain or to exceed the maximal standard set by neighborly intrafaith relations, friendships between Jews and Gentiles must go beyond the neighborhood context where they may have originated and must be pursued in and for themselves. The same requirement seems to be true of friendships that may have originated in voluntary associations within the community. Only those that have emerged from the context of work appear to be capable of transcending the neighborly standard whether they are pursued at work or elsewhere. Should a friendship between a Jew and a Gentile exceed the level of the neighborly, it often continues to grow until it is cherished by our respondents as one of the most meaningful relationships they possess, with Jew or Gentile alike.

The Aura of Unreality

In the final analysis, though, despite the significant contacts between Jews and Gentiles and the benign atmosphere that prevails in Lakeville, an air of uncertainty and fantasy still characterizes their relations. In part, this results from the fact that their relationships rarely go beyond acquaintanceship to acquire the warmth and mutual trust of close friendships. As a result, few Jews and Gentiles appear to be in a position to gauge the feelings of the other with any accuracy, and thus they consult their own underlying anxiety or complacency, as the case may be.

Contributing even more significantly to this air of unreality is the very basis on which the Jew is accepted. He is judged as an individual and is accepted *if* he conforms to the standards set by a Gentile-dominated tradition. The orientation is essentially egalitarian in nature, and the goal is the assimilation of the Jew into the traditional mold of the community. The overall outlook is optimistic, for it is expected that in time even the Jewish newcomer will rid himself of his abrasive behavior and become fully acceptable.

But all Jews do not want to be cast into this mold; what this optimistic theory of acculturation and adaptation fails to confront is the Jewishness of the Jew. Most Gentiles in Lakeville are not concerned with the deeper meaning of Jewishness; they appear to treat it as just another barrier to the incorporation of the Jew into the community. In this they are joined by some Jews, particularly among the oldtimers. However, to the majority of Jews in Lakeville the problem of being a Jew is not confined to that of integration into the community or the development of amicable relations between Jew and Gentile. While deeply favoring intergroup amity, they are also involved in a different and perhaps even more perplexing enterprise: that of working out their identity as Jews and developing a viable pattern of Jewish living. This desire for a religio-ethnic subcommunity which is simultaneously "Jewish" as well as compatible with and integrated into the larger structure of Lakeville and American society is as much a fact of life in present-day Lakeville as is its Gentile past.

Despite the recent changes in Lakeville, most Gentiles and some Jews continue to press for uniformity with and conformity to an older version of the community. In effect, they refuse to legitimate the genuine diversity that already seems to characterize Lakeville. But until they do, or at least come to terms with it more effectively than they have, there will remain an air of fantasy and an undercurrent of unresolved tension between Jew and Gentile in the community.

SUGGESTIONS FOR FURTHER READING

The following information will be helpful in utilizing this bibliography:

1. A current annotated bibliography on the subject matter of this volume is not available. We are in no position to remedy this defect; because of limitations of space the bibliography which follows is selective rather than exhaustive. However, while this bibliography is selective, the items in it are of differing value and are drawn from a variety of sources; in areas where the level of scholarship is not high, for example, items have been included which would otherwise have remained unlisted.

2. As a corollary to the above, we have included some items by individuals active in American Jewish life as leaders or organizational executives, rather than primarily as scholars. We believe the student can often profit as much from analyzing such documents as from studying the results of scholarly investigations.

3. Books and articles reproduced or excerpted in this volume are not listed in the bibliography. In some cases the user will want to consult the original source, which may contain more information on the topic than we utilize, or may contain material on topics other than the one we focus upon.

4. A number of items in the bibliography—particularly those cited in the sections entitled "Background Reading" and "General Treatments"—are readers or collections of articles. Such volumes generally deal with a wide variety of topics. In some cases, in addition to citing the book itself, we cite individual items from it as well; but we have attempted to restrict this practice as much as possible. The user is therefore advised to check individual tables of contents for articles on the particular topic of his interest.

5. In most cases we cite only a single edition of a book, generally the latest hardcover edition. The availability of a paperback edition can be readily ascertained by referring to *Paperbound Books in Print* published by the R.R. Bowker Company.

6. Even a selective bibliography needs to be supplemented by newly published items. Two good sources exist for this purpose, both issued at regular intervals by the Blaustein Library of the American Jewish Committee, 165 East 56 Street, New York, New York 10022: "Articles of Interest in Current Periodicals" and "Recent Additions to the Library." The Committee's bulletins are particularly exhaustive in the field of intergroup relations, but they also include most of the topics dealt with in our bibliography.

ENCYCLOPEDIAS, YEARBOOKS, AND BIBLIOGRAPHIES

American Jewish Year Book, prepared by the staff of the American Jewish Committee and published annually by The American Jewish Committee and The Jewish Publication Society of America. An index to Volumes 1–50 of the *American Jewish Year Book* was prepared by Elfrida C. Solis-Cohen and published by Ktav Publishing House, Inc. (New York: 1967). (Hereafter the *American Jewish Year Book* is abbreviated: *AJYB.*)

Elazar, Daniel J., "The Pursuit of Community: Selections from the Literature of Jewish Public Affairs, 1965–1966," *AJYB 1967* (Vol. 68), pp. 178–229.

———, "The Rediscovered Polity: Selections from the Literature of Jewish Public Affairs, 1967–1968," *AJYB 1969* (Vol. 70), pp. 172–237.

———, "Selections from the Literature of Jewish Public Affairs, 1969–1971," *AJYB 1972* (Vol. 73), pp. 301–383.

Encyclopedia Judaica (Jerusalem: Keter Publishing House Ltd., 1972), 16 vols.

Gartner, Lloyd, "The Contemporary Jewish Community" in *The Study of Judaism: Bibliographical Essays* (New York: Ktav Publishing House, Inc., for The Anti-Defamation League of B'nai B'rith, 1972), pp. 185–206.

Linzer, Norman, ed., *Jewish Communal Services in the United States: 1960–1970, A Selected Bibliography* (New York: Federation of Jewish Philanthropies, 1972).

Universal Jewish Encyclopedia (New York: Universal Jewish Encyclopedia, Inc., 1939), 10 vols.

BACKGROUND READING

Medieval and Modern Jewish History and Culture

Baron, Salo W., *The Jewish Community: Its History and Structure to the American Revolution* (Philadelphia: The Jewish Publication Society of America, 1942), 3 vols.

———, "The Modern Age" in Leo W. Schwarz, ed., *Great Ages and Ideas of the Jewish People* (New York: Random House, 1956), pp. 315–484.

Dawidowicz, Lucy, *The Golden Tradition* (New York: Holt, Rinehart, and Winston, 1967).

Elbogen, Ismar, *A Century of Jewish Life* (Philadelphia: The Jewish Publication Society of America, 1944).

Katz, Jacob, *Exclusiveness and Tolerance: Jewish-Gentile Relations in Medieval and Modern Times* (New York: Oxford University Press, 1961).

———, *Out of the Ghetto: The Social Background of Jewish Emancipation, 1770–1870* (Cambridge, Mass.: Harvard University Press, 1973).

———, *Tradition and Crisis: Jewish Society at the End of the Middle Ages* (Glencoe: The Free Press, 1961).

Sachar, Howard M., *The Course of Modern Jewish History* (Cleveland: World Publishing Co., 1958).

Wischnitzer, Mark, *To Dwell in Safety: The Story of Jewish Migration Since 1800* (Philadelphia: The Jewish Publication Society of America, 1949).

Zborowski, Mark and Herzog, Elizabeth, *Life Is With People* (New York: International Universities Press, 1952).

American Society and American Jewish History

Baron, Salo W. and Blau, Joseph L., eds., *The Jews of the United States, 1790–1840: A Documentary History* (New York and Philadelphia: Columbia University Press and The Jewish Publication Society of America, 1963).

Bremner, Robert H., *American Philanthropy* (Chicago: University of Chicago Press, 1960).

Critical Studies in American Jewish History: Selected Articles from American Jewish Archives (Cincinnati and New York: American Jewish Archives and Ktav Publishing House, Inc., 1971), 3 vols.

Elazar, Daniel J. and Goldstein, Stephen R., "The Legal Status of the American Jewish Community," *AJYB 1972* (Vol. 73), pp. 3–94.

Glanz, Rudolf, *Studies in Judaica Americana* (New York: Ktav Publishing House, Inc., 1970).

Karp, Abraham J., ed., *The Jewish Experience in America: Selected Studies from Publications of The American Jewish Historical Society* (Waltham and New York: American Jewish Historical Society and Ktav Publishing House, Inc., 1969), 5 vols.

Kramer, Judith R., *The American Minority Community* (New York: Crowell, 1970).

Learsi, Rufus, *The Jews in America: A History*, with epilogue by Abraham J. Karp (New York: Ktav Publishing House, Inc., 1972).

Teller, Judd L., *Strangers and Natives* (New York: Delacorte Press, 1968).

Williams, Robin M., Jr., *American Society: A Sociological Interpretation* (third edition, New York: Knopf, 1970).

GENERAL TREATMENTS

Glazer, Nathan and Moynihan, Daniel P., *Beyond the Melting Pot: The Negroes, Puerto Ricans, Jews, Italians, and Irish of New York City* (second edition, Cambridge, Mass.: MIT Press, 1970).

Janowsky, Oscar I., ed., *The American Jew: A Reappraisal* (Philadelphia: The Jewish Publication Society of America, 1964).

Kramer, Judith R. and Leventman, Seymour, *Children of the Gilded Ghetto: Conflict Resolutions of Three Generations of American Jews* (New Haven: Yale University Press, 1961).

Liebman, Charles S., *The Ambivalent American Jew* (Philadelphia: The Jewish Publication Society of America, 1973).

Patai, Raphael, *Tents of Jacob: The Diaspora—Yesterday and Today* (Englewood Cliffs, N.J.: Prentice-Hall, Inc., 1971).

Rose, Peter I., ed., *The Ghetto and Beyond* (New York: Random House, 1969).

Sidorsky, David, ed., *The Future of the Jewish Community in America* (New York: Basic Books, 1973).

Sklare, Marshall, *America's Jews* (New York: Random House, 1971).

———, ed., *The Jews: Social Patterns of an American Group* (New York: Free Press, 1958).

——— and Greenblum, Joseph, *Jewish Identity on the Suburban Frontier: A Study of Group Survival in the Open Society* (New York: Basic Books, 1967).

COMMUNITY SURVEYS AND DEMOGRAPHIC STUDIES

Associated Jewish Charities of Baltimore, *The Jewish Community of Greater Baltimore: A Population Study* (Baltimore: Associated Jewish Charities and Welfare Fund, 1968).

Axelrod, Morris, Fowler, Floyd J., and Gurin, Arnold, *A Community Survey for Long Range Planning: A Study of the Jewish Population of Greater Boston* (Boston: Combined Jewish Philanthropies of Greater Boston, 1967).

Bigman, Stanley K., *The Jewish Population of Greater Washington in 1956* (Washington, D.C.: The Jewish Community Council of Greater Washington, 1957).

Elinson, Jack, Haberman, Paul W., and Gell, Cyrille, *Ethnic and Educational Data on Adults in New York City, 1963–1964* (New York: School of Public Health and Administrative Medicine, Columbia University, 1967).

Goldstein, Sidney, *The Greater Providence Jewish Community: A Population Survey* (Providence, R.I.: General Jewish Committee, 1964).

———, *A Population Survey of the Greater Springfield Jewish Community* (Springfield, Mass.: Jewish Community Council, 1968).

The Jewish Community of Pittsburgh: A Population Survey (Pittsburgh: United Federation of Pittsburgh, 1963).

The Jewish Population of Rochester, New York (Monroe County) 1961 (Rochester: Jewish Community Council, 1961).

Massarik, Fred, *The Jewish Population of Los Angeles* (Los Angeles: Jewish Federation-Council of Greater Los Angeles, 1959).

———, and Chenkin, Alvin, "United States National Jewish Population Study," *AJYB* 1973 (Vol. 74), pp. 264–306.

Mayer, Albert J., *Columbus Jewish Population Study: 1969* (Columbus, O.: Jewish Welfare Federation, 1970).

———, *The Detroit Jewish Community: Geographic Mobility, 1963–1965; and Fertility—A Projection of Future Births* (Detroit: Jewish Welfare Federation, 1966).

———, *Estimate of the Numbers and Age Distribution of the Detroit Metropolitan Area: 1956* (Detroit: Jewish Welfare Federation, 1959).

———, *Flint Jewish Population Study, 1967* (Flint, Mich.: Jewish Community Council, 1969).

———, *Income Characteristics of the Jewish Population in the Detroit Metropolitan Area: 1956* (Detroit: Jewish Welfare Federation, 1960).

———, *Jewish Population Study 1963: Number of Persons, Age and Residential Distribution* (Detroit: Jewish Welfare Federation, 1964).

———, *Milwaukee Jewish Population Study, 1964–1965* (Milwaukee: Jewish Welfare Fund, 1966).

———, *Movement of the Jewish Population in the Detroit Metropolitan Area: 1949–1959* (Detroit: Jewish Welfare Federation, 1964).

———, *Social and Economic Characteristics of the Detroit Jewish Community: 1963* (Detroit: Jewish Welfare Federation, 1964).

Westoff, Charles F., *A Population Survey* (Cherry Hill, N.J.: Jewish Federation of Camden County, 1964).

COMMUNAL HISTORIES

Adler, Selig and Connolly, Thomas, *From Ararat to Suburbia: The History of the Jewish Community of Buffalo* (Philadelphia: The Jewish Publication Society of America, 1960).

Fein, Isaac, *The Making of an American Jewish Community: Baltimore* (Philadelphia: The Jewish Publication Society of America, 1971).

Grinstein, Hyman J., *The Rise of the Jewish Community of New York, 1654–1860* (Philadelphia: The Jewish Publication Society of America, 1945).

Kohn, S. Joshua, *The Jewish Community of Utica, New York, 1847–1948* (New York: American Jewish Historical Society, 1959).

Plaut, W. Gunther, *The Jews in Minnesota* (New York: American Jewish Historical Society, 1959).

Rosenberg, Stuart E., *The Jewish Community in Rochester, 1843–1925* (New York: Columbia Univeristy Press, 1954).

Rudolph, Bernard G., *From a Minyan to a Community: A History of the Jews of Syracuse* (Syracuse: Syracuse University Press, 1970).

Swichkow, Louis J. and Gartner, Lloyd P., *The History of the Jews of Milwaukee* (Philadelphia: The Jewish Publication Society of America, 1963).

Vorspan, Max and Gartner, Lloyd P., *History of the Jews of Los Angeles* (Philadelphia: The Jewish Publication Society of America, 1970).

Whiteman, Maxwell and Wolf, II, Edwin, *The History of the Jews of Philadelphia from Colonial Times to the Age of Jackson* (Philadelphia: The Jewish Publication Society of America, 1957).

THE INFORMAL COMMUNITY

Etzioni, Amitai, "The Ghetto: A Re-Evaluation," *Social Forces*, Vol. 37, No. 3 (March 1959), pp. 255–262.

Bernheimer, Charles S., ed., *The Russian Jew in the United States* (Philadelphia: The John C. Winston Co., 1905). (Reprinted by Jerome S. Ozer, Publisher, Inc., New York, 1971.)

Hapgood, Hutchins, *The Spirit of the Ghetto*, ed. by Moses Rischin (Cambridge, Mass.: Harvard University Press, 1967). (There is also an edition published by Schocken Books in 1965 ed. by Harry L. Golden.)

Hindus, Milton, ed., *The Old East Side* (Philadelphia: The Jewish Publication Society of America, 1969).

Kazin, Alfred, *A Walker in the City* (New York: Harcourt, Brace and Co., 1951).

———, "The Writer and the City," *Harper's* (December 1968), pp. 110–127.

Kranzler, George, *Williamsburg: A Jewish Community in Transition* (New York: P. Feldheim, 1961).

Landesman, Alter F., *Brownsville: The Birth, Development and Passing of a Jewish Community* (New York: Bloch Publishing Co., 1969).

Rischin, Moses, *The Promised City: New York's Jews, 1870–1914* (Cambridge, Mass.: Harvard University Press, 1962).

Rosenthal, Erich, "Acculturation Without Assimilation," *American Journal of Sociology*, Vol. 66, No. 3 (November 1960), pp. 275–288.

———, "This Was North Lawndale: The Transplantation of a Jewish Community," *Jewish Social Studies*, Vol. 22, No. 2 (April 1960), pp. 67–82.

Rossman, Evelyn N., "The Community and I," *Commentary*, Vol. 18, No. 5 (November 1954), pp. 393–405.

———, "The Community and I: Two Years Later," *Commentary*, Vol. 21, No. 3 (March 1956), pp. 230–238.

———, "Judaism in Northrup," *Commentary,* Vol. 24, No. 5 (November 1957), pp. 383–391.

———, "Decade in Northrup," *Commentary,* Vol. 28, No. 3 (September 1959), pp. 214–222.

Schoener, Allon, ed., *Portal to America: The Lower East Side, 1870–1925* (New York: Holt, Rinehart and Winston, 1967).

Sklare, Marshall, "Jews, Ethnics, and the American City," *Commentary,* Vol. 53, No. 4 (April 1972), pp. 70–77.

Welles, Sam, "The Jewish Elan," *Fortune,* Vol. 61, No. 2 (February 1960), pp. 134–139, 160–166.

Wirth, Louis, *The Ghetto* (Chicago: University of Chicago Press, 1966).

THE FORMAL COMMUNITY

Arzt, Max, "The Synagogue Center and the Jewish Community Center," *The Reconstructionist,* Vol. 13, No. 5 (18 April 1947), pp. 10–15.

Bogen, Boris D., *Jewish Philanthropy* (New York: Macmillan, 1917).

Chipkin, Israel S., "Judaism and Social Welfare" in Louis Finkelstein, ed., *The Jews: Their History, Culture, and Religion,* 2 vols. (Philadelphia: The Jewish Publication Society of America, 1949), pp. 713–744.

Elazar, Daniel J., "The Reconstitution of Jewish Communities in the Post-War Period," *The Jewish Journal of Sociology,* Vol. 11, No. 2 (December 1969), pp. 187–226.

Franck, Isaac, "The Community Council Idea," *Jewish Social Service Quarterly,* Vol. 20, No. 4 (June 1944), pp. 191–200.

Freid, Jacob, ed., *Judaism and the Community: New Directions in Jewish Social Work* (New York: Thomas Yoseloff, 1968).

The Future of the Jewish Community in America: A Task Force Report (New York: American Jewish Committee, 1972).

Goldberg, S. P., "Jewish Communal Services: Programs and Finances," *AJYB* 1972 (Vol. 73), pp. 236–287.

Goren, Arthur A., *New York Jews and the Quest for Community: The Kehillah Experimemt, 1908–22* (New York: Columbia University Press, 1970).

Gurin, Arnold, "The Nature of Jewish Community Life" in *Future Directions of American Jewish Life and their Implications for Jewish Community Centers* (New York: National Jewish Welfare Board, 1963), pp. 77–94.

———, "Sectarianism: A Persistent Value Dilemma," *Journal of Jewish Communal Service,* Vol. 43, No. 1 (Fall 1966), pp. 38–48.

Halpern, Ben, "Religious, Educational and Cultural Prospects of the Jewish Community" in *Future Directions of American Jewish Life and their Implications for Jewish Community Centers* (New York: National Jewish Welfare Board, 1963), pp. 4–14.

———, "Sectarianism and the Jewish Community," *Journal of Jewish Communal Service,* Vol. 42, No. 1 (Fall 1965), pp. 6–17.

Hochbaum, Jerry, "The Federation Executive and Our Contemporary Crises: Resistances, Rationalizations and Professional Responsibilities," *Journal of Jewish Communal Service,* Vol. 46, No. 2 (Winter, 1969), pp. 155–162.

Janowsky, Oscar I., *The Jewish Welfare Board Survey* (New York: Dial Press, 1948).

Kaplan, Mordecai M., *Judaism as a Civilization* (New York: Macmillan, 1934). (Also enlarged edition [New York: Reconstructionist Press, 1957].)

Karpf, Maurice J., *Jewish Community Organization in the United States* (New York: Bloch Publishing Company, 1938).

Liebman, Charles S., "Dimensions of Authority in the Contemporary Jewish Community," *The Jewish Journal of Sociology,* Vol. 12, No. 1 (June 1970), pp. 29–37.

Lipset, Seymour Martin, "The Study of Jewish Communities in a Comparative Context," *The Jewish Journal of Sociology,* Vol. 5, No. 2 (December 1963), pp. 157–166.

Lurie, Harry L., *A Heritage Affirmed* (Philadelphia: The Jewish Publication Society of America, 1961).

Morris, Robert and Freund, Michael, eds., *Trends and Issues in Jewish Social Work in the United States, 1899–1952* (Philadelphia: Jewish Publication Society of America, 1962).

Richards, Bernard G., "Organizing American Jewry" in Jacob Freid, ed., *Jews in the Modern World,* Vol. 2 (New York: Twayne Publishers, 1962), pp. 482–508.

Roseman, Kenneth D., "Power in a Midwestern Jewish Community," *American Jewish Archives,* Vol. 21, No. 1 (April 1969), pp. 57–83.

Sherman, Charles B., "Jewish Communal Organization in the U.S.," *Jewish People Past and Present,* Vol. 2 (New York: Jewish Encyclopedic Handbooks, 1948), pp. 217–230.

Sklare, Marshall, "The Future of Jewish Giving," *Commentary,* Vol. 34, No. 5 (November 1962), pp. 416–426.

Stein, Herman D., "Jewish Social Work in the United States, 1654–1954," *AJYB 1956* (Vol. 57) pp. 3–98.

Stock, Ernest, "In the Absence of Hierarchy: Notes on the Organization of the American Jewish Community," *The Jewish Journal of Sociology*, Vol. 12, No. 2 (December 1970), pp. 195–200.

"Symposium on the Relationship Between the Synagogue and the Center," *Conservative Judaism*, Vol. 16, Nos. 2–3 (Winter–Spring 1962), pp. 1–50.

Urbont, Carl, "The Purposes of the Jewish Community Center Movement: An Appraisal of their Operation," *AJYB 1967* (Vol. 68), pp. 29–59.

Weinberger, Paul, "An Empirical Assessment of Priorities in Jewish Community Services," *Journal of Jewish Communal Service*, Vol. 48, No. 2 (Winter 1971), pp. 159–166.

Weisberg, Harold, "Ideologies of American Jews" in Oscar I. Janowsky, ed., *The American Jew: A Reappraisal* (Philadelphia: The Jewish Publication Society of America, 1964), pp. 339–359.

Wischnitzer, Mark, "Jewish Communal Organization in Modern Times," *Jewish People Past and Present*, Vol. 2 (New York: The Jewish Encyclopedic Handbooks, 1948), pp. 201–216.

Zibbell, Charles, "Suburbia and Jewish Community Organization," *Journal of Jewish Communal Service*, Vol. 38, No. 1 (Fall 1961), pp. 69–79.

RELIGIOUS MOVEMENTS

Blau, Joseph L., *Modern Varieties of Judaism* (New York: Columbia University Press, 1966).

Carlin, Jerome and Mendlowitz, Saul, "The American Rabbi" in Marshall Sklare, ed., *The Jews: Social Patterns of an American Group* (New York: Free Press, 1958), pp. 377–414.

Davis, Moshe, *The Emergence of Conservative Judaism* (Philadelphia: The Jewish Publication Society of America, 1963).

———, "Jewish Religious Life and Institutions in America" in Louis Finkelstein, ed., *The Jews: Their History, Culture and Religion*, 2 vols. (Philadelphia: The Jewish Publication Society of America, 1949), pp. 354–453.

———, "The Synagogue in American Judaism" in Harry Schneiderman, ed., *Two Generations in Perspective* (New York: Monde Publishers, 1957), pp. 210–235.

Freehof, Solomon B., *Current Reform Responsa* (Cincinnati: Hebrew Union College Press, 1969).

"The Future of Rabbinic Training in America: A Symposium" (Participants: Daniel Jeremy Silver; Eugene B. Borowitz; Ira Eisenstein; Arthur Green; Charles S. Liebman; Mark Loeb; Emanuel Rackman; Seymour Siegel;

Eugene Weiner; Arnold Jacob Wolf; Sheldon Zimmerman), *Judaism,* Vol. 18, No. 4 (Fall 1969), pp. 387–420.

Glazer, Nathan, *American Judaism* (Chicago: University of Chicago Press, 1972).

Kampf, Avram, *Contemporary Synagogue Art* (New York: Union of American Hebrew Congregations, 1966).

Karp, Abraham J., "Rabbi, Congregation, and the World They Live In," *Conservative Judaism,* Vol. 26, No. 1 (Fall 1971), pp. 25–40.

Kaufman, Michael, "Far Rockaway—Torah-Suburb-by-the-Sea," *Jewish Life,* Vol. 27, No. 6 (August 1960), pp. 20–32.

Kelman, Wolfe, "The Synagogue in America" in David Sidorsky, ed., *The Future of the Jewish Community in America* (New York: Basic Books, 1973).

Klausner, Samuel Z., "Synagogues in Transition: A Planning Prospectus," *Conservative Judaism,* Vol. 25, No. 1 (Fall 1970), pp. 42–54.

Lenn, Theodore I. et al., *Rabbi and Synagogue in Reform Judaism* (New York Central Conference of American Rabbis, 1972).

Lerner, Stephen C., "The Havurot," *Conservative Judaism,* Vol. 24, No. 3 (Spring 1970), pp. 2–15.

Liebman, Charles S., "Reconstructionism in American Jewish Life," *AJYB 1970* (Vol. 71), pp. 3–99.

———, "The Training of American Rabbis," *AJYB 1968* (Vol. 69), pp. 3–112.

Mintz, Jerome R., *Legends of the Hasidim* (Chicago: University of Chicago Press, 1968).

Neusner, Jacob, *American Judaism: Adventure in Modernity* (Englewood Cliffs, N.J.: Prentice-Hall, Inc., 1972).

——— ed., *Contemporary Judaic Fellowship in Theory and in Practice* (New York: Ktav Publishing House, Inc., 1972).

Plaut, W. Gunther, *The Growth of Reform Judaism: American and European Sources until 1948* (New York: World Union for Progressive Judaism, 1965).

Poll, Solomon, *The Hasidic Community of Williamsburg* (New York: Free Press, 1962).

Polsky, Howard W., "A Study of Orthodoxy in Milwaukee: Social Characteristics, Beliefs and Observances" in Marshall Sklare, ed., *The Jews: Social Patterns of an American Group* (New York: Free Press, 1958), pp. 325–335.

Rossman, Evelyn N., "A Fund-Raiser Comes to Northrup," *Commentary,* Vol. 33, No. 3 (March 1962), pp. 218–225.

Rubin, Israel, *Satmar: An Island in the City* (Chicago: Quadrangle Books, 1972).

Sklare, Marshall, "Church and the Laity Among Jews," *The Annals of the American Academy of Political and Social Science,* Vol. 332 (November 1960), pp. 60–69.

Steinberg, Stephen, "Reform Judaism: The Origin and Evolution of a Church Movement," *Journal for the Scientific Study of Religion,* Vol. 5, No. 1 (Fall 1965), pp. 117–129.

Temkin, Sefton D., "A Century of Reform Judaism in America," *AJYB* 1973 (Vol. 74), pp. 3–75.

Waxman, Mordecai, *Tradition and Change: The Development of Conservative Judaism* (New York: Burning Bush Press, 1958).

"What's Wrong with our Seminaries," *Response,* Vol. 3, No. 2 (Fall 1969), pp. 2–20.

JEWISH EDUCATION

Ackerman, Walter I., "Jewish Education—For What?" *AJYB 1969* (Vol. 70), pp. 3–36.

Band, Arnold J., "Jewish Studies in American Liberal Arts Colleges and Universities," *AJYB 1966* (Vol. 67), pp. 4–30.

Berkovits, Eliezer, "Jewish Education in a World Adrift," *Tradition,* Vol. 11, No. 3 (Fall 1970), pp. 5–12.

Borowitz, Eugene B., "Problems Facing Jewish Educational Philosophy in the Sixties," *AJYB 1961* (Vol. 62), pp. 145–153.

Dushkin, Alexander M. and Engelman, Uriah Z., *Jewish Education in the United States* (New York: American Association for Jewish Education, 1959).

Fox, Seymour, "Toward a General Theory of Jewish Education" in David Sidorsky, ed., *The Future of the Jewish Community in America* (New York: Basic Books, 1973), pp. 260–270.

Friedman, Norman L., "Religion's Subsystem: Toward a Sociology of Jewish Education," *Sociology of Education,* Vol. 42, No. 1 (Winter 1969), pp. 104–113.

Goren, Arthur A., "Review Essay: Jewish Education in a Pluralist Society," *American Jewish Historical Quarterly,* Vol. 58, No. 4 (June 1969), pp. 515–520.

Himmelfarb, Milton, "Reflections on the Jewish Day School," *Commentary,* Vol. 30, No. 1 (July 1960), pp. 29–36.

Hochberg, Hillel, "Trends and Developments in Jewish Education," *AJYB* 1972 (Vol. 73), pp. 194–235.

Jick, Leon A., ed., *The Teaching of Judaica in American Universities: The Proceedings of a Colloquium* (New York: Ktav Publishing House, Inc., 1970).

Kaminetsky, Joseph and Friedman, Murray I., eds., *Hebrew Day School Education: An Overview* (New York: Torah Umesorah, 1970).

Kaufman, Jay, "Day Schools: Not Whether, But How?" *The Central Conference of American Rabbis Journal*, Vol. 12, No. 3 (October 1964), pp. 3–9.

Lang, Gerhard, "Jewish Education," *AJYB 1968* (Vol. 69), pp. 370–383.

Pilch, Judah, *A History of Jewish Education in the United States* (New York: American Association for Jewish Education, 1969).

Rothman, Eugene, "Whither the Hebrew Day School?" *Midstream*, Vol. 17, No. 6 (June–July 1971), pp. 19–30.

Schiff, Alvin I., *The Jewish Day School in America* (New York: Jewish Education Committee Press, 1966).

Schwartzman, Sylvan, "Who Wants Reform All-Day Schools?" *The Central Conference of American Rabbis Journal*, Vol. 12, No. 1 (April 1964), pp. 3–10.

Sleeper, James A., "A Radical View of Jewish Culture" in David Sidorsky, ed., *The Future of the Jewish Community in America* (New York: Basic Books, 1973), pp. 239–259.

Weinberger, Paul, "The Effects of Jewish Education," *AJYB 1971* (Vol. 72), pp. 230–249.

Weinstein, David and Yizhar, Michael, *Modern Jewish Educational Thought: Problems and Prospects* (Chicago: College of Jewish Studies, 1964).

Winter, Nathan H., *Jewish Education in a Pluralist Society: Samson Benderly and Jewish Education in the United States* (New York: New York University Press, 1966).

THE JEWISH COMMUNITY AND THE GENERAL SOCIETY

The Politics of American Jewry

Cohen, Henry and Sandrow, Gary, *Philadelphia Chooses a Mayor* (New York: American Jewish Committee, 1972).

Cohn, Werner, "The Politics of American Jews" in Marshall Sklare, ed., *The Jews: Social Patterns of an American Group* (New York: Free Press, 1958), pp. 614–626.

Elazar, Daniel J., "American Political Theory and the Political Notions of American Jews: Convergences and Contradictions," *The Jewish Journal of Sociology*, Vol. 9. No. 1 (June 1967), pp. 5–24.

Fuchs, Lawrence H., *American Ethnic Politics* (New York: Harper & Row, 1968).

———, *The Political Behavior of American Jews* (Glencoe: Free Press, 1956).

Gartner, Lloyd P., "Candidates, Messiahs, and Aristocrats," *Midstream*, Vol. 14, No. 8 (October 1968), pp. 22–29.

Glazer, Nathan, "The Jewish Role in Student Activism," *Fortune*, Vol. 79, No. 1 (January 1969), pp. 112–113, 126, 129.

———, *The Social Basis of American Communism* (New York: Harcourt, Brace and World, 1961).

Himmelfarb, Milton, *The Jews of Modernity* (New York, Basic Books, 1973).

Levy, Mark R. and Kramer, Michael S., *The Ethnic Factor: How America's Minorities Decide Elections* (New York: Simon and Schuster, 1972).

Litt, Edgar, *Beyond Pluralism: Ethnic Politics in America* (Glenview, Ill.: Scott, Foresman and Co., 1970).

Parenti, Michael, "Ethnic Politics and the Persistence of Ethnic Identification," *American Political Science Review*, Vol. 61, No. 3 (September 1967), pp. 717–726.

Tumin, Melvin M., "Conservative Trends in American Jewish Life," *Judaism*, Vol. 13, No. 2 (Spring 1964), pp. 131–142.

Weyl, Nathaniel, *The Jew in American Politics* (New Rochelle, N.Y.: Arlington House, 1968).

Prejudice, Discrimination, and Anti-Semitism

Ackerman, Nathan W. and Jahoda, Marie, *Anti-Semitism and Emotional Disorder: A Psychoanalytic Interpretation* (New York: Harper and Brothers, 1950).

Adorno, Theodor W., et al., *The Authoritarian Personality* (New York: Harper and Brothers, 1950)

Baltzell, E. Digby, *The Protestant Establishment* (New York: Random House, 1964).

Bettelheim, Bruno, "The Dynamism of Anti-Semitism in Gentile and Jew," *Journal of Abnormal and Social Psychology*, Vol. 42, No. 2 (April 1947), pp. 153–168.

——— and Janowitz, Morris, *Dynamics of Prejudice* (New York: Harper and Brothers, 1950).

Cahnman, Werner J., "Socio-Economic Causes of Anti-Semitism," *Social Problems*, Vol. 5, No. 1 (July 1957), pp. 21–29.

Chertoff, Mordecai S., *The New Left and the Jews* (New York: Pitman Publishing Corp., 1971).

Dawidowicz, Lucy, "Can Anti-Semitism be Measured?" *Commentary*, Vol. 50, No. 1 (July 1970), pp. 36–43.

Dinnerstein, Leonard, ed., *Anti-Semitism in the United States* (New York: Holt, Rinehart and Winston, 1971).

Glock, Charles Y. and Siegelman, Ellen, eds., *Prejudice U.S.A.* (New York: Praeger, 1969).

———, Selznick, Gertrude J., and Spaeth, Joe L., *The Apathetic Majority: A Study Based on Public Responses to the Eichmann Trial* (New York: Harper & Row, 1966).

——— and Stark, Rodney, *Christian Beliefs and Anti-Semitism* (New York: Harper & Row, 1966).

Goldberg, Albert I., "Jews in the Legal Profession: A Case of Adjustment to Discrimination," *Jewish Social Studies*, Vol. 32, No. 2 (April 1970), pp. 148–161.

Graeber, Isacque and Britt, Steuart H., eds., *Jews in a Gentile World: The Problem of Anti-Semitism* (New York: Macmillan, 1942).

Higham, John, "Social Discrimination Against Jews in America, 1830–1930," *Publication of the American Jewish Historical Society*, Vol. 47, No. 1 (September 1957), pp. 1–33.

———, *Strangers in the Land: Patterns of American Nativism, 1860–1925* (New Brunswick, N.J.: Rutgers University Press, 1954).

Lipset, Seymour Martin, "The Left, The Jews and Israel," *Encounter*, Vol. 33, No. 6 (December 1969), pp. 24–35.

Lowenstein, Rudolph M., *Christians and Jews: A Psychoanalytic Study* (New York: Dell Publishing Co., 1951).

Lowenthal, Leo and Guterman, Norbert, *Prophets of Deceit: A Study of the Techniques of the American Agitator* (New York: Harper and Brothers, 1949).

Marx, Gary, *Protest and Prejudice: A Study of Belief in the Black Community* (New York: Harper & Row, 1967).

McWilliams, Carey, *A Mask for Privilege: Anti-Semitism in America* (Boston: Little, Brown and Co., 1948).

Morse, Nancy C. and Allport, Floyd H., "Causation of Anti-Semitism: An Investigation of Seven Hypotheses," *Journal of Psychology*, Vol. 34, No. 2 (October 1952), pp. 197–233.

Pinson, Koppel S., ed., *Essays on Anti-Semitism* (New York: Conference on Jewish Relations, 1942).

Rose, Arnold M., "Anti-Semitism's Roots in City-Hatred," *Commentary*, Vol. 6, No. 4 (October 1948), pp. 374–378.

Selznick, Gertrude J. and Steinberg, Steven, *The Tenacity of Prejudice: Anti-Semitism in Contemporary America* (New York: Harper & Row, 1969).

Simpson, George E., and Yinger, J. Milton, *Racial and Cultural Minorities* (fourth edition, New York: Harper & Row, 1972).

Stember, Charles H. et al., *Jews in the Mind of America* (New York: Basic Books, 1966).

Trachtenberg, Joshua, *The Devil and the Jews: The Medieval Conception of the Jews and its Relation to Modern Anti-Semitism* (New Haven: Yale University Press, 1943).

Intergroup Relations and the American Jew

Cohen, Naomi W., *Not Free to Desist: The American Jewish Committee, 1906–1966* (Philadelphia: The Jewish Publication Society of America, 1972).

Duker, Abraham, *Jewish Community Relations: An Analysis of the MacIver Report* (New York: Jewish Reconstructionist Foundation, 1952).

Frieder, Steven E., "Intergroup Relations and Tensions in New York City," *AJYB 1970* (Vol. 71), pp. 217–228.

Friedman, Murray, "Intergroup Relations and Tensions in the United States," *AJYB 1972* (Vol. 73), pp. 97–153.

———, "Politics and Intergroup Relations in the United States," *AJYB 1973* (Vol. 74), pp. 139–193.

Glazer, Nathan, "The New Challenge to Pluralism," *Commentary*, Vol. 30, No. 6 (December 1964), pp. 29–34.

Halpern, Ben, *Jews and Blacks: Classic American Minorities* (New York: Herder and Herder, 1971).

Harris, Louis and Swanson, Bert E., *Black-Jewish Relations in New York City* (New York: Praeger, 1970).

Hentoff, Nat, ed., *Black Anti-Semitism and Jewish Racism* (New York: Richard W. Baron Publishers, Inc., 1969).

Hirsh, Selma G., "Jewish Community Relations," *AJYB 1953* (Vol. 54), pp. 162–177.

Hochbaum, Jerry, "Change and Challenge in Jewish Community Relations in the United States," *The Jewish Journal of Sociology*, Vol. 12, No. 2 (December 1970), pp. 181–186.

Kahane, Meir, *Never Again: A Program for Survival* (Los Angeles: Nash Publishers, 1971).

Katz, Shlomo, ed., *Negro and Jew: An Encounter in America* (New York: Macmillan, 1967).

MacIver, Robert M., *Report on the Jewish Community Relations Agencies* (New York: National Community Relations Advisory Council, 1951).

National Jewish Community Relations Advisory Council—Special Committee on Reassessment, *The Public Schools and American Democratic Pluralism: The Role of the Jewish Community—Report of a Conference* (New York: N.J.C.R.A.C., 1972).

Perlmutter, Philip, "Intergroup Relations and Tensions in the United States," *AJYB 1971* (Vol. 72), pp. 131–159.

Raab, Earl, "The Black Revolution and the Jewish Question," *Commentary,* Vol. 47, No. 1 (January 1969), pp. 23–33.

———, "The Deadly Innocences of American Jews," *Commentary,* Vol. 50, No. 6 (December 1970), pp. 31–39.

———, "Intergroup Relations and Tensions in the United States," *AJYB 1970* (Vol. 71), pp. 191–216.

Ringer, Benjamin B., *The Edge of Friendliness: A Study of Jewish-Gentile Relations* (New York: Basic Books, 1967).

Slawson, John, "An Examination of Some Basic Assumptions Underlying Jewish Community Relations Programs," *Journal of Jewish Communal Service,* Vol. 36, No. 2 (Winter 1959), pp. 111–119.

Sobel, Bernard Zvi and Sobel, May L., "Negro and Jew: American Minority Groups in Conflict," *Judaism,* Vol. 15, No. 1 (Winter 1966), pp. 3–22.

Weisbord, Robert G. and Stein, Arthur, *Bittersweet Encounter: The Afro-American and the American Jew* (Westport, Conn.: Negro Universities Press, 1970).

SOURCES

Herbert J. Gans, "The Origin of a Jewish Community in the Suburbs," in *The Jews: Social Patterns of an American Group,* edited by Marshall Sklare (New York: The Free Press, 1958), pp. 205–248.

Marshall Sklare and Joseph Greenblum, "The Friendship Pattern of the Lakeville Jew," in *Jewish Identity on the Suburban Frontier* by Marshall Sklare and Joseph Greenblum (New York: Basic Books, 1967), pp. 269-290.

Daniel J. Elazar, "Decision-Making in the American Jewish Community," in *The Future of the Jewish Community in America,* edited by David Sidorsky (New York: Basic Books, 1974), pp. 271–315.

Morris Axelrod, Floyd J. Fowler, and Arnold Gurin, "The Jewish Community of Boston: Membership in Synagogues and Jewish Organizations," in *A Community Survey for Long-Range Planning: A Study of the Jewish Population of Greater Boston* by Morris Axelrod, Floyd J. Fowler, and Arnold Gurin (Boston: Combined Jewish Philanthropies of Greater Boston, 1967), pp. 135–138, 143, 160–167.

Charles S. Liebman, "Orthodoxy in American Jewish Life," in *American Jewish Year Book 1965,* Vol. 66, (New York and Philadelphia: The American Jewish Committee and the Jewish Publication Society of America, 1965), pp. 21-92.

Marshall Sklare, "The Conservative Movement: Achievements and Problems," from *Conservative Judaism: An American Religious Movement* by Marshall Sklare (New York: Schocken Books, 1972), pp. 254–282.

Leonard J. Fein, Robert Chin, Jack Dauber, Bernard Reisman, and Herzl Spiro, "Reform Is a Verb," from *Reform Is a Verb: Notes on Reform and Reforming Jews* by Leonard J. Fein, Robert Chin, Jack Dauber, Bernard Reisman, and Herzl Spiro (New York: Union of American Hebrew Congregations, 1972), pp. 135-151.

Lloyd P. Gartner, "Jewish Education in the United States," in *Jewish Education in the United States: A Documentary History,* edited by Lloyd P. Gartner (New York: Teachers College Press, 1969), pp. 1–33.

Walter I. Ackerman, "The Present Moment in Jewish Education," *Midstream,* December 1972.

Lucy S. Dawidowicz and Leon J. Goldstein, "The American Jewish Liberal Tradition," in *Politics in a Pluralist Democracy* by Lucy S. Dawidowicz and Leon J. Goldstein (New York: Institute of Human Relations Press, 1963), pp. 76–90.

Nathan Glazer, "The New Left and the Jews," in *The Jewish Journal of Sociology*, Vol. XI, No. 2, December 1969.

Seymour Martin Lipset, "Intergroup Relations: The Changing Situation of American Jewry," in *Group Life in America: A Task Force Report* (New York: The American Jewish Committee, 1972), pp. 13–24, 26–27, 31–32, 46–58, 89–93.

Benjamin B. Ringer, "Jewish-Gentile Relations in Lakeville," from *The Edge of Friendliness* by Benjamin B. Ringer (New York: Basic Books, 1967), pp. 124–130, 259–268.

INDEX